SEDIMENTS OF TIME

Cultural Memory
in
the
Present

Hent de Vries, Editor

SEDIMENTS OF TIME

On Possible Histories

Reinhart Koselleck

Translated and edited by
Sean Franzel and
Stefan-Ludwig Hoffmann

STANFORD UNIVERSITY PRESS

STANFORD, CALIFORNIA

Stanford University Press
Stanford, California

These essays were originally published in German in 2000 under the title *Zeitschichten: Studien zur Historik;* in 2010 under the title *Vom Sinn und Unsinn der Geschichte: Aufsätze und Vorträge aus vier Jahrzehnten;* and in 2006 under the title *Begriffsgeschichten: Studien zur Semantik und Pragmatik der politischen und sozialen Sprache* © Suhrkamp Verlag AG Berlin.

The translation of this work was funded by Geisteswissenschaften International—Translation Funding for Humanities and Social Sciences from Germany, a joint initiative of the Fritz Thyssen Foundation, the German Federal Foreign Office, the collecting society VG Wort and the Börsenverein des Deutschen Buchhandels (German Publishers & Booksellers Association).

Printed in the United States of America on acid-free, archival-quality paper

Library of Congress Cataloging-in-Publication Data

Names: Koselleck, Reinhart, author. | Hoffmann, Stefan-Ludwig, translator, editor. | Franzel, Sean, translator, editor.
Title: Sediments of time : on possible histories / Reinhart Koselleck ; [translated and edited by] Stefan-Ludwig Hoffmann and Sean Franzel.
Description: Stanford, California : Stanford University Press, 2018. | Series: Cultural memory in the present | Translated from the German. | Includes bibliographical references and index.
Identifiers: LCCN 2017057772 (print) | LCCN 2017058936 (ebook) | ISBN 9781503605978 | ISBN 9781503601512 (cloth : alk. paper) | ISBN 9781503605961 (pbk. : alk. paper)
Subjects: LCSH: History—Philosophy. | Historiography.
Classification: LCC D16.8 (ebook) | LCC D16.8 .K632213 2018 (print) | DDC 901—dc23
LC record available at https://lccn.loc.gov/2017057772

Cover design: Rob Ehle
Cover photo: Stefan-Ludwig Hoffmann

Contents

Introduction: Translating Koselleck   ix

PART I

1   Sediments of Time   3

2   Fiction and Historical Reality   10

3   Space and History   24

4   *Historik* and Hermeneutics   41

5   Goethe's Untimely History   60

PART II

6   Does History Accelerate?   79

7   Constancy and Change of All Contemporary Histories
    Conceptual-Historical Notes   100

8   History, Law, and Justice   117

9   Linguistic Change and the History of Events   137

10 Structures of Repetition in Language and History   158

PART III

11 On the Meaning and Absurdity of History   177

12 Concepts of the Enemy   197

13 Sluices of Memory and Sediments of Experience:
    The Influence of the Two World Wars on Social
    Consciousness   207

14 Behind the Deadly Line: The Age of Totality   225

15 Forms and Traditions of Negative Memory   238

16 Histories in the Plural and the Theory of History:
    An Interview with Carsten Dutt   250

    Notes   *267*

    Index   *291*

Introduction: Translating Koselleck

Stefan-Ludwig Hoffmann and Sean Franzel

Reinhart Koselleck's writings display a keen interest in individual linguistic expressions that are historically specific but also have a more general, formal reach, extending beyond the situations that gave rise to them. To take one example, he opens the essay "Structures of Repetition in Language and History" (chapter 10 in this volume) by quoting a witticism by the mid-nineteenth-century Viennese playwright and actor Johann Nepomuk Nestroy: "'The strange thing with all these love stories is that they always revolve around the same thing, but how they start and end is so endlessly different that watching them never gets boring!'" As Koselleck notes, reading this in standard German (or English), rather than in the original dialect, one misses the unmistakable Viennese cadence of the original, even though the basic idea remains accessible. Koselleck goes on to translate Nestroy's remark, which originated in the world of nineteenth-century comic theater, into a more general thesis about the formal structure of historical events. Events are singular occurrences that surprise those who experience them. Yet this singularity unfolds historically in recurrent ways, recorded by the formulations of singular experiences by previous generations. Koselleck is attuned to historical specificity but also believes in a modest form of translatability, such that experiences captured in language can be applied to historical events that are potentially far afield from their original contexts. If singular events and experiences reoccur and are translated into language at different moments in time, wouldn't it be imperative for the historian to catalogue and theorize such reoccurring structures? To propose, not a philosophy of history that claims to know how all possible human stories start and end, but rather a set of abstract categories, serving as an analytical grid, that tell us what we might expect these stories to revolve around based on historical experience and evidence? A deliberately tentative theory that aims to break with the belief in "history," as it has evolved since the late eighteenth century with all of its ideological burden, and invites us instead to explore theoretically and in historiographical practice some of the conditions from which human conflicts, and hence possible histories, emerge?

I

Koselleck worked on his theory of history for most of his academic life, and there is surely something German about the idea that a discipline needs theoretical foundations. But while other postwar German theorists with similar ambitions for their own disciplines, such as Hans Blumenberg, Jürgen Habermas, or Niklas Luhmann, did produce large systematic works, Koselleck preferred the pointed essay as the vehicle for sketching out his theory; Montaigne's *Essais* was, after all, the third book (after the Bible and Jacob Burckhardt's *Weltgeschichtliche Betrachtungen*) that Koselleck would have wanted to have on a desert island.[1] In stylistic terms this essay form is a careful and precise, yet open-ended, mode of carving out abstract categories that accounts for a set of theoretical issues from a variety of different, yet related, perspectives. Collected and for the most part translated here for the first time into English, these theoretical and historiographical essays were clearly the form he found congenial for illuminating structures of repetition from "the prescient past" (*vorausgewußte Vergangenheit*, one of many untranslatable phrases), a past that is known in advance, because it repeats previous experiences.[2] Koselleck's prose is based upon a careful excavation of semantic layers contained in concepts, as well as upon the coinage of new and evocative concepts or metaphors. This explains why he is considered to be such a masterful stylist in German; but it is also the reason why he is notoriously difficult to translate for an anglophone readership.

It is perhaps not surprising that Koselleck returned time and again to the nineteenth century, the era in which the German philosophy and discipline of history rose to predominance. His first two books dealt with what he termed the *Sattelzeit*, the era between the mid-eighteenth-century Enlightenment and the 1848/49 revolutions, and authors from this period are frequently cited and evoked in his theoretical writings. One of the strengths of this work is that Koselleck mines these German intellectual traditions for his own arguments, making them thus available to readers today. But to describe the original language in which Koselleck thought and wrote, one has to situate his work in post–World War II Germany. Born in 1923, he experienced the Nazi period as an adolescent and young man, served in the German army, and was a Soviet prisoner of war in Central Asia until the fall of 1946; he then studied in postwar Heidelberg under Hans-Georg Gadamer, Karl Löwith, Viktor von Weizsäcker, Karl Jaspers, and others. Koselleck's intellectual concerns were formed by the experiences of World War II and its aftermath, and by the attempts to process these experiences in an academic landscape shaped by the Cold War division of Germany and the world, an era of global convulsions under the ever-present threat of nuclear annihilation.

Like Martin Heidegger and his students Gadamer and Löwith, Koselleck was steeped in the language of German idealist and existential philosophy, an idiom that has often proved challenging for English translators (including for us). Like his teachers, Koselleck tends to avoid latinate formulations, accounting, for example, for the temporal structure of historical events using German terms like *vollziehen, sich ereignen*, or *sich zeitigen*, rather than via cognates of "realize" or "manifest," and preferring *Zusammenhang* (constellation or connection) to *Kontext*. He likewise builds on the centrality of structures of anticipation or priorness in Heidegger's and Gadamer's hermeneutics, as expressed by the *Vor-* or "pre" in words like "preconception" (*Vorgriff*), "prejudice" (*Vorurteil*), or "pre-understanding" (*Vor-Verstehen*). At the heart of his theory of possible histories is an emphatic notion of structural "pregivens" (*Vorgaben*) that have formed experiences and events, and this term is not always easy to translate into English.

But Koselleck is also quick to point out how some concepts coined at earlier historical moments lose their applicability, addressing in particular the experience of being unable to continue to use certain Heideggerian concepts that evoked the conservative, militaristic intellectual milieu complicit with the rise of National Socialism in which Heidegger was situated. (In a late interview he called Heidegger's a "belt-buckle philosophy" [*Koppelschlossphilosophie*],[3] evoking the military uniforms of the world wars.) Despite wanting to salvage certain formal features of Heidegger's analysis of the temporality of human experience, Koselleck rejects polemical esoteric concepts from *Being and Time* such as "being toward death [*Sein zum Tode*]," "calling [*Geschick*]," and "loyalty [*Treue*]" (see the essay "*Historik* and Hermeneutics" in this volume). In all of these essays, Koselleck pursues a strategy of de-escalating, de-polemicizing, and de-ideologizing theoretical language, rejecting a more partisan language in favor of a set of abstract structural and anthropological concepts. Koselleck seeks to translate Heideggerian ideas into a more neutral register, but also to historicize and discard certain overdetermined concepts that might obscure historical fact; for example, he argues that the German term *Totschlagenkönnen*—"ability to kill"—is better suited both historically and anthropologically to capture the human condition than Heidegger's "being toward death." Koselleck does pursue new conceptual coinages, seeking a theoretical register that might translate more generally and pluralistically into a range of historical experiences. Like Heidegger and other twentieth-century thinkers such as Michel Foucault or the early Frankfurt School, Koselleck sought to inaugurate a new conceptual language capable of coming to terms with modernity,[4] but he does not do so in an ideological or insistent way.

2

If time defines history as a discipline, Koselleck posits, then a theory of historical time (or rather of a plurality of times) must be at the heart of the attempt to sketch out the conditions of possible histories. Koselleck's reflections on the challenge of giving expression to multiple temporalities shed light on his own theoretical language. In the introduction to his 2000 essay collection *Zeitschichten*, Koselleck speaks of the dependency of theorists of time upon spatial metaphors. He goes so far as to argue that "the metaphorical power of all images of time emerges initially from spatial visualizations [*Anschauungen*]," and that time can only be visualized through movement in specific units of space, as temporal concepts like progress (*Fortschritt*) or development (*Entwicklung*) indicate. "Every historical space constitutes itself through the time in which it can be measured, thereby becoming controllable politically or economically,"

Koselleck observes. In particular, spatial metaphors are needed to conceive of the simultaneity of the nonsimultaneous (*die Gleichzeitigkeit des Ungleichzeitigen*), and this is why Koselleck coins the concept of sediments or layers of time (*Zeitschichten*).[5]

Time is not linear and progressing from one period to another, as the modern concept of history suggests.[6] Instead, there are multiple historical times present at the same moment, layer upon layer pressed together, some still volatile, others already hardened—this is what the metaphor of sedimented layers or strata of time attempts to capture. It is the tension between different and jarring layers of time that might erupt in historical events, as Koselleck demonstrated for the clash between the times of law, administration, and social change in Prussia before the revolution of 1848–49. In chapter 8 in this volume, "History, Law, and Justice" ("Geschichte, Recht, und Gerechtigkeit"), Koselleck engages with the history of legal concepts through the complex German concept of *Recht*, a notable challenge, for example, to translators of Hegel's *Grundlinien der Philosophie des Rechts* (Elements of the Philosophy of Right). In the German legal and philosophical tradition, *Recht* means law, legal system, and right, and is a cognate of the German word for justice (*Gerechtigkeit*), a term that is central to "Geschichte, Recht, und Gerechtigkeit." In this essay Koselleck explores the different temporalities of law and history, how law is by its very nature dependent on repetition and follows other rhythms than social change or political events, and how the law might generate social injustices or political conflicts because it remains in the continuum of its time. Characteristically, Koselleck then goes on to sketch out five modes, from ancient Greece onward, in which history has been set in relation to justice, ending with the totalizing notion of Friedrich Schiller's "Die Weltgeschichte ist das Weltgericht" (world history is the Last Judgment), which declares that history metes out justice in the here and now.

Other essays in this volume attempt further to differentiate Fernand Braudel's tripartite distinction among the *longue durée* of geographical and social structures, the *moyenne durée* of mid-term economic cycles, and *événements*, or short-term currents of political events. In contrast, "Structures of Repetition in Language and History" (chapter 10 in this volume), one of Koselleck's last essays, is more interested in the interactions between different "times" and identifies five reoccurring structures, all belonging to what Braudel called the *longue durée*: the prehuman conditions of human experience (some of which, like the climate, may be altered by humanity); biological structures that humans share with animals; those humans don't share with animals (e.g., work and the law), structures of repetition contained in events; and, finally, structures of repetition contained in language. Only if we identify and analytically separate natural, biological, social or economic, political and linguistic structures of repetition can we empirically observe how their interactions condition possible histories.

In every repetition there is rupture and therefore the possibility of something new. *Zeitschichten*, Koselleck's portmanteau title for his essay collection, referring to "multiple temporal levels of differing duration and varied origin that are nonetheless simultaneously present and effective," merges "time" (*Zeit*) with "strata" (*Schichten*). (Cf., e.g., the German words *Geschichte* [history], which etymologically comes from *Geschehen* [occurence], and *Gesteinsschichten* [rock strata].)[7] This term presents a spatial image of different coexisting layers, but also alludes to the process of these layers accruing or sedimenting at different speeds. It is in good part to access this process of accretion (and erosion) over time that we have chosen to translate *Zeitschichten* as "sediments" of time rather than the more geologically precise "strata." The metaphor of sediments captures the gathering, building up, and solidifying into layers of experiences and events, as well as the tensions and fault lines that arise between different kinds of sedimented formations (all metaphors that Koselleck uses throughout his writings).[8] Indeed, in the essay "Forms and Traditions of Negative Memory" (chapter 15 in this volume), Koselleck describes the process of memory formation in terms of flow and solidification, here speaking of the events and experiences of the concentration camps: "They fill the memory of those affected by them, they form their memories, flow into their bodies like a mass of lava—immovable and inscribed."

Many of the central formal metahistorical concepts coined by Koselleck likewise seek to visualize complex temporal processes via spatial imagery. These include "sediments of experience" (*Erfahrungsschichten*) and "sluices of memory" (*Erinnerungsschleusen*), which describe how flows of experience, events, and memories are shaped, regulated, or redirected. Another good example is the conceptual pairing of "space of expectation" (*Erwartungsraum*) and "horizon of experience" (*Erfahrungshorizont*), which both establish ideas of a spatial outside or beyond in order to track different kinds of temporal unfolding, including the eclipse or overriding of past experiences by utopian expectations.[9] Another such concept frequently used by Koselleck is "inventory" (*Haushalt*)—he speaks of inventories of language, of experience, of arguments, of emotions and more. The idea of a linguistic or experiential inventory likewise combines spatial and temporal imagery, with the inventory's contents being gathered and stored, organized, and reorganized over time. This is not an easy term to translate: "linguistic" or "experiential economy" might also work, tapping into older notions of the household (*oikos*) often mobilized by models of cultural memory, as might more literal spatial metaphors such as that of a commercial, domestic, or military storehouse, or arsenal. However, the important point here is that Koselleck uses this term to evoke a sense of temporal processes of repeated use, a sense of words and concepts that collect or accumulate over time. These various "inventories" are dynamic archives, for their contents are subject to being replaced by other words, concepts, or arguments, depending on historical shifts or ruptures, although they are more often characterized by stability and constancy.

Another place where Koselleck addresses the sedimentation of experiences in language is in his frequent citation of pithy, almost platitudinous sayings or maxims. In his important essay in *Futures Past* on the topos of history as the teacher of life (*historia magistra vitae*), first published in a Festschrift for Löwith, Koselleck details the dissolution of the rhetorical-topological model of history, which dominated up to the eighteenth century and which posited that history teaches a certain set of moral lessons that recur over time.[10] This earlier model was superseded by the modern concept of history as the unfolding of the new and the unique that could not be captured by the inventory of tropes catalogued by ancient, medieval, and early modern authors frequently evoked by Koselleck.

Seen in this light, it might appear peculiar that Koselleck gravitated toward certain almost axiomatic sayings that grasp structures of repetition in history. These include quotations from Goethe, who pursued a similar theory of history, something Koselleck realized only late in life ("the same event sounds different in the evening than it did in the morning"); the nineteenth-century author and illustrator of cautionary tales Wilhelm Busch: "First, it comes differently, second, not as you think"

(Erstens kommt es anders, zweitens als man denkt); or more universal bits of folk wisdom such as "Time hurries and time heals" (Die Zeit eilt und die Zeit heilt) and "Sticks and stones may break my bones . . ." Furthermore, Koselleck himself often translated his abstract historical theory into pithy new formulations: "One conflict comes to an end only when a new one begins," for example, in the interview with Carsten Dutt at the end of this volume (chapter 16).

At first glance, Koselleck's predilection for succinct formulas or folksy sayings might seem old-fashioned, anachronistic, or untimely (he defends untimeliness in his essay on "Goethe's Untimely History," chapter 5 in this volume), for the nineteenth- and twentieth-century German *Bildungsbürger* (educated bourgeois) was only too inclined to cite Goethe or Busch as moral authorities. But Koselleck is largely interested in adages that deal with the temporal structure of historical events and their experiences, as those cited above indicate. These sayings and maxims—often hard to translate, given their highly idiomatic nature—largely boil down to questions of temporal sequence or change through time, change in perception, change in memory, and so on, and, for Koselleck, they signal the consolidation of human experiences in recurring structures. By attending to certain expressions that are tied to specific historical experiences, but that have broader formal application, he shows how structures of persistence and repetition can manifest themselves. Koselleck's provocation is to ask us to consider how, even in modernity, structures of repetition and constancy persist and relate to one another, and these sayings are sites where these structures can be glimpsed, where repeated and repeatable experiences solidify into knowledge that extends beyond the context of these sayings' initial utterance. This is neither an attempt to reground history writing in certain immutable topoi nor, concomitantly, to detemporalize historical experience and language in an era when all experience and language has been temporalized. Koselleck merely reminds us that the experience of the new is always based on possibilities of repetition, and that we need to know what repeats in order to understand what is new.

3

Arguably, there has been an uptick of interest in Koselleck since his untimely death in 2006, especially since the publication of Niklas Olsen's excellent intellectual biography, *History in the Plural* (2012).[11] Whenever scholars deal with issues of temporality, with present pasts or past futures, Koselleck's writings are invoked. But the recent surge in interest in Koselleck's work makes it even more conspicuous that his name was more or less absent from late twentieth-century anglophone critical theory or in the excruciating methodological debates about linguistic and cultural turns. If there was one historian who had thought long and hard about language and history and, in response to Gadamer, about why history is not a subdiscipline of hermeneutics, it was Koselleck. Yet in the avalanche of manifestos after the arrival of French poststructuralism on American shores, debating whether "all the world is a text," Koselleck is rarely mentioned. This is all the more striking because the debate revolved precisely around questions (such as the evidence of experience or the extralinguistic preconditions of linguistic change) that were at the center, not only of Koselleck's writings on conceptual history, but, more generally, of his theory of the conditions of possible histories, his *Historik*.

Of course, many of Koselleck's theoretical writings were not translated into English. Still, this is only part of the answer and does not explain the puzzlement and skepticism that some of his translated works provoked in the United States—in marked contrast to France, where Koselleck has been recognized as the most inspiring German theorist of history of the late twentieth century, first by Paul Ricœur in his *Temps et récit* (1983–85), especially volume 3, *Le temps raconté,* and, more recently, by François Hartog in his explorations of contemporary experiences of time, what he calls "presentism."[12]

The late 1980s and early 1990s seemed like the perfect moment for a more sustained reception of Koselleck's work in the anglophone world. After a delay of thirty years, his first book, *Kritik und Krise*, was finally published in English translation (1988).[13] Three years earlier, his important collection of essays *Vergangene Zukunft* (1979) had appeared in English translation in MIT Press's series Studies in Contemporary History, edited by Thomas McCarthy. *Futures Past* received prominent reviews by David Carr and Hayden White, the latter calling him "one of Germany's most distinguished philosophers of history."[14] In 1986, Koselleck had been a visiting professor at the New School for Social Research in New York, and in the fall of 1988, he was invited to be a visiting professor in the History Department at the University of Chicago. Earlier that year, he had retired from his position at the University of Bielefeld, and his appointment at Chicago was meant to be renewable. The French historian François Furet, with whom Koselleck had co-authored a book in the late 1960s, and had remained friends, had already been at Chicago on and off since 1980, more permanently since 1985. After 1990, Furet shifted completely to the Committee on Social Thought, an arrangement that Koselleck would probably have also wanted for himself.[15] But Koselleck's impact at Chicago was much more limited than Furet's. After three fall quarters with a total of six courses, Koselleck's appointment was not renewed. He did accept invitations to teach again for the fall quarter at the New School (1991) and at Columbia (1992), but this was the last time that Koselleck taught in the United States.

Irrespective of why Koselleck's appointment at Chicago was not renewed, his work evidently did not translate as well into English as that of Habermas, for example, whose *Structural Transformation of the Public Sphere* appeared in English translation in the same series in 1989. Of course, *Critique and Crisis* was also an important reference point for Habermas's own take on some of the same questions. As Anthony La Vopa asserted in a 1992 review essay, *Critique and Crisis* and *Transformation of the Public Sphere* both "reflect the political preoccupations of the 1950s, though from opposite ends of the ideological spectrum."[16] Both studies take Kantian philosophy as their starting points—and both were influenced by Schmitt. Whereas Koselleck aimed for a conceptual genealogy of the political function of Kant's critiques (the original working title of his 1954 Heidelberg dissertation had been *Dialektik der Aufklärung*),[17] Habermas wrote an affirmative account of Kant's idea of publicity, which, he argued, had been corrupted in the nineteenth century by the rise of capitalism and mass culture. However, it was Habermas's *Transformation of the Public Sphere* that became one of the most influential books by any German theorist in anglophone academe in the 1990s.[18] The question, of course, is why?

One reason was certainly the problem of translation. Part of why *Critique and Crisis* had become an instant classic in 1960s West Germany was Koselleck's suggestive writing style, his use of the different semantic layers of social and political concepts to craft historical arguments. *Critique and Crisis* was itself an early exercise in *Begriffsgeschichte*, conceptual history, a feature of the book that got lost in the literal translation of the English edition (for which, quite unusually, no translator claimed responsibility). The Cambridge historian T. C. W. Blanning articulated what was probably a common reservation for anglophone historians when he complained in his 1989 review about "the gargantuan German footnotes" in *Critique and Crisis*. These footnotes contained many succinct conceptual histories, however. According to Blanning, Koselleck's prose was hard to understand, inasmuch as it "soars into a metaphysical stratosphere and has no discernible relation to what was happening on the ground."[19] Blanning compared *Critique and Crisis* unfavorably to Hans-Ulrich Wehler's *The German Empire*, which was surely no less Germanic in its prose, excessive footnotes, and polemical style. Of course, Wehler was also Koselleck's colleague and intimate enemy at Bielefeld, with close ties to anglophone academe. Never shy to pick a "lively situation of contestation," Wehler had claimed ten years earlier, in Haberman's programmatic edited volume *Stichworte zur »Geistigen Situation der Zeit«*, that Koselleck's conceptual history was a "historicist dead end" at best.[20]

The distance between Koselleck and Wehler (or Habermas) also had to do with different wartime experiences. Whereas Wehler, Habermas, and the "45ers" generation of postwar German intellectuals were too young to have been drafted into the Wehrmacht and embraced American reeducation after the war as liberation, Koselleck's experiences of the catastrophic absurdity of mass death during the war and in its aftermath were deeply formative for his own understanding as being defeated. As he noted in his introduction to *Critique and Crisis*, written only a few years after his return from the war and the Gulag, "[. . .] man as a historic[al] creature is always responsible, for what he willed as well as for what he did not will, and more often, perhaps, for the latter than for the former."[21] A son of a liberal Weimar German professor with some distance from the Nazi regime, Koselleck regarded himself as intellectually neither a former Nazi nor a product of (American or Soviet) reeducation. He was thus happy to talk to anyone he found inspiring in postwar Heidelberg, including Heidegger and Schmitt, both of whom had lost their professorships after the war on grounds of complicity with the Nazi regime.

In his acceptance speech on receiving the Munich Historische Kolleg's prize in 1989, for example, Koselleck explicitly stated that his education at Heidelberg would have been unthinkable without the questions raised by Heidegger and Schmitt, even though he did not necessarily agree with their answers.[22] However, *Critique and Crisis*'s indebtedness to Schmitt, especially to his 1938 *The Leviathan in the State Theory of Thomas Hobbes*, proved to be decisive for its reception, and not only in West Germany. Habermas himself had insinuated in a 1960 review that anyone who wanted to know what Schmitt was then thinking should read *Critique and Crisis*.[23]

In the same year, the Harvard émigré political scientist Carl J. Friedrich reviewed *Critique and Crisis* for the *American Political Science Review*. Together with his young colleague Zbigniew Brezezinski, Friedrich had written *Totalitarian Dictatorship and Autocracy*, one of the most influential books of Cold War American social sciences, which came out in 1956, the year of the Hungarian revolt against Soviet control. Given his staunch anti-communism and critical views of the Enlightenment and French Revolution, one might have expected Friedrich to be sympathetic to *Critique and Crisis*'s anti-totalitarian bent. Instead, he focused entirely on the influence of Carl Schmitt on *Critique and Crisis*. Schmitt, Friedrich wrote, "is singled out for acknowledgment and [his] works are copiously cited. The 'decisionism' of this author leads Dr. Koselleck to think of absolutism primarily in terms of 'sovereign decisions'—only one of the aspects of this complex system of government. The discussion abounds in certain words fashionable in these circles, such as 'sprengen' [to explode], 'Raum' [space] and its various derivates, 'verorten' [emplace] and so on." Some of Friedrich's other criticisms of *Critique and Crisis* may have had something to do with his intimate knowledge of Heidelberg, and especially his close ties to his former mentor Alfred Weber, who was also one of Koselleck's teachers after the war. In any case, Friedrich set the tone for the later reception of *Critique and Crisis*: "Inspired by antiliberal and antibürgerlich sentiments, it is a brilliant exposition of a theme that seems rather dubious, where it deviates from familiar paths."[24]

In 2004, Koselleck himself conceded the "slightly mannered severity of his argumentation" in *Critique and Crisis*, and he never made a secret of the influence of Schmitt's conceptual rigor (but not his politics) on his writings. In fact, Koselleck developed his own intellectual program of a theory of history in his early correspondence with Schmitt.[25] Karl Löwith's *Meaning in History* (1949), which Koselleck helped to translate into German as *Weltgeschichte und Heilsgeschehen. Zur Kritik der Geschichtsphilosophie* (1953) while writing his dissertation and, of course, Hannah Arendt's *Origins of Totalitarianism* (1951), which appeared in an expanded German version in 1955 (now after Stalin's death including a chapter on "Ideology and Terror"), were just as important for his work. Löwith's critique of the philosophy of history as a secularized form of Christian eschatology was one of the starting points for *Critique and Crisis*. And Arendt's work in particular guided Koselleck's argumentation for the published version of his dissertation. However, these and other influences were occluded by Koselleck's affiliation with Schmitt. As Koselleck wrote with indirect reference to Habermas's 1960 review in 2004, two years before he died:

Thus whoever expressed thanks to Carl Schmitt was labeled a mouthpiece of Carl Schmitt. Whoever cited eighteenth-century conspiracy theories became a conspiracy theorist. Whoever criticized a politically or morally inspired dualism became a dualist. The opposite, however, is the case: the mutual dependency of politics and morality was in fact the normative implication of my argumentation. My critique of utopia was based on the disclosure of the polemical juxtapositions of the two entities lurking behind *mauvaise foi* or hypocrisy: the utopian designs for the future, the implementation of which would make princes disappear as tyrants. And for this reason there would no longer be any tyranny, wars as well would be permanently ended, and ultimately peace-loving citizens would make the state disappear [. . .]: All of these—as we now know, dangerous and bloody—illusions arose directly from the inadequacy of thinking or implementing morality without politics or politics without morality.[26]

It was Koselleck's intention to unveil the agonistic utopian philosophies of history, which he considered to dominate the Cold War confrontation of the 1950s between communism and liberal democracy. Like Jacob Talmon in his *Origins of Totalitarian Democracy*, written at the same time in

Jerusalem (part 1 published in 1952 and part 2 in 1960), Koselleck looked to the Enlightenment for the genealogies of twentieth-century utopian ideologies. Koselleck's primary political concern was the ideological potential for global self-annihilation in the Nuclear Age rather than some Schmittian justification for Third Reich expansionism or postwar German self-pity. He was, like Talmon or Arendt, politically a Cold War liberal, "an enlightener of the enlightenment," as Ivan Nagel put it in his 2006 obituary, borrowing a phrase that Koselleck had used to describe himself.[27]

If there is a political lesson contained in Koselleck's theory of history, it is the necessity of consensus and compromise. As he argues in "Concepts of the Enemy" (chapter 12 in this volume)—a postscript to his famous essay on "The Historical-Political Semantics of Asymmetric Counterconcepts"—all human experiences are organized by a here and there, an inside and outside, and it as essential for a political unit of action to solidify these boundaries as it is to transcend them. "Without contacts and contrasts, without conflict and compromises, without the building of this or that form of consensus, no group could exist or survive, at least not in our complex society." In the 1980s Koselleck co-edited a volume on the nuclear arms race that was academic in tone but no less political as an intervention. Characteristically, his introduction urged both sides of the debate in the West—the peace movement as well as those advocating nuclear deterrence against the Soviet Union—to translate their shared apocalyptic visions of nuclear annihilation into rational political arguments.[28]

4

It was not merely the affiliation with Schmitt or Heidegger that made the reception of Koselleck's work difficult in the anglophone world. Koselleck's reputation in German intellectual life, especially among German historians in the 1960s and 1970s, was built on much more than *Critique and Crisis*. In many ways, he became a historian (and received an appointment, a *Lehrstuhl*, in history) as a result of his Heidelberg Habilitation *Preußen zwischen Reform und Revolution* (1967), which has not been translated into English, as well as for his ambitious lexicon project *Geschichtliche Grundbegriffe* (Basic Concepts in History; 8 vols., 1972–92).

Becoming the main editor of *Geschichtliche Grundbegriffe* and participating in the *Poetik und Hermeneutik* group propelled Koselleck into the center of German intellectual life in the 1960s and 1970s. Some of the essays in *Vergangene Zukunft* (1979) were also part and parcel of Koselleck's studies of the history of particular concepts like crisis, critique, revolution, history, and modernity, or the modern era (*Neuzeit*), which had informed his empirical work as a historian.[29]

But the *Geschichtliche Grundbegriffe* lexicon also made Koselleck's theoretical reflections seem primarily like explorations of conceptual history as a method. Conceptual history became almost synonymous with Koselleck's name, and *Geschichtliche Grundbegriffe* was henceforth a straitjacket, not only for his writings, but perhaps also for his reputation abroad.[30] In an interview with the Italian historian Edoardo Tortarolo in 1989, Koselleck himself articulated the intellectual constrains imposed on him by what he called his penal labor (*Strafarbeit*) on *Geschichtliche Grundbegriffe*. "Because I am really not interested in this method anymore. If you've invested a quarter of century in something, it's just no fun anymore to work with this method, it has become boring for me."[31] Koselleck thought of conceptual history as only a methodological and empirical starting point (hence the lexicon format) for historical and theoretical explorations of any kind. Ironically, Koselleck came to be known as a conceptual historian at a time when his interests had shifted toward strikingly new and original theoretical questions, which all came to revolve around the question of the conditions of possible histories. Koselleck's unique theoretical approach allowed him to write about dreams and prognoses, death and iconography, war experiences and memory, and always in new variations on time: the times of law, history, space, humanity and what is now called "deep time," that is the time before the anthropocene.

Koselleck was such a unique and original historian because he was at the same time a theorist. This also explains the failed conversation with Quentin Skinner and John Pocock, who shared an interest in political languages with Koselleck. In retrospect, one has to admire Melvin Richter's advocacy in America since the mid-1980s of conceptual history as a historical method (ultimately, without lasting success) in his pointing out its similarities to the approach of Skinner, Pocock, and the Cambridge School of Intellectual History. There were probably more differences than

similarities between the two approaches, however, and the main differences are less methodological (which was at the center of the debate) and
have more to do with the theoretical implications of Koselleck's work,
something he might have been aware of.[32] In December 1992, Richter
was finally able to put together a symposium on *Geschichtliche Grundbegriffe* at the German Historical Institute in Washington, DC, marking the
completion of the lexicon that same year, which brought Koselleck and
Pocock into direct dialogue for the first time.

Language, ironically enough, turned out to be one of the main bar-
riers for this conversation. Pocock (like Skinner) lacked any first-hand
knowledge of Koselleck's writings (with which he was familiar only
through Richter's summaries). Still, his comments were more cautiously
critical than Skinner's earlier assertion that the notion of a diachronic
history of individual concepts is fundamentally flawed. As Koselleck
later explained to Richter, he had difficulties answering Pocock on the
spot, because he had been unable to understand Pocock's English accent,
with its unique blend of Cambridge and New Zealand. But even years
later, when Koselleck did find the time to write a more formal response
to Pocock, his tone was uncharacteristically brusque. "As my previous
comments indicate, I dealt with the issues he raises already long ago,"
he declared.[33] Thus, the anglophone history of political languages and
German conceptual history continued to exist in parallel after the symposium, Richter's advocacy of combining the two notwithstanding. With
the curious exception of anglophone academia, *Begriffsgeschichte* has gone
global in the past ten years, and it is particularly strong today in Scan-
dinavia, eastern Europe, and the Spanish-speaking world. The theoretical underpinnings of Koselleck's *Begriffsgeschichte*, including his critique
of the ideological use and abuse of modern concepts such as "history"
have more in common with Foucault's archeology than with Pocock's and
Skinner's much more contextual interests.[34]

Up until very recently, however, Koselleck was perceived either as a
conservative historian of the eighteenth and early nineteenth century à la
Furet or, more generally, as a *Begriffshistoriker*, that is, an intellectual his-
torian/historian of concepts à la Pocock and Skinner or a meta-historian
à la White (if not as a "philosopher of history," something Koselleck
always abhorred). Of course, Koselleck repeatedly insisted that all these

different interests belonged together. Yet only the three collections of essays, *Zeitschichten*, *Begriffsgeschichten*, and *Vom Sinn und Unsinn der Geschichte*, published in the years immediately before and after his death in 2006, and from which all the writings in this volume are taken, make apparent how these different interests are laced together in his theory of possible histories.[35] Instead of borrowing theoretical concepts from other disciplines, Koselleck believed that historians should develop their own epistemology, with being in time (following Heidegger's lead)[36] as its defining episteme. From Koselleck's perspective, his studies in conceptual history were only a kind of propaedeutic for a fundamental theory of history, the first systematic outline of an epistemology of history since Johann Gustav Droysen's *Historik* (1858). Consequently, Koselleck speaks emphatically of history as a science (*Wissenschaft*) in the essays in this volume, an ambition that does not translate well into the anglophone "discipline" of history.

A case in point is the ninth essay in this volume, his inaugural public lecture, as Lurcy Visiting Professor at Chicago, on "Language and History," perhaps the most cogent summary of his theory of history that Koselleck delivered for an English-speaking audience. In his lecture, Koselleck insisted on the fundamental difference between language and history. At a time when theoretically infatuated anglophone historians debated whether "all the world is a text," the conceptual historian Koselleck delivered an untimely reminder of the prelinguistic conditions of all possible histories. It is precisely his interest in language that explains why Koselleck is so careful not to confuse *res factae* (historical reality) and *res fictae* (fiction), *res gestae* (things done or *Geschichte*) and *historia rerum gestarum* (things written about it or *Historie*). This was his argument against Gadamer and the hermeneutic tradition, and it was also what sets him apart from intellectual compatriots like Paul Ricœur or Hayden White. For Koselleck, these prelinguistic conditions included the tensions between "earlier" and "later," "inner" and "outer," and "above" and "below"—abstract sets of universal contraries that condition all particular histories, and that he had sketched out in a slightly different form three years earlier in "*Historik* and Hermeneutics" (chapter 4 in this volume) and, more than thirty years earlier, as a graduate student still in Heidelberg.[37] His second set of arguments concerned the temporal differences between language and events. History is always more than language can grasp, and concepts contain more or less than what occurs in the actual course of events. "Language adjudicates above all as to the possibility of an actual history," Koselleck asserts in "Linguistic Change and the History of Events" (our chapter 9), "As a storehouse of experiences, language bundles together the conditions of possible events." We cannot know how a particular event—whether a revolution, civil war, military defeat, or social and economic crisis—might unfold, but we can access some knowledge of the possibilities that are contained within historical experience and captured by language.

For Koselleck, history is above all a science of experience, an *Erfahrungswissenschaft*, and experiences also determine the language of the historian. Here, Koselleck applies his abstract, systematic categories of the prelinguistic conditions of all possible histories to historiography itself. The historian's perspective is conditioned by temporality, the question of whether he or she is a contemporary of the events reported on, or was born later. Next it is important whether he or she is "higher" or "lower"—for example, is among the winners or the losers. And, finally, it is decisive for the historian's perspective whether he or she is on the "inside" or the "outside," that is, part of the polity being described or looking on from the outside. From here, Koselleck moves on to discern three dominant modes of historiographical writing that are likewise structured by temporality and capture past experiences linguistically: writing down (*Aufschreiben*) at the moment when events occur; copying (*Abschreiben*), that is, transmitting the meaning once attached to particular events; and rewriting (*Umschreiben*) under the pressure of new experiences that call for new explanations of familiar events.[38]

5

And yet there are certain experiences that elude capture by language. It seems clear that Koselleck's theoretical interests are refracted through his experience of World War II, and that this lies behind his insistence on the difference between primary and secondary experiences, those that can be put into words and perhaps be transmitted to others, and those that "flow into their bodies like a mass of lava—immovable and inscribed." Koselleck shares with Arendt an existential understanding of the ruptures of the 1940s, which lead both of them to radically critique the modern concept of history.[39] Arendt and Koselleck believed that the catastrophes of the twentieth century were caused by ideologies that claimed to execute the laws of history. This theme of the political hypocrisy of the Enlightenment's philosophy of history was already the argument of Koselleck's dissertation, resurfaces in different essays throughout the 1960s, 1970s, and 1980s (e.g., in "History, Law, and Justice," where Koselleck speaks about the absurdity of history as exemplified by Nazi evil), and comes to the fore again in his late essayistic work. "On the Meaning and Absurdity of History" and "Forms and Traditions of Negative Memory" (chapters 11 and 15 in this volume) are two examples of his polemics against the political evocation of history, as if the meanings of historical events could be contained and controlled. It is the senseless absurdity of mass killing, its "abysmalness" that makes it difficult for the survivors to transform their individual primary experiences into a "history" or "collective memory." Of course, historians can retroactively write an account of the events of World War II and the Holocaust and provide explanations for the course of events. But histories in the moment of their unfolding (*in actu*, as Koselleck would say) are not rational and are only carried out in the perspectively refracted perceptions of the participants, like in the novels of William Faulkner or Leo Tolstoy. "Ideas, formulated intentions, desires, generated linguistically as prelinguistically, taking and holding something to be true, all of these enter into the situation out of which events crystallize. What the different agents hold to be real about a history as it arises and is carried out *in actu* pluralistically constitutes the history to come. [. . .] As events ferment or occurrences are intertwined, as conflicts pile up and then break through, there is no common reality that can be perceived in the same way by the different participants involved" (chapter 11).

Koselleck lost both of his brothers in World War II: the older died at the front a few weeks before the end of the war, the younger at home when his parents' house was hit by an Allied bomb. One of his aunts was gassed during the Nazi euthanasia campaign in 1940. He was conscripted into the army at seventeen and deployed to the Eastern front. In 1942, Koselleck's foot was crushed in an accident when his artillery regiment marched toward Stalingrad—the injury probably saved his life. Koselleck returned home and spent time in hospitals. At the front he had heard rumors about the mass killings of Jews at Babi Yar near Kiev. Visiting family in Weimar after his release from the hospital in February 1943, he also learned about Buchenwald. Eventually, Koselleck was redeployed to a Wehrmacht radar unit in Strasbourg. In the last months of the war, he was again sent to the Eastern front, which by then had reached German territory. His unit fought against the Red Army in Moravia. Once in Soviet captivity on May 9, 1945, he had to march on foot to Auschwitz for two days, together with thousands of other German prisoners of war.

There he took part in the dismantling of the IG Farben chemical factories, which were sent by train to the Soviet Union for reassembly. After a few months, the German prisoners were put on eastbound trains themselves. A few weeks later, Koselleck arrived at Karaganda in Central Asia, an industrial coal-mining city built in the Kazakh steppe primarily by Stalin's convicts and deportees of the 1930s and 1940s, many of them Volga Germans and other Soviet ethnic minorities. Not all prisoners survived the transport, and most were initially not in a condition to work at all. The Karaganda region itself was a dystopian place with harsh cold winters and brutal summer heat, populated by settlements of deportees and Gulag camps, including separate camps for German and Japanese prisoners of war.[40] At his camp in Spassk, south of Karaganda, Koselleck encountered hunger and diseases (the main cause of death everywhere in the Soviet forced labor penal system), but also Marxist-Leninist (or rather Stalinist) ideologies of reeducation and redemption. In 1947, now a student in Heidelberg, Koselleck attended a reeducation seminar at Göhrde castle. One of the teachers was the young Marxist historian Eric J. Hobsbawm, deployed as a British reeducation officer. Hobsbawm recalls in his memoirs the lasting impression of Koselleck's report about Karaganda, how difficult the conditions were for the German prisoners and for the Soviet guards alike, both displaced in the Kazakh steppe, but how the latter were much better able to cope (at least in Koselleck's perception).[41]

Koselleck survived the camp thanks to another inmate, who recognized the symptoms of a fatal illness, and with the help of a German military doctor who had been an assistant to his uncle, a famous pathologist at Leipzig University. After fifteen months at Spassk and another surgery, this doctor declared Koselleck unable to work but strong enough for transport back home. Arriving at the border between Poland and the Soviet zone of occupation in East Germany in September 1946, Koselleck was given a copy of the *Communist Manifesto*. Later in the French zone, where his family lived, he was briefly arrested by the police, who took him for a vagrant. American Baptists replaced his ragtag Soviet prisoner clothes and provided him a copy of the Bible. Upon arrival at home his father politely asked him for his name—he didn't recognize his son.

Two-thirds of Koselleck's class in school didn't return home. He survived by chance but also by social privilege. In "Sluices of Memory and Sediments of Experience" (chapter 13 in this volume), he painstakingly analyzes how war experiences are shaped differently according to social and cultural categories. Dying in a war is unpredictable, but who survives is not necessarily so. Koselleck's fierce critique of moral hypocrisy was itself deeply moralistic, as is often the case. This holds true not only for *Critique and Crisis*. Most essays in this collection, written between 1976 and 2006 as explorations of his theory of history, return at central moments to the questions of Nazism, war, and the Holocaust.

Unsurprisingly, Koselleck's writings become most polemical when concerned with questions of memory and mourning. "Forms and Traditions of Negative Memory" is a case in point. After the end of the Cold War and the division of Germany, Koselleck participated in the debate about the Neue Wache ("New Guardhouse") war memorial and the Holocaust Memorial in Berlin, the only time when he felt compelled to participate directly in German political debates. In his intervention against the planned Neue Wache Memorial (a critique ignored at the time by German Chancellor Helmut Kohl), Koselleck comes back to an argument that guided his research into the iconography of nineteenth- and twentieth-century European war memorials. In modernity, increasingly abstract monuments for fallen soldiers (and, after the two world wars, also for dead civilians) signify a democratization of death. The commemoration of fallen soldiers, as individuals or in groups, replaced war memorials with great personages like monarchs or generals, and the dead came to represent the nation. But this democratization relies on sharp demarcations between "us" and "them," that is, those who belong to a nation and those who are excluded. War memorials thereby become sites of identity formation for the survivors. The dead are not treated equally but are grouped and categorized by the political agendas of different political communities of action (*Handlungsgemeinschaften*). Koselleck was appalled by Kohl's idea of transforming a small and intimate sculpture by Käthe Kollwitz, a pietà of a mother holding her dead son in her arms, into reunified Germany's main war memorial. He passionately pointed out the different forms of exclusion entailed by the visual language of the Kollwitz sculpture (created to commemorate her son who died in World War I). How, he demanded, could a Christian pietà alluding to the Virgin Mary holding the dead body of Jesus commemorate the murdered European Jews?

Koselleck also directed his chagrin against the dedication "To the victims of war and dictatorship" (*Den Opfern von Krieg und Gewaltherrschaft*), which transformed World War II and the Holocaust into a history without perpetrators, only victims. How could a World War II German national memorial portray Germans as victims like any other people? Instead, he proposed emphasizing mourning the dead without social, political, or national-ethnic distinctions, but differentiating how they died: "To the dead—to the fallen, the murdered, the gassed, the perished, the lost" (*Den Toten—gefallen, ermordet, vergast, umgekommen, vermisst*), a dedication that is equally problematic, of course, since it would also have lumped Wehrmacht soldiers and Holocaust victims together. Similarly, he argued only a few years later in 1998 against the Berlin Holocaust Memorial being the central site of the commemoration of German genocidal policies, since its dedication ("To the Murdered Jews of Europe") did not include all the other groups and peoples murdered by the Nazi regime, for example, the Sinti and Roma (who received their own memorial in the proximity of the Holocaust Memorial only in 2012) and the three and a half million Soviet prisoners of war who died in German captivity but are not commemorated at all by a central memorial, either in Germany or in Russia. Instead of a central state memorial that remembers all those murdered by Nazi Germany, the commemorative landscape in Berlin is now splintered into various monuments of various shapes and sizes for different (but not all) victim groups, based on the categories of the SS, exactly as Koselleck had predicted in the 1990s.

"Mourning is not divisible," as Koselleck sums up his position in "Forms and Traditions of Negative Memory." Germans should not only remember the victims but also the perpetrators of World War II, who murdered others and sacrificed their own lives (the *Opfertod*) for an immoral and abysmal cause, a cause that completely transformed the meanings of "victim" (*Opfer*) in German from active sacrifice to passive endurance (*Leiden, Erleiden*), terms Koselleck employs in these essays to avoid the charged concept of victimhood. Koselleck's use of the idiosyncrasies of his own biographical ruptures as a prism for his theoretical essays opens up his experiences to critical reflection and, conversely, makes his theory historically concrete and legible. For Koselleck, the mid-twentieth-century cataclysms of modernity, which he experienced both as a soldier, that is, a "perpetrator" (in the Wehrmacht) and as a camp prisoner, that is, an "endurer" (in the Gulag) completely dissolved any meanings attached to "history." History itself is without meaning, only its analysis can be rational and meaningful—hence the need for a theory of history. This is the leitmotif of Koselleck's *Historik*.

PART I

1

Sediments of Time

My topic is "sediments of time." And I should preface it by noting that, as a historian, I am not capable of making any claims based on the laws of physics or biology. Instead, this essay operates much more in the realm of metaphor: "sediments or layers of time" refers to geological formations that differ in age and depth and that changed and set themselves apart from each other at differing speeds over the course of the so-called history of the earth. We are, then, using a metaphor that first emerged in the eighteenth century, after traditional, static natural history (*historia naturalis*) had become temporalized and thus also historicized. By transposing this metaphor back into human, political, or social history as well as into structural history, we can analytically separate different temporal levels upon which people move and events unfold, and thus ask about the longer-term preconditions for such events.

As is well known, historians usually deal with time in a bipolar manner. Time is either portrayed as linear, as an arrow of time that heads in a teleological direction, or toward an open future, or conceived of as recurrent and cyclical. The first model envisions an irreversible form of sequential unfolding, while the second addresses the recurrence of what is fundamentally the same. This cyclical model is commonly traced back to the Greeks, whereas the Jews and Christians are thought to have developed the linear model. However, Momigliano has already shown that this opposition is ideologically overdetermined.[1] Both models are insufficient, because every historical sequence contains linear as well as recurrent elements. After all, every so-called cycle must also be conceived of teleologically, for the end of its movement is from the outset its predetermined goal: cyclical movement is a line directed back into itself.

In what follows, I use a theoretical approach that draws on the notion of sediments of time to parse historical findings and circumvent the linear-cyclical dichotomy. Historical times consist of multiple layers that refer to each other in a reciprocal way, though without being wholly dependent upon each other. First, though, one more etymological point: in response to Kant and his formal, a priori definition of time, Herder already insisted on the idea of "proper or individual times" [*Eigenzeiten*], the idea that every living thing has its own time and carries within itself its own temporal measure. And a second etymological point, which is also worth noting, given its central importance for history [*Historie*]. In Greek, *historia* originally meant what is called *Erfahrung* (experience) in German, and since the related verb *erfahren* (to have an experience) implies going from one place to another, what is involved is something like a journey of discovery. But as a science [*Wissenschaft*], history [*Historie*] first emerges through the report about this journey and reflective work on this report. By definition, history is the science of experience. When I speak about sediments of time in the following, I am always referring to the results of experience, even if I parse these analytically into three different layers:

1. Upon examining the role of time in historical processes, the first finding based on experience is naturally that of singularity. Events are experienced primarily as surprising and irreversible; this is something that each person knows from his or her own biography. But the same applies to communities of action, which experience their own evolution in terms of political or military histories or social and economic situations simply as the succession of singular constellations. The same applies to all matters that need to be addressed historically. The history of religion, for example, recounts the shift from Saul to Paul, and political history the turning point of 1789 (or, more recently, of 1989). In each case, we are dealing with singular turning points that irreversibly define and launch pent-up processes. The same applies *eo ipso* to military victories or defeats that fundamentally altered the constellations from which they emerged, and to economic crises or discoveries in the history of technology or industry,

where unique innovations have brought about irreversible results. We can thus consider such successions of singular events as linear, and locate all innovations upon such a time line. Progress is conceivable and possible because time, insofar as it is a succession of singularities, gives rise to innovations that can be interpreted as progressive.

2. This singularity is only half the truth, however, because history as a whole is based upon structures of repetition that are not exhausted in singularity. Take the banal case of the mail carrier who comes in the morning and brings you the message of a close relative's death. You might be shocked or perhaps even pleased. In any case, this is a singular occurrence mediated to you via the mail carrier. But the fact that the mail carrier comes each morning at a specific time is a recurrent process, which is made possible, in turn, by a regulated postal administration and its budget that is renewed on a yearly basis. The mail carrier returns at the same time each day regularly in order to transmit singular messages. The same applies to all networks of transportation and communication. The fact that we are gathered together at this conference location and that we arrived at the same time, or at least on time, is based on train schedules that guarantee recurring processes in the railway system. Without the recurrence of the same, or at least of the analogical in planning, and without organization, singular events (such as our conference) could never occur. These might seem to be superficial, everyday occurrences, but more substantial proof exists of recurrence as a precondition for singularity.

Consider the relationship of speaking [*Sprechen*] and language [*Sprache*]. Whoever wants to make her- or himself understood uses the language that she or he already knows and with which her or his listeners will presumably be familiar; communication would otherwise not be possible. And even someone who wants to say something new must still make what she or he wants to say intelligible in a preexisting language. In order to make individual acts of speech understandable, one must be able to recall the entire preexisting linguistic inventory [*Sprachhaushalt*]. Singular acts of speech thus depend upon the recurrence of language. Speaking performs this recurrence again and again, which changes only very slowly, even when something entirely new is put into words.

To take a different example, the same applies to the relationship between laws and justice. Laws must be formulated generally enough to remain repeatedly applicable. They can only secure justice if they can be applied repeatedly. Individual cases might all differ in their singularity, but a minimum of recurrence is necessary if laws are to be applied to specific cases and if justice is to be guaranteed at all. This means that all theories of justice are based upon the relative longevity of laws and legal texts and their reapplicability. The same applies to theology and the Church, to rituals and dogmas, which only by virtue of their repetition offer guarantees of truth.

But enough examples. In all realms of life we can identify phenomena of recurrence that secure the condition of possible singularity. But then a difficult question immediately emerges, namely, whether and how these structures of repetition themselves change. In light of this, long-lasting structures of repetition, too, take on the character of singularity by revealing themselves to be alterable, at least in certain situations. And here we encounter the phenomenon that makes history so exciting: not only does the singularity of sudden events seem to bring historical changes with it, but longer-lasting structures that enable changes, but initially appear to be more static, are themselves also subject to change. The advantage of a theory of sedimentations of time lies in its ability to measure different velocities—accelerations or decelerations—and to thereby reveal different modes of historical change that indicate great temporal complexity.

A case that has been thematized often in recent years is that of the *Wende* in 1989 [preceding German reunification]. The GDR was incorporated relatively quickly into the old Federal Republic through processes, however contested, that made the former GDR into a durable part of the new Federal Republic. Constitutional history, as a history of events, leaves no doubt as to this fact. However, this view of the events does not apply when one examines the economic conditions and the mentality of former citizens of the GDR. The political act was performed quickly, in a short window of time, and with remarkable diplomatic skill, but it could in no way immediately transform economic conditions. Nor could it alter the mind-sets of the people living in the former East. The socioeconomic difficulties of conforming to the new order cannot be directly solved through politics. They can only be addressed through changes in behavior, acclimatizations, or processes of mutual attunement between the populations of the East and the West; in each case these processes seem to last longer than the time span of a half generation. We do not yet know how long exactly. Every empirical investigation of this topic would seem to need to work, at least implicitly, with a multilayered theory of time.

We have spoken thus far of singular events and of structures of repetition without which such singular events would not be possible. In both cases, these different layers of time have been connected to the ways in which individuals or generations living together as a group accumulate experience. Let us take a closer look at this connection. The singularity of a sequence of events can be empirically located at the point when one experiences surprise. To experience a surprise means that something happened differently than one had thought. "First, it comes differently, second, not as you think," Wilhelm Busch observes. Suddenly one encounters a novelty, that is, a temporal minimum generated in the space between before and after. The continuum between previous experience and the expectation of coming events is breached and needs to constitute itself anew. It is this temporal minimum of an irretrievable before and after that inscribes surprises into our bodies, which is why we are always trying anew to interpret them. Historians in particular ask, not simply what has singularly been the case, but also how it could have come to happen the way it did. Hence historians seek causes whose evidential proof lies in their repeatability. Singularity can only be made plausible through causes if these causes repeat themselves. We confirm our recognition of such causes with expressions such as "Aha, I should have known that before," or "One thing leads to another." Therein lies the retrospective reaction that already refers back to causes that can always be called upon. Yet from a strictly historicist perspective, there are also singular causes that seek to gather explanations on the temporal level of pure succession. At any rate, the one-time experience of surprise adds up to a growing knowledge of the possibilities of such singular surprises. Becoming old means to be less surprised than the young. Increase in age is therefore characterized by a decrease in the potential for surprise. The more one internalizes an inventory of possible surprises, the less one is able to be surprised, a characteristic of youth. This is a biological aspect of the human experience of history, which cannot be simply subsumed into political or economic history.

To be sure, the arrogance of age can quickly lead to self-delusion because the resistance to surprise limits possible experiences. By repeating familiar modes of experience, opportunities to perceive anything new are squandered. To this extent, historical times are grounded in biological finitudes. The accumulation of experiences and the ability to process singular surprises create a finite inventory that spans from a person's birth to death, and that cannot be overstretched or overburdened. Not every person can process everything. Herein lies an individual generational determination that can easily be extended to everyone alive at the same time who shares similar social conditioning or thresholds of political experience. This is how generational groups are formed, even if birth and death constantly change the makeup of such groups. Everything that can be said about the experience of repetition and the processing of singularity also always applies to generational groups living together for whom it is plausible to assume that they can communicate with each other.

3. The outlined biological grounding and simultaneous limitation of possible historical experiences point to an additional sediment or layer of time. Some historical times point beyond the experience of individuals and generations. This pertains to preconditions of experience that are in effect *before* their respective generational cohorts, and that will most likely continue *after* these cohorts pass on. Continuous, biologically conditioned reproduction is one especially basic and evident case of this, which is always in play over and above any specific groups of shared experience or action. This is the truly recurrent cycle from conception to birth and death, in which all stories of love and hate, all intergenerational conflicts are imbedded. This biologically grounded cycle has recurred in specific rhythms without undergoing fundamental change as long as the human race has existed, at least in this biological sense.

However, as soon as we move from biological to cultural questions, processes of recurrence that die off more quickly come into view. Nonetheless, many structures of repeatability exist that reach far beyond a single generation, as well as beyond any form of generational succession that can be experienced first hand, that is, where generations can communicate with each other face-to-face. Such phenomena of repetition that go beyond everyday experience might be called "transcendental." This is the realm of religious or metaphysical truths that are based on foundational statements that have been modified over the course of millennia but that remain accessible, even if all people do not share them. We are familiar with the succession of magical modes of behavior and with different religious or modern, scientific attitudes that all span multiple generations. These kinds of human conceptions of the world repeat themselves in rhythms too slow for specific generations to directly experience their alteration over time. These long-term, recurring foundational assumptions only change at a creeping pace, and it is in this sense that they can be called transcendental; they are "transcendent," not in the sense of otherworldliness, but in the sense that they reach beyond and undergird multiple generations. All groups with shared experiences possess a certain minimum need for transcendence: without it, there is no final explanation—however provisional it might be—and it would be impossible to translate experience into knowledge [*Wissenschaft*].

What can be defined, then, in everyday language as long-, mid-, and short-term provokes a complex theory of historical times. To propose the existence of different sediments of time makes it possible to grasp different speeds of change and transformation without falling prey to the false alternative between linear or cyclical temporal processes.[2]

2

Fiction and Historical Reality

Anyone engaging today with the question of the relationship between fiction and historical reality faces a twofold challenge. Tradition poses the first challenge, for the antithesis between *res factae* and *res fictae* belongs to the basic topoi that have been parsed in ever-new ways since antiquity. Examining the history of these topoi allows us to recognize the transformation of what in each case is experienced as historical reality. And, in the process, one also finds that this experience is not independent of what in each case is understood as fiction, especially in the realm of poetry.

The second challenge, which this essay addresses in more detail, takes as its point of departure the current discussion of how historical reality conditions fictional texts, and how this reality is in turn affected by them. This question is new, insofar as it has only become possible to ask it in such a pointed way since the Enlightenment, with its philosophy of history. Of course the notion that this question is particularly current is itself part of a tradition, for the categorization of *res factae* as *res fictae* once belonged to the realm of rhetoric and thus (to put it in modern terms) to an *eo ipso* socially and politically relevant art form.

Let me begin by telling two stories that were compiled through the praxis of the historian, who would seem to be concerned on a professional level with what one might call historical reality. Some more general reflections can be derived from these, culminating in a thesis that casts some light on the relationship between fictional texts and so-called historical reality.

Both of my stories are short.

The first is told by a doctor in 1934: "It was about nine o'clock in the evening. My consultations were over, and I was just stretching out on the couch to relax with a book about Matthias Grünewald when suddenly the walls of my room and then my apartment disappeared. I looked around and discovered to my horror that as far as the eye could see, no apartment had walls any more. Then I heard a loudspeaker boom: 'By the decree of the 17th of this month on the Abolition of Walls.'"

The second story likewise comes from the 1930s, in this case from a Jewish lawyer: "Two benches were standing side by side in Tiergarten Park; one was painted the usual green and the other yellow [at the time Jews were permitted to sit only on specially painted yellow benches]. There was a trash can [*Papierkorb*] between them. I sat down on the trash can and hung a sign around my neck like the ones blind beggars sometimes wear—also like those the government makes 'race violators' wear. It read 'I make room for paper trash [*Papier*] if need be.'"

Both stories come from a collection of dreams from the time of the Third Reich edited by Charlotte Beradt.[1] The dreamers are anonymous, and the dreams are truthfully recorded and transmitted. Each dream tells a story with a beginning and an end, which obviously never happened in the way it is reported.

If we understand our question about fiction and historical reality in terms of two clear alternatives, both of these short stories surely belong to the realm of fictional texts, and one can certainly read them as such. In their condensed, incisive form, they have much in common with the short narratives of Kleist, and even more so of Kafka. No one would want to deny that they possess a poetic quality. They approach poetry, which, in Aristotelian terms, reports not on what has happened and how it by chance occurred, as the historian does, but instead tells of something that could happen.[2] Both dreams contain a different kind of likelihood than what would have seemed empirically possible at the time they were dreamt. They anticipate something that seemed empirically improbable but that would come to pass in the course of catastrophic demise. Both dream stories came to pass and for that reason were not simply fiction, at least they have not remained it.

Apparently, the stories told in these dreams cannot be forced to correspond to the alternatives of either "fictional text or historical reality."

At this point, I might be permitted a historical excursion. The classical history of topoi associates *res fictae* with poetics [*Poetik*] and *res factae* with the theory of history [*Historik*]; formulated more polemically, the one has to do with appearance, the other with being: "Si fingat, peccat in historiam; si non fingat, peccat in poesin" [If you invent, you sin against history; if you don't invent, you sin against poetry].[3] On the basis of these two extreme positions, two camps can be identified, which rank either history or poetry higher. The former camp ranks the truth content of writing history higher than poetry, for whoever deals with *res factae* must depict reality itself, while *res fictae* lead to lies.

Naturally, historians were the ones who mostly took this view, which privileged their own position. Citing the metaphor of the mirror, in use since Lucian, they described their task as depicting "the naked truth" and nothing more. In 1714, Fénelon wrote of history's *nudité si noble et si majestueuse* [nakedness so noble and majestic] that it needs no additional poetic decoration.[4] Gottsched describes the noble task of the historian as "speaking the naked truth . . . to narrate events that have taken place without any varnish, without any makeup."[5] The ethos and pathos of the [nineteenth-century] historical school, especially its subtle philological method, which sought to show everything "the way it actually happened," as Lucian and later Ranke put it, surely derives from this approach. The excavation of events, the turn to the so-called core of the facts then gave rise to a methodological perspective that ruled out things like dreams as possible sources. Ever since the Enlightenment, dreams have belonged to the realm of mere fiction, their difficult accessibility notwithstanding: they do not count as events, as *res factae*, they count as neither actions nor deeds, even though Herodotus and many after him found them worth reporting.

Let us turn to the opposing position emphasizing the author's active, creative role more than any kind of mere reaction, which the mirror metaphor evokes. Indeed, Lucian already conceded that the mirror metaphor is insufficient for describing the task of the historian, and he immediately introduced an additional comparison: the historian must work like [the famous ancient Greek sculptor] Phidias. The material is given to him, but the important task is to properly develop the literary shape, so to speak, of that which happened through one's own activity, through *poiesis*.[6] Already with Lucian, we see, then, the epistemological naïveté of the mirror metaphor being retracted in favor of an alternative position, which invoked Aristotle.

Aristotle famously devalued history vis-à-vis poetry because history only attends to the unfolding of time in which various things happen, however they might occur. In contrast, poetry deals with the possible and the universal. As the eighteenth-century Aristotelian Lessing put it: "accidental historical truths can never become proof of necessary rational truths."[7] The inner likelihood of directionality is thus more powerful than the often all too questionable status of what was assumed to be historically true. In contrast to the historian, (as Lessing puts it in a more modern formulation), "the poet is master of history; and he can move events as closely together as he desires."[8]

Lessing was then also consistent enough to avoid using the term "history" [*Geschichte*] when he wrote as a philosopher of history in his *Education of the Human Race*. There he expressly did not deal with the *res factae* with which only historians would occupy themselves. Lessing may well have been familiar with the collective singular "history as such" intended to encompass the sum of all individual histories, a term that was just starting to be used at that time. But he did not yet allow the modern term to supercede the traditional hierarchy of history [*Historie*]— poetry—philosophy, and thereby present himself as a philosopher who dealt with "history as such"—something that he did do, according to our terminology, when composing his reflections on the progressions and aims of the human race.

Let us cut short this historical excursion on the two-thousand-year use of these two topoi. It remains uncontestable that fiction and facts [*Faktizität*] can be differentiated. It is undeniable that a difference exists between narratives reporting on what actually happened and those reporting on what could have happened, or claiming that it happened, or narratives that dispense with the slightest gesture toward reality. Instead, the question is much more whether an absolute differentiation can be made between fiction and facts that sets one realm aside for the poet and the other for the historian. It would seem that the relationship between *res factae* and *res fictae* is not something that can be distinguished on the basis of how the two function or their status as the objects of study of two different professional groups. As we well know, modern history in the eighteenth century opened up a new horizon of expectation and a new space of experience and *Poetik* and *Historik* have since come to stand in a new relation.

The first empirical test case of this is the osmosis between the novel and historiography in effect since the Enlightenment. The more the novel gained in its claim to present historical reality, the more the writing of history [*Historie*] was propelled toward generating meaningful units, without which history [*Geschichte*] could not be discerned.[9]

If we ask which came first, in Germany at least, it was the novel that was first designated as "history," as "true history," in advance of the transition by historians to deal with "history" rather than to narrate histories [*Historien*] drawn from individual stories [*Geschichten*]. Beginning in the mid-eighteenth century, "history as such" [*die Geschichte*] came to be the common topic of both. In turn, this semantic convergence is relevant to our initial question, for ever since this convergence, the theoretically decisive question no longer addresses the distinction between facts dealt with by historians and fictions created by poets. Indeed, the front line shifts and generates new categorizations by posing the following question: what is the relationship of the linguistic constitution of a history, whether it is the history of a writer of history, poetry, or any kind of text, to what from then on is experienced and designated as historical reality?

To explore this question, I would like to return to the dream stories [*Traumgeschichten*] and their fictional status; we were acquainted above with this status though we were not entirely satisfied with it. Of course, the dreams tell stories that never happened in the way they were narrated. However, something also happens in these dream stories that was unique and pertained directly to the historical reality at that time. These dreams are a liminal case, but they take us to the heart of our question.

For prior to being recollected in narrative form, these dreams played out in the interiority of the dreamers, they occurred in prelinguistic form, if you like. They thus take on a different significance for the psychoanalyst, but, under certain circumstances, also for the historian, than if only the structure of the narrative is considered.

These dreams open up sediments [of historical experience] that even diary entries cannot. And this applies to all the dreams collected and brought to safety in emigration by Charlotte Beradt. These dreams are from around three hundred people from 1930s Berlin; modes of experience are fractured therein with distressing vividness. Insidious conformity to the new regime, submission out of bad conscience, the spirals of fear, the paralysis of the opposition, the interaction between executioner and victim—all of this comes to the fore in these dreams, with slightly estranged imagery, in often strikingly realistic ways. The result is crushing.

Of course these are the dreams of the persecuted, but not theirs alone—these are also the dreams of people who conformed or wanted to conform but were not allowed to. We do not know the dreams of those excited by the new regime and the victors—those dreams also existed, and who knows how often their contents overlapped with the visions of those whom the victors crushed against the wall. At any rate the dream stories quoted here bear witness to terror that was often only silent at first, but whose open escalation they anticipate. With proper methodological care, the historian can therefore make use of them as a source and draw conclusions from these dreamt and then narrated stories. The historian can deduce the effects that the immanent terror of the National Socialist system had, at least in the early years, the kinds of oppressive fears generated by this terror, the images anticipating the coming catastrophe to which it gave rise.

To be sure, these kinds of questions are the result of a methodological limitation. The recorded dreams are presented as written sources in order to infer something that stands behind them, namely, the historical reality of the terror after 1933. The stories presented by the texts as clearly fictional are supposed to provide a glimpse of the factuality of the rising Third Reich. By recounting these methodological steps of the historian, we remain within the orbit of the separation of *res fictae* and *res factae*. The one is inferred on the basis of the other. To varying degrees, every unit of fictional text can in principle be presented as evidence of facts.

However, these particular dream stories are more than just a form of evidence that can be transformed into a historical source with the necessary methodological precautions. Even if they are only accessible as narrative, they already exist as prelinguistic histories that occurred in and to the persons in question. They are embodied ways in which the terror occurred. In other words: they were an element of the historical reality, precisely as fiction. And it is not simply that these dreams point to the conditions that made such dreams, as fictions, possible. As phenomena, these dreams are modes of implementing the terror.

The dreams of the doctor and the lawyer might certainly be interpreted in terms of individual psychology as long as we have access to their biographies. But in both of these dream stories, it stands out that the latent and the manifest contents of the dream overlap almost seamlessly. Even if private conditions are at work in these dreams, their political function is immediately apparent. To stay in the symbolic register of psychoanalysis, the political experiences and threats inundated the doorman and flooded unimpeded into the so-called subconscious. They allowed for images and histories to emerge that are immediately evident in their political valence to consciousness.

The elimination by decree of the walls removes all protection from the private sphere. The loudspeaker does not leave any doubt in the dreamer that his house is being broken into in the interests of a form of monitoring that can be carried out on any person in the name of the *Volksgemeinschaft*. The pressure on the lawyer to make room even for paper trash—indeed, to willingly make room for paper trash—is in need of no interpretive translation for anyone who has experienced history. The improbable becomes real in a self-acting paralysis. The persecuted give themselves over to an absurdity that is as existential as it is banal, before this absurdity is then inflicted upon them. Apparently, a bodily rationality exists that extends beyond the constraints imposed by fear upon the dreamer in his waking hours. Of course, this needn't necessarily be the case. If we may believe his recollections, George Grosz had a similar dream, which caused him to emigrate to America before it was too late.[10]

I will refrain here from continuing these historical dream analyses and breaking society as a whole down into complexes, transferences, and identification compulsions. The methodological difficulties are more significant than many statements about such an approach might lead us to believe.

For example, the dreams that Jean Cayrol collected inside the concentration camps resist any kind of direct political interpretation.[11] In this resistance to political interpretation, Cayrol glimpsed (presumably correctly) a chance at survival, because the complete and utter negation of the empirical self gave inmates the silent, mute weapon with which to confront inevitable death. Based on Cayrol's experiences, those still capable of dreaming socially and politically lost their ability to resist, because they drew this from an unattainable past. They gave death a larger chance than it already had, institutionally speaking, in the camps.

Through these reflections we have surreptitiously come to an insight regarding our opening question as to the relationship between fiction and facts, and I would like to formulate this insight as a thesis: historical reality never entirely overlaps with what can be articulated in it and about it.

By interrogating the contents of our dreams as the expression of political terror rather than in terms of their fictionality, we moved into a prelinguistic sediment in which something like historical reality became recognizable. At first it would seem that a liminal case made this possible, one that bridged the gap between fiction and reality in an uncommon manner. But the result is of more general importance: history is never completely identical to language. We find ourselves in an unresolvable tension, which prevents each and every linguistic action from ever fully capturing historical reality. And this applies to the carrying out of history as well as to the acts of recollection that reassemble the past in writing.

Of course, the reality of history takes place through perpetrators and endurers [*Erleider*] relating to each other linguistically, who act and react in language. No political unit of action is possible without language, without common concepts, orders, contracts, discussion, perhaps without propaganda and without the silence of those who do not or are not allowed to have a voice. However, historical reality first constitutes itself in between, before, or after the linguistic articulations that target it. In each case, language and sociopolitical issues intersect in ways that differ from the ways those speaking about them can grasp.

The reason for this is very simple, for what a history is only ever makes itself known retrospectively. And if this history has been, it is no longer reality, at least no longer in the way that it really is, as long as it is not yet completed.

This temporality of history cannot be captured in any linguistic act. To quote Goethe: "An important event is narrated in the same city differently in the evening than in the morning."[12] And this applies not just to history *ex post*, for also to history *in spe*. What you say today has a different meaning tomorrow. A word spoken once and a sentence written down once congeal irrevocably and unalterably as soon as they are preserved. But reception resists being controlled by the person who has spoken or written. We can therefore assume that no linguistic articulation, no matter of what kind or rank, can ever capture what really happens in history. History certainly never happens without language, but it is likewise always something different to language: something more or less.

If this thesis is correct, we can make an inference on its basis, for it follows that the relationship between fiction and historical reality can only be determined if the line dividing the discipline of history and fictional texts is not pushed too far. The historian, the literary historian, and the poet (or "writer" in contemporary usage) are all faced with the same incommensurability of historical reality and its linguistic processing. However, each of these figures reacts differently to this same challenge, and this is what I would like to explore in conclusion.

1. The historian begins with the assumption that no linguistic testimony entirely captures the reality that he or she is trying to ascertain. He or she does not interrogate a text, a diary, a letter, a record, a chronicle, a depiction for its own sake. In general, these only serve as sources to create a referential framework that aims at something lying behind the texts. Even treaties of international law, which represent the closest thing to the overlap of the text's meaning and its political function, are interrogated by historians for what they remain silent about or stylize, thus drawing conclusions about dynamics that can be discerned from a source text only indirectly.

Such questions differentiate the historian from the linguist and the literary historian, to the extent that the latter thematize a text for its own sake or for the sake of a statement therein. This is apparent, for example, in studies of the reality of fiction, as carried out by Iser [in the context of reception aesthetics].[13] Iser only incorporates extra- and prelinguistic factors into his analyses in order better to explain the structure of a fictional text that is immanent in its language. However, I do not want to suggest that this kind of study has no direct effect upon the task of the historian, for every historical statement exists on the basis of linguistically pregiven grids, which first create the condition for possible historical experience. However, a historical textual linguistics is still in the process of being developed.

At any rate, the majority of professional historians make use of linguistic testimonies in order to access something not immediately intended by these sources. And this applies all the more when a historian moves away from the so-called history of events and takes longer-term procedures, structures, and processes into consideration. Even if written sources can make events directly accessible, they certainly cannot do the same for procedures, structures, and processes. If a historian is justified in assuming that the conditions of possible events are just as interesting as the events themselves, he or she is required to transcend all linguistic and written sources, for every linguistic or written source remains tied to specific situations, and the excess of information that it might contain is never enough to grasp the historical reality that permeates all linguistic events.

Here I do not want to go into the methodological difficulties associated with generating long-term sequences or with establishing source-based proof for structural statements such as the claim that all history is the history of class struggles.

Instead, I am interested much more in the status of a historical utterance about the specific kind of historical reality that repeatedly withholds itself from being fixed linguistically—whether it is because history must always be rewritten, for it is always changing and provoking new questions, and because new expectations always work back upon it, or because fixing past history in writing always remains a risk. The only thing that is real in an accessible and verifiable sense are the sources that have been transmitted to us from the past. The reality of history that we derive from

them, in contrast, is a product of linguistic possibilities, theoretical pregivens, and methodological points of access that come together in a narrative or depiction. The result is not the reproduction of a past reality, but
instead, to put perhaps too much of a point on it, the fiction of the factual.

If I may be permitted to quote Goethe once more, this issue inherent
in language is exactly what he meant when he defined his autobiography
as a "kind of fiction."[14] He called it a fiction in part because he could only
recollect the results, not the events and particularities themselves, in part
in order to do justice to the claim to historical truth that only the medium
of fiction can realize. He described this fiction as narrative or indeed as
poetry, entangled as it is with truth in the title of his autobiography [*Dichtung und Wahrheit* (Poetry and Truth)].

Goethe defined his autobiography on the very linguistic level that
requires us to speak of the fiction of the factual, rather than naïvely of its
simple reproduction.

By no means, though, does the historian thereby achieve the same
freedom that is usually conceded to the poet, which allows the latter, as
Lessing put it, to situate the events he invents as closely together as he
desires.

The historian remains subject to a regulation of compulsory rationality. This regulative instance is negative in nature and is a result of historical method, for it disallows any statement that does not pass through the
test of source consultation, and sources offer a unique kind of resistance.
A source never shows what should be said, but always what cannot be said.
Sources have veto power. For this reason, and with proper methodological
preparation, they create a minimum realm for rational insight, such that
specific results of historical research can be universally communicated and
regulated, no matter the position of the historian.

Of course, this realm of source-based veto power should not be overestimated. But it is grounded in the kind of scientific empirical evidence
that is immune to statements that lay claim to a certain kind of overcon-
fident self-certitude. Historians are subject to a ban on certain kinds of
statements, which is self-imposed due to their source-based method.

It is for this reason that Alexander Kluge's novel *Schlachtbeschreibung* [Battle Description, translated as *The Battle* (of Stalingrad)][15] can
be counted among respectable historical achievements. For regardless of

his cutting and montage technique, Kluge drew upon enough sources to make his thesis testable, namely, that the catastrophe of Stalingrad had its origin in a hierarchical structure of unconscionable rigidity, demonstrable by social history. As an analysis of the conditions for the catastrophe, Kluge's thesis is certainly seriously debatable. Nonetheless, a perhaps more deeply seated and more broadly reaching factor is missing in Kluge's account (as it is in Theodor Plievier's Stalingrad novel),[16] namely, the fear of the Russians, something that can explain many things that were hardly written about at the time, because it was not allowed or it did not seem necessary to articulate them.

2. With Kluge and Plievier, we have shifted unwittingly into the realm of literary observation, without giving up the connection to historical reality. My critique of Kluge (above all, though, of Plievier) seeks to address a realm nearly inaccessible in sources, namely, one where fear is a key motivation for action. Here we confront a question that largely resists the methodological control of the historian, though one that thereby does not cease to be an issue of great significance in terms of historical efficacy. The transition from the factual to the fictional, however concrete, thus occurs on a sliding scale, as we saw with the dreams after 1933.

In other words, what constitutes historical reality is not only decided on the methodological level of source control, but already occurs whenever the attempt is made to articulate this reality linguistically. I said earlier that language and history never fully overlap. Historical events are certainly unthinkable without linguistic actions, and historical experience and memory cannot be transmitted without language. But numerous extra- and prelinguistic factors enter into each given history, and articulating these is certainly yet another linguistic achievement. Historical and fictional texts thus enter into close proximity.

This is because both are always engaged with the differentiation between linguistic articulation and extra-linguistic experience.

Let me demonstrate this through the case of a contemporary writer who dabbles in history and is a rather undistinguished dramatist. Dieter Forte's drama [about Martin Luther and the rebel leader Thomas Münzer] *Die Einführung der Buchhaltung* [The Introduction of Accounting][17] borrows its legitimacy from the use of historical sources—by the claim of the historical accuracy of what it puts on stage. However, the author's claim to have relied on historical evidence can easily be disproven. Chronological changes (e.g., of the date when Luther was assigned the Augustinian cloister) and omissions (e.g., of Luther's critical indictments of the princes) can quickly be challenged and dismissed as simple falsification by the historical sources. But such manipulations, of which historians are also guilty, are not what makes the Luther–Münzer piece a weak drama. The serious objection that must be raised is directed much more at the flawed theory of what history actually should be in this case. This objection functions on a level where writers of history and of fiction meet. Ranke and Forte should be placed on the same level when it comes to the reception history of the Reformation, but we should for this reason also subject them to the same criteria when they claim to depict the Reformation as historical reality.

Forte creates his characters in such a way that the supposed results of the Reformation in later epochs of German history are imputed to the figures acting at the time of the Reformation. This leads to a personalized history with disregard of the actual historical persons in question. Forte's Luther speaks like [Kaiser] Wilhelm II, who was known to be given to Luther-like turns of phrase. But the distinction between someone speaking like Luther and the speech of Luther himself is lost on Forte. To each word its proper place [*jedes Wort an seinem Ort*].

By projecting supposed effects back onto supposed causes, Forte loses sight a fortiori of a key aspect of history, namely, that it can never be derived entirely from its pregivens, or that it can never be entirely identical to its effect thus far. Like many historians, Forte proposes a linear theory of development that interprets the Reformation as an early bourgeois revolution and thereby seeks to inspire the contemporary viewer in a political manner. If the Reformation really is supposed to be a bourgeois revolution in a nutshell (and some things do speak in favor of such an interpretation), then the tragic hero would certainly have to be [the banker Jacob] Fugger, not Münzer, it being the former who was unable to impose his economic interests upon the ruling structures of the nobility. Fugger's debtors, the high nobility of the empire, remained in power longer than he, their financial lender, whose family the nobility attempted thoroughly to integrate into their system.

The historical reality was more complex than Forte perceived, and this is not just a theoretical issue but also one of simple source consultation. For Luther was economically conservative and theologically revolutionary; Fugger, in contrast (whom Forte throws into the same boat as Luther), was economically progressive yet theologically conservative. The lines of conflict did not run linearly, but instead were multilayered and fractured.

To quote Goethe one final time: "The more incommensurable and ungraspable a poetic production is for the understanding, the better."[18] It could well be that Goethe asked something of poetry that applies all the more when this poetry is tasked with depicting historical reality. History can be rationalized through language, but this does not mean that it is anywhere close to becoming rational.

Evidence of this might well be found in Kleist's *Verlobung in St. Domingo* [1811; Betrothal in Santo Domingo], as a representation of the first slave revolt launched under the sign of the French Revolution, or Melville's *Benito Cereno* [1855], as a story key to understanding the American Civil War. The linguistic testimonies of these writers capture more historical reality for the situation around 1800 or around 1860, perhaps, than all historical genres combined, for the distinction that remains pre-given to us is not that between fiction and facts, but between history and linguistic testimonies.

3. A closing remark on literary history, which today takes the form of the social history of literature or reception history: a science [*Wissenschaft*] understood in this way can become historiography in the best sense of the word. Of course, it is burdened with all of the methodological and theoretical difficulties that every historian faces, namely, having to submit to the veto power of the sources without being able to describe historical reality sufficiently on this basis. At any rate, the discipline of history can be thankful for the support that it receives from literary scholarship understood in this way. "History" enters through the back door, though many thought the front door had already been slammed shut in its face.

3

Space and History

To speak of space and history and to correlate the two means to address two concepts that are quite common and well known from everyday usage. In theoretical terms, however, these concepts are anything but clear and agreed upon. Whether I speak of space as four-dimensional or define it as a force field or a form of pure intuition; speak of living space [*Lebensraum*] or of the space of the heart within which the gnat [still] leaps [as Rilke says];[1] define history as narrative or the founding of identity or a reservoir for the consolidation of identity; or circumscribe it as a field for exploring questions posed by the social sciences, all of these various preliminary choices lead us to very different determinations of the relation between space and history. No one will deny that history, whatever it may be, deals in some way with space, or, rather, that histories deal with spaces. But both categories' claims to universality are so high that they either pale under closer scrutiny or become emotionally overburdened.

A glance at the relevant literature on the topic only adds to the confusion. At first glance it stands out that the old *Historie* thematized the human world, its works and actions, and nature without strongly differentiating between the two.[2] This analogy is apparent in Japanese, where the same expression is used for history and space. In Europe, nature and history diverge at the latest in the eighteenth century. At the same time, nature, which up to that point had been conceived of as static, came to be historicized and subject to diachronic laws of development. *Historia naturalis*, previously a subset of knowledge about nature [*Naturkunde*] within the older, all-encompassing *historia*, now took on a life of its own as the history of nature. Nature became temporalized and has been studied ever since as something distinct, with its own inherent patterns of temporal sequence, with scientific methods that diverge from those of the humanities.[3] A questionable opposition thus emerges between nature and history, one that still occupies us today, perhaps now more than ever in light of the various ecological challenges that we face. However, I have omitted the absence of the concept "space" from this sketch. This is simply because we lack a thorough conceptual history of "space," even though many good accounts of the concept in the natural sciences are available.[4] To this extent, then, my theoretical reflections on history and space move on unstable ground, both in the following section and in the conclusion, where I shall try to bring space and time into relation.

I

Ever since the eighteenth century, space and time have been correlated with each other in general ways, but the same does not apply to space and history. The natural sciences developed their own theories and methods of measurement for analyzing space and time, just as the historical sciences have their own theories and methods of measurement that make use of space and time as historical categories. This opposition of scientific and historical categories of space and time is modern. The study of nature, geography in the more limited sense as well as chronology, was part of the older *historia* as a universal science of experience. At the latest with Kant and Herder, it came to be a basic principle of historians that they are concerned with space and time, meaning thereby historical space and historical time, understood within the horizon of their own historicization.

Ever since, geography has found itself in a precarious in-between position, obliged to be part of both the pure natural sciences and the humanities and social sciences, as anthropogeography or cultural geography, and so on.[5] Properly understood, geography can thus only be conceived of as an interdisciplinary science, even though in former times the more self-confident historians categorized it only as an auxiliary science.

Let us explore several foundational accounts of space and time by historians that serve as the premises of their own discipline [*Wissenschaft*].

Droysen explicitly situates himself in the Kantian tradition, defining space and time as "indices of our comprehension" and its sign systems, indices that "as such" do not exist in the external world. He adopts the transcendental orientation of Kant. As he states, space and time "prove to be correlative, so that everything that we can take note of through perception falls in their either-or. [. . .] But space and time, these most universal of intuitions, are empty."[6] They must be filled empirically. Droysen does not address the thought that historical agents and their interactions refer in each case to specific spaces and times, a notion that Herder had already explored in his critique of Kant. It was the achievement of the Humboldt brothers, of Ritter, Kapp, and Ratzel to thematize the spatio-temporal constitution of empirical histories. Lamprecht would then become their heir (or rather colleague) when pursuing this concept in his regional history, which represented a kind of empirically grounded history of society that sought to bundle all conditions and factors of a circumscribed totality.[7]

Faced with the formal alternative of space or time, the overwhelming majority of historians opted for the dominance of time, though this dominance was not very theoretically grounded. Bernheim argued, for example, that historical subject matter allows for no systematic classification. For this reason he simply wrote about historical method as part of a "philosophy of history." For history is grounded, he states, in temporal sequence. As changes in time, events resist any systematic understanding. The axiom of historical singularity prevails, something that is plausible, perhaps. However, more astonishing is his conclusion that a systematic approach to space is even less possible: "The form of appearance in the spatial realm, despite its eminent importance, has so much less uniform significance for historical analysis that one cannot base a general classification upon it, and instead must subordinate it to the temporal realm."[8] Even Helmholt's geographically conceived world history does not organize the material spatially; instead (as Bernheim argues), he organizes it ethnically and culturally, that is to say ultimately merely chronologically, and not according to spaces.

Rieß reaffirms this verdict in his positivistic theory of history [*Historik*] of 1912. On one of the book's four hundred pages he mentions unalterable geographical conditions of historical constellations, concluding:

"But these kinds of self-evident preconditions of historical thought need not detain us in a serious methodology of the science of history." He leaves these self-evident conditions to geographers and statisticians.[9] This preference of time over space in the theories of history I have mentioned is initially plausible. For the historian has always been interested in novelties, in transformation and in change, when he or she asks how it has come to pass that the present is different from the past. There is also a more particular reason, namely, the experience of singularity that has come to prevail with the advent of technical-industrial progress and its unrelenting transformational impulse in Europe ever since the 1770s. Ever since, history in its entirety can be treated as a singular sequence under the predominance of chronology, not simply because events surpass one another, which they have always done, but because the societal formations, that is, the structural preconditions of the events themselves change. However, this empirical experience by no means forces us to privilege the history of events; indeed, it was possible for this year's conference of [German] historians [*Historikertag*] to be held on the topic of space and history.

My thesis then would be the following: categorically speaking, space is just as much a condition of possible history as time. But "space" too has a history. Space is both something that should be metahistorically presupposed for every possible history and something that is historicizable, because it changes socially, economically, and politically. This dual usage of the category of space has thus given rise to several ambiguities, which I now would like to clarify.

First: the history of different conceptions of space that follow upon each other has been well researched and need not be repeated here. This includes the transition from mythical cosmogonies to cosmologies that increasingly lend themselves to empirical verification; the discovery of the spherical shape of the earth (previously held to be flat), which allowed for the breakthrough discovery of Newton's so-called absolute, infinite space; all the way up to this space's relativization, something that had already begun with Leibniz and led all the way to Einstein, whether this relativized four-dimensional space was conceived as a static or dynamic entity. In general, as historians, we can ascribe this history of ideas of space to the history of philosophy and of the natural sciences, fields that have certainly had an influence on economics and politics, though they do not address the history of space that is the topic of historians of political or historical geography.

Second: historical geography emerged from the early modern comparative statistical depiction of different respective spatial units conceived of as territorial states. It reconstructs the past spaces of life and action that were particular to political, legal, economic, ecclesiastical, or social units of action as understood within the framework of their shifting or shifted geographical pregivens and consequences. In contrast to the reconstruction of past conceptions of space, historical geography aims at the reconstruction of past so-called realities. Contemporary cartography of the ancient world, for example, does not collate its data and records with the conceptions of space of that time, but instead depicts these data in maps generated according to contemporary modes of measurement, thereby taking into account the geological or climatic changes that have since occurred and have been recognized by science, but were obviously unknown to antiquity. In the course of justifying their discipline, historical geographers have constantly clashed with their colleagues in the natural sciences, who pursue their geography without accounting for the human being as acting subject. Theoretically, this conflict has now become rather obsolete,[10] for neither the authority of geology as a natural science nor that of anthropogeography are in need of further self-justification.

I would therefore like to approach our question as to the relationship between space and history in terms of a scale between two poles. On the one end of the scale, we find the natural preconditions of every human history, which remain dependent on natural pregivens, or more specifically, to use Ratzel's terminology, on geographical situations [*Lagen*]. At the other end of the scale, we find the kinds of spaces that the human themselves create or that he or she is forced to create in order to survive. It is between these two poles that the productive tension emerges between geologists and morphologists, on the one hand, and anthropogeographers or spatial planners, on the other.

Let me elaborate in regards to history: the natural pregivens of human history are based in what astrophysics, geology, geography, biology, and zoology study as sciences. All of these natural pregivens have their own history, with developmental lines that are calculated in terms of millions and billions of years. In each case we are dealing with histories that occur independent of human consciousness, but that can only be reconstructed *ex post* within our historical consciousness. All of the data that these natural histories offer us should be defined as metahistorical in relation to human history. These metahistorical conditions of possible histories are those that withhold themselves from human intervention and that, as conditions of our action, provoke human activity. To name just a few familiar ones: land and sea, the coasts and the rivers, the mountains and plains, all of the geological formations, including their natural resources. The latter are metahistorical pregivens as well, because they can be exploited but not replenished. Climate and climate change are part of this, without which we could not account for transformation in flora and fauna or the genesis of higher aggregated human cultures. In every case we are dealing with the pregivens of possible histories that escape human control but not human use.

In our century, like it or not, the climate has entered the realm of possible human control, just as for millennia the world of plants and animals increasingly became subject to human control. Our globe might soon be transformed into a single zoo, though one might well ask who holds whom captive, the animals or the humans. Limits on the control and use of resources have shifted enormously over the course of human history, and it would be an exciting story to account for this process—as a contribution to the ecology of the present—as a common undertaking, from the perspectives both of natural science and of political and social history. Theoretically this would entail asking where the metahistorical pregivens of the human *Lebensraum* shift or are transformed into historical pregivens that humans can influence, master, or exploit. To be sure, the weather is still capable of causing famines or decisively altering battles. Seen in this light, the relational scale between space and history shifts depending on whether spatial pregivens are conceived of as metahistorical or historical.

This leads me to the opposite end of the scale, namely, to purely human, historical spaces. This would include the different spaces that humans create, to which they adapt as hunters of animals, which they appropriate, settle, work on, shape, or which they must abandon due to pressure from their enemies. In all cases we are dealing with different spaces that can exclude and include each other—and that increasingly overlap in modernity, depending on the human units of action in question and their various spheres of action. I need only recall the space-opening trade and transportation routes or the medieval and early modern pilgrimages that passed through politically and legally distinct spaces, or through completely unorganized spaces on the high seas. Or I might recall the conquering of the third dimension: this has occurred since the beginning of human history in the case of mining and more recently in the depths of the ocean or in universal airspace. All of this points to the economic and military imbrication of human spaces of action, whose increasing entanglement is the challenge and topic of our world history.

There are numerous scientific accounts that gauge in various ways the transformation of space by human action as well as human agents' dependence upon geographical pregivens. Faber has shown that the research questions of geographers and historians often converge in regional history, and, moreover, that the vision of a so-called total history of society as put forth by Ratzel, Turner, Vidal de la Blache, and Henry Berr can be tested out to a certain extent in historical geography.[11] As I have mentioned above, this concerns the pragmatic construction, through research, of entities that remain small enough that all factors, from climate and geology to the economy and politics, can be taken into account in tandem. Theoretically, though, this kind of regional delimitation is only acceptable if isolating distinct spaces in this way is justifiable. This certainly no longer applies for modernity, where every space has come to stand in relation to the globality of empirically mediated humanity.

Third: this brings me to an observation about so-called geopolitics, an avidly discussed and contested topic. In terms of the history of knowledge, the emergence of geopolitics is not accidental—indeed, it emerged together with an empirically verifiable global interdependency of all economic and political units of action. You will allow me to pass over an ideology critique of proponents of geopolitics, something that the German geopoliticians of the 1920s and 1930s certainly deserve as much as the German literary scholars and historians of the period, as do, to turn westwards, authors such as Homer Lea, Mahan, Mackinder, or Goblet, who were saturated with naturalistic or social Darwinist ideas. Schöller has already given this common critique a more solid scientific grounding,[12] so I only need to mention arguments that place the questions implied by geopolitics into the framework of a theory of history [*Historik*].

Our distinction between metahistorical spatial pregivens and historical spaces of human organization might be useful here. There are natural spatial pregivens that must be taken into account as conditions of possible action in every historical and political analysis according to the varying challenges they present to technical, economic, or political control. The fact that South Africa does not have an opposing European coast like Algeria fundamentally alters the status of the civil war threatening the southern part of Africa. The political solution that de Gaulle brought about and acceded to is not so easily attained in southern Africa. Inescapable geographical location thus conditions the desperate rule of the white minority in a different way than that of the French in Algeria.

To give a different example: the geographical pregiven of the British Channel has remained one of the constant protective conditions of the development of the British world empire. It was first effective with the defeat of the Spanish Armada in 1588 and was only [subsequently] penetrated once, by the successful invasion of William of Orange in 1688. These protective conditions no longer apply today, with the transformed economic power potentials and their corresponding ballistic and atomic weapon systems. Today, in political terms, the Channel has become a river. But as late as 1940, the impossibility of conquering a thirty kilometer–wide landing strip on the other side of the Channel was the first military failure that led Hitler, and thus us Germans, down the road to catastrophe, at least in military-technical terms. The metahistorical condition of the Channel became a historical factor because and to the extent that it resisted the control of a political unit of action: in this case, the German air force and navy.

A third example: the shifting ice cap over the North Pole is a geographical pregiven; in the space of action of the strategy of ballistic missiles, this pregiven has taken on—and here we might risk the word—geopolitical significance. Soviet and American nuclear submarines operating under the ice can surface and carry out annihilative strikes from positions that are difficult to reach.

A fourth example: according to Thucydides, the Trojan War lasted as long as it did due to the small number of ships on the Greek peninsula that could be collected and mobilized at the same time to cross the Aegean Sea and conquer Troy.

The metahistorical geographical conditions of human spaces of action thus change their spatial quality depending on how they come to be economically, politically, or militarily conquerable. Or, to put it theoretically: the conversion of metahistorical situations [*Lagen*] (to use Ratzel's term) into historical spaces is a question for a theory of history. Every historiography makes implicit or explicit use of it. At stake here is not the word "geopolitics," which its proponents have discredited, but historical circumstances in need of conceptualization. Ranke was right, for example, when he stated that the opposition between Asia and Europe is historical and not geographical—an opposition that Herodotus introduced and that has remained valid up to the present day, as it turns out.[13]

And a final reference: in 1919 and in his melodramatic terminology, Mackinder interpreted the opposition between land and sea on the basis of the current military and economic conditions so as to envision the potential border of Europe as running from Lübeck to Trieste. For Mackinder, this represented the border zone between Anglo-Saxon maritime rule and Russian land rule.[14] Should we argue that Mackinder's prognosis rests on pure coincidence, or is it not the case that, under historically unique conditions, he was diagnosing the conversion from a geographically metahistorical pregiven into a historically political spatial determination? At that time, he called for the resettlement of all East Prussians under the control of the Prussian Junkers. He hoped, at Germany's expense, to establish a politically stronger Polish barrier against Asia, that is, against communist Russia, and he thereby developed a train of thought that was effectively put into motion later on by the Germans—with the very result prognosticated by Mackinder.

Let me draw two conclusions. First: viewed within the framework of a general theory of history, so-called geopolitics deals with questions of the determinants of human freedom. There are numerous social, economic, or political determinants that in every case both enable and limit the space for potential action. These determinants also include extrahistorical geographical pregivens that must be incorporated into the canon of historical research questions. This applies today perhaps more than ever before in light of the ecological crisis. The theoretical mistakes (not to mention nonsense) of so-called geopoliticians resulted from turning these determinants of possible action into naturalistic or ontologically fixed laws that were supposedly capable of guiding or mastering history. My critique here is not exclusively directed at geopolitics or at numerous ambiguously formulated passages in the important work of Ratzel, but also, on a theoretical level, at numerous analogous conceptual mistakes in our own historical science, to the extent that historians impute necessities, economic ones, for example, that are not provable. No event has ever been any more likely to occur because it has been defined as necessary.

My second conclusion is likewise a general one. Geopolitics saw itself as a practical science, as providing political information. Here we might merely add that German politics was poorly informed—if it was even capable of being informed under Hitler. Hitler would have never been allowed to begin the war in the first place if a rational geographical and historical analysis of space and its military potential had been applied. If the geopolitics of the time played any kind of role in decision making, such decisions depended on false theoretical premises, for geopolitics took it upon itself to restylize geographical pregivens into agents that had already begun to carry out law-like necessities, or would do so in the future. Uncovering this kind of error puts the critique of ideology on firm scientific footing. But it does not follow from this that it is in all cases wrong for science to inform political judgments. The retreat of contemporary geographers into the geography of cultural landscapes and anthropogeography in order to be active in spatial planning at this level, whether in order to draw new administrative boundaries or to enable higher aggregated units of administration, only confirms on a small scale the challenge that we continue to face on a larger scale, at the level of the European economic community, for example.

In a single sentence: the poorly formulated questions and the quasi-ontological premises of geopolitics nonetheless aimed at the natural pregivens of human possibilities for action, and it remains necessary to incorporate these pregivens into every analysis of historical or political conditions.

II

In a second step let me attempt to correlate our question about spatial, metahistorical, and historical conditions temporally. It is self-evident that every human space of action, whether private or public, whether in the realm of interpersonal gaze and touch or of global interdependencies, always also has a temporal dimension in order for it to be experienced or controlled as space. The diachronic pregivens that constitute the space of experience are part of this temporal dimension just as much as the expectations that are connected to it, whether conveniently or awkwardly. Proximity and distance, which distinguish a space in variously stratified ways, may only be experienced through time, and it is time that allows for immediate proximity or mediated distance to be opened up or bridged in each case. I mention these anthropological findings so as to address the shifting relation of space and time as a foundational context for every human interpretation and self-interpretation. Simmel's sociology of space and the work of Plessner, Gehlen, Heidegger, and Viktor von Weizsäcker raise numerous important questions for historians that have yet to be answered. The beautiful German word *Zeitraum* [space-time] is not simply a metaphor of chronology or of periodization, but instead invites the possibility of examining the mutual relationality of space and time in their respective articulations. Here I would simply like to draft a diachronic sketch that presents more questions than answers. It is a commonplace that spatio-temporal relations have changed over the course of our human history according to a pattern of seemingly ever increasing acceleration. This can be seen in three exponential time curves, which correspond in each case to entirely different spaces.

First, the differentiation of humans takes place in ever shortening intervals.[15] Measured against the five billion years since the earth's crust became solid and against the one billion years of organic life on this crust, the ten million years or so of primate-like humans represent just a small span of time, and the two million years in which there is evidence of self-made tools appear that much shorter in comparison. Without a doubt, geological and geographical, biological and zoological—in short, metahistorical pregivens of human determinations of space have a much more pronounced effect in this period than in later phases of our history.

Humans were able to make use of their environment without being able to control it. Relatedly, however, the minimal space of action for attaining sufficient sustenance for hunter families or hunter-gatherer families or bands was much larger (and had to be much larger) than what individual human groups have access to today. Prehistorians calculate multiple square kilometers per person in the Early and Middle Stone Age.[16] The metahistorical determinants, namely, plant growth for the gatherers or the migrational patterns of the wild animals to be hunted likewise set certain minimal boundaries that extend much further and must necessarily offered larger spaces of action for life than was possible in later phases. The process whereby hunter-gatherer cultures have increasingly been suppressed in favor of a consolidation of our human spaces of action, which are circumscribed through agriculture or industry, has continued all the way into our century.

This takes us to our second phase, which we might conceptualize (contra Bernheim) in ideal-typical terms as the structured period of our history. Compared to the two million years of verifiable history of humanity, the thirty thousand years or so in which products of a differentiated, reflexively applied art appear (as well as the invention of weapons capable of killing other humans) represents a relatively short time span. The introduction of farming and domesticated animals around twelve thousand years ago and finally, based on this, the unfolding of advanced cultures around six thousand years ago—again, in comparison to prehistory, these represent intervals of time that became ever shorter, intervals within which the new appeared. Ever since, the new has become one of the durable preconditions of our own lives. In turn, this time span corresponds to the human ability to organize and divide up space, which then enabled the conditions of all of our histories all the way up to the so-called early modern period, and did so in a quasi-static, that is to say, repetitive, manner. In this period, a structural model emerged that hypostatized the spatio-temporal unity and overlapping effects of our advanced cultures, and this lasted until the eighteenth century at the latest. Since then, the control of geographical as well as other kinds of pregivens, in any case, of metahistorical pregivens, has increased dramatically. One might say that metahistorical pregivens have increasingly been historically incorporated [into human life]—with limits, of course, that could not be surpassed all the way through the early modern period. Rivers were regulated, canals built, dams erected, drainage and irrigation projects planned and carried out, and transport routes built over thousands of kilometers, while inland seas and coastal waters became navigable and masterable. The organizational density of communication, postal, and transport systems had already reached its greatest effectivity in the oriental empires, not to be surpassed by the Romans or the Mongols under Genghis Kahn. This is not to say that this or that aspect could not be perfected, but it was only in terms of what was finitely possible. The speeds at which people traversed the geographically pregiven, and at times expanded and improved routes, remained constrained by nature. Even the invention of the wagon could not accelerate horses or oxen above their inborn maximums. If relay riders were able to cover two hundred kilometers in a single day, it was a record that held throughout the pre-industrial era. Cicero calculated that a letter to Athens would take three weeks to be delivered, and this was the same time span that a Hanseatic merchant had to plan for his message from Danzig to Bruges, or a Florentine merchant for his dispatch to Paris. The goods themselves, even if they were transported via quicker and cheaper but also riskier sea routes, required two, three, or four times as long as message delivery. We might also add, however, that the people of this era or "space-time" also had the corresponding time for themselves in order to pass through this space, conceived of in organizational and legal terms. Space-time relations were stabilized at a level that remained relatively constant and was not raised for around five thousand years, although disrupted by wars, when detours were necessary and transport routes might be entirely closed off in order to keep the analogous space-time open for troop movements. This was the time of the great empires, spread out across different regions, each viewing itself as the center of the earth. Neither the compass, the printing press, nor gunpowder, which were known to them, motivated the Chinese to explore the Pacific.

This brings us to the third phase. If we limit our view to the six thousand years or so of our own advanced cultures, we can once more recognize an exponential time curve. Within this framework, the kind of acceleration that has lasted the past two hundred years and characterizes our own life world occurs.[17] Transformed by science, technology, and industry, our world is now familiar with processes of acceleration that have altered all space-time relations in a fundamental, and, more accurately, fluid, manner. I need only mention the increase of the world population from around a half billion people in the seventeenth century to around six billion in the year 2000. Connected with this is the consolidation of human life through advances in science and technology, emanating from Europe, making possible the transformation of our globe into a self-enclosed spaceship [*geschlossenes Raumschiff*]; the globe as spaceship—is this a metaphor or reality? That is what we have to ask ourselves.

In closing, let me mention several points that characterize the change in space-time relations in our third phase. To continue our example, the European states had already greatly expanded and accelerated communication networks in advance of the Industrial Revolution. It was already possible to double travel time on country roads long before the railway turned a day into an hour and the night into day. Long before steamships came onto the scene, clipper ships doubled the speed of earlier sailing ships. The communication network became more dense, and ever more locations could be reached by mail.[18] It was regulated with schedules accurate down to the hour prior to the introduction of the minute-by-minute schedule of the railway. The measurement of time was standardized, as were the legal status of taxes, custom duties, and the salaries of postal civil servants and transporters. In sixteenth-century Paris, there were just three carriages, one for the king, one for the queen, and one for a nobleman who was too fat to be able to ride a horse. Now, the transportation network was accessible by all, or at least for everyone who could pay for it. And finally, taken together, all of these factors enabled the expansion of rule, the intensification of control, and the increased surveillance of all. This complex, which too has its economic prerequisites and conditions, can be seen as paradigmatic for what might be called a denaturalization of geographically pregiven space: it is a process that has since incorporated all units of action on our globe organized as states.

But this was by no means the end point in the wake of the Industrial Revolution. The scale of what in each case represented optimal units of actions changed in absolute terms. Optimal units of action could be bigger or smaller, depending on the inner organizational density. We know that Portugal in the sixteenth century could be a world power, just like Holland in the seventeenth century, and England in the eighteenth and nineteenth and even into the twentieth century, and this occurred with ever larger expansions that unfolded in phases, as well as with increasing intensification of internal rule.

Today, continental blocs rather than individual states oppose each other, blocs that can assume that the other is capable militarily of making the final possible decision that remains for us to make. These are greater [geopolitical] areas [*Großräume*], and the larger part of the rest of the earth's inhabitants depend on their economies. *Cuius regio, eius oeconomia* [Whose realm, his economy]. Or rather: *Cuius oeconomia, eius regio.*

This then raises the question that concerns our globe as a whole. Even if the normal everyday life of our fellow inhabitants of earth still entirely depends on the form of state organization and rule of the citizens or those affected—take the Chilean democrats or the Polish Solidarity movement or the Palestinians in Israel or the blacks in South Africa—in many ways, all state spaces of organization have become permeable, and in ways much more extensive than before. In other words, state and sovereignty no longer converge today as they did at the beginning of our modern acceleration.

Economic self-reliance—which used to be the mercantilist ideal—would mean the downfall of most states. Regression into what we have described as the second phase of our world history would come at the price of unceasing catastrophe. This means that economic interdependence is designed for a global scale, even if the globe is organized in different ways politically. This also applies to additional aspects: in terms of military technology, the unity of the world has been established by controlling airspace, through airplanes, rockets, and satellites. Air (like water, as Justinian stated) is the property of all: this leads to necessary constraints on action that must be defined as global. Even if launch pads remain tied to the ground or to boats on the water, the attainable targets are ubiquitous.

It would then seem that the historical quality of the elements has changed. Today, international law has been used increasingly to territorialize the space of water [*Wasserraum*], whether it is to exploit the underwater natural resources by extending the zones of control to which states lay claim, to make use of water flora, or in the future to tend oceanic schools of fish like domestic animals and to cultivate them and secure food sources. But even if water ends up being territorialized completely in the twenty-first century—in the sense that the water legally belongs to land powers—the same will never happen to the air, despite all sovereign rights. More than all other elements, the air points to the unity of our living space [*Lebensraum*], however the political borders may run or be drawn. In closing, one final point: the air is also the carrier of our contemporary communication system, with radio, television, and satellites. This has introduced spatio-temporal compression, which does not simply enable our daily routine as couch potatoes in front of the TV, but instead shapes politics to ever-increasing degrees. Events and the reports about the very same events increasingly coincide, at times completely. In Venice around 1500, people were in denial for years [about reports] that the Portuguese had already found a direct maritime route to India.[19] This was an economic threat of the highest order; it was feared as a catastrophe and could thus be repressed. Today, these kinds of repressions and delays in perception are no longer possible. We live under an intensive compulsion and necessity to perceive, which forces politicians to retreat into the future to the same extent that space has shrunken.

With events predictably occurring virtually simultaneously with reports of them, the need to plan ahead is all the greater, because [quick] decisions about how to respond have to be made. Chernobyl, which has impinged on our bodies through the air, is just one instance of the interdependence of our global space in which we are bound to live.

I have thus sketched three exponential time curves that correspond to three completely different spaces of life and action. The first was large-scale space in which natural pregivens dominated. In the second phase, the metahistorical preconditions became increasingly controllable and usable and the natural determinants of human freedom and political spaces of actions were historically subsumed and transformed. Cities, empires, and then states emerged with spaces of action that were to be optimally organized but whose natural conditions could not be transcended. Indeed, there were empires that perished as a result of their (over)extension.

And finally we have sketched a third phase: the acceleration of our own era or space-time, leading to the consolidation of the globe into a single unit of experience. How it will be formed as a unit of action is a question of politics and not of geography. But recalling the fact that natural pregivens of our lives may have longer or shorter durations takes us back to the teachings of history writing of old, which used to view nature and the human world as a single entity.

4

Historik and Hermeneutics

A life can be long or short. When it is short, as with Schiller, Kleist, or Büchner, the individual's story is wrapped in mourning, because life couldn't continue to write the biography. When it is long, as with Kant or Heidegger, one gets the sense that both the past and the historical future are fully contained and elaborated in their late work. We'll never know what Schiller might have said in 1813, Kleist in 1830, Büchner in 1848, but we can extrapolate what Kant would have said about these years, and Heidegger expressed what he had to say about our future.

The duration of a person's life evidently affects the quality of life, with its intervals of time that only ever become—increasingly, biologically—shorter and shorter. With growing age, the scarcity of time gains a certain experiential thickness and intensity that is not possible in lives that are broken off early. Such intensity is at best forced into existence, as with Schiller, or consciously rejected, as with Kleist; or, as with Büchner, physiological reasons prevent any chance of reaching this heightening intensity, allowing for nothing but death.

Seen in this light, our jubilarian Gadamer is a very special case. The older he has become—the older he is—the younger and livelier he has become. He completed his major work *Wahrheit und Methode* [Truth and Method] at the age of sixty; building upon this, he has since explored many more aspects of the past and the future than in the years prior. And here we already have a biographical entry point into the central problem of his philosophical work, the relationship of hermeneutics to time. All understanding that lacks a temporal index remains mute. Whether of a specific text or conceived of ontologically, as a human, existential project [*Entwurf menschlicher Existenz*] in search of meaning, the understanding—all understanding—is fundamentally bound to time. It is bound not simply to the current situation or the contemporary zeitgeist, which synchronically brings people into resonance with each other, not simply to the sequential unfolding of time, to temporal change or transformation; rather, for Gadamer, the understanding is tied to reception history [*Wirkungsgeschichte*]. The origins of reception history cannot be calculated diachronically; instead its main point is that each person can only experience it in his or her own time [*in der je eigenen Zeit*]. Indeed, Gadamer's life elaborates his own hermeneutic experience. Time is not just the linear succession of ontic data—it is fulfilled in the temporalization [*Zeitigung*] of the person who, via the understanding, internalizes his own time, bundles all temporal dimensions within himself or herself, thereby making the most of experience. Gadamer's philosophical hermeneutics is intimately intertwined with the question of the historical conditions of our reliance upon the understanding if we are to live. For this reason Gadamer's hermeneutics deals with what the study of history calls, as part of its purview, *Historik* (the theory of history), namely, the thematization of the conditions of possible histories, which is to say of the aporias of human finitude in its temporality.

The question, then, that I want to pose and attempt to answer here is the relationship of the theory of history and hermeneutics.

Gadamer's hermeneutics makes the implicit (and also in part explicit) claim to encompass the theory of history. Like theology, jurisprudence, poetry, and its interpretation, history falls under the larger heading of existential understanding [*Begreifen*]. Predisposed to understand, the human being cannot but transform his or her experience of history into meaning, cannot but hermeneutically absorb such experience in order to live.

To be sure, written history [*Historie*], as the science of history and the art of its representation or narration, is indisputably part of the hermeneutic cosmos that Gadamer has designed. Through listening and speaking and textual mediation, the historian operates on the same platform as the theologian, the jurist, and the interpreter of poetry, the other paradigmatic figures of Gadamerian hermeneutics. Admittedly, then, Gadamer's existential hermeneutics elastically encompasses and implicates *Historie*. Whoever relies on language and texts cannot evade the claims of Gadamer's hermeneutics; this likewise holds for *Historie*. However, does it also hold for *Historik*, for a theory of history that does not examine empirical findings about past histories, but instead asks as to the conditions of possible history? Are the conditions of possible history exhausted in language and texts? Or do conditions exist that are extra-linguistic, prelinguistic, even if we explore them linguistically? If such preconditions for history exist, preconditions that can neither be exhausted in language nor refer back to texts, then such a theory of history must have a theoretical status that makes it more than simply a subset of hermeneutics. This is the thesis that I hope to ground in what follows, proceeding in two steps.

First, I will sketch what such a theory of history might look like that draws attention to its prelinguistic characteristics. I will pursue this via a reading of [Heidegger's] *Being and Time*, for Gadamer's existential hermeneutics is unthinkable without this work. Secondly, I will compare my outline of a theory of history that addresses prelinguistical conditions of possible histories to positions from Gadamer's central book, *Truth and Method*.

I. *Historik*

Here, then, are several suggestions for how we might conceive of a prelinguistic theory of history. As a theoretical science and in contrast to empirical *Historie*, the theory of history does not deal with individual histories themselves, whose past, present, and potential future realities are examined by historical fields of study. Rather, *Historik* is the theory of the conditions of possible histories. It asks about the theoretically discernible presuppositions that make conceivable why histories occur, how they unfold, and, likewise, how and why they must be examined, represented, or narrated. *Historik* thus aims at grasping the double-sided nature of each history, encompassing both a cluster of events and its representation.

In *Being and Time*, Heidegger offered a fundamental-ontological outline that sought, among other things, to derive the necessary condition for possible *Historie* and the condition for possible history [*Geschichte*] from the existential analysis of finite *Dasein*. Stretched out between birth and death, the foundational structure of human *Dasein* is its temporalization [*Zeitigung*]. This structure emerges from the unsurpassable sense of finitude only encountered in anticipation of death—as Pope Innocent III observed: "We are dying as long as we live, and only when we stop dying do we cease to live."[1]

To be sure, Heidegger's systematic intention was to thematize the possibility of nonbeing in anticipation of death in such a way that the horizon of meaning of every experience of Being would have to surface in the temporalization of *Dasein*. Despite these systematic intentions, Heidegger's analysis of human finitude presented various categories and interpretations that could be read anthropologically and that could thereby be expanded upon, despite the fact that Heidegger sought to limit all such anthropologization. Certain concepts like care and anxiety made their way into his analyses; taking over of fate [*Schicksal*] and history [*Geschichte*] as destiny [*Geschick*]; authenticity and inauthenticity, the people, loyalty, heritage, to be free toward death, as well as death, guilt, conscience, and freedom—in short, no preventative methodological measures could obliterate the political semantics of this terminology. Whoever spoke of resoluteness in anticipation of death prior to 1933 could not avoid being criticized on ideological grounds, at the latest by 1945. Today many of these concepts sound faded, empty, or outmoded, and are in need of historical translation if they are to remain legible as fundamental-ontological categories capable of laying claim to some sort of permanence. But my intention here is not to illuminate the pathos of the 1920s through ideology critique. Rather, the question for us is whether Heidegger's categories and concepts are enough to develop a theory of history that is capable of deriving the conditions of possible histories from the basic determination of finitude and historicity. Indeed, it is in this that Heidegger's concepts seem insufficient to me.

As "*Dasein*," human beings are not yet open to their fellow humans—a topic Löwith explores—and not free in their potential for conflict with them. The times of history are not identical to and also not derivable in their entirety from the existential modalities that emerge on the basis of the human being as "*Dasein*." From the beginning, the times of history are constituted interpersonally, and they always deal with the simultaneity of the nonsimultaneous, with determinations of difference that contain their own finitude and are not traceable back to an [individual human] "existence."

For this reason I would like to expand the categorical options on offer. In order to shed light on how actual histories are made possible, it seems useful to supplement the determinations of finitude at work in Heidegger's analysis of *Dasein*. Additional oppositional determinations can supplement Heidegger's central oppositional pair of "thrownness" (empirically, birth) and anticipation of death (empirically, the fact that we all must die), and they can help us conceive of the temporal horizon of our experiences of finitude more sharply, or at least differently. The fact that these categories suggest an expansion into historical anthropology should not deter us; indeed, in being anthropologically legible and interpretable, Heidegger's categories themselves provoked a theory of history, even if they did not properly ground it. For conditions of possible histories surely cannot be grounded on "provenance," "heritage," "loyalty," "destiny," "people," "fate," "care," and "anxiety," just to recall a few important concepts from *Being and Time.*

To this end, I would like to use five well-known categories that seem well suited for thematizating something like the basic temporal structure of possible histories.

1. In order to make histories possible, we must supplement Heidegger's central determination of running toward death with the category of being able to kill. It is characteristic of histories of human beings that they have not only made survival the primary aim of their efforts within the horizon of their impending death. From hunter-gatherer hordes to highly armed modern superpowers, the struggle for survival has always threatened the death of others, or, perhaps more commonly, death at the hands of others. It is also well known that this threat can limit the use of violence. The actual risk of survival brings with it the chance that various organized groups of people may kill each other and that they believe they need to kill each other to survive. "In one respect a cavalry charge is very like ordinary life. So long as you are all right, firmly in your saddle, your horse in hand, and well armed, lots of enemies will give you a wide berth. But as soon as you have lost a stirrup, have a rein cut, have dropped your weapon, are wounded, or your horse is wounded, then is the moment when

from all quarters enemies rush upon you." Churchill thus described one of the last cavalry battles in the Sudan, in which he himself participated. "Brought to an actual standstill in the enemy's mass, clutched at from every side, stabbed at and hacked at by spear and sword, [my comrades] were dragged from their horses and cut to pieces by the infuriated foe."[2]

In Heidegger's diction, one might well say that being able to kill each other is equiprimordial with the anticipation of death, as long as *Dasein* is considered as historical existence. For this reason it is a historical achievement to hold, preserve, or establish peace at all after a war.

However one might want to approach the various characteristics and temporal manifestations of possible war and possible peace and their techniques and vulgarities, it does seem clear that without the ability to kill other people, to violently shorten other peoples' lives, the histories with which we all are familiar would not exist.

2. An additional opposition lies behind the oppositional pair of necessary death and the ability to kill, namely, that between friend and enemy. As we know this conceptual pair comes from the same political context that gave *Being and Time* its particular tonality, and that has already made this text legible as a historical document. And yet despite the political and ideological pointedness of these terms, we must be clear that the oppositional pair of friend and enemy thematizes finitudes in entirely formal ways, finitudes that crop up in all histories of human organizations. The empirical extension of conflicts in diachronic succession has always presupposed the opposition of friend and enemy, no matter whether it was Greeks and barbarians fighting each other, or Greeks and Greeks; whether Christians fought heathens or other Christians; whether modern units of action constituted themselves in the name of humanity and fought their opponents as unhumans; or whether these groups conceived of themselves as class subjects fighting to do away with all classes.[3] Categorically speaking, we are dealing here with a formal opposition that remains open to various contents, that is, something of a transcendental category of possible histories. Whoever insists upon the Christian commandment to love one's enemy, whether out of cleverness or humanitarian sympathy (to follow it today is, perhaps for purely Machiavellian reasons, a commandment for self-preservation on our globe), presupposes the categorical oppositional pairing of friend and enemy. As existential determinations, these

categories are sturdy enough to resist any ideological cooptation. Friend and enemy contain temporal determinations of the future, such that being toward death [*Sein zum Tode*] can be outpaced at any moment by being toward killing [*Sein zum Totschlagen*]. Anyone familiar with the shifting border between Israel and Lebanon or with the various twists and turns of discussions about military armament at the negotiating table in Geneva knows that there is no form of critique of ideology that can prevent these existential categories from being filled and emptied in each particular case. Indeed, hope for peace begins with the recognition of the other as an enemy and not as an incarnation of evil deserving of extermination. Even those who feel that being forced to differentiate between friend and enemy is something imposed on them, which they would prefer to avoid, share at least the insight that this differentiation is an extreme case that makes future histories possible through its potential for recurrence.

    3. A more general oppositional pair stands in the background of the acute escalation brought about by the friend-enemy distinction, namely, that between inside and outside. If Heidegger described the spatiality of *Dasein* as equiprimordial with his "being-in-the-world," a theory of history must supplement this determination by adding that every historical *Dasein* is split up into inner and outer spaces. No social or political unit of action constitutes itself without excluding other units of action. If all humans are fellow humans [*Mitmenschen*] (something that remains indisputable), from a historical perspective they can nonetheless be fellow humans in a variety of ways. There is no love story that does not create its own relations of inside and outside and that is not at the same time sustained by the tension between these relations. And the same inside-outside opposition arises in all histories, even when the units of action involve more than just two people. Boundary determinations also accompany each inside-outside relation, and its spatial scale and these determinations make each inside and outside space operational. It is natural for spaces to shift and change diachronically; this includes their density and size, as well as how their boundaries are drawn. Conflicts that are called forth or resolved by various boundary determinations, or that are initiated by shifts in boundaries, likewise undergo diachronic changes in similar ways.

    Viewed in terms of content, the epochs of world history can be defined according to various attributions of inside and outside, ranging from various nomadic hunting groups to complex forms of civilizational organization up to today's global society and all of its contested plurality. In the present situation, boundaries have seem to become osmotic, because the growing pressure of economic and technological interdependence has intensified the ways in which all units of action across the globe rely upon each other. And yet osmotic boundaries still remain boundaries, and their porousness is more strictly controlled today than ever before. Indeed, the multilayered quality of overlapping spaces does not disable the force of the foundational opposition between inside and outside, but instead presupposes it. This is the case most strikingly in the military units of action divided into the *Großraum* [greater area] organizations of East and West. Global interdependence has created biologically or economically complex and multilayered spaces that are conditioned by the environment, by now affecting our heating bills and provoking catalysts. Despite all this, this interdependence is not enough to destabilize the existing political spatial divisions.

A further important characteristic of this inside-outside distinction is the dichotomy between the public sphere and secrecy, which are necessarily linked. This opposition likewise structures the conditions of all possible histories, whether we think of initiation rites of cultic societies; professional organizations and economic interest groups; political elections and the ways in which they are financed; or cabinet meetings deciding domestic and foreign policy. By definition, every secret delimits an external public realm, and after being institutionalized, each public space reproduces new secret spaces that enable the continuation of politics. This ranges from the politics of the UN to our newly reorganized academic departments. The incorporation of representatives of different status groups into the plural public of the university has inevitably led to secret discussion forums of these organized groups that must be held before department meetings so as to ensure these meetings' functionality. To the extent that relations between inside and outside aim at doing away with either a secret or a public realm, all such relations always have a temporal coefficient that affects possible action and that is more or less effective, depending on the situation. This is the case because agents' ability to act cannot be preserved otherwise. Of course, there are various ways to regulate the back and forth between secret and public. The boundary is much more porous in Western democracies and enables a certain elasticity between the two that self-corrects in both directions, but as a result it also privileges a certain slowness of action. In the realm of communist rule, the patrolling of this boundary is primarily intended to steer the public sphere toward the opaque internal planning of the Central Committee leadership. Quick action may be possible in this case, but it remains rigid and inflexible as a result.

Even the moral test through publicity that Kant demanded for rational legal provisions cannot prevent that reforms and their implementability remain dependent on phases of confidential planning. Otherwise, every reform would fail by reason of the principles according to which it is being pursued. The history of the Prussian reforms in the early nineteenth century is a good example of how liberalizing principles that called for new forms of publicity could only be established by distancing the ruling political public sphere—which was dominated by the nobility—from decision-making processes long enough to let the reforms take hold in the name of a future public sphere. These economic reforms would not have occurred if the old orders had been part of the planning phase.

And whoever postulates the existence of a discussion free of domination must resort to artificially suspending time, something that is impossible given the action producing boundary distinctions between secret and public sphere. The opposition between secrecy and public sphere operates as a special version of inside and outside and constitutes the structural conditions of possible histories. At all times these conditions are subject to time pressure, and the boundary between secret and public must constantly be drawn and perceived anew in order to release or mitigate this pressure. "Watergate," for example, was a criminal breach of this boundary.

4. The analysis of finitude is likewise in need of further differentiation. Through this analysis, Heidegger derived the horizon of temporality and historicity and sought thereby to disclose the possibility of history in general. Despite the term's associations with the animal world, his so-called "thrownness" implies how one's own existence is forced onto oneself and empirically refers to birth, with which life (and thereby also death) begins; this determination of finitude, the factual pregivenness of which is supposed to be the source of all temporalization, is in need of further differentiation in order to ground the conditions of all possible histories.

Here I want to propose the concept of generativity [*Generativität*], if this neologism is acceptable. Hannah Arendt speaks similarly of "bornness [*Gebürtlichkeit*]" or "natality [*Natalität*]." From a biological perspective, generativity is the natural sexuality [*Geschlechtlichkeit*] from which the procreation of children results. Viewed anthropologically, generativity is a zoological pregiven that is reworked into a universally human reality. Via this concept I simply want to show that the relation between man and woman leads to the relational determination between parents and children, that is, between generations. As a quasi-transcendental determination, generativity has its empirical correlation in human sexuality as well as in the reality and efficacy of generations in their diachronic succession. Contained within generativity is the very finitude that belongs to the temporal preconditions for the generation of ever-new possible histories. The necessary succession of generations in their factual and temporal overlap lead to ever-new exclusions, to distinctions between inside and outside, and to the before and after of generationally specific units of experience. Without these exclusions no history is imaginable. On the most basic level, generation change and shift are constitutive of the temporally finite horizon that allows for histories to take place through the various displacements and generative overlaps characteristic of that horizon. Experiences are specific to generations, and are, for this reason, not immediately transferable.

The student revolts of the late 1960s were carried out by the first generation that no longer had firsthand experience of World War II. Still, this generation was confronted with the experience of those who, as their parents, were shaped in and through the Nazi period. It was as if the break between the generations was preprogrammed in the form of an accusation; the forms of confrontation were predisposed in the generation break, and their content can be historically substantiated in this way. The only thing in this case that the more general pattern of generational break cannot directly explain is the structure of accusation inherent in this specific generational conflict.

All actual histories can be untangled in one of two ways: either the break between generations can be successfully bridged, or it cannot. An example might be attempts to ritualize generational succession that regulate various forms of entry into the so-called adult world through initiation or examination, that is, through entering into new relationships of inside and outside. Another example might be institutional forms derived from oaths, originally given personally, that seek to renew the identity of the group with each new generation. Or recurring acts of voting that try to integrate the shifting experiences of subsequent generations politically into a democratic system. Or the institution of emancipation, whose iterative structure first allows for the achievements of emancipation to persist and be transformational. Emancipation is always conditioned by generation, and it would be a mistake to believe that a certain form of emancipation could ever be final and universal. Political maturity cannot be made ontologically eternal or reified in its content. The moving dictum "Don't trust anyone over thirty" that the students were so proud of can only be true if, ten years later, it proves the very same students to be in the wrong.

In terms of the temporal manifestation [*Zeitigung*] of generations, every emancipation can only be realized legally, politically, or socially if it can be repeated as a formal act, if it never allows itself to become codified and made eternal as any kind of supposed end point of history.

To be sure, the experience of generational breaks pregiven by generativity can certainly also lead to violent changes, as are common in civil wars or revolutions. Whether contained within institutions or transformed by revolutions, the generational break [*Verwerfung*] is one of the most elementary preconditions for every history manifesting itself in time,—but this is a question for the facts of history, whose conditions of possibility are included in generativity.

5. We should include an additional oppositional pair that is characterized by the same formal structure and power of explanation as the previously mentioned categories, despite its old-European outmodedness. I am thinking here of "master and slave [*Herr und Knecht*]." Plato names six different relations through which dependencies naturally come into being, relations that help to found ruling relationships as well as conflicts in the realm of the political. He only defines one of these relations as a dependency that, by nature, would not call into being any heteronomous claims or conflicts, namely, living according to laws. Put in formal terms, we are dealing here with relations of above and below. These, too, belong to the conditions of finitude without which histories are not possible,

despite all the achievements of political self-organization. One of these relations is the position of sheer power of the strong over the weak. The Melian Dialogue in Thucydides was undoubtedly repeated in Moscow when Dubček tried to preserve Prague's freedom. It is empirically evident who was below in the dialogue between the Athenians and the Melians and between Moscow and Prague. Discerning that ever-new dependencies come into play, even in those cases that seek mastery over the finite conditions of possible histories, does not change this finding. Despotism or tyranny, as blatantly unlawful forms, are merely extreme cases that indicate dangers that are possible but not necessary, as long as authority, custom, or tradition make relations of dependence possible; by agreement and law; or by transformation and change of course. Every revolution that changes power relations by force leads to new power relations being established. The legitimation may be new, legal relations may be different, perhaps they are improved, but nothing has been changed in terms of the return of newly organized and legally regulated forms of dependency, that is, in terms of the relations of above and below. Even an agreement among equals deploys political force to stabilize relations.

What, then, do these five oppositional pairs provided by a theory of history have in common? Following Heidegger, these are existential determinations—in a sense, transcendental categories—that name the possibility of histories without, however, thereby making concrete histories sufficiently describable. The catalogue of categories is intended for empirical usage and is not able to grasp the manifold nature of actual histories. Additional conditions must come into play in order to give a history its specifically constructed character of reality. These may be religious, cultural, economic, political, social, or any other sphere of life that must be included in order to make a history representable or narratable.

Why then even rehearse these transcendental minimal conditions? As oppositional pairings, they are well suited to reveal structures of finitude, which, through mutual exclusion, evoke tensions in time that must necessarily crop up within and between units of action. Histories only occur because the possibilities contained within them extend beyond what can be realized later on. This excess of possibilities must be worked off so that something can be realized "in time." For this reason, oppositional conditions that push temporal finitude forward are needed. Within the horizon of finitude, tensions, conflicts, breaks, and inconsistencies open up that always remain unsolvable in the specific moment but that all units of action must take part in and make an effort to solve diachronically, whether in order to survive or to perish. Friend and enemy, parents and children, generational succession, earlier or later, the tensions between above and below and the tensions between inside and outside, secret and public—all of these remain constitutive for the emergence, course, and efficacy of histories.

Up to now I have pursued a theoretical outline (albeit brief and pointed) that is intended to think Heidegger's existential analysis several steps further and in a direction that he himself did not envision, namely, toward conceptualizing the possibility of multiple histories. Heidegger himself found the category of historicity to be sufficient. This category had the effect of positively perpetuating the experience of relativity characteristic of historicism, but it did not ground the multiplicity of actual histories transcendentally.

II. *Historik* and Hermeneutics

I have intentionally left one category out of my sketch of a possible theory of history, a category that every listener must have anticipated in connection with my topic, especially today and on this occasion, namely, that of linguisticality [*Sprachlichkeit*]. Gadamer placed this pregiven at the center of his philosophical hermeneutics, building on Heidegger but also surpassing him (not least thanks to his humanistic and scientific *grandezza*). Heidegger and Dilthey had already situated the hermeneutic circle one level deeper than in the traditional sense, showing it to be at work in the procedure of understanding of all texts and oral discourses through the presupposition of both part and whole. Human existence [*Existenz*] is a historical existence [*Dasein*], because it is always already oriented toward understanding a world that is grasped and at the same time constituted linguistically through this very act of understanding. The interdependence of every experience of the world with the interpretation of the world is thus equiprimordial with language enabling this process of the understanding, and this interdependence is, like each language, historical in nature. Prior to all theoretical differentiations and methodological manipulations, hermeneutics is the theory of the existential dependence upon what one might call linguistically enabled and linguistically mediated history. Gadamer is concerned primarily with historical truth, and only secondarily with method; the title *Truth and Method* has something of a productive deception to it. The copula "and" does not bind truth and method like man and wife. But method is also not the doling out of truth in coin, like so many pennies or dimes. Instead, if the analogy is permitted, we are dealing with a general theory of the climate within which a brief downpour too finds its place.

As a theory of understanding, hermeneutics thus has a historical-ontological status, and linguisticality is the mode of realization inherent to it, a mode that resists being objectified into any single method. It is impossible to conceive of human existence prior to all sciences without this kind of pregiven possibility of experiencing the world. This undoubtedly then sheds new light on the relationship between hermeneutics and *Historik*.

To return to the above outline of opposing categories, what characterizes the theory of history in its outline of the transcendental conditions of possible histories? In each case, we are dealing with determinations that aim at pre- and extralinguistic structures. The general formal distinctions of inside and outside, above and below, earlier or later, as well as the more concrete formal distinctions of friend and enemy, generativity, master and slave, and public and secret, these all represent categorical determinations that aim at modes of being that certainly must be mediated linguistically, but that nonetheless are not wholly subsumed into linguistic mediation, and instead stand on their own as independent entities. We are thus dealing with categories that aim at the mode of being of possible histories and that first provoke something like understanding and conceptualizing. On this model, hermeneutics would be condemned to respond to a state of affairs already predetermined theoretically by *Historik*. To oversimplify, the theory of history draws our attention to situations of action, to formations of finitude that occur in a realm that can be extra-linguistic, while hermeneutics points to the understanding of this realm. This line of thinking undoubtedly has something to it, but it is too simple to be mereley true.

In closing, then, we should ask once more about the linguistic status of the categories employed by our description of the transcendental conditions of possible histories. A possible rejoinder from hermeneutics might be that the opposing concepts in question can only ever be grasped linguistically. On this line of thinking, the type of *Historik* I have sketched here is simply a linguistic excerpt, an aspect, just one possible theory of history among conceivably many others. Or it is a *Historik* that aims at the same metahistorical conditions of possibility that humans share with animals; it is not a *Historik* that, for example, can be derived from Marxian categories of work and the division of labor. The ways in which one arrives at this or that theory of history can only ever be understood within the horizon of their linguistic genesis. A certain amount of textual debris floats around in the stream of transmitted events, theoretical set phrases stemming, above all, from the reception history of political theory from Plato to Carl Schmitt, and the poor historian is standing at the banks of this stream (or so he believes), fishing out specific pieces of the debris that may help him or her swim back out into the stream of occurrences well prepared with new theoretical equipment.

Despite any off-kilter metaphors, this description is not entirely false. In terms of linguistic origin, the adoption of heritage, and engagement with the tradition of earlier theories of history (or whatever else the connecting definitions in the horizon of continuity might be called), it is accurate. Nonetheless, this exemplary outline of a *Historik* does not become a subcategory of hermeneutics simply because the origins of a historical theory can be linguistically identified or because this theory can be thought of as a linguistic answer to a pregiven question.

The important thing for the scholarly task of a *Historik* is to know what it achieves analytically in its attempt to extract rational order from the chaos of historical findings or from preconceptual familiarity with history. History itself (if we accept for once this deeply ideological term) is irrational—at most, its analysis is rational. What matters, then, seems to be the following: does a *Historik* thematize the structures of possibility for histories, to which a theory of understanding [*Verstehenslehre*] then first reacts? Even if it can be shown how the historian has come to his theory of history, this has nothing to say about whether the result is applicable to the preconceived evidence; in other words, it has nothing to say about whether the historian makes truth visible and controllable through method. The medium of linguistic genesis does not decide as to the finding determined via language. The primary experience lies in the difference between language and the facts of the matter [*Sachverhalt*]. Undoubtedly, this relationship gets even more complicated if we assume that hermeneutics and *Historik* both rely on their linguistic character [*Sprachlichkeit*] in order to reflect their mutual status. Let us take two strong theses as points of departure, theses that Gadamer repeatedly defended and that seem plausible. First of all, Gadamer argues that language certainly enables and mediates our experience of the world, but that this experience is never simply a linguistic act or exhausted in language. Just the opposite: every act of speech has to do with the issue being put into language. To this extent, then, the issue dealt with by the theory of history remains within the realm of general hermeneutics. In his debates with Habermas and Apel, however, Gadamer goes so far as to stress the inaccessibility and unattainability of pregiven meaning with which history confronts all understanding and through which history retains the advantage over all hermeneutic efforts. "This [insight] is nothing less than uncovering the true hermeneutical subject matter. Its true legitimation is to be found entirely in the experience of history."[4] No interpretation can ever fully access the predominance of what one seeks to understand. This then would make the subject matter of a *Historik* a very special case, which all language tries in vain to grasp.

Secondly, Gadamer asserts that, within the methodologically more limited framework of fields of study tied to historical texts and their interpretation, the historical approach to sources differs considerably from neighboring fields in the humanities that likewise work closely with texts. Among the fields that interpret texts, the science of history has a rank that nearly surpasses all other hermeneutic procedures.

To briefly explain this second claim: legal, theological, and philological procedures share in attributing a genuine and, to a certain extent, unquestionable role to the text in question.

Exegesis of the law organizes each individual case history such that the facts can be subsumed under the statement of law, thus enabling a just judgment. A juridical case subsumed under the law is linguistically structured in a different way than if the case had been elucidated in psychological or sociohistorical terms. Dependence upon the wording of the law prestructures the case history in such a way as to affect possible decisions about the case and to make the application of the law easier. Within the interpretation of history, the text of the law thus has a regulative function, and this interpretation of history is subordinated to the law. Viewed in terms of its other components, the same case that led to a guilty judgment might well reveal lack of guilt when considered from a psychological, moral, or ideology-critical perspective standing in tension with the application of the law.

If the interpretation of the law shifts in the wake of changing political and social conditions, text exegesis rushes to catch up with history. There must be factors in place prior to shifts in interpretive analysis and application. And when a creative, transformative legal judgment sheds new light on a case, breaking with previous exegeses of the law, then the productive role in response to history is stronger than the interpretationally receptive role played by legal hermeneutics up to that point. But the productive decision to interpret a text in a new manner or to suggest an actual change in the law belongs primarily to *Historik* as theoretical foundation and only secondarily to hermeneutics. It is a thesis of Gadamer's that history takes place above the heads of individuals. But linguistic understanding that has recourse to a given legal text needs to be preceded by a conceptualization of history, more precisely, of historical change; this conceptualization is also linguistic, though in a different way, and it plays itself out in the formation of new laws or in radical new interpretations of old texts.

Measured against legal texts, theologians and philologists are even more closely bound to the status of their sources. The theologian remains directed toward the word of God as revealed in the text of the Bible. And even if, as Nietzsche said, God proved himself a bad student of Greek when dictating the New Testament, the text of Revelation nonetheless retains its potential for dogmatic authority. Issues dealt with in the text of the Bible can certainly be historically relativized and viewed in light of new challenges, but as revelatory text, the Bible maintains its unique claim, to which the believer must immediately respond.

The philologist, too, tends to attribute an inherent weight to the text that he or she edits and comments upon, a weight that is all the larger when the linguistic form has taken on the irreplaceability and unsurpass-ability of a poetic work. The issue brought to language in the text remains subject to its linguistic form.

Yet the historian is different: he or she makes use of texts solely as pieces of evidence, so as to determine a reality that lies behind the texts. More than all other textual exegetes, the historian thematizes a state of affairs that is in every case extra-textual, even if he or she only ever constitutes its reality by linguistic means. This sounds almost ironic. Among colleagues in the humanities, the historian is less beholden to texts—on principle, if not in the research he or she carries out—than the jurist, theologian, or philologist. By being transformed into sources through research questions, the historian's texts only ever have the quality of pointing to a history that the he or she is trying to understand.

To write the history of a particular time means to make statements that could never have been made in that period. To construct a history that aims to understand economic conditions entails the attempt to analyze factors that cannot be directly derived from any one source.

When *Historik* seeks to grasp the conditions of possible history, it points to long-term processes that are not found in any text as such, but instead first provoke the creation of texts. They point to unsolvable conflicts, breaks, discontinuities, to elementary modes of behavior that might well come to inhibit one another; to name these modes with language already represents a form of rationalization, especially when the named or discussed states of affairs are entirely unrational. Linguistic absurdity [*Unsinn*] can be revealed through language. But absurdity that, with the help of language, emerges from motives and necessities that defy language can only be channeled into the realm of rational observation through a supplementary procedure of translation. This approaches but does not surpass the limits of absurdity.

Let me elaborate via a notorious, and more or less familiar, example: Hitler's *Mein Kampf.* On the basis of this text's statements, one could gather that the extermination of the Jews was a possible maxim for a future political course of action. If taken literally, the words leave no doubt, even though the book was considered to be an antisemitic screed and not taken entirely seriously. At least initially.

That said, the history leading to Auschwitz that followed cannot necessarily be deduced from *Mein Kampf.* It could always have happened differently. But the fact that it did happen the way it did is no longer a question of the text and of textual exegesis. The reality that set in, in that humans produced it—literally produced it, the factory-like mass murder—this history is stronger than any *ex post* textual deduction or documentation.

After Auschwitz, the status of *Mein Kampf* was thereby transformed. What Hitler had written was immeasurably outmatched by actions, and his speech gained new meaning that could not have been perceived beforehand.

One must thus differentiate, at least methodologically, between directing one's understanding toward texts in order to grasp their linguistic statements, on the one hand, and inquiring about something that speaks unintentionally through the texts and that only establishes itself as historical truth after the fact, on the other. There is no source text that contains the history first constituted and brought to language with the help of textual sources.

We must differentiate between the kind of reception history that unfolds as part of the continuity of textually bound tradition and its exegesis and the kind of reception history that certainly is enabled and mediated by language, while at the same time being more than language can ever gather up. There are historical processes that defy each and every linguistic compensation or reading. This is the realm to which *Historik* turns, at least theoretically, and the realm that distinguishes it, even if *Historik* seems to be encompassed by philosophical hermeneutics.

In both theory and method, history is more than a philological, text-bound discipline. The theory of history can thus easily be differentiated from a text-bound hermeneutics. But can it be distinguished from a hermeneutics that seeks to incorporate any *Historik* as a linguistic achievement? Certainly, in the sense that history, its predetermined topic, precedes all understanding. What was it, again, that Fichte said? "And the whole of reality as such [. . .] is nothing more than the graveyard of the concept, which tries to find itself in the light."[5] It may be that the concept of history is likewise the kind of concept that is consumed by reality. Consequently, I am happy to let Professor Gadamer have the final word.

5

Goethe's Untimely History

Whoever sits down to read Goethe has an experience similar to that of reading Hegel. Once taken at his word, Goethe does not let you find your way back out of his writings. Complicating the matter is the fact that nothing that has been said about Goethe can match what he said himself.

In 1932, Albert Schweitzer gave a speech in honor of the one hundredth anniversary of Goethe's death. With the worldwide economic crisis and the looming collapse of the Weimar Republic in mind, Schweitzer spoke of the "greatest hour of fate that has ever tolled for humanity." Though this formulation was perhaps not entirely false, it was certainly un-Goethean. Invoking and rewriting Goethe in an attempt to master the current crisis, Schweitzer conjured up "the old, singularly true ideal of personal humanity" that must prevail over superficial materialism and egoism.[1]

And in 1945, when "the German catastrophe" seemed to have severed all bridges to the past and the future, Friedrich Meinecke implored the Germans to rebuild their country via Goethe. Only through the "internalization of our existence [*Verinnerlichung unseres Daseins*]"—again, an entirely un-Goethean expression—, only through routes "back to the era of Goethe" could Germany be saved.[2] This internalization was to be cultivated in "Goethe Communities," which, as he cautiously added, were not to be confused with the existing Goethe Society.

As we know, these and other invocations of Goethe have neither accomplished nor impeded anything. It would seem that it was untimely to invoke his name. The question, however, is whether it has been the voices of our century who sought, anachronistically, to apply Goethe to their own historical situation—or whether Goethe himself has always prevented any attempt to co-opt him in the name of "history." If so, then Goethe must be protected from Goethe. Living as an émigré, Löwith saw with more clarity that it was no longer possible to return to Goethe, but that it was equally impossible to transcend him.[3] This is, by the way, the common definition of a classic: impossible to return to, but just as impossible to transcend. And this is the aporia with which Goethe has left us. In turn, this aporia is inherently connected to the way that Goethe experienced, lived, and conceptualized "history," namely, in a manner that was always untimely.

In order to show this, I will seek to answer two questions. First: how does Goethe's life relate to the history of his time? Second: how did Goethe personally experience and interpret history?

I

If we examine Goethe's biography from the outside, at a historical distance, it is squarely representative of its time [*zeitgemäß*]. He was successful and fortunate, the third of three generations of social climbers, from master tailor to privy councilor; he was financially well provided for, which allowed him to study law, rather than theology, and to avoid earning a meager keep as a private tutor. He did not need to become a grumpy professor or a lifelong civil servant in order to make possible a life of writing poetry and books. Nor did he find it necessary to marry the daughter of a nobleman to gain recognition in society. Goethe's ascent began in the upper reaches of the burghers [*Bürgerstand*], and it continued upward on a steep and rapid path. He joined a privy council as a minister and was granted noble status by the emperor at thirty-three; in his extensive contact with the middle and upper nobility he maintained the distance proper to his social position, but was also quite friendly. And he felt himself superior to all. This career, based in talent, or, better put, in genius, and (we must not forget) in merit, was thus successful and thereby also entirely of its time. Goethe was often enjoined to be a ruler himself, or at least to be able to be one. And for this reason, he also saw mere bureaucratic administration, if it did not entail becoming a governing lord, as a philistine task, which only fools or rogues were capable of performing.[4] But Goethe never once claimed to play the role of the philosopher who knew better and who could guide or even replace his ruler. However much he liked to compare himself to Friedrich the Great, Julius Caesar, or Napoleon in this or that regard, he always knew how to restrain himself. He was no revolutionary. He remained true to the muse that, as he put it, only accompanies [*begleite*] but does not determine [*leite*] life.[5]

Also representative of their time were the circumstances under which Goethe took part in the task of governing (if not in the task of ruling, which was, of course, reserved for the prince). Indeed, how could it be otherwise? These circumstances were those of "world history," as it began to be called in those days, something, however, that Goethe did not invoke when defining his own position. He spoke instead of the "immense currents of the general political course of the world [*des allgemeinen politischen Weltlaufs*], which had the largest influence upon me as well as upon the entirety of my contemporaries."[6] Seen from a historical distance, this "political course of the world" spanned two forty-year periods, straddling the year 1789, [the first] from the Seven Years' War—the first war that took place on (though not between) multiple continents at the same time—and the American and the French Revolutions up to Napoleon, and [the second] from Napoleon through the Restoration, all the way to the beginnings of technological industrialization and the July Revolution.

Here, too, Goethe was fortunate, even a bit elevated: Weimar lay in the geopolitical safe haven between Austria and Prussia and later between France and Prussia, which together guaranteed peace for ten years after 1795. This was the neutral era of Weimar Classicism in a narrow chronological sense. In the following years, Napoleon even tolerated Weimar's continuation, which ultimately allowed Weimar to advance to the status of a grand duchy in 1814. And in 1816 it became the first state in the German Confederation to bestow a written constitution on its subjects, though this was not entirely to the liking of our state minister Goethe. He mistrusted the voice of the majority his whole life, and he was inclined, like Rousseau, to prefer the true voice of the people—"peoplehood [*Volkheit*]," as he put it—over and against the empirical *Volk*.[7] He was a man of the

Enlightenment, prerevolutionary and revolutionary at the same time, just like Rousseau.

Caught in a web of courtly and bureaucratic interests, Goethe was thoroughly criticized, however eager for reform he may have been. A *Stürmer und Dränger* who had opened the gate to freedom, he seemed to have betrayed his Götz von Berlichingen and was now considered a courtier—something that he himself notably affirmed—lacking any patriotism, someone who forbade his own son to volunteer for the wars of liberation against Napoleon.

From the perspective of those who did not grow up before the French Revolution but instead with it, Goethe fell into the conservative, anti-revolutionary, anti-patriotic camp. From a modern ideological-critical perspective, he came to be categorized as untimely, as not belonging to his time.

This was only possible because, since the Enlightenment, all histories had come to be alienated [*verfremdet*] by the philosophy of history. It was not today, but instead yesterday or tomorrow that decided whether a person was thinking or acting in congruence with the breathtaking transformations taking place. It became customary thenceforth to question each and every decision or event depending on how the past was valued and how the future was anticipated. As a result, each contemporary quickly came under suspicion of thinking or acting incorrectly. Goethe refrained from making such impositions, though he was himself subjected to them.

Goethe's sober neighbor Wieland wrote astute commentaries on the Revolution, which he derived from classical constitutional theories, and which allowed him to view the events critically and with prognostic accuracy. For Goethe, each aristocrat or democrat murdered was one dead person too many. Herder, his other neighbor, continued to hold that the human race remained on its path toward humanity. On the basis of moral certainty, Kant postulated the ability to disclose and pursue the progressive path to the one true republic. And all intellectuals born in their footsteps, idealists or romantics, designed philosophies of history in order to redeem the achievements of the French Revolution as an initial pledge toward a rational future. Three- or five-phase models were constructed that enabled interpretations of the contemporary situation as a singular moment located between a notional beginning and a notional end of world history. This was the case whether or not the present was viewed as the transformative nadir of history; whether the alienation of humans from themselves and others was viewed as necessarily leading to genuine self-determination—all the way to the abolition of the state and of all domination, as in Fichte's vision; or whether the traditional social orders still in existence were seen gradually to disintegrate and thus finally usher in genuine democracy. Lastly, this democracy came to be inscribed into the organic body of the sovereign nation, especially that of the German nation, to the exclusion of its neighbors.

All of these philosophical-historical interpretations went out of their way to conceive of the present day as a necessarily transitional phase on the way to a better future. In each case, differing partisan hopes and desires helped shape these aims. Yet common to all was the view that history was an agent of higher necessity that could redeem these different hopes and desires. All of these perspectives, which codified history teleologically, cast a shadow over the minister Goethe, who meanwhile grappled with more mundane questions of taxation and recruitment, streets and mines, diplomatic missions, theater and education. Through no fault of his own, Goethe apparently became untimely. And Goethe was in fact untimely, but in a different sense than both his critics and his critical admirers were able to realize.[8]

If one traces Goethe's career on the basis of what he said and wrote rather than according to external dates (however one might want to organize these dates from the perspective of the philosophy of history), it becomes clear that he defies all critique of ideology.

Goethe always knew more than he said. Not that he wrote ambiguously, but his writing was always multivalent and false-bottomed. He was able to fuse the canonical four senses of Scripture into spontaneous speech and writing: whether realistic, literal, or spiritual, whether allegorical or symbolic, even typological: he could kaleidoscopically intermingle, imply, or withhold each and every one of these modes. "For I know what I have written into it, and this cannot be read out if it all at once."[9] He stored up three thousand years of the myths and stories of world cultures so as to recall them in a variety of ways: hermeneutically, metaphorically, ironically, sarcastically or mockingly, didactically, daringly or hubristically, defiantly or gently and tolerantly, at any rate, so as to recast them in his works. This was, so to speak, a singular theater that enabled many different productions. And this is why a critique of ideology can never codify what Goethe said. Goethe was untimely, not because he could be defined via his social and political role as a conservative or as an enemy of the revolution, but because, through his language, he evaded all such reductive operations. His language produced a surplus value that cannot be exhausted by any one exegesis, a surplus value that allows for no exploitation.

For this reason let us consider Goethe's internal biography, the ways in which he has imparted it to us in writing. Via the medium of his own self-interpretation, Goethe's is the first authentic case of a methodically consistent autobiography. There is hardly another writer in German who has reflected on his own life, works, and their external as well as internal conditions as rigorously as Goethe. This is already evident in his poetic production. Who else has transformed completed first versions of poems into similarly completed second versions as much as Goethe, versions that he then worked on for years or decades? It was Goethe's personal experience that history must always be rewritten, because new situations raise new questions, and this long before any such maxim became a commonplace of modern historians. But he also rethought works that he left behind and no longer wished to read or see performed. The idea that every recorded, written, and spoken word changes its meaning with time and needs, for this reason, to be considered anew, this foundational hermeneutical experience was something that Goethe personally lived out. We can only know and recognize ourselves through temporalization. It is time that "we cannot save without spending."[10] As he got older, Goethe entered into a historical relationship to himself, he understood himself as historical, even as others came to see him as worthy of monumentalization while he was still alive.

But Goethe was no archivist simply wanting to hold onto the past. He destroyed countless letters and diaries, in retrospect often more than he wished. Goethe did not intend to sneak up on his own character, knowing full well that a person cannot unmask him- or herself, that every experience is only half the experience.[11]

Goethe measured out the temporal refractions of all experiences into specific genres. His annalistic diaries, retrospective chronicles, and reflective memoirs overlap and augment each other. If we leave his poetry aside, nearly half of his work claims to be of a directly autobiographical nature. Composed in a multiplicity of styles, his recollections always aim to monitor and call into question his personal history as reception history [*Wirkungsgeschichte*]. He sought to find traces of the external influences that made his works possible, both past and present. And he was also concerned with the various channels of transmission and reception his works took. Via this twofold reception history, Goethe was able to extricate the memoir genre from the stale alternatives it had faced up to that point, namely, either subjective reflection or objective observation. The transformation of his biography into an autobiography is thus genuinely "historical," both subjective and objective. Goethe brings external conditions and personal accomplishments to bear upon each other, a process for which he found the seemingly paradoxical formulation of "self-conditioning [*Sichbedingen*]."[12] His activity of writing, speaking, acting, and thereby transforming himself was the topic of his self-historicization, not of any kind of hidden or withheld inwardness. But the other extreme was also not his topic: the political history of the world.

To the extent that Goethe integrated the world into his life, productively transformed it, and externalized it in literary form, world history itself retreated to a threatening distance. At all times it had surprises in store, lastly with the July Revolution—a legitimate but not natural daughter of the French Revolution. But world history itself, that historians' charnel house,[13] retreats from the history of the individual life. If Hegel could understand the entirety of world history as the phenomenology of a spirit ever on its way to itself, then Goethe completed this work for himself by excluding world history. At a time when philosophies of history were springing up from the ground like mushrooms, Goethe firmly held on to his own historical self-reflection in an altogether untimely manner. He never expected general history to be responsible for his self-formation [*Bildung*]. He did not equip incommensurable basic conditions with their own meaning, with immanent importance, or with the cunning of reason. World historical events are exciting, gripping, provocative, inexhaustible, bitter, surprising, and bloody, but they are not teleologically legible. Here I turn to my second question.

II

Goethe's untimely history—not how he lived it, but how he thought of it. For Goethe, history offers no theodicy, no providence to which he owed his self-formation. History is not equipped with the divine power of infinite justice. If Schiller and Hegel both saw world history as a world tribunal, Goethe knew it to be otherwise: "The Last Judgment has been postponed / so that they can all murder each other [Damit sie sich alle einander ermorden / ist der jüngste Tag vertagt geworden]."[14]

And while the victors of the French Revolution or the wars of liberation erected their monuments, Goethe proposed something different. He suggested that the soldiers of all sides were all equally moral, religious, and uninformed; only trade and business interests led them to kill one another on the battlefield. "We only see handsome people murdering one another, as if the tragic destiny of Eteocles and Polynices needed to be repeated again and again, without the existence of the Furies, which alone lent the motif its significance."[15] This is, by all accounts, an untimely insight of Goethe's, one drawn from the presence of myth in his life, and one that proved to outlive him, without anyone taking notice.

But before we sketch history from Goethe's point of view, a word about historical method and what we might *ex post* call Goethe's epistemology. Goethe never addressed questions of method in an isolated way; instead, he always embedded such questions in the anthropological paradigms that accompanied all of his research. He was no professional historian, and he viewed such professionals with mistrust and irony, in particular, those scholars of his time who felt secure in contemptuously looking down on chronicles and annals, and who approached legends, myths, and the preliterate period in general only with critical skepticism. For Goethe, in contrast, these were the very genres that originated hand in hand with the writing of history itself.

In his historical research, Goethe let himself be guided by pairs of opposing concepts and categories; he never thought of these as contradictory, however, but rather as concepts that were relational, that conditioned and referred to each other, as concepts in exchange with each other [*Wechselbegriffe*]. Goethe thus always juxtaposed matters of fact and their meaning, facts and fictions. It is only in representation, in narration that so-called facts achieve their historical status, namely, by having a large enough effect to manifest [*zeitigen*] results that the historian must take into consideration. Two different modes of experience thus come into conflict with each other: the authority of what is past and no longer present, and the experience of the present, which can only be gathered on the basis of the authority of the individual. "The history of the sciences is actually the conflict of the individual with immediate experience and mediated tradition."[16]

In his search for objectivity, Goethe followed the very "maxim to renounce as much of myself as possible,"[17] that is, to renounce, but not to extinguish his personal self, as Ranke said he expected of himself. For Goethe was "deeply convinced that the individual person models the external world according to his own idiosyncrasies in the present day, and does so even more when recollecting."[18] The conditional binary between poetry and truth is likewise relevant here, for according to the Aristotelian triad (the written history [*Historie*] of the accidental, the poetry of the probable, and the philosophy of the true), history [*Geschichte*] is not mentioned because poetry and truth both already contain it in equal measures.

For Goethe, the fact that impartiality must guide all research—and all poets—did not prevent him from recognizing that all knowledge was subject to perspectival refractions. Moreover, every gain accomplished by recollection thrives on forgetting: the same event sounds different in the evening than it did in the morning.[19] And every historical insight emerges from generational cohorts who unavoidably only have their own particular experiences and thus only grasp things in light of them.[20] The perspectivization of space likewise goes hand in hand with that of time: the conclusions of every nation are different from those of its neighbors. "How different the views of the French about English history sound in comparison to those of the English."[21] And history must be written in different ways, depending on the knowledge and ability of its readers: for the already knowledgeable or for those who are not.[22]

But enough evidence and references: all the opposing conceptual pairs used by Goethe that are legible in methodological terms share a common trait: they do not deal with philological techniques of source exegesis—though he did follow and value these—but are instead grounded in an anthropology of historical experience. Moving from sensuality through intuition to perception, from perception via the imagination to judgment and to conviction: this might well serve as an abbreviated formula for attaining historical knowledge, before it comes to be temporally refracted. And all of this based on the "truth of the five senses."[23]

But let us turn from questions about historical knowledge to history itself, even though Goethe never considered the two in isolation.

What, for Goethe, was "history" [*Geschichte*], as it came to be called in the second half of the eighteenth century? "History," in other words, that is both its own subject and object. Whenever possible, Goethe tried to avoid this weighty collective singular, a term that was supposed to encompass all individual histories as well as their representation. He thus knew neither of the progress of history nor of a history of progress.

Of course, he knew of many particular steps forward, along with their limitations, and steps backward, always tied to very specific realms of experience. As a Protestant, he did not reject out of hand the idea of relative religious progress leading to spiritualization. But here, too, he was inclined not to read polytheism, pantheism, and monotheism diachronically, instead stressing their simultaneity, depending, in each case, on the sediment of experience in question.[24]

And when he did, on occasion and in two short pages, sketch out four spiritual epochs that followed on each other as characteristic of the entirety of history, the final epoch ended in confusion: "Each individual steps forward as a teacher and a leader and presents his complete folly as a completed whole."[25] Goethe speaks here of his own epoch, which he thought would not likely last very long (here Goethe was wrong).

One would hardly want to deny Goethe that the history of German literature was without any traces of progress, especially in the case of someone whose poetry paved the way for the invention of a modern classicism [*Klassik*]. But Goethe was never quite sure whether one could hope for similar progress in the visual arts.

But he did in fact commit over half of his life—indeed, his whole existence—to the idea that the history of the natural sciences leads to advances in knowledge.[26] Whoever reads the historical part of Goethe's *Theory of Colors* can certainly learn one specific thing about the progress of natural knowledge, namely, that it is always embedded in cultural history, a postulate that contemporary historians of science still painstakingly try to recapture. Every advance in knowledge is tied up with prejudices specific to generation and group, Goethe argues, and these can only be overcome by individuals, at first only in solitary efforts. As in his theory of knowledge, Goethe traces advances back to the experiences and achievements of specific individuals, however much he situates these individuals in specific life circumstances and spheres of activity. No element of progress can be generalized in a world historical manner, and regression undermines each advance. But Goethe puts even stricter limitations on progress: "experience and knowledge progress and can be enriched; reflection, thought, and association" remain "contained within a certain sphere of human capabilities."[27] Here, too, Goethe makes use of an oppositional pairing, although it is asymmetrical. Progress is possible diachronically, but synchronically it remains limited, both at every specific moment and across time. Goethe thus interweaves temporal transformation with its ever-present pregivens [*Vorgaben*]. The human capacity for thought may discover new things, but it itself remains the same.

What, then, is left of history in and for itself, of "history" in general? After all that has been said about different modes of knowledge and the relativity of progress, it should not be surprising that Goethe never claimed to observe history as a totality. Instead, he was much more inclined to approach it via oppositional categories such as progress and regress. Viewed formally, such dichotomous concepts continuously recur throughout Goethe's thought, but he fills out their content in a variety of ways. Linguistically speaking, Goethe is a structuralist, someone who uses semantic alternatives for possible histories in order to describe ever-new constellations, without ever needing to postulate a finalistic history. Indeed, he uses such oppositional pairings to preclude any kind of teleological direction. His remarks about nature likewise apply to his view of all conceivable histories: "With quiet weight and counterweight nature weighs itself back and forth, and an 'over here' and 'over there' thus arise, an 'above' and 'below,' a 'before' and 'after,' through which all phenomena we encounter in space and time are conditioned."[28] It is always via these kinds of formal conceptual pairings—inside-outside, above-below, earlier-later—that Goethe seeks to identify history's conditions of possibility. They overlap amid continuous distortions, a further reason why a purely chronological representation of true history remains impossible.

Through their formal structure, all such oppositional pairs make a metahistorical claim, for they precede concrete particular histories, while at the same time being inextricably linked back to human nature. For this reason, writing to the Kantian Schiller, Goethe no longer "laughs" "about the idea of writing a history a priori: for everything truly develops out of the progressing and regressing qualities of the human mind, out of nature and its striving and self-retardation."[29] Here Goethe argues neither transcendentally nor with Kant, whose historical a priori points to the predominance of practical reason, which claims not only to think but to enforce history via moral premises. With his temporal oppositional pair of progress and regress, Goethe is more concerned with understanding "the incommensurable of world history," as he puts it. Goethe works in similar fashion with the dichotomy of law [*Gesetz*] and chance [*Zufall*]— confusing the two is a common mistake of the historian, who is thereby led, sometimes unwittingly, to seek partisan advantage.[30]

To name another such opposition, for Goethe, "the conflict between unbelief and faith" remains "the true, unique, and deepest theme of world and human history, the one under which all others are subordinated."[31] Before structuring the content of individual historical epochs according to this dichotomy, Goethe opts, axiomatically, for faith. Entirely in line with the Enlightenment, Goethe fears superstition; in contrast to common enlightened opinion, however, he aligns superstition more closely with unbelief than with faith.[32]

To offer a different example: "there are two moments of world history that reveal themselves in individuals and peoples, sometimes in close succession, sometimes simultaneously, sometimes alone and separate, sometimes entirely imbricated."[33] These are first the epochs of becoming and reason, which turn inward and end in anarchy; and second the epochs of technology, knowledge, and the mind, which are turned outward and end in the tyranny of individuals or entire masses. Via this theory of oppositions that require formal distinction, but are de facto always imbricated and intertwined, Goethe is able to transcend the traditional doctrine of the cyclical rise and fall of political constitutions, something that was always only ever conceptualized in linear terms. Even if Goethe occasionally used traditional metaphors of the cycle or the spiral, his multiple oppositional concepts enabled adequate interpretations of the combinational plurality of each historical situation without imputing any unilinear direction to it.

The ability to follow one's own entelechy that Goethe ascribes to the individual person is something that he considers impossible when forces, individuals, social orders, or peoples come into conflict with one another. So-called world history is always repeating itself in structure (if not in the sequence of events); the key, then, to understanding world history lies in rediscovering and reformulating old, well-known elements in what is new. "The most original modern authors are original not because they produce something new, but only because they are capable of saying things as if they had never been said before."[34] Here Goethe might well be adapting an old turn of phrase from the fifth century by Vincent of Lérins, an opponent of the Augustinian doctrine of predestination: "Do not say anything new; instead, say it in a new way."[35]

For this reason you might allow me to express this age-old concept of history, well-known to Goethe, via a dual formulation: history consists in risk and recurrence, in daring and repeatability. Viewed from this perspective, all individual cases lend themselves to being solidified into symbols without relinquishing their uniqueness. Goethe experienced the random sites that bore witness to the bleak misery of the revolutionary wars as "symbols of contemporaneous world history," without having "the slightest idea" as to "anything better, or merely different that should come out of it."[36]

It is here where we can find the key to the long-standing question of why Goethe refrained from incorporating politics and current events into his memoirs or his literary works. His reticence in dealing with political history in his writings certainly bears the mark of a proper amount of political prudence vis-à-vis his prince. His literary distantiation of politics was thereby anything but unpolitical. He knew all too well how to analyze sequences of actions and to identify diachronic rules that applied to their unpredictability, unrepeatability, and shortcomings: "Only the next day will tell you what you did today."[37] No one can forestall the "unrolling of world history."[38] The supremacy of historical constraints upon human action limits any attempt to control historical events.

For this reason Goethe used a further oppositional pair to interpret the irreversibility and inescapability of the French Revolution, namely, nature versus freedom. This pairing helped uncover the absurdity of sequences of actions beyond the control of human agency. The Revolution was a "natural necessity" for Goethe that engulfed each and everything like a raging river, "in which everyone perishes, those who predicted it along with those who did not have the slightest idea it was coming. Visible in this monstrous empirical evidence is nothing but nature, nothing of what we philosophers"—here directed at Schiller—"are so keen to call freedom."[39] For Goethe, each revolution is a relapse into the state of nature, which devours all freedom.

We must surely be wary of mistaking the natural force of a revolution for the natural pregivens that help bring forth individual histories, and that we have depicted thus far in terms of Goethe's binary or dual conceptual pairings. The categorial status of Goethe's concepts frequently shifts according to the metaphorical power and direction with which he invests them. But this feature of his thought perhaps helps us to better grasp why his memoirs, novels, and even his dramas are so slow. They are calibrated for long time periods, for repetitive structures. Aside from the so-called heroes, all of his dramatis personae are figures or types who bundle and personally reflect on their inner and outer conditions, who let their social or political situation shine through. Goethe makes visible backgrounds and preconditions that foment conflicts but cannot resolve them. But it is exactly for this reason that his works are exciting in a much different way—especially for the historian—and bear witness to a tension below the surface, something that only Bertolt Brecht was able to recreate. This is not a tension engendered by a specific situation—something that Schiller so frequently found to be absent in Goethe's works—because Goethe did not let his conflicts arise from political actions and their chain of events.

In closing let me give three examples. The situations of conflict in *Egmont* are derived from the rights and privileges of the social orders and their reworking by church and state. The four orders of the court-centered upper nobility, the nobility, the bourgeoisie, and the common people and lower classes appear on stage via figures that are representative types. It is then hardly surprising that situations of conflict analogous to the ones Goethe identified in the sixteenth century flared up on the eve of the French Revolution, when Brabant was able to deflect the patronizing interventions of Joseph II in 1787, this time successfully. Goethe showed surprise—at least rhetorically—at the fact that "the revolutionary scenes [. . .] were repeated exactly. I took from this that the world always remains the same, and that my depiction must have had some life in it."[40] Goethe uncovered social and political refractions between different sediments in a quasi-geological manner; because these sediments are repetitive, they contain a prognostic potential, though this does not necessarily mean that individual events occurring later could have been predicted.

Goethe took an entirely different tack in his "Fleeting Depiction of Florentine Conditions" which he appended to his *Cellini*.[41] Here Goethe managed to depict the viscous webs of conditions that makes palpable the uniqueness of Florentine history, something that no chronicle he consulted had ever been able to do. In the few short pages of this masterful sketch—which owes much to Machiavelli—, the reader learns about how the economic interests of the cosmopolitan citizens collided with the military constitution and the interests of the mercenary army collided with familial egoisms; how foreign and civil wars impelled each other forward; how religious fanaticism brought about policy shifts and yet how an incomparable level of artistic production nonetheless blossomed. Today this type of historical account is called structural analysis.

In his French *Campaign*, Goethe took yet another approach. Goethe philology has long since proven that he was mistaken about dates and names throughout nearly the entire piece,[42] or that he self-assuredly backdated his famous prognosis about the epochal battle at Valmy that never happened. Nonetheless, this work belongs to the unredeemed models for the kind of history of mentalities that historians pursue today. Goethe weaves a history into his autobiographical artwork that is unfolded out of the perception of those who participate and are affected by historical events. Here one can learn how history only ever manifests itself by the way it is perceived, and that things only ever come into being or fail—that is to say, have specific effects—in this manner; how collective judgments brew together and create reality by being wrong about it—or perhaps more to the point, how historical reality is being wrong about it; how anecdotes condense events; how war, as "pre-death [*Vortod*],"[43] makes all people the same; how international law can evaporate and give way to fanatical bloodlust in a matter of seconds (i.e., the behavior typical of civil war, against which Goethe boldly railed); how, despite everything, all help is rendered useless; in a word, how occurrences happen *in actu* and become history without being named as such, this is what Goethe's *Campaign* teaches us. The fact that the lacking diplomacy and strategy failed miserably was something that Goethe likewise appended to his work, placing this conclusion into the mouths of those affected and betrayed by it, thereby concealing his own criticism. He does not deliver any kind of rationalizable history of events that is generated by the difference between planning and failed result; instead, he shows how wishes run rampant and spread misery, dragging those who hold them to their deaths.

Goethe brings to light what remains hidden behind the events. Indeed, he suggested that the fate of the Jacobin Republic of Mainz—which, as he put it, was worn down both from within and without—was not caused by the war, but by the decline of civil society, which had come before the war and in fact had instigated it.[44]

Goethe was thus of his time and yet untimely. Our judgment today depends upon whether we follow his perspective that makes repetitive, durable structures visible, or whether we let ourselves be involved in the kind of political engagement that must guide us from day to day. When Heine saw Goethe as the "genius of dismissing the times" that finds "its own purpose in itself," this was only half of the truth.[45] Via his formal oppositional pairings, Goethe was better able to discern how histories came into being than his critics, who reproached him for not having his Mignon fall on the battlefield during the Tyrolean fight for freedom in 1809.[46] Goethe's history of events remained open to the future, but its multilayered conditions repeated themselves, overturned each other, again and again, without ever becoming timeless as a result. They bear witness to a different rhythm than what the events themselves can manifest. "The fact that Moscow is burned to the ground does not matter to me at all," Goethe wrote in 1812 to Count Reinhard [later grand duke of Saxe-Weimar-Eisenach], two of whose siblings had gone missing there. "World history will also want something to narrate in the future." And here a new oppositional pairing immediately comes to his mind: "Delhi also first perished after being conquered, but as a result of the conquerors,—Moscow perishes after being conquered, but as a result of the conquered. Teasing out this kind of a contradiction would be tremendously enjoyable if I were an orator."[47] Goethe was no orator. He hints at the desperate cynicism

of the realist who unfortunately knows better and who must strain to
ironize his knowledge so as to contain its implications. "World history
is collecting very great treasures at our cost."[48] But he quickly corrects
himself vis-à-vis the relatives and friends gone missing in Moscow: "thus
we do have a sense of the times we live in and of how deeply serious we
must be so that we can remain cheerful in the fashion of the ancients."[49]
Here Goethe approaches the kind of cheerfulness that only thrives when
hovering over the abyss.

Imprisoned in the [Carmelite] Convent in 1793, shortly before he was
beheaded by the terror machine, [the Girondist deputy Pierre-Victurnien]
Vergniaud invoked the myth of Saturn in order to stave it off: the Revolution devours its children.[50] Goethe might well have known this citation of
the myth when he thought it one step further, with an additional, bitter
nuance: not only the Revolution, but also—

> The good cause seems to me
> to be like Saturn, the sinner:
> No sooner are they brought to light
> Than he devours his children.
>
> [Die Gute Sache kommt mir vor
> Als wie Saturn, der Sünder:
> Kaum sind sie an das Licht gebracht,
> So frißt er seine Kinder.][51]

By the way, this was transcribed by his [Goethe's] son.

PART II

6

Does History Accelerate?

> Make haste, my smith, to fit the steed!
> Day passes away as you tarry o'er the deed.—
> "How your great horse steams in its might!
> Where do you rush to, my worthy knight?"[1]

The first German railroad poem, Adelbert von Chamisso's "Das Dampfroß" (The Steam Steed), written in 1830, five years before the first German rail car rolled from Nuremberg to Fürth, starts with these somewhat hackneyed couplets, portraying a half-familiar, half-uncanny scene, all-too-typical of late romantic ballads.[2]

As the title shows, the poem thematizes the shift from horse to locomotive, to a monstrous horse, or, to put it nonmetaphorically, to acceleration. For one, our locomotive gains a day in traveling around the world from east to west. This still is situated with the framework of calendrical experience. But then its speed increases: "My steam steed, model of all that is fast, / Leaves the course of time itself in the past. / Now racing off into the setting sun, / It appears from the east 'fore the day has begun."[3] It is as if Chamisso's locomotive casts the shadow that time itself lets fall back from the future onto the past. The train subverts not only clock time but historical time; it circles the earth so quickly that, aided by the turning of the earth, it can even catch up with the past. "I have robbed time of its secret, / wound it back from yesterday to yesterday."[4] The knight of the locomotive thus comes to witness his own birth; he disturbs his grandfather the bridegroom flirting with his bride and is angrily turned away; he conveys posterity's greetings to Napoleon on St. Helena, then finds him earlier in 1804 and warns him before he crowns himself emperor—"Oh, if only he had heeded the warning!" the critical Bonapartist Chamisso added.

The blacksmith, who wants 1,900 gold pieces as payment for his services—the nineteenth century settles its debts in gold—wants to know something else, though, namely, the future of the stock market, and whether, "entirely confidentially," it is wise to bet on Rothschild? But by then the rider, pressing a lever, had already disappeared with his steam horse.

Chamisso's poem is not just the first in Germany, but also the most striking contemporary poem lyricizing railroad technology. The soon quite fashionable poetry of steam came to represent the entire range of social and political attitudes on offer at the time: from hymns to progress—"with every rail that we lay, new life is brought into the world" (Louise Otto-Peters)[5]—to fear of the energies that threaten to destroy culture and spirit once released. The increase in speed remained a constant challenge and elicited genuine shock. Machines could now accomplish what had previously been done by horses, wind, or water, and it was difficult to describe the transition from the nature-bound time of forward movement to a time made technically controllable. At first, natural metaphors were used: exotic animals or mythical forms were attributed to the locomotive. Rhinoceros, dragon, elephant, colossus, giants, all were evoked to show that the locomotive could do more than a single horse: it could cover six miles or twenty-four kilometers in an hour, could draw an entire train of wagons from one location to another with people, luggage, freight, and even horses on them.

But Chamisso was the only author who outdid these metaphors of the technological generation of power and thematized acceleration itself. Here something unexpected emerged. In a fairy-tale-like inversion, he saw acceleration increasing to the point where the past could be caught up with, although not the future. The more the one opens up, the more the other escapes from view. After reading Chamisso's poem, one is almost forced to conclude that historicism is the true essence of progress. For it becomes increasingly clear what the past was, but increasingly unclear what the future will bring.

Chamisso was not alone in his interpretation dressed up like a fairy tale. It was part of the experience of acceleration typical of the Vormärz [the pre-1848 period]. "A new era of world history is beginning," as Heine reported from Paris on the opening of the Rouen-Orléans line, "and our generation can be proud to proclaim that it was there." This generation experiences both more and less here than in the thunder of cannons at Valmy [during the French revolutionary wars]: "we merely note that our entire existence is thrown, tossed onto new tracks, that new relations, new joys, and new struggles await us, and the unknown holds a fearful attraction, seductive and at the same time alarming."[6]

Because of this new unpredictability of the future, another contemporary, Eduard Beurmann, wrote of governments that they "distrust these enterprises [e.g., railroads] because they cannot calculate their end, but time cannot be made to stand still."[7] And even Ludwig I of Bavaria, a monarch who called for new railroads to be built, took up his quill to write against the new future: for it is written that the earth will go up in smoke. "At home everywhere and nowhere, the human race moves vagrantly over the earth, like steam / the racing wagon has began its revolving course / Now, its goal obscured from view" (1847).[8]

Even today's generation, which has witnessed live television coverage, rockets, jet airplanes, moon landings and earth satellites, has not incurred a shift in experience similar to that of the generation of the Vormärz. It is as though, not the flight and its acceleration, but the plane lifting up off the ground were itself the experience. Indeed, it would seem that accelerating events could become part of everyday life. The Brockhaus encyclopedia anticipated something similar in 1838, writing that flight would not approximate the breakthrough that was achieved by the railroad in terms of the technological mastery of time. Does this acceleration exist in history, or is it history itself that accelerates? I will divide this question into two subquestions:

First, I will take up the uniqueness of the experience of acceleration in the empirical context of the Industrial Revolution, which was beginning at that time. My thesis is that acceleration corresponds to a denaturalization of the hitherto traditional experience of time. It is an indicator of a specifically modern history.

Second, with recourse to intellectual history, I will examine theorems or myths that addressed something resembling historical acceleration prior to the Industrial Revolution. My second thesis is that as a category of historical expectation, acceleration is old, that it came to incorporate new expectational contents beginning in the sixteenth century, but that it could only become a fully saturated concept of experience with the Industrial Revolution. In other words, starting in the sixteenth century, the foreshortening of time already envisioned by apocalyptic thought became a metaphor of acceleration expressing new, different contents than originally intended by Christian eschatology.

I. The Denaturalization of the Experience of Time through Factors of Technological Acceleration

I recognize that the expression "denaturalization of time" runs the risk of criticism. For time always deals with nature, with the stars and with the biological cycles of humans, no matter how these cycles are used, reworked, or transformed by human society. We need only recall the famous Soviet joke "Sleep faster, comrade!" to indicate a boundary that no planning can surpass. My aim here is to show that the factors that the human, as historical being, has introduced into his experience of time lead to a relatively larger independence from nature, on which the human being always remains dependent. The acceleration brought about by humans themselves is unmistakable evidence of this process.

The introduction of mechanical clocks in the fourteenth century had already effected a denaturalization of the experience of time. It led to the quantification of the day into twenty-four identical hours. Jacques Le Goff speaks of mercantile time, the time of businesspeople, which entered into competition with religious-liturgical time and then, under the influence of the developing science of physics, represented an enormous achievement of abstraction.[9] In terms of its social function, the entire history of the measurement of time can be described as a history of increasing abstraction.

Ethnologists report of how deeply the earlier measures of time remain embedded in the context of human action.[10] On Madagascar, for example, there is a unit of time for "the duration it takes to cook rice" or for the split second required "to roast a grasshopper." Temporal measure and the course of action still converge almost entirely. Such expressions remain much more concrete than something like the German *Augenblick* [moment, or literally the "blink of an eye"], which itself also represents a unit of time, or the "present," which originally meant "in the presence of" and only mutated into a determination of time around 1800.

The elementary modes of measuring time of advanced cultures, which indicate the passing of time by the dwindling of material—sand or water—were also based in concrete actions: they measured the length of a sermon or determined the hour of Mass, or as with Cicero's water clock, the duration of a plea in court. Sundials are also part of this group of elementary modes of measuring time; they indicated different times depending on season and geographical location, because they showed the time on the basis of the natural orbit of the sun.

Mechanical clocks were also made to approximate sundials. Into the nineteenth century, the Japanese still used clocks whose particular artistry was their ability to variably mark the telling of the hours so that daytime hours stood in reverse relation to nighttime hours, being longer in the summer and shorter in the winter, depending on the season. Through these clocks, the seasonal difference between day and night hours was directly integrated into the rhythm of work, which gave them their purpose. Like elementary measures of time, these kinds of clocks corresponded to everyday rhythms of agriculture or manual labor rather than to a mechanized work world, whose temporal rhythms, derived from the machine and all equal, are prescribed for humans.

Introduced in the fourteenth century, the mechanical clock descended from the castle or church tower to the town hall, then to the living room and finally into the vest pocket. These clocks, which could display minutes by the sixteenth century and then seconds by the seventeenth—certainly indicated but also stimulated the disciplinization and the rationalization of the human work world and its realms of action. In the first half of the nineteenth century, many industrial workers in England already carried their own watches, not least to verify those of their overseers. Standardized time was eventually introduced with the creation of the railroad network and its standardized timetables—in Prussia prior to the 1848 Revolution—which differed completely from the given time in a locality and the position of the sun. Henry Ford began his career as an entrepreneur by making watches with two hands so that they could show both standard and local time. This was final evidence of the development of technologically determined units of time, which broke with the traditional nature-bound rhythms of time. Day and night came to seem identical as soon as railroad times made it possible to solve the problem of night travel, thanks to their tracks. This process corresponds to the rise of nightshifts in the great nineteenth-century factories, which had already existed in mining in the sixteenth century and were now being introduced ever more often to increase production.

All these processes have been frequently described, though not sufficiently studied. We can distinguish, roughly speaking, between three phases of increasing abstraction:

1. At first, the measurement of time was embedded in the context of human action.

2. The sundial made it possible to objectivize natural time, so to speak.

3. The mechanical clock and later the pendulum clock began a process of reworking the everyday through quantified units of time, which helped to secure and promote a far-reaching organization of society, a process that extended from the fourteenth to eighteenth century. The Sun King, Louis XIV, was celebrated as the *mâitre du temps*[11] because he ruled the present by his wisdom, the past by his memory, and the future by his foresight: clocks dedicated to him and those he had erected symbolized this.

For our purposes, it is important to recognize that the regularly running clocks that intruded into everyday life instigated and were signs of a lasting order, but not of acceleration,[12] however much they allowed for it to be measured in the physical realm. The dwindling hourglass and its fluid time became the allegory of evanescence (*Vergänglichkeit*), of *vanitas*; the mechanical clock, in turn, became the allegory of constancy, of wisdom, and utility. It was only at the end of the eighteenth century, when the clock was fully integrated into everyday life, that it could also represent *vanitas* iconographically.

The metaphor of the machine, especially of clockwork, that came to encompass the cosmos, society, and humanity in the seventeenth century, was still a pre-progressive metaphor: it evoked regularity, the stable household of God, nature, or humans that had been set up and then ran steadily, but not their acceleration.[13] The clock could measure acceleration but not symbolize it. This first became possible with the railroad and its metaphorics: Marx spoke of revolutions as the "locomotives of history," not the clocks of history. This new metaphor indicates the threshold only after which acceleration could coalesce into the dominant mode of experience of a new generation.[14]

Our findings about this epochal threshold [*Epochenschwelle*] include the fact that an increase in the speed in life as a whole had already been registered prior to the invention of the steam engine, mechanical looms, and the telegraph, which accelerated transportation, textile production, and the transmission of news. We are dealing with an initial running-up phase that led to a new dimension of temporal experience only after crossing the threshold. "One began to live more quickly and more intensively than before," Niebuhr observed, looking back at the eighteenth century, "but this was still taking shape at the time of the Revolution and has primarily developed since."[15]

Premechanical increases in speed have been registered in many ways since the seventeenth century. The expansion of networks of roads and canals increased the volume of freight and the distance it could be transported. The motivation for this expansion could be mercantile or political. In England, which had always enjoyed the advantage of cheap, fast waterways, a network of roads was constructed after [the Jacobite Pretender] Bonnie Prince Charlie had penetrated so far into England in 1745 that no troops could be mustered quickly to counter him. But we are not concerned here with explanations, but with the phenomena themselves.

The average speed of private carriages on French roads more than doubled between 1814 and 1848, from four and a half kilometers per hour to nine and a half. In Prussia in the same period, the mail coach journey from Berlin to Cologne likewise shrank from 130 to 78 hours. Government investments in [toll] roads also made governments long hesitate to subsidize railways, thus creating cheaper competition for themselves—as we know, this was one of the indirect causes of the 1848 revolutions.

We also can witness a similar process of increasing speed in sea routes.[16] In the first decade of the nineteenth century, North Americans invented the clipper ship, a narrow sailing ship with tall masts that cut the time to travel from New York to San Francisco around Cape Horn (19,000 kilometers) from 150–90 to 90 days. The record for a day was more than 750 kilometers, that is, around fifteen nautical miles per hour, which steam would only surpass much later.

We can observe something similar in communications. Prior to the establishment of the electrical telegraph—Thomas Sömmering had invented one in 1810, but it proved unusable—optical telegraph networks, whose tradition stretched back to antiquity, were developed to perfection.[17] The speed of signaling was increased enormously, whether through the necessary abbreviation of baroque administrative texts or the construction of a system of signals transmitted from tower to tower. In the French Revolution, this system of communication—which was also a system of control—was systematically developed. The fall [to the Austrians] of Condé-sur-L'Escaut in 1794 was reported from Lille to Paris by optical telegraph many hours earlier before the mounted courier arrived. Napoleon's successes were also aided by the acceleration of the transmission of messages in this way, which also led to the execution of [the Tyrolean rebel leader] Andreas Hofer after receipt of a [supposedly] direct order transmitted by optical telegraph [from Napoleon], even though the majority of judges had voted against it. As so often is the case, business only later caught up with political and military interests. "Cases are conceivable in which having messages arrive just a few hours earlier could be worth much more than the yearly cost of the telegraph lines and all their equipment," Professor Büsch noted in 1800[18]—a guiding principle of the world of trade and finance in the coming centuries. Saving time increases costs, and profits even more.

What, then, is the takeaway from all of this? Prior to the invention of [new] technological instruments of acceleration, the modern state and civil society had already achieved an astounding velocity in their transportation systems. However, they ran up against an absolute limit dictated by nature. Roads could be improved, coaches refined, but the power of horses remained limited. Sailing ships could be perfected, but in the end, their speed depended on the wind. The optical telegraph could be rationalized, but transmission was thwarted by nightfall, or by rain and clouds in the day, not infrequently for days or weeks. Sometimes a partial report was all there was for days: thus, victory was reported from Spain without anyone in Paris learning whether Wellington or Napoleon was the victor.

Once acceleration was unleashed in interpersonal traffic, it could only be driven further once technological inventions allowed it to surpass nature-given limits. Only in the wake of the French and Industrial Revolutions did acceleration begin to become a universal principle of experience.

Let me list several criteria of the principle of experience formulated at the time.

The most frequent benchmark for acceleration was the disappearance of space. In 1838, the *Brockhaus der Gegenwart* [Brockhaus Dictionary of the Present] pointedly defined the essence of the railroad as follows: "It does away with spatial separations by bringing things closer in time. [. . .] Thus, all spaces are only distances for us by virtue of the time we need to pass through them; if we accelerate these times, it limits the influence of space on life and transport." The writer makes individual calculations for the world of work and politics with touching naïveté, and the railroad's coming military significance is intentionally overlooked. Traveling by train, the itinerant manual laborer would gain four and a half days of working time per week. Adjacent cities would grow together into an "artificially concentrated space." The division of city and countryside would be overcome by a common economic space. "Land and sea will exchange roles." "Railroads will reduce Europe to approximately the territory of Germany."[19]

We need not include any further examples. Ignoring political or social factors of change, the data of acceleration are projected linearly into the future. But this is not without political purpose. The enemies of the railroad recognized and feared the democratizing effect of the railroad, which transported all the existing estates [*Stände*] in four classes at the same speed. It was a commonplace that the railroad initiated the age of equality. And it is almost unnecessary to mention that the unification of legal spaces at the cost of traditional regional titles was part of the same inventory of experience.

But acceleration was also registered in other areas unrelated to the railroad. In 1793, Adam Smith's calculations made their way into the German *Realenzyklopädie*. The division of labor "does not simply induce corresponding growth of the productive powers, but also helps to save time by gaining time that otherwise would have been lost on moving from one kind of work to another. This gain in time significantly increases the quantity of work." Ultimately, wages are saved with the gain in time, and machines are to thank for it all. The working time freed up in this way should in turn be used for the satisfaction of new needs, which emerge because the machines have already satisfied existing needs.[20]

Another component of this is the analysis of structures of needs, which came to be seen in temporal terms beginning in the 1790s. Luxury lost the stigma of being the purview merely of the upper classes. Instead, need was transformed into the need for the increase of need through the accelerated shift in fashions, something recognized by Garve. Instead of simply satisfying the most basic needs required by nature, growing needs now put pressure on the order of the estates. There was a growing perception of widespread processes that were experienced as acceleration and could not be reversed. This is why the static metaphor of the machine falls apart from the economic side: in 1800, Büsch, in analyzing the circulation of money, described the classes as different driving wheels, based on their occupation. But he then goes on: "We must not take these comparisons too far. Because these wheels do not simply work individually and all as a whole, namely, for the welfare of the state, but also back on one another, and each promotes and accelerates the course of the other; I am not able to find an example in mechanics that can adequately capture this kind of interaction."[21]

In each case it is acceleration that distinguishes the temporal experience of this time from all previous times. But the metaphor for a self-induced, self-accelerating system was still sought in vain. Acceleration seemed to take hold of one realm after the other, not merely the technical world of industry, the empirically verifiable core of all acceleration, but everyday life, politics, the economy, and population increases as well.[22]

The bourgeois world unfolded under the sign of acceleration. Ever more pianos—the mark of distinction of every bourgeois salon—were produced in ever-shorter periods of time. In 1750, a piano maker produced around twenty instruments. Thanks to the mechanical production of metal frames, Broadwood of London manufactured four hundred pianos in 1802 and fifteen hundred in 1824. "Prices sank, pitch rose" and reached the brilliant frequency of 435. Mozart and Beethoven were irritated that their pieces were being played faster than they had intended. Reading in the bourgeois household was likewise accelerated. Repeated readings of the Bible and the classics shifted to include the consumption of constantly new literary products, above all the novel. Starting in 1814, the rotary press helped increase volume, and Brockhaus, one of our key witnesses, sought to adapt. The publisher's first encyclopedia was brought up to date through supplemental volumes, but in 1830 and 1840, it shifted to offer a separate *Brockhaus der Gegenwart*, which provided a cross section of modernity. This cross section then became the journal *Die Gegenwart*, which reported the events of a bustling time to [German readers'] homes every month.

Let us pause with these empirical findings and their nineteenth-century interpretations and ask what the effect of acceleration as a principle of experience was.

First, the increasing use of the term "acceleration" since the turn of the nineteenth century bears witness to a change in the sensation and consciousness of time [*Zeitgefühl und Zeitbewußtsein*], without the everyday use of language necessarily having any kind of theoretical or systematic stringency. It would seem that the term served to register an experience that had not existed before: of course, this is precisely the point of acceleration. It is the moment of surprise that is articulated here. Let me try briefly to explain.

The question as to acceleration is part of the more general question of what constitutes historical time. If we may characterize progress as the first genuinely historical category of time—which it is, despite its historical-theological implications—then acceleration is a specific variety of this progress. Theoretically, there also can be progress that moves uniformly, so that the simple speed of a change or improvement does not present an additional criterion for something progressively changing. Rise in production, for example, can remain the same in uniform intervals of time. It is only if productivity is increased that it becomes an acceleration of production. (As we know, this is a question for economic history that has not yet been adequately researched. The transition from manual to mechanical spinning and weaving is just one symptom of many that could be weighted in a variety of ways.)

It is only when rates measured in identical intervals of time increase geometrically rather than arithmetically that we can register something like acceleration. Thus, around 1900 Henry Adams considered the entirety of modern history in terms of the "the law of acceleration."[23] This model is useful as a heuristic determination for the technological-industrial conditions of modern history, but it cannot be applied in an unmediated way to general history. At any rate, it is clear to us that acceleration is more than simple change and more than mere progress. It qualifies the "progress of history," a phrase first employed after 1800.

Change, *mutatio rerum*, is reported in all histories. The kind of change that calls forth a new experience of time—the sense that everything is changing more quickly than one had expected or experienced up to that point—is modern, however. Shorter time spans bring a component of unfamiliarity into the everyday life of those affected, and this component cannot be derived from any previous experience. As Goethe has Eduard say in *Elective Affinities*: "It is a great annoyance that one can no longer learn anything once and for all. Our ancestors observed their whole life long the instruction they received in their youth; but we have to learn anew every five years if we do not want to fall completely out of fashion."[24]

In other words, rhythms and processes of times are articulated that can no longer be derived from the natural time of any sequence of generations. The former constant reproducibility of learning and the lasting application of what had been learned are interrupted for the mastery of what is now new. Compared to the preceding experience of learning, the temporal rhythms of relearning become shorter and shorter, which calls forth the experience of an accelerated transformation. This kind of acceleration refers to a history that is conceived of as a time that is always outpacing itself, as it were, as modernity [*Neuzeit*] in an emphatic sense.

Here it is necessary to make a second point, which should serve as a warning against positing this concept of modernity as absolute in its singularity. Acceleration is always also a perspectival concept that takes its evidence from the comparison of contemporaneous generations who share a common space of experience, even if this space is also perspectivally refracted. Wondering at the "unbelievable speed" with which his age transformed all thought and intention, [the German publisher] Perthes formulated this in a letter to Jacobi.[25] Previously there had only been transformations in experience over the course of centuries, now the sequence of different experiences is compressed together and expands the discord accordingly. "Our time [. . .] has unified what is completely ununifiable in the three generations that are now currently alive. The immense contrasts of 1750, 1789, and 1815 lack any and all transition and appear not as a sequence but as coexistence in the people now alive, depending on whether one is a grandfather, father, or grandson." It is the chronological contemporaneity of those who are not politically or socially contemporaneous that calls forth conflicts, where attempts to resolve these conflicts are experienced as acceleration when measured against previous epochs.

Our category of "acceleration" can thus also serve as an instrument of knowledge that aims at a theory of political crisis, though one that would not necessarily claim future accelerations. The French Revolution and its course were conventionally understood in this way. Georg Friedrich Rebmann, for example, composed a funeral elegy for the [French] revolutionary calendar (revoked in 1805), in which he offers a typology of the Revolution that had created it, adding: "In short, the calendar saw everything that had happened in the twenty centuries before it in the space of just a few years, and just as child prodigies rarely grow old, it finally died of a stroke, even though doctors had prophesized a death by consumption. Oh, if the calendar had only been able to experience how people had become cleverer and better, how their experiences had become useful for them and their descendants! Requiescat in pace!"[26]

Here the topos of the compressed and therefore accelerated time of revolutionary events ends in partial resignation, since progress did not ensue to the degree Rebmann hoped for.

Görres reacted similarly after the Restoration in a traditional sense seemed to have been reinstated once more: he came to the conclusion that one could learn little from earlier history: "If you want to study history, then take the Revolution as your instructor: in it the course of many sluggish centuries accelerated into a cycle of just a few years."[27] Here, then, we encounter an interpretational concept of acceleration that starts with the dimension of surprise at an unknown future and points back to structural possibilities of a history that can repeat itself in analogous ways. A revolution is just the accelerated concentrate of all possible history, so to speak.

In this regard, accelerated history still remains a history that is not only modern.

To be sure, these two last examples come from political experience, not of industrialization. Over the course of the technologizing society of the nineteenth century, this political variety of acceleration was always invoked whenever revolutionary shifts occurred, but on the whole they did not determine the interpretation of all occurrences. For this reason, we must differentiate theoretically between two types of acceleration:

1. The acceleration registered in periods of crisis in constitutional-political life. There have been examples of this going back to Thucydides that continue to apply to present experience, just as the word *Geschwindigkeit* (speed) in early modern usage also referred to unrest and civil war. Characteristic of the interpretations of the French Revolution is the oft-repeated thesis that, with the recent cascade of events, Polybius's model of constitutional cycles spread out over nine generations is now being compressed into the cataracts of events within a single generation, or become even shorter. This kind of acceleration draws on something long familiar, merely seeing it as taking place in a much shorter time period.

2. The acceleration that has resulted from technological-industrial progress and—in contrast to the past—can be registered as the experience of a new time. Of course, both types of acceleration, which a theory of time must strictly differentiate, naturally blend together and influence each other in everyday speech and can provide arguments for a more universal-historical theory of crisis, like the one masterfully assembled by Jacob Burckhardt.[28]

A first preliminary finding, then, is that there surely are accelerations, but not accelerations of history but rather in history, depending on the sediments of experience, whether they are primarily political or technical and economic. "History itself" or "history in and for itself" is hardly suited to be considered an acting subject capable of accelerated action. For this history in and for itself contains all standards of comparison within itself, according to which one would have to measure if it was accelerating on decelerating. The concept of a history [*Geschichte*] that is theoretically abstracted away from empirical histories [*Geschichten*], that constitutes both its own subject and object, a history, that is to say, that contains the condition of all possible histories within it, this concept, first developed in the eighteenth century, does not allow for standards of measurement outside of itself that could register or even calculate an acceleration "of history." Hegel, who derived the stages of world history from the work of the world spirit, saw this clearly, though he conceded that the writing of history has accelerated: "in recent times, all relations have been altered. Our culture grasps everything immediately and trans-forms all occurrences directly into historical representations."[29] But the world spirit, which works its way through nations and individuals at their own cost, and only progresses via detours and mediations, "it not only has plenty of time," time is irrelevant for it. "In terms of the slowness of the world spirit, we must remember that it needn't hurry, it has plenty of time—before you, thousands of years are like a day—it has enough time because it is outside of time, because it is eternal." Moreover, this slowness is "increased by each seeming regression, by times of barbarity."[30]

It is not by chance that Hegel, who sought to develop and com-prehend "history itself" out of the spirit of a formerly Christian divinity, quotes the verse of Psalm 90 to demonstrate that each situation could equally call for deceleration and for acceleration: "For a thousand years in your sight are but as yesterday when it is past, and as a watch in the night." This multivalent allegory leads us back to the apocalyptic preconditions of modern axioms of acceleration.

II. The Category of Temporal Foreshortening between Apocalypse and Progress

Up to now we have become acquainted with acceleration as a con-cept of experience of modernity and have thereby encountered two variet-ies: we can theorize acceleration either as the possibility of self-repeating histories or as a result of technological-industrial innovation. In order to gain a new perspective, let us now look at the criteria for acceleration in use prior, as it were, to the transitional threshold leading into our period.

The apocalyptic texts of the Judeo-Christian tradition repeatedly take up the foreshortening of time. One might define temporal foreshort-ening as a concept of religious experience, but it draws its meaning from Christian expectation, by which temporal foreshortening is a favor of God, who does not want to suffer us to wait so long for the end of the world

(Mark 13:20; Matt. 24:22). The end should [thus] come about sooner than it otherwise would. The standard of this temporal foreshortening is the prophesized overcoming of time itself.[31]

The longer the Second Coming of Christ is delayed, the more another variant of expectation leads to the question: How much longer? The basis for this expectation is the stubborn wish of the faithful to see time shortened so as to be able to participate in salvation as soon as possible. In 2 Peter 3:8 the answer (from Psalm 90) is given, that a day before the Lord is like a thousand years and a thousand years like a day. This should offer consolation in the face of all-too empirical hopes, for it points to God's grace, who wants to first let his message reach all inhabitants of earth and complete the number of the chosen. Delaying the end was therefore just as much an indication of God's grace as the prophesized foreshortening of time. There is no contradiction here, to the extent that both variants could account for the Pauline transposition of expectation into the certainty of belief. For our purposes, what is decisive is that temporal foreshortening or delay both have their guiding points entirely outside of time. Both ideas secure evidence solely from the eternal nature of God, whose renewed entry into this world would give rise to a new world. We are therefore faced with two relational determinations of time in apocalyptic thought, which would, to be sure, allow for the interpretation of historical events, but whose interpretive grid cannot be primarily derived from the temporal structures of these events themselves. We are dealing not with a historical foreshortening of temporal processes, but rather with a foreshortening of the time of history, an anticipated end of the world.

Finally, a third variety represents the chiliastic interpretation of the intermediary condition between expectation and the arrival of the end. This too drew on the same passage from Peter's epistles and especially John's Apocalypse. If a thousand years are only a day to God, they are inserted as a time of blessed expectation of the final return of Christ to the earth. This theory of an intermediate phase in which the foreshortening and the delay of the expiration date are temporarily deactivated, so to speak, also depends on a pregiven telos that is extrahistorical in nature. Whenever apocalyptic images were time and again applied to empirical occurrences, institutional problems repeatedly arose concerning who is qualified to make the correct exegesis. Heresy lurked behind every empirical verification of apocalyptic interpretation, even if these interpretations themselves influenced and advanced the history of Christianity.

Even after the Church Fathers, and especially Augustine, made the doctrine of the thousand-year empire taboo, determinations of both temporal foreshortening and delay remained an inherent moment of Christian expectation. Luther's table talk is a good example of this, for it contains down-to-earth apocalyptic expectations, in contrast to his theological writings; there he both asks for a delay and prophesizes and longs for the arrival of the Last Judgment. In this way, the two arguments for delay sometimes blend together: that for God, a thousand years are just a day, and that empirical history is becoming shorter.

One criterion for the extrahistorical determination of time of apocalyptic prophesy is its repeatability. An unfulfilled prophesy or apocalyptic expectation can be repeated continually; indeed, the likelihood that what is prophesized and expected will still occur grows with each disappointed expectation. That is, evidence of its future fulfillment lies precisely in the error about the timing and makes this fulfillment all the more certain. In this way, the temporal framework for the formula for foreshortening is metahistorically pregiven. The empirical data for confirming the fact that accelerating events are also signs of the end times can in each case be exchanged with one another. This holds through Luther and deep into the seventeenth century, but in the further course of modernity [*Neuzeit*], the circle of those who evoked these texts decreases to a small one, with no access to the realm of political decision making.

On the basis of this heuristically simplified position, we can gain a new perspective on the proliferation of sixteenth-century statements that time was being foreshortened that did not invoke the Apocalypse. The notion of self-foreshortening spaces of time still remained enclosed within a horizon of expectation (namely, that in the future ever-faster progress will ensue), but the notion is also enriched by other, new kinds of experience that were not interpreted in a Christian sense. The discoveries and inventions of the emerging natural sciences constituted the hard kernel of experience from which it initially derived. Here we can note a general tendency for the time span between the sixteenth and the nineteenth centuries: the hopes and expectations, initially stimulated by Christianity, enriched by utopianism, and then applied to the history of inventions and discoveries, were increasingly overtaken by principles of experience from the natural sciences.

From the foreshortening of time that had previously posited an early end to history from outside of history, an acceleration of determinable sectors of experience was now registered within history itself. What is new here is that the end was no longer approaching more quickly; rather, compared to the slow progress of the previous centuries, the current steps of progress come about ever more quickly. The telos of mastering nature and organizing society more justly became a sliding goal and every over-ambitious intention lent itself well to being interpreted as long-delayed progress.

We are thus dealing with something more than and different from mere secularization. However many apocalyptic expectations might have entered into the new concept of acceleration in the guise of millenarian hopes, the kernel of experience to which these new expectations referred was no longer deducible from the Apocalypse.

However, the engagement with the apocalyptic tradition would continue. It has always reemerged, mediated in many ways, when the telos of history is at stake, which it is humanity's task to reach ever more quickly. This becomes evident in the eighteenth century, when the category of acceleration is expanded from increasing mastery of nature to include society, the unfolding of morality, and history as a whole. Indeed, one can say that history itself was first revealed as a particular human way of being [*Seinsweise*] when interpreted as progressive and accelerated.

Toward the end of the eighteenth century, above all during the French Revolution, voices proliferated that came to see all of history from the perspective of increasing acceleration. Most authors implicitly or explicitly address the question of whether the succession of foreshortening periods is objectively verifiable or whether it was only a matter of subjective perception. Still keeping his distance from the enlightened chiliasts, Lessing attested that he wanted to bring about the future in an accelerated manner. This, then, is the aim of connecting the actual course of history to human hopes, plans, and actions, something that Kant also sought to justify in a way that is as subtle as it is engaged. Kant believed that he could find empirical proof of the moral duty of attempting and promoting progress in the events of the French Revolution, and especially in people's reactions to these events, generating hope that a just republic and a peaceful world order could be brought about in ever shorter intervals of time.

Kant never went as far as Condorcet, who was convinced of his ability to predict, direct, and accelerate the progress of the human race, "as soon as one has found the correct guiding thread in the history of previous progress."[32] But in both theories the duty, the desirability, or the establishing of an accelerated progression is tied back to human action itself, however much philosophical-historical reinsurance was taken out in a plan of nature (Kant) or a universal law (Condorcet).

The experience of a series of natural scientific successes and the start of technologization may well have helped Condorcet in his self-assurance. In any case, for the eighteenth-century concept of acceleration laden with the philosophy of history, this meant that it could only be used meaningfully if there was a goal to be attained via acceleration. Herein lies the formal analogy to the extratemporal determination of the goal long familiar from apocalyptic texts.

Thus, at the Festival of the Constitution in 1793, Robespierre invoked happiness and freedom as the destiny of humankind, which it had now, with the Revolution, become the duty of all citizens to attain in an accelerated manner. And in the same year Condorcet formulated the "revolutionary law" whose goal it was to maintain, guide, and accelerate the Revolution.[33]

And Joseph Görres's deduction a quarter century later: that "the great world course of history [. . .] is uniformly accelerating," that the "foreshortening of the periods as they approach the present" is undeniable[34]— this transmutation of apocalyptic expectation into the interpretation of history also impregnated the French positivist school. People should now bring about what was expected in the Apocalypse from the secret decision of God. With recourse to Condorcet, Saint-Simon likewise demanded the organization of previous centuries according to the successive steps forward of the human spirit, "et vous verrez clairement les moyens à employer pour accélérer son perfectionnement."[35] All the interrelated social, economic, and political analyses of world history by Saint-Simon and his student Comte remain within the framework of factually observed increases in speed as well as according to the guiding imperative of continuing to accelerate them. Here the Last Judgment, as with Schiller, is incorporated into history itself. The French Revolution is the "great final crisis" prior to the peaceful reordering of society, whose precondition for Comte is, of course, sociological theory: only long-range planning of the future based on knowledge of the past can achieve the complete reorganization that will end the crisis ("la reorganization totale, qui peut seule terminer la grand crise moderne").[36] Even if the words of the Last Judgment are still intact, the apocalyptic imagery fades.

Now, what unites all of this evidence? Clearly, the acceleration claimed and invoked for the entirety of world history is less a controlled concept of experience and more a utopian concept of expectation.

A quasi-religious promise had colored the span of time that was to have been covered in an accelerated manner. But the goals remain of this world and found new support, in the nineteenth century, in technological progress. For example, in the 1838 essay on the railroads cited earlier, the *Brockhaus* defined the organization of world peace by self-determining humanity as a morally necessary postulate. "Indeed, history has been directed toward this truly divine goal all along, but it will reach it centuries earlier on the wheels of the railroad rolling furiously forward," the author observes.[37]

One might well argue that this represents the formal temporal structure of an apocalyptic expectation. But this is as far as the claim can go, for the instance of experience remained a technical instrument, which, as very quickly became apparent, was unable to redeem the demand of future salvation. Whoever still wanted to continue to cling to inner-worldly determinations of the destiny of history had to search for other accelerators.

By returning to the apocalyptic tradition and its transformation since the early modern period, we have thus found another answer. Historical acceleration can be registered in two possible cases:

First, it can be traced back to the temporal foreshortening arising from the expectation of a goal: in this case, processes of acceleration are always possible as a postulate and can be repeatedly invoked anew, irrespective of whether they can be fulfilled. In this case we are dealing with a concept of expectation that can be repeated at any time. Decelerations, hesitations, or delays are deduced purely on the subjective level, qua categories of wishful things or of disappointed hopes.

Second, acceleration can be deduced from comparison with past events: in this way they remain empirically verifiable and can provide data for subsequent planning. In this case, we are dealing with a pure concept of experience.

Finally, and in conclusion, the two possibilities can be combined, and this is perhaps the most common variation today, consisting in the idea that the technological-industrial condition achieved by developed countries in the past is to be made up by the less-developed countries in the future. It necessarily follows that acceleration alone can satisfy the need to catch up. Here again we have a determination of the contemporaneity of the noncontemporaneous, which carries a great potential for conflict. Moreover, this presents an imbrication of experience and expectation; the gap between the two demands to be bridged in an accelerated manner. The experience of the one is the expectation of the other. Condorcet, Comte, and Friedrich List investigated and promoted the acceleration of historical events primarily with this third possibility in view. In our time, it does not simply inform the day-to-day tasks of political planning (consider Khrushchev or Mao Zedong [who both believed in the need for accelerated development]) but is an indispensable part of politics and economics in a global context, though we do not know how long this will hold.

Let us listen once more to Chamisso, with whose help we entered the orbit of acceleration: "In the fall of 1837 I was in Leipzig to fulfill my vow to ride the train, harnessing the zeitgeist—I could not have died in peace had I not looked from the high seat of this triumphal car into the unrolling future."[38] A year later, Chamisso was dead.

7

Constancy and Change of All
Contemporary Histories:
Conceptual-Historical Notes

I

Zeitgeschichte [the history of the present or contemporary history; literally, the "history of time"] is a lovely word, but a difficult concept. At first glance, the concept seems simple and clear. It aims to describe our own history, the history of the present, our "times," as one says. This is the standard use of the word and its meaning is intuitive. Otherwise, there would be no Commission and no Working Group for *Zeitgeschichte*, no Institute for *Zeitgeschichte*, names adopted because of its simple, frequent use and its higher claim to generality. The *Institut für Zeitgeschichte* was initially supposed to be called the "German Institute for the History of the National-Socialist Time."[1] This subject-oriented name gave way to a formal, general concept that could be repeatedly refilled with new content, depending on what comes to be newly experienced and defined as *Zeitgeschichte*, for example, the history of the Federal Republic or of the Cold War.

The fact that it is plausible that this general concept can be refilled with new content presents us with our first difficulty. Why is X now part of *Zeitgeschichte* and not Y, or not any longer? Where do we draw the boundary between what belongs to *Zeitgeschichte* and what is no longer part of it? Does not every history deal with time? Why is our own history *Zeitgeschichte* in a special sense, while earlier histories are not? Was Alsted wrong three hundred years ago when he defined history [*Historie*] in the following manner: "Historia omnis chronica est, quoniam in tempora fit [History is a chronicle of everything that happens in the course of time]"?[2] All history is a chronicle, a representation along a chronological order, for history, after all, manifests itself in times. For this reason, it used to be common to differentiate between older and newer times about which one was reporting; however, the "times," *tempora*, referred to all histories being reported about. There can be no history without the relation to time. Why, then, does so-called *Zeitgeschichte* stand out? With this finding, which might well be called banal,[3] a second difficulty arises.

Granting that all histories deal with time (as all historians would), we might follow conventional parlance and say that the term *Zeitgeschichte* refers to the history of our own time, our present day—"contemporary chronicling," to quote Fritz Ernst.[4] Here, however, our initial problem reoccurs, though perhaps on a more limited level. For what exactly does "the present" mean? We might identify two extreme answers.

First, the "present" can refer to that point of intersection where the future becomes the past, the point where the three dimensions of time meet and which always brings about the disappearance of the present. In this case, the present is a notional zero point on a notional axis of time. As long as the human being has a future ahead of him or her, he or she is always already past. And only when he or she has stopped being both past and future, is he or she dead. Presentness thus becomes a notional nothingness that always draws our attention to the fact that we belong both to the past and the future. It becomes the moment that continuously eludes capture. "In life, nothing is the present," as Goethe once translated Byron.[5]

But whoever cites Goethe can also find the opposite in his works—as in all adages about time. Indeed, Goethe likewise wrote: "You must always enjoy the present / and especially hate no one / and leave the future to God."[6] This takes us to our second extreme answer.

One might well invert the first conclusion—that the present can be brought to disappear between past and future—and suggest that all time is presence in an exceptional sense. For the future is not yet and the past no longer. The future only exists as a present future, the past only as a present past. The three dimensions of time are bundled in the presentness of human existence, to speak with St. Augustine in his *De anima*. Time is only present in its constant withdrawal: in the *expectatio futurorum* [expectation of things to come] the future, in the *memoria praeteritorum* [memory of things past] the past.[7] The so-called being of the future or the past is their presence, in that they are present, made present.

Our thought experiment, which has produced two extreme answers, still does not solve the question of what the "present" actually is, if we choose to speak of the history of the present rather than of *Zeitgeschichte*. In fact, this only compounds our difficulties, for the present can just as well encompass all dimensions of time—our second extreme—as it can disappear in favor of the past and future, as a permanent tension in which every present is caught by vanishing—our first extreme. The seemingly precise redefinition of *Zeitgeschichte* as the history of the present thus does not lead us out of our dilemma, namely, that all histories are *Zeitgeschichten*, and that each history, viewed in terms of its temporal dimensions, relates to a particular present that either contains all dimensions within it or can only ever be interpreted in light of the past and the future. From a theoretical perspective, then, conventional language is insufficient, if not misleading.

We might find a way out of this dilemma if we think our thought experiment through to its conclusion. If all dimensions of time are contained within a specific present and they can be unfolded from there, but if it is not possible to connect these dimensions back to that present because it is in a state of continuous withdrawal, then each of the three dimensions of time must themselves be temporalized. Heidegger makes this approach possible with *Being and Time*, Raymond Aron and Richard Wittram have taken this up, and Luhmann has executed it in a formally consistent manner.[8] Corresponding to the three temporal dimensions, we therefore have, again, through temporalization, three times three possible combinations.

First, as our thought experiment already revealed, there exist a present past and a present future, which correspond to a present present, whether it is conceived of as a disappearing point or as something that encompasses all dimensions.

Second, if each present expands backward and forward at the same time, there exists a past present with its past pasts and its past futures.

Third, there is consequently a future present, along with future pasts and future futures. With the help of these categories, we can grasp all historical determinations of time in a formally sufficient manner without getting lost in the opaqueness of concepts such as *Zeitgeschichte* or history of the present. The duration, change, and singularity of events and their sequences can be determined on the basis of this model. Something that has duration, for example, spans from a past present (not from a past past) into the present future and perhaps into the future future. Change can also be located within this formal framework as something that leads from a past past into a past present (think, e.g., of the institution of feudal law and its dissolution in the wake of secularization or the freeing of the peasants)—or from the past future of earlier life worlds to our present pasts (e.g., the utopias of the French Revolution, whose hopes are still present). And finally, singularity arises out of the succession of every conceivable present with its shifting pasts and futures, which themselves likewise shift. Further examples are unnecessary, for we have formally determined the kaleidoscope of historical possibilities enough to be able to reflect on the relationship of time and history.

And a first result already comes into view. Every history is *Zeitgeschichte* and every history was, is, and will be a history of the present. Duration, change, and singularity can be aligned with particular relational determinations of the temporal dimensions. In terms of our theoretical formalization, one might then argue that so-called *Zeitgeschichte* in no way differentiates itself from other histories that occurred earlier and that have been narrated or represented.

But—one might object—times themselves change, times have their own history, otherwise it would be impossible to speak of different, clearly distinguishable time periods. I would like to take up this objection by retracing the preceding line of thought, but historically rather than formally.

II

What do histories of the word, concept, and issue of what is meant by and experienced as *Zeitgeschichte* tell us? The issue itself is naturally quite old; the term *Zeitgeschichte* emerged in Germany in the seventeenth century, and after it became more widely used around 1800, the concept evolved. Our formal problem of what *Zeitgeschichte* is thus also has its own genesis in linguistic history, even if we can apply the results of the emergence of the word, changes in its meaning, and the designations to which these changes refer to periods before our term emerged, that is, retroactively.

As far as we know, the history of the word begins with the baroque poet Sigmund von Birken, who made a name for himself with his theoretical reflections on the relationship between poetry, theology, and history. *Zeitgeschichte* comes up incidentally in a 1657 hymn to Emperor Matthias, who ruled between 1612 and 1619: "The *Zeitgeschichten* prove / how wisely he prevented / all misfortunes, including / his own and the Empire's."[9] The meaning is clear: at stake are histories in which the emperor played a role, and about which the singer reports, who, as a poet, felt especially indebted to history. He specifically evokes the past future, for the actual achievement of the monarch lay in preventing looming misfortune, in fending off something that could have but did not happen.

The issue designated by this new word had existed previously and continued to exist, namely, the history of those living at the same time and their own or others' reporting about it. *Zeitgeschichte* in this respect is always a history of contemporaneity. In this sense, it is a lovely euphemism for *historia sui temporis*—something that histories of our cultural sphere [*Kulturraum*] have been ever since their scholarly grounding. In this sense, Herodotus devoted a third of his *Histories* to the great Persian War that had occurred just a brief generation before, and it was in this sense that Thucydides was a pure "historian of the time [*Zeithistoriker*]," as were Polybius and Tacitus. But the *Actus (praxeis) Apostolorum* and Caesar's *Gallic* and *Civil Wars* also belong to this genre as do the *Mémoires* of Commynes and of Cardinal Retz and the *Denkwürdigkeiten* composed by Friedrich the Great about his wars. This line can be easily extended to the histories for which Churchill won the Nobel Prize, or to

Grosser's exemplary *L'Allemagne de notre temps* (Paris, 1970), which covers the period up to one year before the book's publication. In this partially scientific and partially literary sense—but the one does not exclude the other—, *Zeitgeschichte* has "always" existed and one can only hope that this will remain the case.

One can certainly object that this line from Herodotus to Churchill is forced and lumps together a heterogeneous variety of themes, interests, styles, genres, and scientific (and unscientific) methods. At least initially, however, let us stress the commonalities.

First: in almost every case, participants experienced particular thrusts of events as high points of all previous histories, whether they belonged to the victors or the vanquished, although the vanquished were often compelled to write better, more clear-sighted history. This applies to Thucydides as well as to the Marx of the *18th Brumaire*, who was a defeated party, even though he wrote like a victor.

Second: the fact that the narrator was a participant, whether as a witness or—even better—an actor, is an important criterion for the authenticity and the truth of the history being recorded [*Historie*]. And even if critical history [*Historie*]—at the latest after it developed the philological method—learned to cast doubt upon the truth content of agents' statements: the "contemporary-historical [*zeithistorisch*]" truth findings of these formally contemporary histories [*Historien*] count in every case for more than any later compilations or compositions. The false testimony of a contemporary will always remain a more immediate source even if it is later unmasked.

Third: the practice of questioning witnesses' interests or blind spots, their believability or propensity to lie, indeed, their inescapable mendacity, this all was part of the methodology of Thucydides or Tacitus long before our philological, critical method.

Fourth: weighing different witness statements in a manner analogous to legal proceedings was an integral part of genuine contemporary history writing in antiquity ever since Herodotus, the inventor, and (so to speak) unsurpassed master of "oral history."

Herodotus already made the important distinction between immediate eyewitnesses and mediated earwitnesses in order to ascertain degrees of reliability. Even something like analyzing myths in order to measure their relationship to reality (a task undertaken by Hecataeus) can be compared to Vico's method or with the analysis of rumors, for reality may lurk in hiding behind rumors, which as rumors are already part of reality. To this day, Tacitus can still teach us that the political reality of rumors lies in the psychic dispositions of those who hear and retell them and that their content is effective precisely for that reason.

This list could be extended to find similarities in approach of all histories of distinct worlds of experience from antiquity up to the present day, even as they are filtered methodologically to varying degrees. In this sense, *Zeitgeschichte* was and always is current, or at least always conceivable, despite all actual fluctuations, constrictions, or differentiations to which it has been subjected over the succession of different times. To this extent, the contemporary history writing that I have depicted thus far has always been concerned with experiences of and modes of processing current, generationally specific events, that is, it has always been concerned with synchronicity. This finding was first formulated as a concept in German in the seventeenth century with the term *Zeitgeschichte*.

Yet the same word encompassed a second field of meaning, namely, that of diachronicity, a field that *Zeitgeschichte* came to describe as early as the seventeenth century as well. In 1691, Stieler included an entry for "Zeitgeschichte / Chronologica" in his dictionary[10] in a specifically diachronic sense as the doctrine of the sequence of time [*Zeitabfolge*]. It is hard to extract from this short text whether Stieler meant this more in terms of an ancillary field of study or in terms of history writing proper [*realgeschichtlich*].

This duality, the fact that the term was used both synchronically and diachronically at the time of its coinage, is surely not accidental. Given our initial reflections, it is clear that there can be no pure *Zeitgeschichte* in the sense of a mere history of the present, and that, at the very least, it must refer to a past present and its past: first comes the history, then its narration (which does not rule out the existence of histories that consist only of their narration).

Recourse to the sequence of time periods [*Zeitenfolge*] is thus part and parcel of the concept of *Zeitgeschichte* in its earliest usage (put in terms of the lifeworld, this entails looking from today back into the past; but in terms of written presentation, looking back from the past up to today). Indeed, as late as 1800, Schwan's lexicon defined *Zeitgeschichte* as "l'histoire qui rapporte les événemens du temps où l'on est," that is, a synchronic conception, but also that the *Zeitbuch* [book of time] is "die Zeitgeschichte; la chronique, l'histoire dressée suivant l'ordre des temps," that is, a diachronic conception.[11] Diachronic sequence thus has also been a part of *Zeitgeschichte* since the word's formation, and it is theoretically impetuous to allow this conceptually crucial aspect to recede into the background.

At stake in this diachronic understanding is neither simply the imperative of establishing exact dating or exact temporal sequences [*Zeit-folgen*], which might at first seem only ancillary, nor any kind of narrative chronicle that is recounted after the fact and that is meant to have new occurrences added to it day after day, year after year, as in annalistics. However important these simple forms of history writing are, however, Herodotus and Thucydides had long before gone beyond them. Herodotus achieved something that had been previously inconceivable, namely, the synchronization (as far as possible) of the various empires and cultural spaces [of the ancient world], each with its own temporal sequences—put in modern terms, he placed them all within a common *zeitgeschichtlich* horizon to uncover the constellations that led to the great conflict between the Greeks and the Persians. Thucydides wrote his diachronic introduction (*proemium*) in order to derive the conflict potential and power constellation of the Peloponnesian War from its genesis.

Synchronic analysis and diachronic derivation thus belong in equal parts to the concept of *Zeitgeschichte* introduced in the seventeenth century, which continued to be used around 1800, when the term explicitly combined the two. Hence, the concept did not yet thematize one's own *Zeitgeschichte* (e.g., that of the French Revolution) but rather events particular to one's own times more generally. This is why, for example, Gottlieb Jakob Planck's 1805 history of the papacy could repeatedly stress "how and where, in each time period, the history of the papacy entered into the *Zeitgeschichte* and likewise emerged out of the same *Zeitgeschichte*." Planck applies this finding to the late Middle Ages. He also invokes the concept of the spirit of the time [*Zeitgeist*] that influenced and was influenced by the papacy.[12]

In line with our evidence, then, we can say that *Zeitgeschichte* has been used as a systematic concept whose formal structure made it applicable to all periods, to the past present, the past past, and the past future (to return to our formal categorization). In this sense, Goethe investigated (as he put it) "that *Zeitgeschichte*," about Götz von Berlichingen [1480–1562], which he then dramatized under that name.[13]

Campe's definition in his dictionary is especially lucid.[14] Campe formulated the systematic claim that *Zeitgeschichte* is both diachronous and synchronous in a single concept: *Zeitgeschichte* is, "first of all, history in general, ordered according to the sequence of time periods [*Zeitenfolge*] (i.e., chronological history)." Here Campe is describing history itself, not simply each additional continuation of the chronicle: in other words, the theoretical meta-concept [*Oberbegriff*] of history that was first coined in this era and that self-reflexively collects the entirety of all conceivable histories. Secondly, Campe added the synchronic aspect, namely, *Zeitgeschichte* as "the history of a certain time, especially our time, including a single history of our time or of the present time." However, this systematic aspect of the term—namely, that history as a whole is *Zeitgeschichte* directed toward both the past and the present—was almost entirely lost over the course of the nineteenth century.

Of course, this systematic claim did not emerge out of nowhere around 1800. The Enlightenment and the French Revolution had occasioned a shift in experience expressed in the concepts of "history as such," "process," "revolution," "progress," or "development." These were all new leading concepts [*Leitbegriffe*] whose commonality lay in the consciously self-reflective presupposition that all events are structured in a specifically temporal manner. Attempts to clarify how and in what way led to the great systems of German idealism from Kant to Hegel and Schelling. But there are also empirical ways to interrogate the elusive concept of "time" that allow us to describe the historical location when the concept of *Zeitgeschichte* first became a new challenge. Starting around 1800, everything that was understood to have lasting significance or that was targeted for change was legitimated in the same way, namely, with reference to "time"; depending on the political interests being pursued, time as constancy and time as change both came to serve as equally irrefutable titles of legitimation.

The extent to which "time" became a specifically historical concept of interpretation in this period—however ambivalent—is shown by the

Grimm brothers' *Deutsches Wörterbuch*. Despite all caveats, we can draw authoritative conclusions on the basis of the many compound terms it lists that include "time." The Grimms record 216 time compounds prior to 1750.[15] These refer primarily to the many realms of the human lifeworld, to their moral interpretation, or—in connection with the Bible—to their theological meanings. A further 342 new time compounds were added between 1750 and 1850, with an emphasis in the realms of politics and history. Zeitgeist is a striking example from this new group. The extent to which these innovations anticipated our own ways of conceptualizing the historical experience of time is revealed by the striking finding that only 52 new time compounds were recorded as new terms between 1850 and 1956.

One further empirical finding shows why *Zeitgeschichte* in particular gained currency as a concept around 1800. The diachronic framework of the doctrine of different time periods or ages [*Zeitalter*] changed slowly but fundamentally after the so-called Renaissance and so-called Reformation. It is not possible here to recreate the complicated semantic history of our conventional concepts of time periods, but we might sketch a few suggestions pertaining to the altered experience of time that gave rise to the triad antiquity–Middle Ages–modernity [*Neuzeit*] as well as to the Renaissance and Reformation as concepts of threshold [*Schwellenbegriffe*].

As long as the Christian world moved toward the Last Judgment, it knew itself to be in the last time period or age [*Zeitalter*] in which there was nothing fundamentally new to anticipate. Whether one followed the doctrine of the four empires, as in Germany, or the three-phase model of salvation history—before the law, under the law, and in the age of mercy—all people fundamentally lived in the final age. Within this theologically extended horizon of expectation, in expectation of the *res novissima*, that is, of the Last Judgment, chronicles could update and record each new subsequent event, case by case. Chronological order arose from the biological dates of the duration of the ruling princes' lives, their dynasties, or those of the popes, a schema that to this day has not entirely fallen out of use. Genealogical and biological neutrality corresponded to an age that was identical to itself and that would conclude with the end of history.

Beginning in the late eighteenth century, however, once the future came to be experienced as open-ended, and history experienced as a process, as progress or development, the concept of a new, modern time

(*Neuzeit*) with an unknown end or outcome emerged. As a logical sequential element that corresponded to that of the Middle Ages, this concept established itself only very slowly. And after it become established in the seventeenth century, it became necessary, in the eighteenth century, to introduce the concept of a newest time [*die neueste Zeit*], and later, in the nineteenth century to differentiate the *Neuzeit* from more recent time [*der neueren Zeit*]. As a word, *Neuzeit* was first coined in the German language of the Vormärz, and it was first registered in lexicons only at the end of the nineteenth century. In short, in the progression "Renaissance, Reformation, newer history, newest history, *Neuzeit*," the sequential unfolding of historical time periods seemed to be accelerating. It became necessary to invent ever-new in-between periods in order to delineate so-called modern history.[16] So-called *Zeitgeschichte* has also become this same kind of connecting concept related to the newest time, to our time, to day-to-day history (*Tagesgeschichte*), promising actuality per se.

Beginning with the French Revolution, we can witness a boom in journals and book series that were to inform the reader about current events; these often contained over thirty volumes and appeared yearly. Viewed according to their common theme, these journals continue the project of traditional annalistics but apply it to revolutionary world history, a genre that seems to have its empirical origin in the French Revolution. The short-lived stages of the Revolution offered a typological structure of constitutional succession that became applicable for all other forms of historical interpretation, regardless of the partisan perspective from which current events were viewed.

Subsequently, the concept of *Zeitgeschichte* was narrowed to refer to the synchronous actuality of the most recent past. The concept was limited to the modernity of recently occurring histories. It thereby became a formal concept of duration that only recorded the newest history, namely so-called *Zeitgeschichte*. Examples include *Die Geschichte unserer Zeit* [The History of Our Time] (33 vols., 1826–30) by Karl Strahlheim, a former French Army officer, and *Die Geschichte unserer Tage* [The History of Our Days] compiled volume for volume by Dr. Mährlen in the wake of the July 1830 Revolution in France.

The concept of *Zeitgeschichte* came to be displaced into the realm of journalism, of day-to-day scribbling. But this, too, had its distinguished representatives. We might recall the left Hegelians Bruno Bauer and Karl Marx, but also Heine, Lorenz von Stein, Michelet, and Thiers, whose writings on contemporary history remain required reading for any scholar seeking to reconsider the nineteenth century (an increasingly common undertaking in recent years). In the mid-nineteenth century, professional historians were skeptical as to whether the actuality of daily events could be processed in a scholarly [*wissenschaftlich*] manner. Perthes, for example, found it extremely difficult to find authors for his history of European states; this was not simply because there did not seem to be enough source material to write the history with the tools of philological-historical method—in archives that were barely accessible, if at all—, but above all because the shifts in politics and transformations of society seemed to be occurring too rapidly for anyone to risk definitive statements. In contrast to Christian and humanistic modes of history writing, the incompleteness of history became an objection to the attempt to process it in any *zeitgeschichtlich*, historical way.

The accelerated history of the everyday and the secure location of archives seemed incompatible. However, we should recall that the retention period before archives holdings were made available to the public first started to shorten in the wake of accelerated history. In the Vormärz period, the holdings in the Prussian archives covering the times reaching back to Luther still remained closed in principle and were only accessible with special permission. At the end of the nineteenth century, the retention period still covered the entire period back to 1700. Access to all more recent archival materials necessitated ministerial permission. The actuality of history was still calibrated to a duration that lasted centuries. Archival materials retained political, legal, or theological topicality for over two hundred years. Today's thirty-year retention period remained far beyond the hopes of nineteenth-century professional historians— apart from the official court historians, who could forfeit their access to material, as Sybel did at the hands of Wilhelm II. In other words: for the politicians of the nineteenth century, the explosive power of historical topics extended not simply to what we today call *Zeitgeschichte*, but to the entire so-called *Neuzeit*. Titles of legitimation tied to archives were not yet subject to such rapid expiration as today, when archives are opened after thirty years (with the protection of personal privacy rights and excluding economic archives and special political holds, including those made public or kept secret).[17]

In defense of professional historians, however, it must be said that they dealt intensively with *Zeitgeschichte* even in the nineteenth century, despite having to contend with files that were difficult or impossible to access. They did so almost always in lectures, but occasionally also in publications, like Ranke, Droysen, or Sybel, to name only German historians. And the posthumously printed lectures on *Zeitgeschichte* by Niebuhr and Jacob Burckhardt are not only some of the most important sources for contemporary views from that period, but remain worth reading, because they developed a theory of historical times that enabled them to immerse their own time in long-term perspectives and to distinguish it consciously and qualitatively from the past. Niebuhr gave lectures on the history of the epoch of the French Revolution, interpreting it as an age of acceleration. Similarly, Droysen and Burckhardt both thought that they had discovered the singularity of their own time in the accelerated succession of events. It is no surprise, then, that, in light of its acceleration, the time of history (and thereby also *Zeitgeschichte*) gave rise to new kinds of research questions. *Zeitgeschichte* began to take on the meaning of a new and, in each case, singular actuality, departing from the term's beginnings as both a diachronic and synchronic possibility, and it did so via new, previously unexperienced determinations of historical content.

III

Thus far, we have dealt with the formal difficulties that arise when *Zeitgeschichte* is applied solely to a specific contemporary time period rather than to the entirety of history. Additionally, we have identified the historical location where *Zeitgeschichte* was articulated as both a diachronic and synchronic concept, although the issue is as old as history writing itself. We then showed how the novelty of *Zeitgeschichte* took on new meaning in the wake of the French Revolution, namely, as constantly changing actuality. Ever since, one's own *Zeitgeschichte* has appeared to be constitutively different from all previous histories. In conclusion, we will examine this last position more closely and call it into question.

Historicism's axiom that everything in history is singular—each epoch stands in immediate relation to God—and that history does not repeat itself but instead finds itself in a state of constant development is the epiphenomenon of the primary experience that ever since the French and Industrial Revolutions, history has in fact seemed to be continuously changing at an accelerated rate: to this extent, nothing was comparable and everything singular.

This experience had a retroactive effect upon the entire past. Only after history had undergone accelerated change in the past twenty years, as Wilhelm von Humboldt noted under the pressure of the French Revolution,[18] only then, and with the distance thereby attained, is one capable of recognizing both the particular characteristics of ancient and medieval history and their otherness as a precondition for one's own time. Only then did it become possible to rewrite [*umschreiben*] history from a newly attained perspective, rather than simply copying [*fortschreiben*] it. History always has to be rewritten, not only because new sources are discovered, but also because the times themselves change; this observation of Goethe's continues to be redeemed and confirmed to this day. For Machiavelli, in contrast, who still evaluated his Livy systematically rather than historically, the writing of history meant the rediscovery of new truths in old ones, not rewriting it. Frederick the Great—who carried Plutarch in his pocket whenever he was at war—would have found the compulsion to rewrite history completely inconceivable as he continued to copy [*fortschreiben*] his own history. Rewriting to correct errors has always existed; rewriting because the transformable perspective of the present has discovered something new has only existed since the end of the eighteenth century. The movement from recording and copying to rewriting and the compulsion to rewrite characterizes the threshold crossed between 1750 and 1800.[19] Thenceforth, the time of history, the historical quality of time, its unrepeatability and singularity have gained a dominance that continues to influence professional *Zeitgeschichte* to this day.

Much seems to speak for the claim that what we today call *Zeitgeschichte* is a unique, sui generis history of the present. The technical and industrial preconditions of our own history have immeasurably refined the means of political control; they have infinitely expanded the means of destruction, and yet they have also constricted spaces for possible decisions enormously; they have extended, beyond recognition, the reach of the so-called compulsion of relations [*Zwang der Verhältnisse*] across the entire globe, where it used to be possible to live in a regionally bounded way; and they have opened up an increasingly maneuverable space of movement for the actions of partisans, resistance fighters, and rebels, whose power was once more limited. More than ever before, the axiom of singularity seems to force upon our own *Zeitgeschichte* a specific compulsion for cognition.

The [social] sciences of economics and sociology (in part also of politics) have helped to uncover new ways of studying modern society and its incomparability as yet. Raymond Aron, Hannah Arendt, Schumpeter, and Keynes call to mind diagnoses of the contemporary that possess the power of scientific interpretation, something historians would have been responsible for up until the eighteenth century. This differentiation [of scholarship] cannot be reversed, but it should caution us against limiting the writing of *Zeitgeschichte* to the history of events and to political history in particular. There are certainly singular situations, singular actions, and singular individuals, and to bear witness to them remains an inalienable task of the historian. Church historians are duty-bound to tell the stories of Dietrich Bonhoeffer and Father Maximilian Kolbe, *testes indelebiles*, which retain their testimonial character. And no one wants to divest today's historians of the present of the task of reconstructing the unique pressures whereby everything became different on January 30th, 1933 [when Hitler was named German chancellor] and after [the failed attempt to assassinate Hitler on] July 20th, 1944.

But the theoretically richer notion of *Zeitgeschichte*, outlined by Campe around 1800, should remind us that this concept seeks to do more than simply study the current sequence of events and their connection to persons and actions. There are diachronic and synchronic dimensions at work at various temporal depths, about which historians from distant epochs can still help us gain insight for today, because history repeats itself structurally, something that is often forgotten when "singularity" is stressed. In what follows I want to mention several examples that bear witness to how the present past is likewise a past present.

Thucydides' Melian Dialogue on power and justice remains mutatis mutandis a key for the situation in which [the Czechoslovakian president] Hácha found himself vis-à-vis Hitler in 1939 and Dubček vis-à-vis

Brezhnev in 1968.—As a topic of long-term historical duration, the Christian sources or shares in modern antisemitism remain of current importance, as something that moral theology, for example, must deal with. Even if Hochhuth made several mistakes of historical fact in his 1963 play *The Deputy* [portraying the failure of Pope Pius XII to speak out against the Holocaust], his question posed to the Church cannot be dismissed. This question was raised by those who came before him, and it is characterized by potential repeatability.—The collective biography of the bourgeois elite in the France of the French Revolution and under Napoleon, their ability to conform and adapt to the events that they helped bring about, but could not control, events in which they participated and made possible, but which did not suit their tastes, remains a model of experience that provides a plausible set of conditions for understanding the twelve years under Hitler, as well the years before and after. We are dealing with social-psychological processes that are constants throughout the history of events. The dosage of cowardice and hubris at work therein might better be understood via the Year of Three Emperors in [the *Annals* of] Tacitus than on the basis of questionable memoirs written by Germans after 1945 under pressures of self-justification. Conclusions about the present are possible on the basis of analogy with Tacitus, conclusions that testify to structural repeatability in order to make present-day actuality more visible.—Or take the literary admission by Ernst Jünger that prisoners were killed during the trench warfare of World War I and its suicidal conditions. This was something the Allies initially thought only the Germans were capable of, and contemporary English historians have only just caught up with this admission,[20] shortly before the death of the last of the survivors of the generation of 1914, and only after 1945, after an entirely different scale of planned mass murder had made the smaller, spontaneous murderous actions easier to communicate to others.

What do these examples reveal to us? Everywhere one looks, there are phenomena of recurrence: time hurries and time heals, it brings new things and reclaims what can only be discerned from a distance. Our *Zeitgeschichte* contains structures that are characteristic of more than just our own *Zeitgeschichte*. There are repeatable constellations, long-term effects, contemporary manifestations of archaic attitudes, regularities of sequences of events, and the contemporary historian can inform himself about their actuality from history. For, as I have been arguing, as a concept, *Zeitgeschichte* is more than the history of our time. Only when we know what can repeat itself at any time (though not always all at once) can we ascertain what is truly new in our time. Indeed, this might be less than what we would like to imagine. It then comes down to this little bit.

8

History, Law, and Justice

The topic that I have chosen—history, law, and justice—sounds rather presumptuous and overstated. Three important concepts are to be put in relation to one another, concepts that have come to imply or describe very different issues or claims for action with the eighteenth-century emergence of so-called history. The historicity of these concepts is uncontroversial, for otherwise they would not be the subject of and interpretive challenge facing the historical disciplines and legal history in particular.

But in what follows, I will not attempt to sketch or recast a history of these central concepts.[1] Instead, I was asked to address the relationship of general history [*allgemeine Geschichte*] to legal history. I attempt to deal with this issue from the distance of a general historian, that is to say from the distance of a professionalized layman. I will circumvent avid recent debates in legal history for I lack a familiarity with the legal doctrine that structures certain aspects of them.[2] To the extent that these debates have operated within the framework of a general theory of history, I am able to determine that these questions have been formulated analogously to the ones that have preoccupied the discipline of history more generally in recent decades. The relationship of a general hermeneutics to textual hermeneutics, questions as to criteria for objectivity and for fixed positionality [*Standortbindung*], questions as to structure, event, and process or development, determining the relationship to neighboring disciplines, especially those of social history and economic history: general historians

and legal historians alike have debated these issues, however, with the latter having done so in a less vehement, more subdued and understated way,
without losing their tempers. But the commonality of the problem horizon, the osmosis of the two camps divided by academic schools or departments is unmistakable. Despite the usual differences in detail caused by
generations or politics, it would seem that there is a relatively far-reaching
consensus about how questions and problems are posed, as well as about
many theoretical determinations and answers.

In what follows, I will attempt to demarcate several integral areas
that connect legal history and general history. As much as possible I will
try to avoid the shifting sands of pure methodological debates, even if I
make myself vulnerable to the criticism that I am operating on too general
a level—generality is, after all, the only (perhaps dubious) privilege to
which the universal historian can lay claim when among specialists.

I will proceed in two steps, seeking thereby to keep to at least a minimum of method: first, I address the relation between history and justice.
More precisely: can we typologize the different ways in which historical
experience is related to something like justice? It would seem that history
and justice stand in a constant, unresolvable tension that generates ever-
new attempts at resolution, without the two concepts ever fully becoming
synonymous. How should we interpret this relationship in a theoretical
manner?

My second point follows from this, namely, that history and law
[*Recht*] are likewise always interrelated, with the law defined as the institutionalized treatment and administration of justice, however justice is
determined. In particular, I suggest several temporal determinations that
should make it possible to deal with general history and the history of law
in an integrated way, even if the two can be differentiated systematically,
or, to speak with Luhmann, even if they are fully differentiated as separate
systems.

I. History and Justice

The idea that historical study and writing are indebted to the
ethos of justice has been attributed to history [*Historie*] since its birth
with Herodotus. To this day, the metaphor of a judicial trial—even

if, according to Cicero, the historian should proceed "without the roughness of court proceedings and without the prickliness of judges' decisions"[3]—still applies: to determine the truth of the matter, the best witnesses need to be questioned, their statements weighed against each other, and the opposing side should be heard as well. This claim is still valid today, despite all methodological differentiation. The principles of just proceedings thus belong to the process of determining truth. Critiques of the historian's moral judicial office are as old as the claim to occupy it, of course. Hellenistic and Christian history writing asserted, for instance, that the historian must do more than pass judgment on the issue at hand and also judge those involved and their actions, but this expansion has been rejected, at the latest by Ranke. The rhetorical tradition dictates that the historian should let the issue in question speak for itself, if possible, so as to allow the reader to pass judgment. Indirect directions for the formation of moral judgment are lurking behind this directive. From our perspective, in any case, the two directives converge: professional historians must not only do justice to their subject matter, but also judge it—or at least make a judgment possible. At stake is thus a concept of justice that is both more limited and more expansive, a concept that aims either for a methodologically just procedure, for identifying cases of fact, or for the just formation of judgment. Put in modern terms, both concepts of justice are deployed in the dispute about so-called value judgments. The two concepts, whether related to method or value judgment, are always interrelated. The determination of fact and the formation of judgment cannot be separated from each other.

I would therefore like to reformulate our initial question for the historians, for it is not simply that the historians' procedure nor merely their judgments be just—again, a demand that historians have had to face since the beginning. Rather, the question that should be raised here pertains to the kind of justice attributed to the history narrated or constituted by historians. Was or is an inherent justice attributed to the history that historians have explored? Is justice inherent in a history once it is constructed in such a way that the judgment about it emerges, as if on its own accord, from the historical issue at hand, rather than as a result of its rhetorical or literary constitution?[4] At stake, therefore, is primarily a question for a theory of possible histories and only secondarily a question for the discipline of history and its various methods. A five-part typology emerges from responses to this question, which I would briefly like to develop.

First: the *Herodotean answer*. No matter what the different histories of Herodotus offer, the element of a justice that permeates all individual histories is always present for him.[5] Humans create their own doom through their own arrogance or blindness. They are responsible, but not sovereign, for the gods reign above them and fate reigns over the gods, which ensures that injustice is punished and crimes are atoned for across time, across generations, as in the Old Testament. An immanent justice is inherent to all histories, a justice that the historian comes upon, as it were, in order to be able to retell it. Herodotus's rationally reflected reliance on the mythical stories of the gods and their pregiven meanings should not prevent us from finding an evidentiary basis in his interpretive framework today. Any historian who examines the Russian campaigns of Charles XII of Sweden, Napoleon, or Hitler can hardly deny the plausibility that here blindness led to catastrophe, and that history can thus be interrogated for a justice that is inherent in it, however one might want to construct scholarly explanations for the causes and processes of the various military campaigns.

Linnaeus's secret diary contains histories from the daily life of northern Europe in the eighteenth century that unfolded in patterns that could have been drawn from Herodotus.[6] The nephew of a treasonous subject arbitrarily pardoned by Peter the Great came back to kill the tsar's own nephew. The interpretive framework at work here is one of a justice that is inherent in the historical constellations. These histories have their beginning and their end, and in this respect they resemble the cases that find their analogy in criminal, civil, or administrative trials. It would be worth investigating where exactly the difference between the two lies. The judge fashions history with an eye to the law and its application. In relation to the carrying out of justice, the judge's role in administering and applying the law should be appraised higher than that of the historian. The latter also constitutes a history through narrative, which he or she also pieces together through interrogating witnesses or analyzing sources (the genre of the Pitaval [collections of famous criminal cases] offers histories for both the historian and the judge). But the judge must bring the case to its end, something that the historian does better to avoid.

And finally, justice motivates one of the oldest forms of historiography, the memoir, where the roles of agent and narrator converge. Whether Caesar, Frederick the Great, or Napoleon is telling of the histories that he influenced and in part produced, none of these authors escaped the drive to justify themselves, however much they might have sublimated it. And the same applies to Churchill's great wartime histories in which he was a leading agent. Every justification presupposes a kind of justice inherent in history to which one must answer affirmatively or defensively.

Second, the *Thucydidean model.* Thucydides has taught us that the Herodotean interpretive framework apparently did not cover all historical experience available to individuals caught up in their own histories. Thucydides explicated something that Herodotus was already able to see. The individual can find him- or herself faced with unavoidable alternatives that he or she did not search out, he or she can become responsible for situations that are forced upon him or her. Chance comes into play and the individual must take guilt upon him- or herself, even if a legal court could not substantiate this guilt.[7] Thucydides thereby does without any rights granted by the gods. He wrote in the century in which the conflict between old and new legal systems [*Recht*] produced intractable situations that could only end tragically.[8] The theoretical or sophistic answer offered by Thucydides is the separation of power and law [*Recht*]. He thus introduced a topic that has remained relevant to this day.

Power, as invoked by the Athenians in the Melian dialogue, follows its own laws, and an appeal to the law does nothing to diminish this. Measured against naked power, the insistence on legal rights can even be transformed into a blindness that leads to death. This is a thought that Agrippa d'Aubigné voiced anew amid the confessional civil wars of the sixteenth and seventeenth centuries. The person who invokes his conscience perishes and is at fault for doing so.[9]

To be sure, Thucydides remains influenced by Herodotus when he moves without commentary to the next historical act directly following the extermination of the Melians, namely, the Athenians' failed Sicilian expedition, the last survivors of which end up in the stone quarries of Syracuse. But the Melians who were murdered, enslaved, and sold off do not become any less murdered, enslaved and sold off as a result, their city does not become any less destroyed. Thucydides refuses to establish a connection of guilt and atonement; at most he allows the law of cause and effect to run its course, even if he sometimes likes to conceal it behind a simple description of the events. The end of the Athenians is better explained through their insufficient power or their misguided appraisals of the situation. Recourse to a justice inherent in history becomes superfluous. The historically recorded invocation of law and justice by the Melians becomes a point of contrast as Thucydides works out his larger argument about the autonomy of power, its rise and fall, and its role as the true nature of every history. Dubček accepted this fact in Moscow when the structure of the Melian dialogue repeated itself between the Czechs and the Russians in 1968, though we do not know the details of this encounter. And the same applies to Hácha's dialogue with Hitler in Berlin in 1939.

Thucydides thus discovered a pattern of experience located in the opposition between power and law that allowed for the interpretation of histories of all varieties and that could serve, moreover, as a model for action. "The history of the world as the history of power" has remained a possible and consistent model from Thucydides and Machiavelli all the way to Alexander Cartellieri (who coined this phrase in the title of his 1927 book),[10] even if laments over the lack of justice accompany this model or go so far as to call it into being.

Who would seek to legitimize, as the effect of a higher justice, the liquidation of the countless political units of action who have "justifiably" perished in the course of history without further ado?[11] Thucydides has taught us that histories do not embody any kind of justice. But his interpretation remains dependent on the unstated differentiation between power and law that is still invoked to this day. The one is the silent negative foil of the other. Absent this theoretical pregiven, the history of international law cannot be conceptualized. In his work on European expansion and international law, Jörg Fisch has shown how and where special rights are packed into the statements of equality justified by natural law and how the legal disguising of these special rights masks different powers and their various interests.[12]

All empires are basically large-scale theft, as Augustine concluded eight hundred years after Thucydides. This takes us to a third interpretive model, which compensates for the unresolvable tension between power and law by theological means.

Third, the *Augustinian model.* Augustine certainly adopted interpretive frameworks transmitted to him via the Hellenistic-Roman tradition. This can be seen in the ideas both that the hand of God punishes the glaring injustices of the world already in this world (a notion compatible with Herodotus) and that unatoned injustices in the use of power constantly create new ones (which is compatible with Thucydides). The actually new component in Augustine's response to the crisis around 400 CE was the idea that true justice rested solely with God, and that Christians may participate in this justice through the grace of God, but that they can only expect its execution with certainty in the *iudicium maximum* after the end times.[13]

Histories are thus unburdened of the assumption that they generate or carry out justice in and of themselves, without humans having to cease presupposing a higher, invisible justice. God's judgments are justifiably secret and secretly just.[14] Of course, this interpretive framework is based in an unprovable belief in the justice of God, a justice that humans can only partake of after the end of all history. Despite all potential participation by humans in the justice of God, all justice in this world remains unfulfillable, unattainable, and if attainable, only in an incomplete manner.

The theoretical consequences of the Augustinian model gave rise to two new responses that are inherently related and diametrically opposed to each other.

Fourth: *absurd history.* History taken in and for itself—a thought that could only first be considered post-theologically—becomes absurd if the equalizing justice of the Last Judgment falls away. Even if humans are tasked with seeking justice and exercising it if possible: everything that happens in this world withholds itself from invisible Justitia. Over the course of medieval history, Augustine's own extreme position was transposed to the extent that his asymmetry was applied to the Church and to worldly units of action and served to territorialize the two realms. And to the extent that the Church could represent the realm of God and the Christian imperium could subsume the world, historical events could also be justified in the interpretive frameworks of Herodotus and Thucydides. But the potential absurdity, the historically unresolvable injustice that Augustine made thinkable for the first time, this absurdity is a mode of experience that still has a hold on us—think, for example, of Voltaire's *Candide.*

Whatever explanations or attributions of guilt are ventured in the case of Auschwitz, none will suffice, according to the standards of any kind of justice, to interpret or "pass judgment upon" the absurdity and inexplicability that became event. And whoever looks for analogies cannot escape the senselessness of a justice that is withheld if one seeks to understand this history. No attribution of guilt and no explanation can capture the event itself. Regardless of his own personal, theologically grounded hope, Augustine opened up for us the possible experience that all justice vanishes into the so-called beyond. He thereby surpasses Thucydides' position.

And one might answer whoever claims to interpret the expulsion of the Germans from eastern Europe as a just punishment for Auschwitz, as implied by the Stuttgart Declaration of 1945, with the Thucydidean argument that the expulsion would have happened without Auschwitz. But with Herodotus one could say that neither event would have come to pass without the delusion of the Germans. Only the war, unleashed by the Germans, made Auschwitz possible; and the Germans of the East could be expelled as a result of the same war. Both can be related back to a common cause without one having to be causally linked to the other.

But the event itself—the "obliteration" of millions of Jews and other ethnic groups—cannot be adequately interpreted by history, either morally or rationally. Rather, absurdity, or to use Hannah Arendt's terms, evil in its banality must be endured, even if one seeks to draw lessons for the future from it. For humans—the Germans, in this case—must also take responsibility for the absurd that they have produced.

The post-Augustinian experience of negativity first opened up by the Church Father's interpretive framework is a mark of our modernity. Every parallel or structural analogy to other forms of "obliteration" fails as explanation. No matter the form of explanation offered, it is an element of our experience that certain histories are fundamentally incommensurable with any kind of idea of justice and that they therefore remain absurd.

This takes us to a *fifth position*, also unthinkable without Augustine, that claims the opposite: Schiller's dictum that "world history is the Last Judgment [*die Weltgeschichte ist das Weltgericht*]," first formulated in a version of a love poem to Laura that was reworked many times. This formula was then systematized by Hegel and has since claimed, as an ideal type, to square Herodotus's and Thucydides's divergent interpretations and to integrate both within the ordo temporum of the Augustinian history of salvation. The phrase can be infused with Herodotus: as Schiller continued, "what the minute beats out / is not returned by any eternity" (Was man von der Minute ausgeschlagen / gibt keine Ewigkeit zurück). Every situation is irreplaceable, just as every epoch is equally immediate to God for Ranke. The individual is responsible for all results that he or she has *nolens volens* set in motion. Error or blindness irrevocably take their revenge. But the justice inherent in history becomes the mover, not just of individual histories, but also of world history as a whole, mercilessly and without any compensation, as in the Last Judgment.

The thought of a reward or punishment that is only to be expected in the beyond is something deeply immoral for Kant because heteronomous determinations such as hope of reward and fear of punishment corrupt pure morality. Morality must prove itself in the *hic et nunc* and not have its eye on the beyond. Due to this rigorous claim, the Thucydidean differentiation between power and law only became more pronounced, and Kant was never able to resolve this difference. It too was dissolved, however, through an oversimplified version of Hegel. Even the history of power, of power exerted immorally or illegally, is graced with the sanctification of justice. The Last Judgment already realizes itself in history itself: every day is the last. The thought that the success [of power] could be unjust is sublated with Hegel: no final judgment ensures compensation; rather, history itself becomes a trial or process, its realization becomes the final authority. The individual human is thus at the mercy of a massive imposition that likewise borders on the absurd.

The Thucydidean difference between power and law, seen diachronically, comes to function as world spirit's vehicle for implementing a "higher law." If properly conceptualized, history as the history of power reveals itself as the history of justice on the way to liberty. Things that seem situationally immoral or illegal can serve to realize justice over time. As Hegel continues: "The only law that applies is that of absolute spirit, and the only relations that can come under consideration are those that implement a higher principle of the spirit. But no state can lay claim to this law." We should keep this in mind, for it runs counter to interpretations of Hegel that focus solely on power politics: history always holds the advantage over, if not transcends, the acting individual. In this regard, Hegel remains compatible with Augustine. Political units of action are not allowed to lay claim to the higher law of world history, to legitimate evident injustices, for example. "We have to observe the right [*Recht*] of the world spirit as opposed to the states." Hegel insists that no political agent can empower himself to act in the name of world history. In situations where power structures are draped with legal justifications—in the relations between Greeks and barbarians, Christians and heathens, Muslims and unbelievers—"no true legal condition" exists, as Hegel continued, in an almost Kantian manner.[15]

This, then, would be the fifth position, which has been sketched here via certain fragmented sources of German idealism. The new and common element of this idealist position lies in consistent and systematic temporalization. Justice, whatever it might be, is realized in and through the entirety of world history. In their relation to world history, humans are always given over to structures of "already" and "not yet" and these structures force them to realize justice, though with full, self-conscious knowledge of their own limitation. This also makes it possible to conceive of history in its diachronicity as a path toward the rule of law [*Rechtsstaat*], toward a league of nations, and to act accordingly.

It is no longer the individual history that displays a justice inherent in it; instead, as an open-ended totality, world history is subject to the rational necessity of progressively transforming the human expression of power into legally secured and, even more important, just conditions.

We know that this interpretive framework that shapes our modern experience has also impregnated historicism and has given rise to all liberal, democratic, and socialist models of history. But we also know that our own experience balks at the allure of this hopeful utopian interpretation of history. Still, we cannot fully avoid this proposition, because our chances of survival depend upon a minimum of legal order, even if this order must be newly attained and reproduced from day to day.

Here, the experience that has been stored and interpreted historiographically can be helpful. The three premodern accounts of the relationship between history and justice retain their force: as formulated by Herodotus, the notion that something like a person's fitting and just fate can shine through the plurality of individual histories; Thucydides' contention that social, political, or economic power cannot be directly correlated with either common or newly posited law; and, finally, Augustine's claim that the world experienced as godless is absurd and it is impossible for human beings to achieve justice in this world. These interpretive frameworks remind us of the burden placed upon human beings forced to have recourse to law in order to survive. Any attempt to relate history and justice to each other leads to disillusionment.

Now, everyone familiar with this material will know that the models of experience described here by no means represent all of Herodotus, Thucydides, Augustine, Kant, or Hegel. And we could expand upon other variants if texts of other authors were brought in, or if, for example, Augustine was read from the perspective of the Stoic-Christian doctrine of natural law rather than that of negative theology.

Here I just want to reinforce one argument as a thesis: there are certain historical experiences that have been enriched, disproven, or expanded over time, and they have all been only possible because the individual histories or the entirety of history remained saturated with interpretive frameworks of possible justice. However it might be conceptualized and varied historically, justice is a necessary (though certainly not sufficient) condition for experiencing history.

We could also stylize the five variants I have sketched here as anthropological possibilities that reference to one another after two and a half thousand years of self-reflective historical experience. If we consider them as they were formulated over time, we could read them as an intellectual-historical sequence. In fact, however, these interpretations all remain accessible, and it would not be possible to carry historical experience over into the disciplinary study of history if they did not. In other words, the five models for experience exist prior to all methodological steps that a professional historian might take when investigating the historical past.

Examined more precisely, all modern historical hypotheses and scholarly representations that construct historical findings can be traced back to these five modes of experience. The justice or injustice of a historical situation, transformation, or catastrophe is always expressed, whether implicitly or explicitly. This does not simply apply to moralizing history [*Historie*], which has been practiced since Hellenism, outlasted Ranke and Max Weber, and persists to this day. Even so-called value-neutral historical accounts cannot avoid imputing justice or the lack thereof to history; such justice necessarily plays a role in the historian's formation of judgment. Even an acceptance of absurdity that is foreign to other cultures remains a part of the Judeo-Christian tradition to the extent that it presupposes a just God whose death unleashed a senselessness.

The terror of the French Revolution, for example, was experienced primarily in moral terms, by the perpetrators as the execution of true morality and by the victims as a breach in the existing moral system. But the next generation of researchers (starting initially with Forster and at the latest with Lorenz von Stein) already started to interpret the terror functionally, as a necessary means for doing away with the unjust society of estates, and they thereby imputed a higher justice to the terror, a justice carried out by the Jacobins in their role of the acting subject of world history. This "value-neutral" interpretation depends on the idea of a form of justice that is immanent to history or upon a *logificatio ex post*, a justice that we will forever be unable to recognize in Auschwitz. No one would attempt to interpret Auschwitz as a necessary step leading to the founding of the state of Israel or to the introduction of the democratic constitution of the Federal Republic [of Germany], in the service of any kind of higher law of world history. To even conceive this thought is to distort the historical findings one seeks to describe. This, by the way, was the kind of legality that the Marxist Russians claimed for themselves—unjustly, in Hegel's terms—apropos of the extirpation of the kulaks.

To interpret history according to criteria of justice is thus necessary but never sufficient. This is the reasoning behind my first thesis, which might sound self-evident to every legal historian. I now turn to the second part of this essay.

II. History and Law—Some Questions for Legal History

We began by interpreting the carrying out of justice as a methodological commitment of the professional historian. Then we turned to consider the extent to which justice is an interpretive element of every historical representation. In the process, we found that certain interpretations remain compatible while others rule each other out. But none of the interpretive options have become completely obsolete due to their age or altered constellations. Experiences had once captured by concepts allow themselves to be repeated and transposed. History offers more than just an unalterable and singular progression. It is such a sequence, but it is also something more. As the models of justice at work in general historiography have shown, history is always simultaneously subject to a chronological sequence and systematic structuring.

Now, no special discipline within the study of history can confirm this finding as well as legal history (and constitutional history, I might add).

We only need recall Wieacker's studies in order to measure the systematic contribution of the Romanist school of law to the adaptation of civil and economic law to the conditions of industrialization. Certain legal rules and formal pregivens about what is just both outlast and make possible the transformation and innovation of material and procedural law.[16]

For this reason, the alternative formulated by Betti and Wieacker—whether legal history is more contemplative and seeks to discover and reconstruct past subject areas, or whether it is carried out in a more applied manner—cannot be resolved one way or the other. One can only go in the one direction or the other pragmatically, in specific research. Both approaches condition each other in the same way that history is not exhausted by its diachronic singularity and instead repeats itself in particular structures. It would then be worth asking whether, in analogy to the models of justice that have long been called upon to conceptualize histories, older legal findings or institutional regulations from earlier times could be called upon today and claim validity in more or less mediated ways, or whether they point to functional equivalents that presuppose common problems.

In the case of constitutional history, it is easy to show structural transferability and thus the possibility of repetition. Aristotelian politics contains modes of procedure and forms of rule that could still to this day be formulated as legal rules without losing their efficacy.

German history offers examples of federal patterns of organization and regulations that were structurally preformed in the Greek Amphiktyonic leagues [alliances of neighboring cities] and that were not singular. Instead, they lend themselves to being transformed and applied in the future. I would mention the Hanseatic League here, which as a merchant union was never completely identical to the sum of the cities where these merchants were in control. Put in modern terms, state and sovereignty are not always identical to each other, and federal regulations necessarily emerge and impose themselves. Conversely, we might also recall that Switzerland and the Netherlands first attained state sovereignty as federations, via the German federal tradition. Or we might recall the German Customs Union, which from a legal perspective served to solve problems analogous to those faced by the European Economic Community today.

Naturally, we must concede that each of these unions, communities, or societies faced singular challenges particular to their time. The political and economic problems of the [German] Customs Union, for example, lay in the shadow of British dominance and had as their horizon the desire for national unification, whereas the problems of the EU are larger in scale and relate to global power structures and are thus economically and politically singular from the perspective of worldwide interdependencies and complex technology. Granted the diachronic singularity of the situation, the structural analogy between organizational and legal forms of regulation of both inter- and supra-corporatist [with the Customs Union] and both inter- and supra-national [with the EU] institutions remains all the more remarkable. If there is a historical discipline that is topically responsible for repeated application, this would seem to be constitutional and legal history more than any other.

Law, in order to be law, is dependent upon its repeated applicability. This requires a maximum of formality and regularity that spans across a plurality of cases. Duration, however limited in the individual empirical case (i.e., relative duration that is secured via procedural rules), allows for individual cases to be subsumed under statutes and laws. To perhaps overstate this: as a series of events, the negotiations that led to the German Civil Code (BGB) belong to political history. Individuals negotiated and acted in order to found law through legislation. As a legal act as well, the issuance and proclamation of the Civil Code is part of political history, and it can thus be located diachronically as a singular event. However, the history of law has a different temporal structure. Here, the legal propositions that were transmitted, adopted, transformed, or formulated anew lay claim to enduring applicability in the very same way as the newly proclaimed laws that went into effect in 1900.

Of course, no one would want to prevent a legal historian from investigating the genesis of legislation, but viewed from the perspective of the theory of historical times, such an approach would intervene in the field of the diachronic history of events in their singular succession. In contrast, the historical scales of the time of law, no matter what law, are determined by their structural repeatability, no matter whether they lay claim to eternal duration or already envision their own expiration date. We know empirically that the history of law [*Geschichte des Rechts*] follows different temporal rhythms than political history, just as the latter follows different rhythms than social or economic history. For example, the German Civil Code remained in effect for the autochthonous Germans in Upper Silesia, who were held back and reclaimed as Poles after 1945, long after the occupation; just as the [French] *Code civil* and the Prussian Civil Code (ALR) remained in effect in the Rhineland and in Ansbach-Bayreuth, respectively, across regime change.

We should thus hold onto the theoretical point that the history of law as well as of all individual legal determinations are dependent upon repeated application and subject to the necessity of repetition, and that the history of law thus thematizes longer-term frames of time and relative duration, that it thematizes structures, if you will, rather than events. The case of the miller Arnold[17] is fascinating, not as an individual one—though its particulars are naturally quite interesting—but as part of legal history, namely, as a symptom of a structural transformation that rules out the repeatability of exceptional decrees in order to set in motion and write into law a new regularity of independent judicial proceedings.

This temporal aspect that ascribes a genuine role in general history to legal history has consequences for both specific source exegesis and legal history's relationship to neighboring disciplines and their objects of study. I would like to briefly expand on this in conclusion.

1. To the extent that legal source texts claim or have claimed legal validity, they aim for duration, for repeated application, very much in contrast to narrative texts, even if these deal with legal matters. Narrative texts or documents refer to singular processes to which they testify. Texts that constitute laws, certificates that might well be the result of the processing

of specific files, legal verdicts that rely on prior procedures and laws, and contracts based on earlier negotiations all interrupt the preceding chain of events and establish a new duration. In order to enable this kind of duration, customary, unwritten laws are transmitted orally or fixed in writing, and this, then, is the purpose of the laws themselves: on the basis of their linguistic self-assertion, all of these texts claim a repeated applicability above and beyond any specific individual application. To this extent, legal history [*Rechtshistorie*] deals with the kind of text that reveals law of its own accord, analogous to the relationship between theologians and the Bible. These texts' conceptual apparatus—their linguistically formulated issue or case—is different from what a parliamentarian uses in proposing a new law and persuading a majority to vote for it. The one textual statement is consciously temporary, while the other aims at duration. This is why dogmatics is a part of legal history just as much and as fundamentally as hermeneutics, which seeks to interpret the text as a singular text. This temporal dimension of depth that aims at the relative duration of law thus imparts to the specific legal source a unique status that should not be confused with the status of a political, commercial, or narrative source.

There are therefore genuinely legal sources that aim at application on the basis of their self-statement, sources whose meaning cannot be reduced to the singular situation in which they emerged or to their singular history of effect. Procedural regulations as well as material regulatory actions aim at their repeated application and have an iterative temporal structure that differs from sources that remain imprisoned in the history of events.

2. But this is only one aspect, which must be immediately supplemented. This brings me to my second point, namely, the relationship of legal history to neighboring historical fields. It is common to all sources that they point to a reality outside of the text. Legal source texts share this status with the texts of all historical disciplines. Every text can serve as a source for every kind of historical inquiry. One might therefore ask of a text making a specific claim to legal validity what its economic, political, social-historical, theological, or linguistic-historical implications might be. The same applies in the opposite direction as well. Legal historians have made extensive use of this shift in perspective to the benefit of their own writing of history, with the ancillary services performed by

neighboring disciplines then being integrated methodologically into the writing of legal history. I might mention Fehr for literary history, Ernst Rudolf Huber for political and social history, Sohm for Church history, Max Weber for economic history, and Radbruch for art history: all of the historical genres mentioned here, along with their specific sources, have been used by legal historians.

We can thus identify two ways in which legal history differs from its neighboring disciplines. A strict demarcation of legal history concentrates on texts that transport genuinely legal contents and uses neighboring disciplines only in a supplementary way. A flexible differentiation reaches out to other fields, revealing that legal history cannot in any way do without political, social, or economic history, without the history of religion, language, or literature, and so forth. This is the situation of contemporary scholarship. Today, mutual interdependencies [between disciplines] are being demonstrated, which offer consistent interpretations, despite all caveats of revision. Of course, every law [*Recht*] can be read as the preservation of the interest of the powerful, thereby following the Thucydidean model, however augmented by ideology-critical additions. Every law can also self-evidently be interpreted as the expression of linguistic possibilities of a particular community under law. Of course, every law can be interpreted as an answer to social grievances or economical challenges, whether one is dealing with (to name a few examples) the regulation of abortion or contract law or international law, which is currently being drawn upon to redefine the status of the continental shelf. Every law can be read as a reaction to hitherto unregulated or newly emerging problems, or as a regulative instance for certain conflicts that take place outside legal boundaries. To this extent, legal history remains embedded in general history, in political and social and socioeconomic history, and, more recently, the history of technology.

These determinations of interdependency are not arbitrary, and instead result necessarily from the immanent source exegesis performed by legal history. Every conflicting interpretation of legal principles aiming for duration points us to pre- and extralegal challenges in need of new answers. Every determination of a difference between is and ought evokes the extra- or prelegal factors conditioning this difference. Or when old wrongs become legal, as with divorce law since the Enlightenment or in the contemporary regulation of abortion, extralegal social and political forces operate whose pressure generates a potential legal quality.

But even legal innovations that emerged under the pressures of industrialization as well as those that will emerge as a result of increasing global and ecological interdependencies can only take on legal status if they help form repeatable structures. Therein lies the test of the justice of these innovations. This applies to administrative acts and verdicts to the same extent as it does for laws as such and for international agreements.

To name a well-known historical example: the Prussian reform laws introduced by Stein and Hardenberg were reacting to a social structural transformation in the midterm, and to a political and economic catastrophe in the short term. We may appraise the extent of their innovative thrust differently; in any case, the success of the innovation depended on the repeatability of the new legal codes. In his municipal ordinance [*Städteordnung*], Stein drew on transmitted frameworks of corporative order. At stake was a municipal reform of the order of estates [*stadtbürgerliche Standesreform*], and it was successful for this reason. A minimum of distinguishing the social orders was regulated in new ways in order to secure a maximum of financial and civic self-government. Without the recourse to or the renewal of older, feudal customs and legal rules, the municipal reform would (presumably) have failed. In comparison, Hardenberg's economic reforms were much more innovative and (partially) failed precisely for that reason. These reforms both reshaped and replaced Stein's municipal ordinances by forcing a common, statewide economic ordinance upon the entirety of the Prussian population. Countless administrative acts and legal verdicts were necessary, as were additional laws and international agreements in order to bring into being the economic space that was intended at the outset and that was organized by common legal rules.

Feudal interests—and rights—worked against [these reforms], while the economic interests and legal claims of the new bourgeoisie pushed for accelerated transformation. The specifically legal answer to the challenges of this diversity of social interests was a search for legal rules that could be preserved across repeated applications and thereby vouch for justice. To work out such a scenario is properly the task of legal history, which should not lose itself in general social history even though legal history has to take up some of social history's questions.

Stein's theory of public administration [*Verwaltungslehre*]—which was saturated with social history—seems to have been the first, and thus far the last, attempt to investigate such mutual dependencies and circumstances in a systematic, comparative manner. On the basis of the differentiated methods and new questions of today, it would have to be rewritten.

Our strict demarcation of a legal history tied to genuinely legal sources has led us to the necessary expansion of such history and the incorporation of the other branches of historical research. But it does not suffice to posit dependencies and speculate about what can be traced back to what (e.g., whether law can be traced back to interests' power relations). Some aspects of general history can only be conceptualized and explained in terms of legal history. In terms of general history, the reduction of legal history to shifting sets of interests and diachronic histories of power is a matter of course, but it destroys the unique content of legal history, whose temporal structure is oriented toward repeatability. In conclusion, I would therefore like to pose the question in reverse: what would general history look like if one did not ask to what extent it is legally conditioned and structured?

Our initial historiographical question about the conceivability, possibility, or impossibility of justice would [in that case] lack any institutional foundation. In other words, legal history is a necessary but not sufficient condition of general history. We should therefore call for an integral legal history able to provide an empirically saturated equivalent to my first thesis that no interpretation of history can inhibit the question of justice.

Writers of such integrated legal history would have to investigate the temporal differentiations that result from the claim to duration and the repeatability of every law. There are different velocities of change in political, social, economic, linguistic, and legal history, and these all converge in the experience of the everyday from yesterday to today to tomorrow. But in every today, frictions emerge from the differences between each of these different issues, and solving these frictions has been and remains one of the most durable tasks of the law. I would suspect that it is for this reason that the history of law proceeds more slowly and has a different speed of transformation than the sequence of events that is characteristic at least of political history. Duration, after all, needs its time. Perhaps this is also why jurists are more conservative than other academics: conservative not for political reasons, but because it is their good right [*ihr gutes Recht*] to be.

Linguistic Change and the History of Events

"Sticks and Stones will break my bones, but words (or names) will never hurt me." Like all sayings, this one embodies an unambiguous truth: anyone who has ever been beaten up knows from experience that words do not capture all that happened there. But like all sayings, this one also only reveals a partial truth, for whoever invokes "sticks and stones" seeks to evade a form of aggression in language. Words can destroy a person too. Herodotus reports, for example, how reading letters from Darius out loud was enough to change the minds of Oroites' bodyguards and lead them to kill the very person whom they were tasked to protect, Oroites himself (*Histories* 3.128.5).

At any rate, we can draw the following conclusion from these observations: history, in the actual course of its occurrence, has a different mode of being from that of language spoken about it (whether before, after, or concomitant with the events). Current methodological debates about intellectual history[1] tend to downplay any strong dichotomy between reality and thought, being and consciousness, history and language. Instead, softer dichotomies are used that can be more easily connected to each other, such as "meaning and experience," terms that mutually condition or elucidate each other, or even "text and context," where both linguistic and nonlinguistic conditions are at work. Placing "meaning" and "experience" in relation thus brings together the sociology of knowledge and the analysis of language, and it would seem that such methodological moves are justified and uncontroversial, for every language is historically conditioned, and every history is conditioned by language. Who would deny that all our concrete experiences only first become experiences by being mediated through language, making history possible in the first place. However, I nonetheless want to insist on separating language and history analytically, because neither can be brought fully into conformity with the other. This is the thesis that I explore in this essay. A difference inheres between speaking and acting or between speaking and enduring, even if speaking is a linguistic action and even if acting and enduring are linguistically mediated. This difference is what will concern us in this essay.

I will proceed in three steps.[2] First, I will draw our attention to several pre- and extralinguistic conditions of human history; second, I will sketch the relation between language and history in the moment that generates the event, namely, of the occurrence itself; third, I will sketch the relation between language and history *ex post*, after the experienced event and its context have receded into the past.

Prelinguistic Conditions of Human History

Humans share many natural geological, geographical, biological, and zoological conditions with animals. Precisely to the degree that they are shared with animals, these conditions are pre- or extralinguistic, and they might well be called metahistorical. In any case, however, they are also necessary conditions of human history, and any historical anthropology must deal with them. I would like to explore three such metahistorical conditions of possible histories.

The first pertains to the time span between birth and death shared by humans and animals. This time span corresponds to the bipolarity of the sexes, the generativity without which there would be no sequence of generations following on each other. The time between birth and death is thus a determination of finitude that makes possible and generates histories. The succession of generations leads to distinct, yet overlapping spaces of experience that do not and cannot fully converge, like different strata. Diachronic conflicts are latent in these different spaces of experience that cannot be mediated without certain institutional rules. The tension constitutive of all histories between earlier and later, and, indeed, the very notions of too early and too late, are based upon this natural pregiven of generativity, birth, and death. And as we know, the human is capable of bringing about his or her own death or the death of others, supposedly in order to better control his or her own history. The naturally conditioned, anthropological pregivens of multiple histories with which we are familiar thus include not just the necessity of death, which can be postponed through precaution, but also the ability to kill, which shortens the life of the other.

Second, humans share with animals the differentiation between inside and outside, which, like generativity, is always in effect. There is no human unit of action that does not delimit itself internally and externally. This formal oppositional pair likewise also contains conditions of possible histories, whether it is the embattled retreat into a cave or the contested fencing in of a house; the drawing of a boundary that causes or ends a conflict; or whether it is initiation rites, asylum spots, groups tied together through an oath [*Schwurverbände*], testing systems and admission requirements, all the things that in today's world condition units of action or that form the conditions for one's belonging to a political community. In each case, these conflicts and their regulations, the histories of which we all are familiar with, remain constituted by the differentiation between inside and outside. This remains true in the present day even as the increased complexity of overlapping and entangled internal and external spaces across the globe puts tremendous pressure on our ability to properly understand world history.

I would like to mention a third differentiation shared by humans and their animal relatives, namely, the pecking order, or in classical terminology, the difference between master and slave. Formally, this is the opposition between above and below. Even if the political art of human self-organization seeks to make "above" and "below" interchangeable through procedural rules and thus to make equality possible, or to secure freedom by making mutual interdependency something that can be consented to and voted upon, this does not change anything in terms of the formal pregiven of necessary relations of above and below. Even the functional differentiation of our society that transforms personal rule into supposedly anonymous administration cannot do away with the above-below relations operating in each case.

To summarize: earlier-later, inside-outside, above-below, these are three oppositional pairs without which no history would come into being, regardless of the form they take on in particular cases—whether on the basis of economic, religious, political, social, or any other factor. This sketch is quite broad and simple, to be sure, but it is intended to lend support to my initial argument that language and history cannot simply be equated. These three formal oppositional pairs prelinguistically condition all concrete histories.

Of course all of these formal determinations—birth and death, generativity, differentiation between inside and outside, above and below—shared by humans and animals are grasped in language and are socially transformed or politically regulated in and through language. There is no community of action that does not define itself through language. It is almost always the case that participating in a particular linguistic community is what decides whether one does or does not belong to that group. The ability to master particular ways of speaking or specialized languages is almost always what determines whether one can move in higher or lower circles of society. There are almost always different linguistic norms that differentiate the experiences and hopes of the young and the old diachronically. As linguistic beings, humans cannot avoid linguistically absorbing metahistorical pregivens in order to regulate and control them through language to the extent that they can. However, these elemental pregivens deducible from nature remain in effect, and all language seeks in vain to come to terms with them. That which comes together into an event within the framework of these pregivens is more than what can be mastered by language.

When the flexible distinction between inside and outside is intensified into a impassioned dichotomy between friend and enemy, when unavoidable, natural death is preempted by killing or self-sacrifice, when the relation between above and below leads to slavery and irrevocable humiliation or to exploitation and class struggle, or even when the tension between the sexes leads to degradation—this is when events emerge: chains of events, cascades of events that withhold themselves from language, to which every word, every sentence, every speech can only react. Indeed, there are events for which words fail us, that leave us speechless, and to which we can (perhaps) only respond with silence. We only need to recall the speechlessness of the Germans when they were confronted with their catastrophe, which drew innumerable people and peoples into it. To this day, every attempt to find a language adequate to mass extermination seems to fail. And every attempt to stabilize memory through language arrives too late for those affected, too late for the event itself. This difference between a history in the moment of its occurrence and its linguistic processing remains in each case constitutive for the relationship between the two. This also applies to language that exists prior to the events and that helps to bring the events about as spoken or written speech. This brings me to my second point.

Spoken Language, Alternatives for Action, and Consequences of Events

"There are certain things that cannot be explained in words, but only in action. Other things can be explained in words, but no exemplary deed emerges from them." This is Herodotus's astute distinction (*Histories* 3.72.2). He placed it in Darius's mouth amid the well-known debates about the succession to the throne in Persia, whose outcome was still completely open. Few linguistic testimonies in world history have been cited as much as this debate about the best constitution, which was decided in favor of monarchy and against either aristocracy or democracy by means of arguments that at that time were, if not better, at any rate stronger.

We need not be concerned with the philological question of whether this constitutional debate was a sophistic insertion, whether Herodotus invented the arguments and simply put them into the mouths of the Persians, or whether these kinds of arguments did in fact emerge during this open and contested royal succession (a version that has much to recommend it).[3] At any rate Herodotus did achieve one thing in particular; namely, he depicted the linguistic preparations, the concepts of actions that preceded a specific political action, the enthronement of Darius. In other words, he drew attention in a methodologically deliberate way to the tension that prevails between spoken speech and the succession of events. The debating Persians turned their experiences of possible forms of political organization into concepts. As a result, they articulated structural alternatives for action rather than simply singular, one-time options.

In other words, they spoke about desirable and less desirable histories, about possible histories rather than about the actual history that would then later occur as a singular, particular event.

Thanks to Herodotus, we have here an initial finding. Spoken language is always either more or less than what is realized in the actual course of history. Language adjudicates above all as to the possibility of a history *in actu* and thus has a different temporal structure than the sequence of events. Concepts [*Begriffe*] become preconceptions [*Vorgriffe*]. This can also be seen in the reception history of Herodotus's text. By thematizing possibilities for forms of political organization and doing so in a way that is situationally singular but more general in argument, the text contains a prognostic potential that extends out beyond the singular situation that occasioned it. By discussing an ongoing decision making process, arguments are drawn from experience that lay claim to more general validity (and the same applies mutatis mutandis to the debates described by Herodotus that occur in advance of every outbreak of war): the advantages and disadvantages of democracy, aristocracy, and monarchy are weighed against each other. The arguments themselves are not exhausted by the situation to which they are related, and for this reason become capable of transposition and repetition. The numerous eighteenth-century prognoses of revolution that predicted the events of 1789 and after—not in detail, but structurally—are evidence of this.

There are many similar kinds of predictions, driven partially by the desire for a singular, complete transformation of all previous history, and partially by prior historical experience that is stored within language and that can thus be called up. No matter the empirical arguments that entered into these prognoses—the analysis of French affairs; the predicted parallels to the English revolution, including the trial of the king and the threatening example of Cromwell; or the texts of Tacitus, Sallust, Polybius, and Thucydides—one element emerges across all the different layers of time called up here, namely, Herodotus's constitutional typology and specifically the immanent course of events predicted by Darius, the victor of the dispute. Darius defended the monarchy, arguing that every democracy leads to bloody partisan divisions; that these partisans would then coalesce around an aristocracy; that the competition between the aristocrats would lead to the self-assertion of the strongest; and that it would be better to establish a monarchy from the start and avoid all of the bloody detours. This very same interpretative scheme returns in the eighteenth century. Frederick the Great offered the most realistic prognosis of the revolution, while Diderot's was the most far-reaching and astute. Both authors came to the same conclusion, that the coming revolution would be a civil war that would lead to the fall of the current monarchies and that would end with the dictatorship of a strong man, to whom the feuding citizens, drunk on freedom, would voluntarily submit—this was Diderot's view. Wieland, one of the foremost authorities on ancient texts, even anticipated the dictatorship of Bonaparte one and a half years before his coup d'état.[4]

It is a common signature of Herodotus's argument and of the prognoses implicitly based upon his principles that language transforms sets of experiences into concepts that influence political actions before their unfolding. These are diagnoses with prognostic as well as pragmatic intent that seek to influence a future that is unknown in its particulars but recognizable in its historical possibilities. It was Herodotus who first set out the conflict situations immanent to political constitutions and their alternatives for action, these basic patterns of human self-organization and the dangers contained therein. Language alone is capable of communicating this kind of information, across each and every reformulation, translation, and addition, so that it can be reapplied at some point.

Yet it is one of the unique achievements of Thucydides to have made this tension between speech and action the central axis of his historical work.[5] All of his (invented) speeches and dialogues are conceived of in such a way that they are always spoken into a still uncertain future, in accordance with the actual situation of the agents themselves. More so than Herodotus, Thucydides thematized the contradiction between actual history and what is spoken before, during, and after historical events, a contradiction that emerges again and again. And what's more, he showed us that this contradiction is in fact constitutive of the experience of history itself. Thucydides' methodological accomplishment was to communicate this by narrating the actual events diachronically through the speeches of the participants that had generated these events. Today we would say that these speeches and dialogues contain a theory of that history. But Thucydides did not develop these theoretical premises abstractly and generally; instead, he depicted them as concrete principles of action for conflicting groups of agents, that is, he thematized the linguistic preconditions of histories *in actu*. He taught us how arguments can both change and miss the point of the conflict situation. Methodologically speaking, the (often invoked) longevity of the political lessons revealed by Thucydides lies in the tension he depicted between speech and action, between *logoi* and *erga*, but also between speaking and opining, between extralinguistic reasons and stated pretenses, in short, between language and historical reality, which in this way, and not otherwise, constitutes history.

We might well recall the Melian dialogue, which, put in modern terms, gives voice to alternative "if/then" statements, to prognoses of conditions. By confusing their legally justified hopes for the coming reality, the Melians brought their own death upon themselves, which they did not foresee. The Athenians overtly invoked their power, which they then brutally applied, and to which at first the Melians could still freely submit. Thucydides then adds in three sentences what actually happened: the Melians were executed and their women and children enslaved. No language is capable of capturing this. And the dialogue was itself incapable of anticipating what actually happened. But it did show which structures of possible action were contained within the speech. And these structures are the kinds that can be linguistically retrieved, that are applicable through analogy and thus repeatable.

Emil Hácha in Berlin in 1939 and Alexander Dubček in Moscow in 1968 were both very aware of this when they agreed to capitulate. They took the repercussions from the conflict between power and legality [*Recht*] onto themselves, the repercussions that the Melians sought to evade, at the cost of their death, as it would later turn out. What you say becomes an event that evades you.

Certainly, the empirical conditions of action were completely different in Melos, Berlin, and Moscow, as were the social, economic, and ideological preconditions. But the linguistically preformulated alternatives under the compulsion of which it was necessary to act were analogous, even if twenty-five centuries had intervened: the Athenian decision to attack Melos, the orders in Berlin and Moscow to occupy Prague. How often in history would one gladly retract a word after it has been uttered, because the word has changed the situation irrevocably. But with their unrelenting clarity, Herodotus and Thucydides have shown us that there is more contained within spoken language than what can be discerned at the unique moment of its utterance. They have shown us that singular alternatives for action bring to light historical structures of possibility, structures that can be called upon again and that are, to that extent, not unique but repeatable.

We are therefore faced with different levels of reality: on the one, the irrevocable succession of events plays out; on the other, language anticipates possible events, which, under different circumstances, may, but need not, recur. As a storehouse of experiences, language bundles together the conditions of possible events. And there are countless histories that have never come to pass, having been prevented or avoided. These kinds of histories, the preventive war against France that Bismarck avoided in 1875, for example, are only accessible as linguistically transmitted alternatives, and the bloody alternative here was later realized, in 1914, with results that no one had wanted or anticipated. One conclusion therefore emerges from the difference we have been describing: the linguistic repeatabilities and the irrevocable sequence of events describe temporal structures that can be distinguished from one another, even if both inseparably influence each other in everyday life. This is a point I would now like to expand upon.

Every language is an enormous effort of abstraction. As John Stuart Mill put it in his essay "Use and Abuse of Political Terms," human beings "have many ideas, and but few words." The number of words is limited, while the issues, ideas, opinions, objects, possibilities, and realities articulated in language are potentially unlimited. Syntax and semantics, too, are limited; it is for this reason that they are more stable over longer periods of time. To this extent (and as we saw with Herodotus and Thucydides) the capacity for repetition of principles of experience after having been first formulated is part of the even greater permanence of statements after having been first put to words. Such statements can outlast the events that occasioned them and that have become part of history. And even if the linguistic inventory integrates new experiences, as with the centuries-old constitutional debates[6] or with the conflict between power and legality that is always breaking out anew and in different ways, semantics have a slower tempo of change than the events themselves. The linguistic formulation of uniquely grasped experiences limits their being subject to the kind of radical transformation with which we are familiar from the history of events.

The consideration of concrete linguistic actions within specific languages can solidify this thesis. It becomes clear that a language does more than just store experiences that outlast the individual occurrence. Indeed, each spoken language also places limits on these experiences because, within the framework of that language, they can only be expressed in a certain way and not otherwise.

Let us consider a comparative example, namely, the debates about enfranchisement in Great Britain, France, and Germany after the French Revolution. From the perspective of actual history [*realgeschichtlich*] these debates undoubtedly reveal the common European phenomenon of democratization.[7] But this so-called trend occurs linguistically at very different temporal rhythms.

In France we find the clear opposition between *citoyen* and bourgeois, which has structured the political discourse ever since it was introduced by Diderot in the *Encyclopédie*. Whoever invoked the rights of property ownership, as in the elections of 1795, 1814–15, and 1830, was suspected on the semantic level of representing limited bourgeois interests instead of more general civil rights, which were to be accorded to all following the revolution. Both the Bonapartists and the radical republicans shared this view and each based their constitutions on the foundation of universal [male] suffrage.

In Germany, the debate was semantically preformed in an entirely different manner. There, only the *Bürger* was known, but this referred to a specific estate [*Stand*]. Colloquially this meant *Stadtbürger* [the townsman, or burgher] in contrast to the peasantry and the nobility. In the wake of the late Enlightenment, the artificial concept of the *Staatsbürger* was invented in analogy to the *citoyen*, but this term was not widely used in the everyday language of politics. Further differentiations of this same basic concept followed: not only the *Kleinbürger* [petit bourgeois] and the *Großbürger* [grand bourgeois], but also the *Spießbürger* [philistine]; in the process, though, the concept of *Bürger* increasingly lost the more the theoretical precision and political efficacy inherent in the concept of *citoyen*. Prior to 1848, the German debate about enfranchisement was caught up in the tangle of the competing interests of property owners and feudal privileges, with the latter differing quite significantly from region to region.

For its part, the British Parliament was able to unite precisely these three factors pragmatically. Without having recourse to universal civil rights in the French sense, the debate in Britain took place on two separate tracks. In the traditional legal language going back to the Middle Ages, the number of privileged "freemen," "burgesses," or "burghers" was determined differently depending on voting district and region. The tradition of very concrete, singular legal determinations was thus preserved. Their legitimation, however, was modern and innovative. At stake was the attempt to include the hitherto unrepresented interests of the new "middle classes" in Parliament's argumentative inventory, which succeeded.

What does this comparison reveal? The so-called trend of democratization, that is, the growing participation of increasing strata of the population in legislation and the exercise of political power appears to be one and the same process on an extralinguistic level, but it is a process that is mastered by each language in completely different ways. Or, perhaps more accurately, we might say that the trend of democratization is registered on the linguistic level in very different ways.

The French debate was one about fundamental principles and drew its leading polemical concepts [*Leitbegriffe*] from the Enlightenment (e.g., feudal privilege versus equality on the basis of citizenship). The same arguments were deployed in Germany, but could not be traced in any unambiguous way back to the *Bürger* concept, which remained plurivalent, having de facto stored up feudal modes of experience that reached back much further in time. And in Great Britain, these traditional legal determinations were preserved while at the same time being expanded and modernized, allowing for the incorporation of new kinds of experience, such as bringing the interests of the "middle classes" into the political area, but also not going much further than this.

What follows from this in terms of our initial question about the relationship between language and history? The concrete concepts that organize political debate link back to political contents of experience that entered into these concepts at some point. In other words, the larger permanence that is characteristic more generally of language—our first argument—reveals in each individual, singular speech situation a variety of temporal deep structures that are stratified in different ways.

In France, once the platform of the language of the revolution was attained in 1789, it quickly and fundamentally limited the legitimacy of feudal privileges. These feudal privileges were exactly the semantic pre-givens that destabilized the enfranchisement debate in Germany. The *Bürger* concept oscillated between feudal connotations and the postulates of citizenship that were not easy to reduce to a common denominator. In Britain, the problem found a pragmatic resolution. Citizenship rights were not mentioned at all. Instead, the centuries-old legal power of concepts that were tied to the townsmen, or burghers, and to specific regional voting districts, was preserved, while these concepts were simultaneously superseded through a sociological terminology that was capable of transforming the new experiences of industrial society into new concepts such as that of the "interests" of the "middle classes."

Every synchronically spoken language whose arsenal was used to make arguments thus contained pregivens that were stratified at diachronically different depths, making the content of the argumentation accessible while at the same time also limiting it. The concepts used each had a diachronic thrust with varied temporal origins, and those who used these concepts could not do so arbitrarily or with sovereign control.

In this way, concepts have a different internal temporal structure than the events that help generate them or that are supposed to be captured by the concepts. This finding applies to the modern concepts of movement [*Bewegungsbegriffe*] that arose in the eighteenth century and that have organized our entire linguistic inventory around the idea of necessary transformation, of shift and plannable change. The central concepts here are development, progress, history itself, reform, crisis, evolution, and, of course, revolution. And in a peculiar twist, these very concepts, on the semantic level, have an altogether stabilizing effect. They produced commonalities in language across all political viewpoints, even if particular points were still disputed. It became increasingly difficult to defend the status quo as such after the French Revolution, and even more so with the advent of the Industrial Revolution. And even the reactionaries did not claim to be reactionary. All political camps accepted a minimum of pressure to change. Semantically, concepts of movement allowed no other choice. The only question separating them was if and how the pressure to change was to be resisted, accepted, or embraced.

To give an example, the radical Left Hegelian Ruge and the Catholic conservative Baader both argued that "reform or revolution" were the only alternatives.[8] Both sought to avoid bloody revolution through reforms, and they only disputed the amount of necessary reforms. To be sure, they disagreed about the direction and tempo of change, but the necessity of change was commonly presupposed in the conceptual framework particular to the modern concepts of movement in which they worked.

Even when modern concepts of movement point to or compel constant change, epoch-specific concepts themselves betray a remarkable constancy and capacity for repeated use, even if in practice they help to legitimate wholly different programs for action. (This, by the way, is the semantic threshold that Marx and Engels could not cross over. Their ultimate goal of a final and decisive revolution did not allow them to perceive in a pragmatically appropriate way the actual changes of a capitalistic society that was continuously reforming itself.)

Our thesis that language is transformed more slowly than the chain of events that it helps to trigger and ground is thus also applicable to accelerated modernity and not simply to the large span of time between Herodotus and Diderot referenced earlier.

Of course there are always counterexamples of spontaneous innovation in language that take on the status of an event in linguistic history, cases where there is a strong enough pragmatic impulse that can evade the pregiven semantics at work. We already mentioned how the theory of "interests" was applied to the new, so-called middle classes, as well as how Diderot invented the praxis-oriented dichotomy between citizen and bourgeois that from the start placed the bourgeois under ideological suspicion. Both innovations were extremely consequential, but both also had stabilizing effects. We might add an example from German, and one that is quite paradigmatic for this linguistic and historical context. *Bund* [union] is a foundational concept of the German language. It was coined in the late Middle Ages and has since become a structural feature of constitutional history in Germany that differentiates the German context from the history of neighboring states in essential ways. Luther used this political concept in order to translate *berith* from the Old Testament. This had theological and hence political consequences as well.

A *Bund*, according to this doctrine, could only be established by God and it was something beyond human control. Bund thus diverged from the legal language of the Holy Roman Empire employed by political Protestantism. What is today called the Schmalkaldian Bund never called itself that. Claims to political autonomy derived from religious reformation remained restricted to the rulers and cities that were privileged by the law of the Holy Roman Empire and that merged into "leagues [*Ligen*]" and "unions [*Unionen*]." Political autonomy was denied to the faithful as participants in the Bund with God. The theological Bund concept remained limited to the realm of pure religion, and this in marked contrast to the English concept of the "covenant," whose overlapping religious and political meanings reinforced each other so much as to legitimate the revolution of 1640 and after.

The diachronic thrust of the Lutheran, antipolitical, theological Bund concept lasted for a long time. We might name its end point: in 1847, Marx and Engels were called upon to write a "Confession of Faith of the Bund of Communists." The specifically German, theological implications of this formulation are unmistakable, and Marx and Engels therefore opted for a radical new formulation. Rather than a "Confession of Faith of the Bund of Communists," they wrote the *Manifesto of the Communist Party.* This was an act of conscious linguistic politics, and it became innovative and effective in the long term. The authors resisted the diachronic thrust of the theological Bund semantics (although their *manifestatio* too remained a profession of faith) and instead used a concept of the "party," which at that time was just beginning to be legible in revolutionary terms and also capable of garnering broad support. They tried to enforce this trend, not without long-term success.

In this way, even language that we can prove is semantically unique and innovative supports our thesis that linguistic transformation proceeds more slowly than the concrete series of events that this transformation helps to call forth. Luther's anti-revolutionary, theological *Bund* concept and Marx's turn to a revolutionary concept of the party opened up new experiences, but limited and lent stability to them over the long run.

History after the Events—and the Language
of Historiography

Thus far we have approached the relationship between language and
history from the perspective of impending events, that is, in terms of history *in actu*. Let us now cast a glance backwards. What does language
retroactively accomplish in allowing a history to emerge, in constituting
a history out of a sequence of events *ex eventu*? Here I am using the term
"history" in the Greek and Latin sense, namely, as an experienced, investigated, narrated, or represented history, not as *res gestae* [things done], but
as *historia* that deals with the *res gestae*. In other words, we are now con-
sidering the language of the historian more specifically.

Every historical representation is a selection from a potentially
unlimited realm of past, endured and enacted histories. Of course this
selection is never purely determined by language. Every selection is already
structured prelinguistically; here too the anthropological pregivens mentioned at the beginning of this essay circumscribe the scope of possible
representation.

First, it is decisive whether the historian is a contemporary of the
events he is reporting on or whether he belongs to a future generation
and lived after they occurred. Up until the eighteenth century, being an
eyewitness or (even better) a participant was considered to be a cognitive
advantage that guaranteed the truth of this history. Only after the experience of progress—methodologically speaking, only with the development
of historical-philological critique—did increased temporal distance from
past events come to count as a prerequisite for better cognition. But who
would want to do without the memoirs of Philippe de Commynes, of
Frederick the Great, or of Churchill, who wrote as active participants and
as eyewitnesses? Being born earlier or later only determines the perspective, not the quality of the work.

Second, it is decisive for the historian's perspective whether he was
born higher or lower in the social or political hierarchy, whether he belongs
to the victors or the vanquished. Thucydides, Polybius, Sallust, Tacitus,
Augustine, Commynes, Machiavelli, Guiccardini, and even Marx all
belonged to the vanquished in analyzing and representing the events of
their time. As vanquished, they were forced to develop new questions and

methods, for their history had unfolded differently than they had hoped. They wrote under greater need of explanation, under greater urgency for evidence than what applies to the victors, because success itself speaks for the victors.

A third decisive factor predetermining the selection of the historian is whether he belongs to the political, religious, social, or economic unit of action on which he is reporting and with which he critically or approvingly identifies, or whether he regards this group from the outside, writes as if he is without a "polis" (is *apolis*), as Lucian demands of the historian. In either case his options are predetermined on a prelinguistic level. Each in its own way, therefore, our metahistorical pregivens—earlier-later, above-below, and inside-outside—determine the cognitive possibilities and thus circumscribe the status of a historical narrative [*Historie*].

Our observation that no history completely overlaps with what is said before and during its occurrence applies all the more if we look at the events retrospectively, that is, to what was said after them. Every history always contains both more and less than what historians can say about it, each from their individual perspectives. How, then is a history linguistically constituted retroactively? Following oral testimony there are three possibilities, which we might express in a simple formula: writing down [*Aufschreiben*], copying [*Abschreiben*], or rewriting a history [*Umschreiben*].

First: every history we do not experience ourselves or learn about through word of mouth was written down for the first time at some point. It was felt that something should be recorded, which otherwise would be lost to future generations. Whether these histories are preceded by old or new narratives, by epics, sagas, legends, or anecdotes; whether and how many witnesses were consulted if such consultation was still possible; whether written sources were sought out, interrogated, and weighed against each other in order to learn about these past histories—these are all questions of method. For the constitution of history, the fundamentally decisive action is that of being written down for the first time.

The past reality is transitioned into the status of a written history, and its fixation in writing establishes the difference between the history that once occurred and the linguistic form that it takes on at a later point. Epistemologically speaking, this is of considerable consequence, for, from then on the fixed linguistic form of a history takes epistemological precedence over what once might have been the case.

A history that has run its course remains as singular as it is past. And if it is held to be memorable, this is mostly because it contains a surprise that humans try to explain. It is only after taking on its linguistic form that we can access all of the reasons that make the singular, often surprising course of a history explainable, evident, and comprehensible. These reasons last longer than the individual, singular events themselves, for otherwise they would not be justifications. However, in contrast to the events themselves and their consequences, these justifications are solely connected to their linguistic transmission.

We all are familiar with implicit or explicit ultimate justifications that lend a history consistency, perhaps even meaning. Whether it is the gods or spirits who step in to explain change as something durable; whether *fortuna* or fate is invoked, or the Christian God from whose will everything can be derived; or whether individual histories draw their explanations from political, social, psychological, or economic conditions or even processes: in each case, singular events are lent their relatively durable meaning or a specific importance through linguistically fixed reasons. This should make the second mode of historiography, copying, easy to grasp.

Second: As long as histories are copied and thus transmitted over time, one can assume that the experiences stored linguistically in the justifications for these histories remain relatively similar or even identical. Or, in other words, as long as no contradiction arises between the justifications contained within the transmitted histories on the one hand and the justifications needed for the newly experienced histories on the other, the job of the historian is comparatively simple. Old histories are copied down and new ones are added to them. The justifications—whether they are religious and theological or political and psychological, whether social or economic—are then stabilized and protect against any kind of basic surprises, even if certain individual cases might have been surprising. All histories remain understandable as long as the presuppositions justifying them are not called into question. From this perspective it thus becomes comprehensible how, for over a millennium, the telling of history [*die Historie*] could be understood as an element of rhetoric, with all its linguistic stability, or why the Christian interpretation of history remained so stable for so long. Biblical history was the axis of all histories.

Third: the rewriting of history is more exciting and requires more explanation. The process of rewriting is comparatively clear and rational in the context of historical-philological source criticism as it has been refined since the Renaissance; this criticism disassembles texts on the basis of their copied and original parts, uncovers falsifications, and discovers motives and interests of the writer lurking behind the texts. Or new sources appear that require reading previous sources in new or different ways. Errors of older readings are corrected. In short, at stake here is a genuine case of scholarly progress occurring within the confines of historical-philological method, which necessitates the rewriting of history. But this form of progress imma-nent in historical research is by no means mandatory and does not fully address why previously credible histories should be rewritten at all.

Histories first come to be rewritten at the point when the context of justification that had been credible up to that point becomes unbelievable and fractured. The linguistic pregivens in which a history is imbedded and that lend it meaning are no longer accepted; explanations that had been capable of being integrated into one's own inventory of experience up to that point now start to lose their plausibility. New questions thus arise that can no longer be answered by the histories transmitted thus far. Old histories need to be written anew, need to be rewritten. Transmitted histories are thus retroactively inserted into new contexts of justification in order to remain compatible with one's own, new and transformed expe-rience. In other words: the new justifications themselves come to require justification, and this is the genuine place where source criticism inter-venes. Source criticism itself only becomes possible when new questions arise; in itself, it is only a means to answer new questions that could not be answered by the history previously transmitted.

Every rewriting of history exists under the pressure of a transforma-tion of experience that forces the historian to substitute new explanations for existing ones or to supplement existing explanations. And this thereby alters the linguistic status of a past history without necessarily ceasing to remain "the same" history.

Yet it would certainly be an error to believe that adaptation of an older history on the basis of one's own new experience is something that first began with historical-philological criticism subsequent to the Renaissance and the Reformation. Rather, the rewriting of history begins with the writing down of history itself.

Herodotus's great accomplishment was not simply to write down what had thus far only been transmitted orally, but critically to call into question these mythic, epic, or orally transmitted reports. In turn, Thucydides did not simply copy Herodotus (though he did do this); above all, he rewrote him. Wherever Thucydides dealt with the same time period as Herodotus, he altered the line of reasoning. Whatever cultural-historical, archaeological, religious, military-historical, semantic, or any other types of reports that Thucydides drew upon, he no longer reported them one after the other and each for their own sake, but instead bundled them all into arguments in order to show that the Peloponnesian War was greater than the Persian-Greek war as recorded by Herodotus. And, furthermore, Thucydides developed a model of diachronic process that made the one-time escalation of power by the Athenians comprehensible as a historical reason for war. Shining through this diachronic description of the process of a single event is the ultimate justification of all histories, in that everything can be connected back to the pathology of human power and its capacity for delusion. In the process, the religious background disappeared, at least on the level of the history's linguistic constitution of the history, a background that Herodotus could still draw on in deriving a basic justice inherent to all histories. One is hard pressed to find any kind of religiously motivated justice inherent to historical processes in Thucydides.[9]

The simple step from Herodotus to Thucydides, the shift from one generation to the next, was more than just the copying of old histories and the addition of new ones; it launched the rewriting of history. Writing down the story of the Peloponnesian War, based on his own experience, Thucydides perceived it as a pathological battle for power that consumed its adversaries. And to the extent that Thucydides reduced his history to this kind of political history, he recast all of the historical reports that he had from Herodotus (e.g., such as those about tyrannicide) and inserted them into his new contexts of justification.

This first, classical case of rewriting is paradigmatic for everything that followed it. We might recall the geographical entanglement of individual histories in Polybius, who was able retrospectively to recognize constellations that had not been perceived up to that point. This was a process that would later repeat itself on a global scale beginning in the eighteenth century. Or we might recall the psychology of terror developed by Tacitus, and that has since been applied in various contexts in order to retroactively find new insights in old realities. Or we might recall Eusebius, Augustine, and Orosius, who ignored the entire inventory of experience of antiquity to the extent that it was not compatible with the Christian interpretation of the world. We might recall the rediscovery of the political in the late Middle Ages, above all through Machiavelli, which allowed the entire Christian history of the Middle Ages to be rewritten through the invention of the Middle Ages as a historical period. We might recall the history of social relations and economic constitutions through which the Scots rewrote history to conform to their own new experience. Or we might recall Marx, who did not in fact disprove Ranke's political history. In fact, Marx supplemented Ranke by integrating political history into new, different, and longer-term contexts of justification, namely, in networks of economic conditions. And we can predict with all certainty that we soon will have an ecological history, which, in analogy to our own experience, will situate our entire past in light of the shortage of natural resources and the dependence of human action upon the environment.

But what do these cases teach us about the relationship obtaining in each case between a reality that is once and for all part of the past and its linguistic elaboration? History *ex post* only exists for us to the extent that it is written down, copied, and rewritten.

Whatever the prelinguistic preconditions that enter or have entered into history, the reality of past histories is only present in their linguistic forms. Many features of events and sequences of events can be credibly transmitted, with the proper methodological precaution, and it is for this reason that we can continue to copy down things that we already know because of linguistic transfer.

But every historian must answer the question in the here and now as to which justifications aimed at repeated use he or she accepts. For the justifications that tell us why something took place this way and not that way must be rationally credible, they must correspond to our experiences or allow us to access new experiences. Many experiences had by the ancients are repeatable, perhaps many more than we moderns would have it. And if we are forced to have new experiences, we cannot get around seeing old histories in a new light and rewriting them accordingly, histories, though, that do not thereby stop being "the same" histories.

The discrepancy between past reality and its linguistic processing will never be closed. What was it that Epictetus said? "It is not what has been done that shocks people, but what is said about it" (*Enchiridion*, cap. V).

10

Structures of Repetition
in Language and History

> "The strange thing with all these love stories is that they always revolve around the same thing, but how they start and end is so endlessly different that watching them never gets boring!"

Whoever reads this in [standard] German rather than in the original dialect will miss its Viennese cadence, but should still be able to guess the author: Johann Nepomuk Nestroy.[1]

The beginnings and ends of all love stories—the alpha and omega of every love—are endlessly different, as long as lovers find their way together and separate or are separated. And yet the same thing is always at stake, namely, the love that, inspired by the sexual drive, is continuously and consistently repeated across the diversity of all individual histories. However different ethnic and cultural contexts orient, direct, and reshape the sexual drive, sexual difference and tension compel repetition with every new relationship, and neither our human race [*Menschengeschlecht*] nor its histories would exist without this repetition.

With this observation we are already at the central question of this essay. As individuals, as persons who find their way together through love, people are as unique as they believe themselves to be: that their love in particular lies outside history, that it is irreplaceable, unique, one-of-a-kind, or however else their pledges to each other are formulated. There is an anthropological finding behind all of this, which has slowly shifted over the course of European history. The Latin term *persona* belongs—like the Greek *prosopon*—to a pregiven typology, to a mask into which a person must slide so as to take up a specific role. Changing roles is conceivable, but the development of a character or a (modern) personality is not.[2] With and following the individualization of the concept of the person, the enlightened-romantic concept of marriage emerged; this concept no longer referenced the objective reproduction and securing of a family tied to a household but instead envisioned the subjective and autonomous self-formation [*Selbstbildung*] and self-commitment [*Selbstbindung*] of two persons to each other through their love. The rituals of other cultures take up zoologically pregiven sexuality [*Geschlecht*] in significantly different ways. But viewed at this level of abstraction, both the realization of these sexually determined givens, repeated over millions of years, as well as the concrete action of at least two people (and also potentially more) who uniquely meet and find each other remain identical at the level of a general formal description. In each unique case the "time after time" repeats itself, and yet the unique case is not subsumed into the repeatability that conditions and occasions it, which is predisposed in sexuality. The ways in which actions are carried out and the modes of behavior are endlessly diverse, but the sexuality [*Geschlechtlichkeit*] to be realized remains structurally identical.

Derived from Nestroy's observation, our line of thinking can be generalized even further. Persons (whom Nestroy does not name) and their stories, occurrences, and conflicts as well as their solutions, whether catastrophes or compromises, remain unique and unrepeatable on the temporal track of events. The thesis I would like to develop in the following essay is, however, that these events are predisposed by or contained within self-repeating pregivens, without ever being identical to these.

To begin, allow me a thought experiment that can help us shed light on Nestroy's curiosity about the story of love that is always the same but nonetheless always new in new ways.

If everything always repeated itself identically, there would be no change and no surprise—either in love or in politics, either in the economy or anywhere else. Gaping boredom would spread.

If, in contrast, everything were new or innovative, humankind would fall into a black hole from one day to the next, helpless and bare of all orientation.

These logically constraining propositions alone teach us that neither the category of duration, which is evidenced by the repetition of the same, nor the category of diachronically aligned singular events (no matter whether these are viewed from a progressive or historicist perspective) are sufficient on their own for interpreting human histories. The historical nature of the human being, or, put in terms of the theory of knowledge [*wissenschaftstheoretisch*], historical anthropology, is located between these two poles of our thought experiment, between constant repeatability and durable innovation. The question then is how we can analyze and represent the sediments and mixtures of both repetition and innovation.

Our conceptual model, which needs to be capable of variably combining repetition and innovation, allows us to register delays and accelerations, depending on how often we can correlate repetition and singularity with one another. Acceleration would occur when, in a given set of cases, increasingly fewer cases were found to repeat themselves and ever more innovations came about that departed from the old pregivens. Delays would arise when traditional repetitions grind into place or solidify in such a way that every form of change would be inhibited or even made impossible.

This thought experiment seeks to circumscribe all conceivable singular events of possible histories theoretically in such a way that they be described in temporal terms with the categories in question, and it likewise aims to uncover the longer-lasting preconditions, that is, the structures of repetition, without which no events would ever come to pass. All actual changes, whether faster, slower, or in long periods of time (to make Braudel's categories more precise), thus remain tied back to the variable interaction between repetition and singularity.

This would then allow us to distinguish between what in our so-called *Neuzeit* (modernity) is really new—that is, repeats nothing of what was earlier the case—and what was actually there previously and has returned in new form. And finally we can thereby also determine the kinds of durable structures that distinguish all human histories regardless of the time period or cultural realms in which we situate them. Formulated even more generally: we may ask what is specific about all people, what is specific about only certain people, or what is specific about only one single person. Diachronicity would then stagger itself in overlapping sediments, which would then enable manifold associations that cut across the conventional historical epochs. Depending on the ratio between repetition and singularity, we could then pluralize historical epochs without falling prey to more or less vacuous periodizing categories such as "old," "middle," or "new." For we cannot derive what is old, middle, or new from these terms. But these formal ratios of repetition and singularity posited here do offer substantive classifications that are well suited for disposing of the traditional three epochs that organize our Eurocentric textbooks and constrict our professorial chairs. We could gain ethnological perspectives that span from preliterate times to our so-called advanced civilizations; inter- and innercontinental comparisons would be called for that describe ethnogenesis as well as the migrations, mixing, and melting together of different cultures and units of action—all the way to the economic, ecological, and religious challenges, the rifts and fractures that span across our entire globe and that all cry out for alternative courses of action. In short, all specialized histories would be called upon to deliver their contribution to our common world history. Historical anthropology is suited, at any rate, to open up vistas in this direction.

Before we come to empirically enriched structures of repetition, I might offer two explanatory warnings. First: A structure of repetition has little or nothing to do with the traditional doctrine of cyclical return. The cyclical model reduces possible repetitions down to a linear, irreversible figure of sequential unfolding that is teleologically programmed (this is the case all the way to Spengler and Toynbee). From the perspective of a theory of time, this model is barely distinguishable from a linear model of progress, except that it is directed, quasi-decadently, back in upon itself. This applies to cosmological doctrines of cyclical return, in Plato or for Leibniz with his *apokatastasis panton* [restoration of everything], without accounting for these theories in their entirety. And it applies to Polybius's doctrine of cyclical return, derived as an ideal type from Plato and Aristotle, which viewed all conceivable and humanly possible constitutional forms as unfolding out of each other over the course of three times three generations.

In contrast to this comparatively simple (and hence easily grasped) doctrine of return, "structures of repetition" aim at conditions for individual events and their consequences that are always possible and actualizable to varying degrees, but that only ever recur situationally. A stochastic [randomly determined] theory of probability may draw on these kinds of ever-present possibilities, but their realization is always dependent upon an unknown series of coincidences. A given singularity can be explained in this way, or, as it were, made probable.

A second observation should caution against causal correlations. All historians can conjure up causes for every event, as many as they like or as public approbation allows them. Our conceptual model aims at an aporia that opens up between the repeating conditions of possible events and these events themselves, including their acting and enduring persons. No event can be completely and sufficiently derived from synchronic conditions or from diachronic preconditions, no matter whether these are economic, religious, political, psychological, cultural, or whatever else. There are countless (synchronic) conditions and (diachronic) preconditions that are not reducible to regularities, which motivate, occasion, enable, and limit the concrete actions of agents, who contradict or compete or struggle with each other. Indeed, the mere plurality of open realms of action [*Handlungsspielräume*] of those involved forbids the invention of unilinear or determining chains of cause and effect (apart from heuristic reasonings). It is the structures of repetition themselves that always at the same time contain both more and less than what comes to light in the occurrences.

Structures of repetition therefore do not attest to any simple recurrence of the same. And structures of repetition condition the singularity of events, but do not explain them sufficiently.

In a second pass through this topic I would like to survey structures of repetition that are staggered at varying depths: (a) extrahuman conditions of our experiences; (b) the biological preconditions of life we share with animals; (c) structures of repetition unique to humankind, that is, institutions; (d) structures of repetition embodied in singularly occurring sequences of events; and (e) linguistic structures of repetition, within which all previously named repetitions or repeatabilities were generated and recognized, and within which they are still generated and discovered.

(a) After having started with human sexual [*geschlechtlich*] needs, we might expand our view to include the natural preconditions that make human life possible, independent of human action. We should first mention the cosmos, in which the orbit of the earth (which turns upon itself) around the sun as well as the orbit of the moon around the earth structure our daily life in regulated recurrence. The turn from day to night, as well as the seasons north and south of the equator, determine our rhythms of sleeping and waking along with our work life, despite all technological advances. Climatically variable, the sowing, harvesting, and rotation of crops depends upon the regular orbits of our planet. Tidal patterns, but also shifts in climate going back to the Ice Ages, which themselves were experienced in a historical manner, remain embedded in the recurrent paths of our solar system. The primary experiences of all known historical cultures are identical or similar in this regard. And one of their first efforts, across the globe, consisted in the measurement of the planetary orbits in order to create calendars—the precondition for the ritualized or rationalized rules for repetition that help give order to our daily life.

Up to the eighteenth century, this cosmos, whether conceived of as created or eternal, was considered to be stable, such that temporally neutral laws could be derived from it or read into it. Of course, with the historicization of the traditional study of nature (*historia naturalis*) and its transformation into natural history—beginning with Buffon and Kant—the temporal status of all natural sciences investigating the cosmos changed. Even the natural laws themselves have come to be located on a continuum between their beginning and possible end. Cosmology, physics, chemistry, biology, and likewise anthropology all need their own theories of time in order to correlate individual hypotheses about courses of events with relevant structures of repetition accurately and adequately. In the meantime, Herder's metacritique of Kant's formal conception of time as a nonempirical precondition of all experience has expanded its reach to apply to all sciences: "Actually, each changeable thing contains the measure of its time within itself; this would exist, even if no other thing were there; no two things of the world have the same measure of time. My pulse, the pace or flight of my thoughts is no measure of time for others; the course of a single river, the growth of a single tree is no meter of time for all rivers, trees, and plants [. . .] there thus exists (one can actually and boldly state it) in the universe infinitely many times at the same time."[3] As Herder conceived of it following Leibniz and in anticipation of Einstein (and as Friedrich Cramer has described it from the perspective of the philosophy of science),[4] the relativity of time within the spectrum of multiple times requires new and unique definitions of the relation between repeatability and singularity for each realm of knowledge and experience, in order to be able to analyze processes that in each case are different from each other, even if they depend upon each other.

(b) The more paleontology has extended back into the depths of billions of years, approaching cosmogenesis, and the more the microprocesses of biological and physical chemistry come to be imbricated, all the way to genetic engineering, the more biological, animal, and human natural history come to be intertwined with each other, however much they remain distinguishable.

Numerous repetitions belong to the biological pregivens of human nature, which we share in varying degrees with many animals. The difference of the sexes, reproduction, birth and death, but also the killing not just of prey but of one's own species, all the different ways of satisfying basic needs, above all that of hunger, which lead to longer-term planning—we share all of this with many animals, even if humans adapt and rework these fundamental processes culturally.

Three formal fundamental determinations can be added here: above-below, inside-outside, and earlier-later, which set each and every human history into motion and thereby propel the temporal realization [Zeitigung] of events. These, too, are preprogrammed in a quasi-natural way.

Demarcations between inside and outside constitute all animal territories, but they also fulfill the minimal requirement for human needs to differentiate themselves from others in order to becoming and remaining actionable. Over the course of history, boundary determinations have multiplied and overlapped all the way up to so-called globalization, which itself calls forth new internal differentiations on our common globe.

The hierarchy-producing determinations of above and below—the pecking order, in animal terms—come to be transformed in all human constitutions and organizations even if these aim to secure equality and freedom for all involved. Only direct democracy as the rule of all over all has never been realized.

The tension between earlier and later is predisposed naturally in sexuality and the genealogical line that follows from it. However much natural, social, and political generational cohorts differ, they remain embedded in the naturally given difference between entering earlier or later into particular units of experience or action, which gives rise to the sequences of action. Animals and humans obviously make use of the tension between childhood and youth and old age in quite different ways, but this tension contains at least some minimal natural commonality that harbors all conflicts and their chances for being solved for human history.

Inside-outside, above-below, and earlier-later are thus each determinations of difference that both animals and humans can intensify into radical oppositions; in their formal structure they characterize structures of self-organization and capability of action, structures that continuously repeat themselves while generating singular sequences of event. To this extent they indicate the biologically conditioned basis of historical anthropology.

If ever more novelties, of which one could only dream in the past, emerge in the meantime thanks to science, technology, and industry, the relationship between innovation and repetition might in fact shift in a modern [*neuzeitlich*] way, so to speak. In that case, we would have to relativize the previously valid insight of Rahel Varnhagen: "We have no new experiences; it's just that new people have the old experiences."[5]

(c) Even if modern inventions evoke truly new experiences, the tension between innovation and repetitions will never be done away with. Only the determination of their relation changes over the course of history. This is something that [human] institutions evidence. They are based on structures of repetition generated solely by humans. We might allude to a few here:

Work (upon which the young Marx based all history) depends upon learnable and teachable repeatabilities. Learning techniques for a craft feeds on a model to be imitated, that is, repeated and practiced. For millennia, rural work remained embedded in comparatively stable geographical and climatic conditions, and hunters and farmers were forced to come to terms with them in different ways in order to survive. The transition from farming and manual labor to machine-based, industrialized, and capitalized production generated structures of repetition, once more and in a quasi-artificial manner, structures that were in effect in advance of the individual product. Ever since, every empirically given individual case is preceded by planned productivity that is in need of being increased. Assembly-line work and automatized and electronic production of individual products feed on the repeatabilities embedded in each individual production facility—as well as on the chances for market profit that have been projected on the basis of the past and that thus call upon a minimum of repeatability. The expansion from the *oikos* [household] to *Oikonomie* [economy] in a territorial, national, or global framework thus reproduces ever-renewed conditions of repeatable continuities, without which every economy would disintegrate.

Law [*Recht*], like all institutions, feeds on its repeatable application. Justice and the rule of law can only be realized if a law brought to bear in one instance is applied again. Otherwise pure arbitrariness would reign, no matter who carries it out. The minimal amount of necessary trust in the law is predicated upon its repeated—and for that reason expected—reapplication. Here, of course, the entire course of history teaches us that again and again, from case to case, new legal findings and new legislation have been called for. And a shift occurs with the beginning of our "new," modern era, which increasingly grants legally effective ad hoc acts and sovereignly proclaimed laws vis-à-vis traditional or long-established rules of laws or customs, which may have been in effect for decades, even centuries. Our accelerated conditions of life evoke prompt legal acts, but also acts that are valid for ever-shorter periods of time, and their increase ensures less and less justice. At the same time, the realm of law only remains secure and capable of guaranteeing justice if a core standard for reapplying laws allows for the incorporation of all newly appearing individual cases.

The same applies to all other social institutions that shape or regulate our daily lives. Religious dogmas must remain (relatively) stable in order to remain believable. If their repeatable proclamation is withheld, the congregation or Church will fall apart, as long as their faith is fixed dogmatically. The same applies to all rituals and cultic actions, which must be repeated regularly to remain effective.

We can mutatis mutandis identify a similar reciprocal relationship between the program committed to by a political party or ideological organization over time and that party's concrete, singular actions. Without repeatedly stating its goals, the party would lose its efficacy and believability and thus its electability.

And certain dictates meant for constant repetition are legally prescribed, such as those that protect individual laws in constitutional law from being changed as such require their repeated application. In our [German] Basic Law, these include the respect of human dignity and the guarantee of the federal separation of powers.

But in parliaments, parties, companies, and businesses, the prescription of rules of procedure likewise belong to the constant temporal pregivens that are necessary for unique decision-making processes to be made possible and set in motion.

Transportation and media sectors have likewise come to be characterized by a similar interplay, which has become increasingly precise over centuries. The designation of the budget and timetables dependent upon it ensure that service recurs on a regular basis over the course of the year. All modes of transportation by land, by water, and by air are operated in this way, and if possible coordinated with each other so that they can all be used continuously. The death notice brought to you in the morning by a mail carrier is singular, but the fact that he or she can bring this message at a regular time is dependent upon the regulated recurrence of transport and delivery.

Of course, the telegraph, telephone, and computer have put control increasingly into the hands of individuals, but the entire electronic network continues to enable the continuous and recurrent ability to be contacted or to contact others. Communicative repeatability has thus been fused with the sum of individual services. It is via interpersonal communication rather than the transportation sector that synchronic preconditions increasingly converge with singular communications. For both the sender and receiver, a picture and message sent via mobile phone is identical to the simultaneous event, an event that only thus comes into existence.

(d) If thus far we have thematized synchronic conditions of possible events whether these be external, non-human pregivens, whether they apply biologically and thus equally to both human and animal, or whether they are generated purely in a human manner, by institutions, I would now like to add several diachronic preconditions for the unfolding of events. Indeed, it may be surprising that even events—which by definition presuppose or generate their own singularity or even utter uniqueness—have repeatable regularities. In his comparative anatomy of the English, French, and Russian revolutions, for example, Crane Brinton has provided graphic models of process that demonstrate the diachronic repeatability of similar kinds of events.[6]

I would like to add three examples. They are related to prophesy, prognosis, and planning. In each case we are dealing with projections into the future whose power of proof depends on the repeatability of earlier procedural sequences.

Prophesies may be drawn from astrological calculations of repeating constellations of recurring planetary orbits, whose astral consequences are then incorporated into personal or political diagnoses. Or prophesies rest upon the text that has been biblically revealed once and for all, a text from which a system—mediating the Old and New Testaments—of apocalyptic or shorter-term expectations was derived that was pieced together over centuries and that could be readily called upon, that is, repeated. The law of the repeatability of biblical expectations rested upon the belief that with every unfulfilled prophecy, the probability increases of it coming to pass all the more certainly in the future. Non-fulfillment in the past made the prophecy's fulfillment in the future all the more likely. In this way, even failed prophecies retained their increasing claim on future realization. This theological *manifestatio Dei* in history led from Bengel and Oetinger to Hegel's *Phenomenology of Spirit*, and finally to Marx's and Engel's *Manifesto of the Communist Party* and their constant, infallible certainty about the final victory in class conflict. Of course, after one and a half centuries of ersatz and supplemental prophesies added on after the fact, this certainty has by all accounts melted away.

Prognoses are fundamentally different from prophetic statements, even if, from the perspective of the history of experience, they are based on prophesies or remain entangled with them. For a prognosis is directed at singular political, social or economic events in the future. These events may occur or they may not. Prognoses are directed at future events, which, as imminent actualities, can only be validated once. All alternative variants dissipate with the arrival of the events themselves. In Leibniz's terms, we are dealing here with a singular truth of fact, a *vérité de fait*—in contrast to the *vérités de la raison*, which remain repeatable, that is, durably true.

What is remarkable is that prognoses that aim for singularity must also thematize repeatable preconditions that themselves are likewise directed toward a possible future, that are not exhausted with the arrival of individual events called forth by individual persons. At stake, then, alongside countless other types, is a repetition prognosis about basic conditions [*wiederholbare Bedingungsprognose*]. Take the following example:

After his bloody defeat at Kunersdorf in 1759, Frederick the Great wrote a brief essay about Charles XII of Sweden, whose forces had been decimated exactly a half-century earlier at Poltava by Peter the Great's Russian army. And Frederick deduced an enduring prediction from this: that everyone who advances from western Europe to the east without taking into account conditions of geography and climate will be cut off from his supplies and squander any chance at victory. If Napoleon or Hitler had read this text and had also realized the threatening sequences of actions that were anticipated there, they would have never—under comparable logistical premises—begun their Russian campaigns. They experienced their Poltavas in Moscow and Stalingrad.

It was only the potential destruction of Russia through atomic weapons in under thirty minutes, from Leningrad to Vladivostok that made Frederick's structural prognosis about conditions obsolete, though not entirely: Frederick's warning about overextending the sphere of influence of a European unit of action remains in effect.

Another example is the ability to plan future events that one's own actions are to bring about. These events necessarily take up preceding occurrences, which are thought to contain repeatable preconditions for possible futures. Hitler did not yet seek to unleash a World War II in 1939; rather, he sought to prevent it. He wanted war, but not the war he got. Hitler made the pact with Stalin in order to avoid fighting on two fronts as in 1914. And he was initially successful, all the more as he rapidly achieved the planned revision of World War I on the western front. And after nonetheless triggering the war with Russia, he disregarded the lessons from 1709 and from 1812 and instead sought to extract lessons for his plans from three more proximate events—history, after all, teaches everything, including the opposite. First, Hitler could refer to the years between 1914 and 1917, which led to the clear defeat of the tsarist empire following the two Russian revolutions. Second, he could point to the murder of almost the entire Politburo and the senior Russian generals, which had done away with the ruling elite of the Soviet Union. And, third, the humiliating result of the campaign against undersized Finland begun by Stalin seemed to be further proof of how helpless the Russian military had become. Hitler's initial successes in the Russian campaign seemed to confirm the three key moments he had derived from recent history.

This example should be adequate for describing the structures of repetition at work in rational planning, even if Hitler's war against the Soviet Union (and moreover against Great Britain and the United States) cannot be sufficiently interpreted through mere recourse to reason. Utopian delusion and fanatical terror—directed against the mentally ill, against Jews, gypsies, Slavs, and other people defined eugenically or racially as unhuman—evade the rational criteria offered here for a model of planning.

Our reflections on structures of repetition in history have taken two extreme positions as their point of departure: that neither constant repetition nor continuous innovation suffices to explain historical change. Both positions are necessary, however, in order to be able to circumscribe specific relations of mixture. Two apparently contradictory conclusions can be drawn from this: especially when a situation should be kept stable, the conditions that once allowed this situation to emerge need to be changed as much as possible. And the reverse likewise seems true: that a situation is all the more likely to change as long as the preconditions affecting it remain the same over time.

We might well derive the reason that this is the case from our series of examples. Due to the different speeds of change of what in a chronological sense are synchronous series of events—in the political, military, social, psychological, religious, or economic realms—analytically distinguishable structures of repetition emerge, which then themselves effect the series of events. This results in displacements, breaks, ruptures, eruptions, and revolutions—to stay in the realm of geological metaphors, which is not altogether misplaced given our dependence on the history of the earth.

(e) At any rate, these metaphors lead us to our final question, about structures of repetition in language. Each and every metaphor—in the broadest sense—shows us that both listener and speaker must already be aware of the potential for comparison of a given turn of phrase if it is to be comprehended and transmitted in the first place. The ostensibly nonsensical sentence "Alexander is a lion" is only understood by someone who can follow the comparison, that Alexander fights boldly, bravely, or victoriously like a lion. Regardless of the psycholinguistically and ethnologically multivalent background of this kind of metaphor, it depends on linguistic pre-knowledge and the repeated application thereof in order to be effective. It is impossible to understand a spoken or written sentence that does not have recourse to what is linguistically known ahead of time, to "pre-understanding" in Gadamer's sense. Even novelties, that is, something newly recognized or discovered, can only be turned into knowledge if language as transmitted allows for them to be expressed.

Of course, purely linguistic innovations may be necessary in order to formulate entirely new phenomena as new concepts. The formulaic language of nuclear physics, genetic engineering, or electronics provides evidence of this on a daily basis. But even expressions that are generated purely linguistically, in a manner immanent to language, so to speak, that shift the meanings of neighboring concepts or that might have an effect upon syntax or even perhaps upon the entire linguistic system: even these kinds of linguistically immanent innovations are only successful and can only be understood if they are embedded in the handed-down linguistic inventory and coined in analogy to previous formulations.[7]

The tension between repetition and singular innovation that we have shown thus far in the plurality of histories also characterizes language in the plurality of its geographical, social, historical, and other articulations. But here we should make clear that the change of issues in histories and the change in languages can never be expressed in a one-to-one relationship. The dual-sidedness of each language alone prohibits this: on the one hand, language refers to issues or states of affairs outside itself, on the other, it is subject to its own linguistic regulations or innovations. The two sides relate and to some extent condition each other, but never entirely converge. The world-disclosing referential character of language, on the one hand, and its own internal power of formation, on the other, do certainly stimulate each other: but extralinguistic world histories always contain more than what can be said about them in language—in the same way that, in reverse, either more or less can be said before, during, or after a history than what is or was actually the case.

Following this methodologically necessary caveat, we might venture a few statements that help to illuminate the relation between repetition and singularity in the reciprocal relationship between language and history.

It is certainly helpful to distinguish between syntax, pragmatics (or rhetoric), and semantics, for each realm has its own unique, that is, different, speed of change. Syntax and grammar remain comparatively stable over long periods of time, while semantics is often required to adapt rather quickly, due, not least, to external challenges. But political and military history often accelerate in quick bursts given the hiatus that opens up again and again between the history of issues and of language [*Sach- und Sprachgeschichte*]. Political change, which is always also induced by language (*ex ante*) and registered by language (*ex post*) tends to occur more rapidly than the linguistic change that is potentially contained within political change but that cannot fully keep up with it. It is usually only semantics that is politically colored; even when semantics must conform to propagandistic language, this does not mean that syntax and pragmatics change. One might recall the triumphant semantics of the Nazi era, which was likewise also intoned by pacifist phrases about reeducation after the war, or one might recall the crisp, staccato way of speaking of the weekly newsreel (*Wochenschau*), which lasted long after the German defeat until it was replaced by a new, milder style of persuasion. [Nazi] modes of speaking and the semantics outlived the political, military, and social collapse for a good while. Both slowly died off long after the Nazi system. But despite the slogans spat out by Nazi propaganda, the basic structure of the German language hardly changed in the twelve years between 1933 and 1945. The words themselves are not responsible for their use and their many nuances of meaning, only the speakers are.

A more general rhetorical problem arises against the backdrop of these kinds of temporal displacements between urgent statements about states of affairs and the longer-lasting history of language, a problem for each and every rhetoric that seeks to build upon repeatable arguments in order to have a unique, one-time effect. Heinrich Lausberg has discussed this:[8] rhetorical topoi are overvalued if they are not identified as recurrent and instead misunderstood as singular or new; however, if they are viewed as repeatable, empty formulas, they are undervalued and likewise misunderstood. What applies to rhetoric also especially applies to the entirety of pragmatics: in order to make judgments that are true to fact, one must differentiate between the propensity for innovation and structures of repetition and weigh them against each other. The uniqueness of a particular, successful speech or the uniqueness of a new line of argument are based on the art of calling up and combining repeatable, well-known elements of language so as to present something unique or new. And in the process one must always keep in mind the difference between linguistic structure [*Sprachgestalt*] and state of affairs [*Sachverhalt*]. The order to kill (or the applause accompanying it) or a report about death are not identical to death itself.

Anthropologically speaking, the fact that each person is mortal is a constantly recurring durably valid statement, and this can be expanded upon linguistically as well as in reality—how, why, where someone dies—without language ever being able to capture the singular event of death as such. It is for this reason that semantics, in contrast to syntax, is most commonly and most quickly prone to face difficulties of proof or crises of believability. Language's difference from factual history is ineradicably inscribed into it. In closing, we might recall an exciting example from the history of concepts in German:

In his Bible translation, Luther used the German concept *Bund* [union or league] for the Old Testament word *berith*, meaning God's covenant with his people. This word was a successful neologism of the preceding constitutional history and referred in the collective singular to the institutionalized carrying out of accords between different social estates or within a single estate. In the late Middle Ages this concept took on increased importance in legal language; at the same time, Luther simplified it theologically. A *Bund* could only be established by God, not between humans. This new theological message absorbed the juridical meaning in its entirety. *Bund* thereby lost its status as a constitutional-political term in the language so influenced by Luther, and the Schmalkaldian Bund, as referred to in our school books, never called itself that. It was a pragmatic, worldly alliance to protect the Protestant concession, but it was not a *Bund* created by God. The explosive and revolutionary political theological mixture that was brought to language with the English word "covenant" remained suppressed in Germany. The extent to which the semantics of Bund remained theologically saturated—despite all the constitutional-political and social uses of the word that were implemented in the age of Enlightenment—is evidenced by the task that Marx and Engels received in 1847: to write a "Confession of Faith of the Bund of the Communists." They rejected this theological imperative to repeat. Instead, they formulated a new text impregnated with the future, a text that was to incite and overshadow the coming century and a half: *Das Manifest der kommunistischen Partei.* The confession of faith was replaced by a philosophical-historical manifestation, the divine covenant by a self-consciously and combatively one-sided party that now knew itself to be in league [*im Bunde*] with history interpreted in a philosophical-historical manner.

The century-old semantic force with a theological background was closed off and guided in a new direction through an innovative linguistic convention—at the expense of a simple repetition. Of course, the old German theological lining shone through in Marx's linguistic usage as well. The path of God through history known in advance, a *manifestatio Dei*, likewise lent the new party program its apparently surprising plausibility.

Our final example thus also shows that no innovation, whether linguistic or related to issues of fact, can be so revolutionary that it ceases to depend on prior structures of repetition.

PART III

11

On the Meaning and Absurdity of History

Anyone who ascribes meaning [*Sinn*] to history should also ask what the opposite of meaning would be: is it absurdity [*Unsinn*] or meaninglessness [*Sinnlosigkeit*]? Choosing between these alternatives involves first deciding what is to be conceived of as "meaning." For "meaninglessness" is a neutral expression that avoids the question of meaning, and I am partial to applying this position to history. "Absurdity," as the negation of "meaning," remains tied to meaningfulness [*Sinnhaftigkeit*]. In contrast, "meaninglessness" opens up a different dimension to the one faced by the science of history [*Geschichtswissenschaft*], insofar as the science understands itself as compelled to look for meaning and thus for absurdity in history. In the following we will not ask about the meaning of the science of "history." In other words, the question of the meaning or absurdity of history as an academic discipline [*Historie*] is not up for debate here, even if [that discipline] likes to claim that it can squeeze meaning out of so-called history and deal it out in controlled doses.

I

There is a collection of letters from soldiers from Stalingrad who did not return home but whose messages—almost like obituaries for themselves—were brought back to Germany in the last mailbags.[1]

Goebbels withheld these letters in the hope of being able to edit a selection that would have provided evidence of the heroism of those who had gone missing. Containing a few thousand letters that never reached their addressees, these four or five mailbags have left behind an abundance of interpretations that sought in vain to find meaning in the catastrophe. These interpretations ranged from absolute desperation to sarcastic commentaries and ironic observations, from cynical bons mots of those about to die to lethargic and reticent reports and to signs of humility or deep piety. Abandonment and helplessness dominate these letters, and there are only a few affirmations of the Nazi system, whose calls to persevere dominated the official public sphere. We are thus confronted with a wide spectrum of perceptions of this event that was in so many ways a crucial turning point, an event about which we are now taught by thousands of books, films, or video clips. Today, we are inclined to interpret these events in terms of meaninglessness or even as total absurdity. Yet the eyewitnesses also failed to invest these events at the time and before their death with meaning—the reality of the battle would not allow for it.

Aggravatingly, however, this compelling collection of "last letters" is a forgery. One of Goebbels's propagandists who knew of these letters apparently wrote those that were published himself, which appeared in a volume that went through two editions. His involvement was anonymous, and my attempts to track the forger down have been unsuccessful, because he is long since dead. We need not review all the clues that prove this to be a forgery. What is fascinating is the fact that this forgery was so well received. The clever fiction of the letters went so far as to create agreement among readers that "meaninglessness" reigned in Stalingrad and that those affected by it also perceived this to be the case. The group of readers would seem to have retroactively shared the same horizon of experience that the forger was able to create to great stylistic effect. All ideological interpretations of the propagandistic language of his time fell by the wayside.

In retrospect, only purely military-historical reasoning might be able instrumentally to redeem the "meaning" of Stalingrad. The downfall of the Sixth Army allowed the troops who had become bogged down in the Caucasus to escape over the course of the two months in which the cauldron of Stalingrad was sealed up and annihilated. The deaths of the

Stalingrad soldiers enabled the survival of the troops who were able to escape across the Don River. However, it would be ridiculous to presume that this secondary purpose of the deadly battle provided the primary meaning of Stalingrad.

Today, viewed within the larger context of the course of the war, the battle of Stalingrad is commonly depicted as a peripeteia, a sudden change in fortune, as the beginning of the end of the German world war. To be sure, political and military historians still disagree about whether this turning point occurred prior to Moscow 1941 or whether it occurred long before in the initial decision to embark upon the Russian campaign, even if this was not yet apparent at the time. We need not concern ourselves here with the interesting question (especially as posed by Ernst Topitsch)[2] as to whether the Russian campaign was rationally justifiable, namely, as a preventive strike against Stalin's expansionistic intentions (as part of the horizon of expectation stemming from the German victory over Russia in 1917). Indeed, viewed over the long term, we can locate the turning point prior to the outbreak of war in 1939, for in light of the global political constellation, the beginning already contained the seeds of the downfall. From this perspective, the entire war would not just be meaningless in itself, but would from the start also be absurd [*unsinnig*] vis-à-vis the rational calculations and embellishments. Stalingrad would then become a symptom of a war of aggression motivated by utopian visions, a war that eventually became World War II, and that was instigated for ideological reasons without any kind of political or military rationale. The criteria for meaninglessness would then lie in the ideology critique of Hitler's racist and expansionistic plans that *Mein Kampf* had already openly stated.

Seen in this light, all other interpretations can be conceived of as establishing meaning [*Sinnstiftung*], for example, if they are being grounded theologically. If at any time we transpose events to the ground of theological interpretation, we can attribute meaning to any event, for we can then explain them via theodicean arguments. If a good person is rewarded, it is God's reward; if a good person is punished, it is a warning. If an evil person is rewarded, it is also a warning, for God's decisions can resolve everything in ways not immediately apparent; and if evil is finally punished, then we are dealing with retributive justice. Theologically speaking, then, everything can be interpreted as meaningful, and there is an abundance of these kinds of arguments that accompany all wars. During World War I, for example, Catholic newspapers did not abandon the age-old interpretation that war should be tolerated as God's punishment for human hubris. The consistency of these sorts of interpretations for believers cannot be denied, even if they are not able to deliver any kind of rational arguments in the sense of statements that can be tested or proved methodologically. They remain indisputable for a believer; in Popper's terms, they exist outside of scholarly discourse.

As mentioned above, an additional method of retrospectively applying the question of meaning to the battle of Stalingrad would be to reconstruct the overall military planning. On this account, though, "Stalingrad" would remain the result of a grandiose miscalculation: not just the result of an excessively utopian strategy, but that of a rational error that makes the battle absurd from the very beginning. Anyone familiar with the writings of Frederick the Great knows of the twenty or so pages he dedicated to the history of Charles XII of Sweden, who experienced his own Stalingrad at Poltava.[3] In several short pages, Frederick shows that it was impossible for a European power to win a war against Russia. And if Napoleon or Hitler had read this text by Frederick from 1759, they would have never begun their wars against Russia—despite the contrary experience of 1917, something that Hitler and his generals at least could reference. But Frederick, who was not lacking in tactical and strategic talent, was unfortunately not able to transmit his line of reasoning to his successors. If he had, the deaths of millions of soldiers and, even more important, the murder of millions of civilians would (perhaps) have been avoided.

We might include another question pertaining to the reception history of Stalingrad, one that has taken on new meaning in particular through the *Historikerstreit*: does the extermination of the Jews occurring at the same time illuminate the meaning or purpose of Stalingrad? The question then arises: did Stalingrad intensify or slow down the murdering of the Jews? Indeed, it would seem that Stalingrad only intensified the excesses of extermination, for the *menetekel* [warning of coming calamity] of Stalingrad never once put the brakes on the actions occurring in parallel in Maidanek, Treblinka, Auschwitz, and other similar locations.

If one assumes that the peripeteia of the entire war was already contained in its beginning, one might relate the battle of Stalingrad to the extermination of the Jews. Political zoology determined Hitler's decisions, and Nazi ideology's racial doctrine had a long prehistory. If in the purely military sequence of the war, Stalingrad was the result of delusion, and if the extermination of the Jews was what it has always been outside the confines of that ideology, which is to say, meaningless, or rather, absurd, then despite all their differences, the two have a common root, dating from before the war. They had their common ground in an ideology of salvation, eagerness to make sacrifices and find victims, and the racist ideology of obliteration, which mutually conditioned and intensified each other in the Nazi worldview. Stalingrad and Auschwitz coalesce in this sense, even if the one cannot be derived from the other. They should not, however, be connected causally: Stalingrad was not fought because of the extermination going on in the hinterland; it did not occur in order to make Auschwitz possible.

In his addresses to the German people in the fall of 1942, after having become aware of the gassing of the Jews, Thomas Mann bore witness to the extent to which racist semantics had influenced the educated bourgeoisie. He calls the perpetrators "SS-kaffirs" and "SS-Hottentots,"[4] even though the black uniform of the SS troops was surely not enough to justify the ethnologically despicable metaphors that he deploys. Indeed, the linguistic inventory of the educated bourgeoisie was saturated with such racist clichés, which belong to the web of conditions that made the catastrophe possible.

On the other, Soviet side, soldiers had to cope with the same frost, the same hunger, the same fear, before perhaps seeking some kind of meaning in the battle. Thousands of deserters on the Russian side were executed. Apparently, calls for liberation from the German "pigs" and "barbarians" were not sufficient to influence the life-and-death considerations of the soldiers and convince them not to desert. But the credit column of the liberators was retrospectively structured in such a way that Russian deserters lost their ability to be memorialized—in contrast to [German] deserters. De facto, on the subjective horizon of perception of those involved, the former were naturally also *Frontschweine* (front-line pigs), as the soldiers on the German side called themselves.

In Russia, the reception of the battle of Stalingrad did not in any way proceed in a straight line in accordance with the ideology of liberation, an ideology that was immediately and directly comprehensible. During Stalin's lifetime, there was no comparable cult of liberation in Stalingrad similar to what occurred in the European countries conquered by the Soviet Union. The gigantic memorial grounds in Volgograd were first initiated after Stalin's death: in other words, the rituals that continue to be performed to this day around the victory of the battle of Stalingrad are specifically post-Stalinist. The official message spread continuously up until the end of the Soviet Union established a hierarchy of the dead heroes, and the memory of their names was only selectively preserved. It was not the number of all individual dead that was memorialized, but rather a selection, which was to restyle the dead heroes as heroes of labor. As Sabine Arnold has shown, the victory at Stalingrad was repurposed into a beacon for the struggle of production, for the struggle that was to characterize the peaceful process of communism all the way to its eventual victory.[5] Military jargon refashioned the heroic struggle of the soldiers into a heroic struggle of the workers to increase their productivity, that is, outpace their quotas. This became the primary message attributed to those who were involved in and survived Stalingrad, and it is only with the fall of the Soviet Union that doubts about the meaningfulness of this message could be expressed publicly in the attempt to remember the countless dead from the battle (who naturally continued to be mourned).

Thus far I have extracted several strands of significance from the complex event designated by the name "Stalingrad." In the context of this essay I am only concerned with deriving a few conclusions that might also apply mutatis mutandis to other frameworks of events. This battle only had "meaning" for the Russians in the sense of achieving an intended goal: this was the first large stroke leading to the liberation of their country from the German invaders. However, this could not have been the meaning or rationale of the battle for the Germans, for whom it could only have served the secondary, purely military purpose of easing the burden on the rest of the German army. As soon as the two rivals are asked together about the battle's meaning, it resists any shared answer, save perhaps that of a macabre massacre. Every additional attribution of meaning [*Sinnstiftung*] by those kinds of political authorities that lay claim to a monopoly on interpretation lacks evidence in light of the many hundreds of thousands of deaths. For this reason, meaning in the sense of an entelechy, a teleology *ex post*, or a *causa finalis* that is clearly realized—all of these attributions of meaning can never be derived from the event itself in a way that applies to all participants. And the believability of these kinds of attributions of meaning stands in an inverse relationship to the absurdity of what became an event there, on the Volga. The five decades that have intervened since this event have not been enough to gather up the lack of meaning or the absurdity, no matter whether it was the Russians who styled their victory as a programmatic step on the way to world revolution, or whether in our case the battle occasioned a moral self-critique that certainly comes far too late to give the past meaninglessness any meaning retrospectively. This is the absurd situation in which we find ourselves as a result of the reception history of Stalingrad.

One can thus venture a first thesis, namely, that the history recorded here was in itself irrational, certain tactical and military rational criteria notwithstanding that by nature always offer situational evidence. History in its entirety remains irrational; at best its analysis is rational. The absurd, the aporetic, the unsolvable, the absurdities and everything that defies meaning that we identify in the set of issues related to this battle, one might formulate it all analytically in a concept, and one might also communicate and visualize it all through narration. Indeed, we are in need of narration if we are to visualize the aporetic, if we are ever to make it comprehensible, even if it can never be rationally understood or conceptualized. Understanding only ever rests on *ex post* analysis. To this extent, analysis and narration supplement each other in sharpening our power of judgment, and to make it possible for us to come to terms with absurdity. What additional general conclusions can we then derive from this multilayered history of the efficacy and the reception of this battle that was only ever experienced as singular?

II

Histories themselves are only ever carried out in the medium of the perception of those involved in them. The ideas of the agents about what they should and should not do are the elements, refracted perspectivally, through which histories coalesce. Ideas, formulated intentions, desires, generated linguistically as well as prelinguistically, taking and holding something to be true, all of these enter into the situation out of which events crystalize. What the different agents hold to be real about a history as it arises and is carried out pluralistically *in actu* constitutes the history to come. We are dealing with a mutual perspectivization of all participants involved, all of whom undertook a form of cognitive selection in order to be capable of perception and action at all. As events ferment or occurrences are intertwined, as conflicts pile up and then break through, there is no common reality that can be perceived in the same way by the different participants involved. The history of perceptions [*Wahrnehmungsgeschichte*] is always pluralistically refracted. "History" thus happens by occurrences being scaffolded into something that might later be called a history. One can even go so far as to say that the realities, as they are perceived, are from the start always already mistaken or even false realities in light of what will later actually be the case. The realities that one perceives are never realizable in the way they were perceived because of their perspectival refraction. We are thus dealing with mistaken realities: first, it comes differently, second, not as you think (to simplify Wilhelm Busch). The reality of the occurrences *in actu* consists of mistaken realities.

An extreme, subjectivist thesis that we might derive from this finding could be that every history is only ever constituted by the multiplicity of its perceptions (similarly to the novels of Faulkner). Actual history would only ever be actual to the extent that in any given case it was perceived to be true, held to be true, and on this basis only ever made true.

A further consequence of this subjective hypothesis of perception might also be found in Hayden White's theory that reality exists only in its being linguistically and culturally processed, such that reality can only ever be fixed literarily in the medium of its so-called discourse and thus only ever analyzed rhetorically. On this account, the reality of history would be limited to each attribution of meaning mediated by language. But this would certainly miss what was initially contained in the plurality of the opening situation. Which formerly perceived realities that had helped to create a later reality were repressed, forgotten, or silenced? Which sources still exist and still provide a perspective outside the perception that has continued to progress and perhaps also offer a chance for controlling what actually was the case, in addition or in contrast? Having recourse to the plurality of the histories of perceptions that constitute a history leads us to doubt whether the continuation of just one variant can ever capture the "meaning" of an individual history. Presupposing its meaninglessness is for this reason a better epistemological basis for dealing with what we commonly call history.

But, then, what was, "actually," the case (to modify Ranke)? Presumably not what the sum of the perceiving participants each experienced individually. What actually was the case in situ withholds itself from any question as to meaning. In the case of history as it takes place, we seem to be dealing with a reality that Kant would have described as the thing in itself and could be defined with Schopenhauer as the difference between will and representation. Behind or before or between the levels of perception of those involved, something constitutes itself that is only *ex post*, after the fact, defined as the actual, the true, or the real history. What is in fact the case or the so-called actual history that one speaks of later is thus always something different than the sum of the modalities of action in each respective inventory of experience of the individuals involved.

An additional consideration in reconstructing so-called actual history is what was preconscious, unconscious, subconscious, or entirely unknown to the agents in this history—that is, the historian must examine all of the factors that predetermine or limit a given space of action. At stake are thus the conditions of possible actions that come to have an effect exactly by not being present for the agents. *In actu*, these conditions can never be gathered up or realized. Of course, one is much cleverer after the fact than beforehand. This sentence is only banal at first glance—in fact, it calls into question our very potential for attributing meaning. After the fact one knows more than one could ahead of time, and this finding from the lifeworld brings with it the naïve hypothesis that is all too often deployed in the most abbreviated form of an explanation: *post hoc ergo propter hoc* [after this, therefore resulting from it]. Only someone who always knows better ever makes use of this type of causal explanation attributed to the progression of time, but it does not answer the question as to what, amid all of the plurality of perceptions, the actual history was. What played itself out in truth can only ever be stated when all parties, including the dead condemned to silence, all reciprocally have their say. To this day, all historians still remain subject to the legal rule *audiatur et alter pars* [let the other side be heard as well]. The reciprocity of perceptions that do not match up with each other must be analyzable before one can begin addressing so-called true or actual history.

Actual history is thus always both more and less than what is contained in the sum of the errors, perceptions, or states of consciousness that entered into this history. Here we might quote the Jewish philosopher Theodor Lessing, who was persecuted by the Nazis, fled Hannover, and was murdered in Marienbad in 1933: every history that we analyze as something completed in the past is a *logificatio post festum* [rationalization after the fact].[6] This necessarily presupposes, however, that every history is *in actu* without meaning [*sinnlos*]. The irony or paradox of this idea is thus that actual history first reveals its truth when it is over. In other words, the truth of a history is always a truth *ex post*. It first presents itself when it no longer exists. The past must become past for us before it can reveal its historical truth. Viewed anthropologically, what is at stake is a transposition of the primary experiences of all individuals involved into a secondary science that must start out by analyzing primary experiences and their sources in order to derive a third element, namely, models of explanation that first make it possible to understand the complex structures of a past history. Such an act of research also precedes all attributions of meaning that might—in vain—be sought in causalities that are intended to explain why something occurred in this and not another way.

We must therefore learn to cope with the paradox that a history that first generates itself over the course of time is always different from what is retroactively declared to be a "history." In addition, this difference always opens up anew, for each history that is reconstructed through the science of history is only ever a preliminary grasp at incompleteness [*Vorgriff auf Unvollkommenheit*], because the actual history continues on. The difference between the history that constantly changes from situation to situation and the history that is temporarily fixed or stabilized through historical research contains an unsolvable paradox, inasmuch as it constantly reproduces itself anew.

Our paradox brings with it another question that we need to address. For the criteria of selection through which an occurring event is perceived derive—in terms of a history of the present—from the same inventory of experience that also enters into the argumentation at work in the science of history. Thus the same prejudices that helped constitute the event itself cannot but also become relevant for its analysis. The cognitive-constitutive interests also produce their own cognitive-preventive interests. Objections are repressed into the unconscious and are not allowed to emerge as argument or questioning. In other words, the everyday modes of perception of the lifeworld that continually enter into the constitution of actual histories both make possible and limit the genesis of the history that is retroactively established through research. The difference between the patterns of perception in the carrying out of action and the categories of explanation that analyze action *ex post* thus gives rise to creeping and sliding displacements that are quite difficult to manage methodologically.

To be sure, these kinds of methodological difficulties have first emerged relatively recently. When did the paradox arise that a scientific history must be structured differently than immediate experience, despite the fact that they are always connected in the lifeworld? I would say that in terms of history of knowledge, this tension first emerged in the wake of the transcendental turn that gave history its modern conception. "History itself" is a modern expression that did not exist prior to 1780. Before, there was history writing [*die Historie*], *historein* on the one side and the *res gestae,* the *pragmata,* the occurrences, that is, the actions and the suffering of those involved and those affected, on the other. This terminological opposition persisted from the pre-Christian into the Christian world until it was subverted in the Enlightenment, especially in the German language.

We might briefly elaborate the transformation of this opposition. Beginning with Herodotus, *historein* means "investigating," "questioning," "researching," and "telling about," that is, what the German "to experience [*erfahren*]," "experience [*Erfahrung*]," and "relating experience [*Erfahrung mitteilen*]" refer to. One collects experience by proceeding step by step, methodically, investigating and researching and then communicating or narrating what has been experienced. Like the analogous Greek concept, the German concept of experience primarily remained an active concept of action, and Kant continued to conceive of it in this manner. It was only at the end of the eighteenth century that a more receptive, passive concept of experience came to the fore, a concept referring to what should be taken as an experience because it has come over me. From that point on, the *res gestae,* the *pragmata,* that is, the realm of acts and of action, take on a larger self-sufficiency to which, then, experience increasingly only comes to react. "History in and for itself" or "History itself" comes to be conceivable: it exists prior to all experience and is experienced as all-powerful. History becomes "fate." What once was the realm of human action, activity, and suffering is transformed into a power that manifests itself as necessary and just, in analogy to God. History then coalesces into a collective singular that devours all individual histories. Prior to 1780, only histories of something ever existed, a history of France or of the papacy or of other units of action. Every history had its subjects, which therefore could become the objects of narrating historians.

These histories always still presupposed the difference between activity and action and the narratives about it, but they disappeared in the moment when all-powerful "history in and for itself" came to be thought. The idea that history is its own subject and object alike is a theoretical assumption that first was expressed in German. Semantically speaking, the source of this assumption was German transcendental idealism, which posited reality as the consciousness of reality.

And this, then, is precisely the second meaning of the new collective singular "history," for the modern concept of history absorbs history writing [*die Historie*] into itself. What had been previously separated as the experience and investigation of, research into, and narration of reality now vanished into the concept of history, a concept that up to that point had only meant a given constellation of events but not its interpretation. Narrated history [*Historie*] was subsumed into so-called actual history and vice versa. From that point on, narration of and knowledge about history could not be separated from actual history. Philosophical reflection and reality were brought together in the term "history." In other words, history from that point on becomes alienated via the philosophy of history.

This then leads to certain theoretical ambiguities and imprecisions that helped give rise to numerous political ideologies. French and English were less susceptible to this, because notions of *histoire* or "history" were still primarily understood from the perspective of the rhetorical tradition of narrated histories. In these neighboring languages, history also certainly took on a similar kind of drive to all-powerful "meaning" the way that the German "history in and for itself" did. When Napoleon believed that he was responsible in the face of *histoire*, he was not just thinking about the usual judgment of a future history [*Historie*] that would report on his actions, but also the power that had come to take the place of God: *histoire* conceived of as all-powerful, all-just, and all-wise, and before which one must be responsible as a human being and especially as a ruler. These were philosophical-historical connotations that the premodern concept of *historia* did not yet contain and that flooded into our conceptual usage through the modern concept of history, without ever being thought through theoretically or channeled philosophically. "World history is the Last Judgment [*die Weltgeschichte ist das Weltgericht*]," [Schiller says].[7]

III

Wilhelm von Humboldt insightfully analyzed the transcendental turn that the collective singular of the concept of history signaled.[8] He shows how a modern reflective concept was developed by bidding farewell to the writing of old history [*Historie*]. With increasing distance [in time], reflection on history by contemporaries as it was unfolding demanded that the old histories also always be considered as well. For Humboldt, the conditions of actual history are identical to the knowledge of them. Humboldt thus traces the differentiation between history that generates itself *in actu* and reflection *ex post* back to shared features of experience that provide the foundation for both the events and knowledge about and narration of these events. Their transmission is a linguistic effort.

The idea that history should be thought of both as its own subject and as the object of narration and science arises from the common foundation of experience that can only be articulated in and through language. For this reason, the same history can be thought both as subject and as object; it can be unfolded actively through actions just as it can be experienced and endured. The individual can conceive of history both as an all-powerful subject and as the object of his own activity—in action and in reflection. The different sediments of experience only converge in linguistic reflection and are thus aesthetically conditioned and grounded.

However, the following age of so-called historicism proved to be extremely susceptible to philosophical-historical and metaphysical incursions that presorted and retroactively impregnated the entirety of historical experiences. Working with the pregiven of teleological attributions of meaning [*Sinnstiftungen*] and believing in historical necessities, various parties, classes, or states touted their good conscience, which was historiographically blessed by the interest that in each case guided their particular self-understanding. The difference between subjective perceptions, holding things to be objectively true, and what actually was the case was voluntaristically eroded. The plurality of competing pregivens of meaning [*Sinnvorgaben*] that mutually excluded each other (and that together indicated a common meaninglessness) was selectively coopted, simplified, and posited as absolute in each case to benefit individual interests, like rulers or saints in the past, classes, states, and nations came to be instituted and accepted as pregiven instances of final authority. And these units of action—which each could have been interpreted as scaffolding or epiphenomena via alternative theoretical premises—thrived on confirming that the meaning of history spoke exclusively on their behalf.

The young Nietzsche was the first to develop an argumentative line of attack against all attributions of meaning ascribed to history as such. However, Nietzsche was also not able to extricate himself from the traps that had resulted from the ambiguity of our concept of history. It was almost a provocation that Nietzsche sought in his 1873 text "On the Uses and Abuses of History [*Historie*] for Life" to revalue the concept of history writing [*Historie*] as it had resulted from the classical rhetorical-philological line of tradition. For he primarily spoke of *Historie* and almost only in passing of *Geschichte*, though he made a point of disabusing *Historie* of its longtime claim to be life's teacher. Instead, he reversed the topos *historia magistra vitae* and summarily declared *Historie* to be *ancilla vitae* [ancillary to life]. *Historie* thus became a scholarship-immanent vehicle for its own ideology critique—a non plus ultra of modernity that cannot be outdone, not even by any notion of the postmodern. In view of the concept of life in whose service Nietzsche placed history, it became evident that the spontaneously vital, the unhistorical, and the superhistorical had the same life force as the rest of *Historie*, if not more. With his ideology critique of the concept of *Historie*, Nietzsche thus implicitly bid farewell to four philosophical-historical axioms that had seemed to ground the modern concept of history up to that point.

First, he denied that history in its entirety had any telos. There is no *causa finalis*, no telos that could somehow be derived from so-called history in general. And Nietzsche debunked the assumption that with God no longer serving as the master of history, the divine epithets—being all-powerful, all-just, being purposive and hence meaningful—could be conferred on "history itself." Life, in contrast, knows many goals, and acting in the service of these goals calls upon one to behave directly and immediately, that is, unhistorically or superhistorically—while normal history writing [*Historie*] can only operate as an amplifier of variously pre-layered needs.

A second axiom under attack by Nietzsche is thereby also toppled, namely, the thesis of [history's] so-called necessity. To the same extent that Nietzsche denied that teleology, as a projective determination of purpose, was able to grant meaning to history, a meaning humans were then tasked with implementing, he also rejected the retroactive ascription of a *causa efficiens* to history. For if I retrospectively ascribe a causally conditioned necessity to history, I say nothing about the past other than that it came to pass in the way it came to pass. The additional criterion of a neces-sary "must" only duplicates the assessment of the same state of affairs. Ascribing a necessity to history represents nothing more than submitting oneself to history, to defer to it, in order to promote a supposed necessity. This assumed necessity injects meaning into history that disenfranchises human agents. In contrast, Nietzsche calls for a freedom that evokes a new beginning from every situation, if possible from a *kairos*. This then transforms necessities or so-called practical constraints into determina-tions of boundaries that both limit and enable possible action. This reveals a certain similarity here between Nietzsche and Marx. For the conditions of action that we experience as pregiven are always ones that we humans ourselves produce. Nietzsche thus discards both teleology and causal necessity—here implicitly against Marx—as a philosophical-historical superdetermination of what has already taken place in one way or the other. For an event that takes place does not take place to any greater degree because it necessarily had to take place.

Nietzsche criticizes an additional argument dealing with the attribu-tion of meaning, namely, that of the so-called justice with which history is overburdened. He does not hold back in his mockery of those historians who *ex post* attribute justice to sequences of events and thus ask us to lend a kind of victorious support to their own interests. Not that Nietzsche sought to impede the criterion of justice or the possibility of forming a moral or legal judgment. But if the criterion of executed justice were to be applied to an unfolding history, it then would become evident that this assumption implies its own fundamental injustice. Every experience seems to confirm that history has perpetuated injustices more often than not. Nietzsche then concludes from this that the task of opposing this injustice in the name of justice can only be carried out by especially capable and engaged individuals, by individuals who think suprahistorically, as predecessors to the *Übermensch*, which he later theorized. In the same way as the unhistorical human who is closer to the animal becomes a variant of the unhuman [*Unmensch*], the human active on a suprahistorical level should attempt to exercise the kind of justice in history that is inaccessible to the historical, that is, to the normal human being. However, it soon becomes clear that this strong human or great politician would have to be lenient, practice magnanimity, and let love reign if he wanted to be just. Thus, the traditional catalogue of rulers' virtues suddenly reemerges if justice is to be done on a trial basis under the normal historical conditions.

But an abyss opens up for Nietzsche here, the first step into a tragic situation that prohibits modernity from transforming the Furies into the Eumenides. Nietzsche can no longer trace this kind of encoded message of mercy: whoever seeks today to realize love, magnanimity, and leniency becomes enmeshed in the meaninglessness of failure. Even the pregivens of meaning that determine just action bring with them the suspicion that they will end in absurdity. Nietzsche thus unburdens the concept of history of any modern attributions of meaning in order to replace it with a concept of life that is free of meaning [*sinnfrei*], and in whose service he places history writing [*Historie*].

This does not make Nietzsche into an ideologue of biology, however. For his fourth critique of historical sense making [*Sinnstiftungen*] takes aim at metaphors of aging. Nietzsche avoids metaphors of aging for peoples or ages in order to resist the necessities of procedural unfolding contained therein. It is part and parcel of the tropes of applying ages of life to history that those engaged in such definitions like to associate themselves with youth in order to then attribute to others or the enemy the necessity of early aging and thus the certainty of premature death. All determinations of age are thus occupiable by ideology and are mutually interchangeable, depending on perspective. Fontenelle was the first to decouple human history from metaphors of aging.[9] If history reaches a certain level of maturity and reason, it starts to function as if independent from earlier stages of life. Fontenelle thus opts for self-determining and self-generating reason, which leaves behind all previous developmental stages—here he is a forerunner of Hegel, though purely on the semantic level. Measured on these terms, even Nietzsche was inconsistent to a certain extent, for he too made use of metaphors of aging, especially on behalf of the youth whom he encouraged, with help from the critique of history writing, to achieve suprahistorical self-reliance and independence. But Nietzsche undertook this by doing without any kind of biologistical reinterpretation of universal history slanted in the direction of decadence or maturity. Overall, he strove to use of the concept of life, which arched over the concept of history, in repetitive and not linear and diachronic ways. New beginnings can occur at any time.

But Nietzsche does not extricate us from the paradox in which he too was caught as a result of his reliance on the ambiguous concept of history. By placing *Historie* in the service of life—*historia ancilla vitae* instead of *historia magistra vitae*—he was able to relieve the superconcept of history from being burdened with meaning, and he certainly did not withhold his sarcasm in criticizing ideological formulas, which he was able to read as self-deception and as the harbinger of coming catastrophes. But just when *Historie* is downgraded to the servant of life, all of the problems of which Nietzsche had absolved history return through the back door. For the concept of life, too, evokes questions of purpose and thus of meaning. If extrahuman life, animal life above all, is subject to the guarantee of innocence and freedom from meaning, then our paradoxes continue to reproduce themselves as soon as the concept of human histories is incorporated back into the concept of life. Nietzsche's concept of life was not able to resolve the ambiguity of the transcendental doubling of history, both as activity and actions and as perception and knowledge.

Nietzsche's true achievement can be found in the epistemologically justifiable excavation of a pluralistic field of action that can only be analyzed devoid of pregivens or attributions of meaning. The need for meaning is no guarantee that what happens in and through us is meaningful in and of itself. Every historical statement remains philosophically historically malformed as long as its justification is unwittingly taken from metaphysics, religion, or theology. In the realm of what empirical science can determine within the range of its own theories, every creation of meaning remains partisan and always is an attribution *ex post*. It follows, then, that meaning for one person cannot be the same meaning for another person as long as humans continue to act—notwithstanding converging or common interests or intentions. History is composed of a multiplicity of meanings [*Vielsinnigkeit*]. There is no "history in and for itself," no "history in general." This construction is itself a glue trap that we set linguistically and that we get stuck in as long as we impute to others the meaning that we have evoked for ourselves. To be sure, this does not imply (to return to Nietzsche once more) that we are not allowed to make use of moral categories that invoke meaning. But to claim that history itself is an executor of morality remains a grand illusion—as Karl Löwith has shown—that is taken from the Christian idea of salvation and injected into the modern philosophy of history.[10]

In closing, we might remind ourselves of an example invoked by Paul Ricœur, namely, Franco-German reconciliation in the twentieth century.[11] It is impossible that François Mitterand and Helmut Kohl shaking hands at Verdun was the purpose or meaning of the mass slaughter of 1916. To suggest that hundreds of thousands of people had to kill each other in order to make a kind of understanding possible on this blood-soaked ground of mass murder is nothing other than retroactively imposing teleological meaning onto constellations of events that had been experienced by those involved as increasingly meaningless. Franco-German reconciliation is certainly sensible [*sinnvoll*] in and of itself, but it should not be derived from the battle of Verdun, either as a historically necessary result or as its moral meaning. History does not provide aid for those seeking psychological plausibilities, unless—and this is Nietzsche's unresolvable contradiction—it is instrumentalized. As soon as history writing is functionalized or even enslaved to the cause of life, it loses all autonomy and proof of rational evidence. In this case, history writing too can be paid off and politicized as an amplifier of meaning.

With Kant, we might well want to justify teleology *ex post* in a hypothetical manner. For history then behaves as if fulfilling secret intentions of nature,[12] such that the bloody conflict between the Germans and

French served the end of making possible lasting peace, "perpetual peace," as it were. For Kant this teleology was still something to be elaborated hypothetically and argumentatively, whereas for Hegel, it became a statement of fact: the "cunning of reason"; the reason of history directs and surpasses all individual human capabilities and actions.[13] Along this line of thinking, one could go so far as to claim that the meaning and purpose of Verdun was to force the Germans and the French to come to an understanding. To translate the absurd mass slaughter of hundreds of thousands in the space of several square kilometers and in just a few weeks into meaningfulness is truly to declare the absurd itself to be meaningful. This certainly surpasses the experiential ability of our generation. Absurdity having become event, it should not also receive some kind of absolution via attributions of meaning after the fact. The invocation repeated by war memorials that those who fell may not have died in vain has in mind a different death than the death that we must mourn today.

One final observation on this point: reconciliation between Germany and France was easier to attain because both countries fought with the same weapons. Reciprocal mass murder was carried out according to the principle of *do ut des* (I give that you might give). The give and take was based on reciprocity, even if no single death allowed for retributive justice. This kind of relation fundamentally no longer applies with the Germans and the Jews. For where mass executions and mass exterminations eliminated innocent civilians, entire peoples, or parts of the population, no reciprocal equality inheres the way it still did, despite all the mass slaughter, in World War I between Germany and France (and the British Empire, Russia, and the United States). It would be completely absurd to interpret Auschwitz as meaningful because it led to the founding of Israel, something that Eichmann's prosecutor was prone to suggesting.[14] To use the acceleration of the founding of Israel as a case for the meaning of Auschwitz would be the epitome of documented absurdity, for it would effectively document and codify absurdity itself.

The costs with which "History" burdens us with its impositions of meaning are too high for us today if we intend to act. Let us therefore dispatch them back to their origins: to the realm of—difficult to bear— absurdity. Instead, we should modestly attempt to do what we ourselves can make possible in a sensible, meaningful manner. And if the results that emerge from conflicting agents and parties do not correspond to what the one or the other intended or expected, these results should not be burdened with the meaning of a self-realizing history. To do so would be to deceive humans about their responsibility to themselves and to others, a responsibility that they cannot, in any case, evade. History is neither a tribunal nor an alibi.

Concepts of the Enemy

All human spheres of life recognize a "here" and a "there," an "on this side" and "on that side." The known and the unknown, the familiar and the foreign organize all experience, however much such boundaries shift over the course of a single life. As soon as individuals gather to act as groups and organize themselves socially, economically, politically, religiously, or however else, "on this or that side" becomes "inside" and "outside." Boundaries solidify, demarcations become socially institutionalized, and rituals or procedures seal and guard forms of entry or exit, from baptism and confirmation to entrance and graduation exams, from the delivery of a document to the granting of a passport. The more such memberships or roles govern the life of a person—as in our industrial society—the more such demarcations of inside and outside overlap. The other can be foreign or familiar, depending on where one encounters him or her: in the family, in the hallway of a shared apartment building, at work, or abroad. Such relations are constantly changing. All of this is well known, and it shapes our everyday lives.

In order to continue to exist, it is just as necessary that all units of action do not simply consolidate themselves internally and close themselves off to the outside, but that they likewise constantly transgress institutionalized boundaries. Without contacts and contrasts, without conflict and compromises, without the building of this or that form of consensus, no group could exist or survive, at least not in our complex society. This applies to groups of all size, significance, and level of intimacy, from romantic relationships to the United Nations. This is also a well-known fact that is instantiated on a daily basis in every newspaper and on every television channel.

These essential inside-outside demarcations first become threatening when they block contacts, inhibit compromises, when consensus-building only serves to stoke conflict, unleash civil or foreign wars, and enable mass murder.

The entirety of history (though not every individual history) can be understood according to the various inside-outside constellations at play therein. A threshold is crossed when the other or foreigner is experienced or conceptualized as an enemy, as someone to be combatted, or when the other is defined as inhuman in order to exterminate him. Whether it is warring tribes or cities; churches that persecute or destroy each other in the name of religion; groups defined as classes or parties that repress or eradicate each other—all of these historical groups are capable of strengthening each other, radicalizing conflict, perfecting murder. This, too, is well known and can be read about in countless history books.

The demarcation between inside and outside always exists and is continuously being drawn in new ways. However, it is only when the other or foreigner becomes an enemy that the bloody path ending—or, put better, temporarily ending—in victory or defeat, in triumph or extermination, opens up. This end is temporary because the history of the survivors continues in contacts, conflicts, compromises, or consensus building, in the minimal conditions for all forms of peace. Put in anthropological terms, what is at stake here are constant pregivens that enter into every history by first constituting it.

The question that this essay seeks to answer, then, is whether and how the other is experienced, perceived, and conceptualized as an enemy. Concepts of the enemy in particular—that is, primarily linguistic creations—will guide us.

One limitation to this approach should be mentioned in advance: the linguistic specifics, the who, where, and why of an enemy are by no means sufficient to create enmity. Psychological dispositions or economic, religious, social, geographic, and political pregivens help generate enmity. Such extralinguistic pregivens are certainly always mediated by language, but they are not initiated by a linguistic act. Language is a necessary but not sufficient condition for fielding enemies, for finding and entering into conflict with them.

And this limited reach of language also applies to the results, that is, to death by violence. Though every form of speech is an action, each action is far from being an act of speech. Killing the enemy may have long been—and perhaps still is—a ritualized event that occurs outside of language, but for us it is solely a form of politically motivated murder, which leaves us speechless. Examining concepts of the enemy thus engages with both the power and impotence of language.

I will proceed in two steps. First, I will sketch the semantic structure of opposing concepts [*Gegenbegriffe*] that generate enmity. Second, I will explore the relationship of preexisting linguistic structures to discrete acts of spoken and written speech, for concepts of the enemy are contained in both, in language as well as in the spoken and written word.

I

Opposing concepts are well suited not only to articulating the self-determination of a unit of action, a "we" opposed to others, but also to solidifying this self-determination as a mark of differentiation. Enmity lurks behind such marks. Barbarians, stammering foreigners, had been marked as enemies long before the Hellenes came up with this name for them. In this and other cases, foreign- and self-determination reciprocally evoke each other. It was in part an achievement of the Greeks to recognize and appreciate foreigners as others. But the low esteem in which non-Greeks were held had many pejorative aspects: the barbarians were wild, less civilized, incapable of having a constitution, even slavish and in need of subjugation by their very nature. Having human relations with barbarians was certainly possible—the Stoics saw such relations as a matter of course and even as prescribed by nature—but exclusion dominated the political use of language. For the barbarians were physically different, ugly, and vicious, and at any rate situated outside of the territory of the Hellenistic and later Greco-Roman culture. As barbarians, the enemies lived at a spatial distance and were of lesser quality, something that was readily apparent to the senses according to the common topos. The "barbarian" is a natural, territorialized, pejorative determination of foreignness that can ground or establish enmity at any time. This concept coalesced at a variety of different moments, in the fight against the Persians, the Scythians, the Gauls, and later against the Germans, the Huns, the Mongols, or anyone else who emerged at the borders and met the pregiven criteria.

We thus are confronted with an astonishing finding: something that had an effect on experience on a single occasion is repeated structurally again and again. New names fill the semantic opposition between Greeks and barbarians, but the barbarians remain. Whether it is the Normans, the Hungarians, the Tartars, the Turks, the Indians, the Russians, or the Germans, the structure of opposing concepts extends into the epithets attributed to the specific barbarians who happen to be approaching at the time. And ever since, there have been caricatures, stereotypical markers are repeated, used interchangeably, and bound together in a tight web of possible variants. Once ingrained in language as an opposing conceptual apparatus, this structure lives on iconically and semantically, always ready to be invoked. Even the self-critical, inwardly directed positive valuations of the brave barbarian, the noble heathen, or the *bon sauvage* that emerge intermittently are identical in structure.

These kinds of opposing concepts tend toward escalation, and this brings us to a new concept of the enemy that began with the introduction of Christianity. The non-Christian is relegated to damnation, only the Christian has the prospect—perhaps even the certainty—that he will be delivered from the evil of this world. The forced alternatives converge, then, in a temporal vanishing line. There are those who are not yet Christians: the pagans, the heathens, the Jews, but also the Hellenes as well as the barbarians—all are addressees of the mission. Indeed, this was how the crusades were motivated: *ubi nunc paganismus est, christianitas fiat.* And then there are those who are no longer Christians, the heretics, the apostates, those who are completely lost (unless—if possible—one burns them so that they might be saved).

Of course, certain theological lines of tolerance can be added to this simplifying sketch. But the exclusion of the not yet converted—even more of the unconvertible—surpasses every territorial or physical determination of the enemy ever attributed to various "barbarians." The enemy excluded on the basis of religion is spiritualized and becomes trapped in an inescapable situation unknown to pre-Christian antiquity.

The unbelieving enemy is blamed for his own extermination, long before worldly execution could or did take effect. The killing of heathens and heretics was therefore not only justified, but even necessary before God. The prospect of delivery and salvation, not simply of combat and sub-jugation, was what discriminated the enemy as unbeliever much more radically than the enemy who is merely a barbarian. The Last Judgment must be preempted as much as possible. Wherever God or the devil are involved, the actual enemy is simply an epiphenomenon of the process of salvation to come.

Who could deny that these temporalized oppositions, once formu-lated as concepts, are then also transferable. The modern revolution to end all domination, and the modern war to end all wars include the escha-tological certainty of salvation, which is unthinkable (despite its secular self-fashioning) without its Christian precursors.

But our modernity brought with it a further radicalization of con-cepts of the enemy. Ever since humanity took the place of God as autono-mous, final authority and was elevated to the status of being both subject and object of its own history, the enemy also came to inhabit new con-ceptual fields.

The enemy of human beings then comes to be the unhuman (*Unmensch*), or, even more radically, the subhuman (*Untermensch*), which are contrasted with the *Übermensch*. To be sure, the unhuman was already available to Stoicism as a concept (a tyrant deserved to be deposed as an unhuman); Christians also used this term to stigmatize heretics, and the self-satisfied Christian could certainly be revealed to be an *Übermensch*.

But the opposing determinations of human-unhuman or *Übermensch*-subhuman radicalize enmity in a language that was previ-ously inconceivable. The barbarian could be naturally or territorially extracted, and the heathen or heretic could be theologically excluded. And whoever was a Hellene or a Christian could also be identified through self-determinations. These communities of action did not live from their exclusionary concepts of the enemy alone, but primarily used their own self-determinations to legitimate themselves.

As for the concept of the enemy that is semantically based on the "human" as such: the unhuman is a blind formula [*Blindformel*] into which each can plug the other so as to prove their own credentials as a human. This achieves nothing more but also nothing less than to recognize the enemy as a function of one's own intentions or interests.

And the subhuman is fully subject to the whims of those who, *per negationem* of the other, establish themselves as a suprahuman. We are thus dealing with empty formulas that can be occupied by a variety of ideologies; being defined into such a formula robs the other of the possibility of being an enemy. He is forced into a position below the bare life of human possibilities, he is literally dehumanized, turned into potential nonexistence, "unworthy to live [*lebensunwert*]," and thus devoured.

Thus far we have described three different thresholds that must be crossed in order to even conceive of the other as an enemy or to think of him or her as an enemy in a new way. For centuries concepts of the enemy have accumulated and been radicalized: from barbarians to heathens and heretics to un- and subhumans. I refrain from mentioning the concrete names to which these concepts of the enemy have been fixed. These names are too many to count empirically, but the semantic structures through which the other is first conceptualized as an enemy persist, are transferable, and are capable of being translated into all languages.[1]

We should, however, be careful not to view these opposing concepts, in their single-minded and one-sided oppositional structure, which always excludes the enemy effectively and pejoratively, as historical reality itself. The reality often looked different and was usually worse than the semantics of concepts of the enemy can ever make apparent.

But we might be allowed one conclusion here: however actual events and enduring is experienced, and however it is interpreted *ex post*, in the unfolding of the events themselves, history only ever occurs in the way that it is perceived and grasped by the agents involved. Certainly, every event is induced and at times even guided by concepts of the enemy deployed in reciprocal fashion, even when it later becomes clear that the concepts of the enemy were based on misapprehension, illusion, or self-deception, on good faith or unquestioned premises. In fact, the other is usually different from what the antagonistic concept purports him or her to be. Whether the other is worse or better remains an open question. Indeed, the efficacy of concepts of the enemy lies precisely in how they mistake the other.

II

For this reason, and in conclusion, we should attempt to evaluate the roles played in semantic opposing structures by preexisting or pregiven language and concepts. Concepts of the enemy are not created overnight, they are preconditioned, and yet they are formulated in singular moments, *in actu*, and put into action.

First, we must counter the assumption that any pregiven language should as such contain some kind of determination of the enemy. Language certainly plays a role in inclusion and exclusion, for each language is at the service of specific linguistic communities: the ability to speak a dialect, a jargon, or a technical language, mastery of an educated or esoteric language, opens and closes doors for individuals. This is the way we regulate all "we" and "they" determinations and their demarcations between inside and outside required by society. But concepts of the enemy cannot be *eo ipso* deduced from these linguistic pregivens, which are, by the way, learnable.

To make a language as such into a criterion for enmity, it is always necessary to form political will, which might well be based on extralinguistic factors such as economics, religion, society, and geography, but is always politically motivated. The status of a language then shifts, it becomes instrumentalized politically—this has occurred with increasing intensity since the French Revolution. The revolutionaries' political usage of language turned the ability to speak French into a defining criterion for implementing the laws of liberty and equality and fraternity. Saint-Just, for example, called for renaming Alsatian towns with the names of French soldier-martyrs so as to elevate the poor citizens still trapped in their regional dialects to the level of the achievements of the revolution. This was only a prelude to later events.

In comparison, Herder's discovery of linguistic nationalities was still a pre-political act. In contrast, the creation of the German linguistic people by the intellectual resistance fighters against Napoleonic occupation became a political action. Without any unity on the level of political constitution, the German language as such became construed as the medium of self-determination and at the same time—with Arndt, Fichte, and Jahn—as a supposedly pre-political and therefore eternally valid criterion of exclusion vis-à-vis the French enemy. "The language of the German people in opposition to the language of civilization as the criterion of hereditary enmity": this is the short version of the formula that would continue to be transmitted for over a century. Those who make their own language into a singular criterion for self-invention isolate themselves, and find themselves faced with a "world full of enemies," as the Germans then were forced to experience in World War I. What's more, they made themselves into their own enemy.

It is the signature of European modernity that languages themselves—not just ways of speaking—have been instrumentalized and turned into modes of inclusion and exclusion of political units of action. The consequences are well known. I will name just three. After World War I, the Flemish gravestones of Belgian soldiers were destroyed because they were not inscribed in French. In South Tyrol, Germans had to be buried under Italian inscriptions. And at Christmas 1935, Goebbels ordered that the names of all fallen Jewish soldiers be purged from all war memorials. In each case, enmity reached beyond death, seized the dead in order to do away with their identity and (in the German case) prove their nonexistence. And again, as we know, this was only a prelude to later events.

Of course, it is not sufficient to trace the catastrophes of the twentieth century solely back to the political invention of linguistic nationality [*Sprachnation*]. But this criterion for exclusion did certainly add to determination of the enemy that had seemed unalterable previously. For this is authentic evidence for the fact that those who are excluded as enemies are made guilty of something for which they cannot take responsibility, namely, the ability to speak a specific language and bear their own name. The heretic lurks behind the barbarian, the unhuman behind the heretic, and behind the subhuman—the nobody.

Clearly, one can offer many counterexamples to the claim that language per se generates enemies. Most civil wars—and perhaps the most brutal ones—have been carried out where both or all parties employ the same language to define each other as enemies and justify murdering each other. It suffices to consider the age of religious civil wars or, more recently, [the fate of] Yugoslavia. Reds and Whites in Russian, Republicans and Royalists in French, Protestants and Catholics in German, Serbs and Croats in "Yugoslavian," the North and the South in the United States in

American—they all killed each other with help from concepts expressed in the same language.

It is the political instrumentalization of languages that creates enmity, not the languages themselves. Put more precisely, it is the semantic oppositional structures manifest in all languages that call forth each concept of the enemy. Once stored away in the linguistic inventory, they both enable and limit perception. Concepts of the enemy remain available to be called upon, whether reflectively or unreflectively, but at the same time they become nets in which speakers get themselves caught. Strictly speaking, we are not dealing with concepts capable of grasping the other, even as enemy, but instead with stereotypes that can be called upon and implemented. Yet the reality of murderous events undercuts language. The German-French writer René Schickele formulated the extent to which concepts themselves break down. As a bilingual Alsatian, he was recognized neither by the Germans nor the French throughout his entire life, and he found himself forced into conformity "for the first time" at the outbreak of war in 1939 under the pressure of the pact between Hitler and Stalin. In 1940, two weeks before his death, he wrote to Thomas Mann opting for the French side even if it meant defeat. "The world is separating into two camps, and that is good. These camps will step forward ever more clearly, ever more powerfully, and, because it is not worth it to continue living when anti-spirit [*Ungeist*] is victorious, it will become a frightful battle of life and death above and beyond all concepts that we have previously applied to similarly decisive historical battles. The battle will have to be fought *extra muros et intra*. It is *worldwide civil war* [*Welt-Bürgerkrieg*]."[2]

The most notorious German orator of the twentieth century offers proof of this. [Hitler] devoutly adopted the *völkisch* vocabulary that he found in books, pamphlets, and brochures in the nineteenth century's wastepaper basket. After devouring the entire vocabulary salad of the autistic language of awakening and salvation, he then cynically reproduced what he had read in a rhetorically adept and calculated manner. His clichés put each and every oppositional concept to ideological use: the Aryan versus the Jew, the supreme value of the German people versus the deficient neighboring peoples, the Nordic race versus the Russian subhuman, and so on. The concept of the enemy reaches its full potential reality only in oral speech—we know how this is done.

What does this mean then, for us, today? Three minimum conclusions suggest themselves: Caution in the face of all stereotypes, for they become conceptual cages that obstruct thinking and impede action. Caution in the face of every dualism—fictive enemies lurk behind it. And, finally, let us use the language of others. It will hinder us from setting out upon the futile search for a German identity. This is something that we can only have when we know the other, a first step toward mutual recognition. And then, presumably, the other will not be an enemy.

13

Sluices of Memory and Sediments of Experience: The Influence of the Two World Wars on Social Consciousness

Everyone experiences breaks and caesuras that seem to open up a new chapter of life—shifts that force us to depart from familiar, previous paths and turn onto new, different pathways. New experiences then also force consciousness to work through them. Thresholds are crossed, as it were, changing the appearance of many things (perhaps everything), depending on the extent to which one is affected and one's consciousness thereof. Forms of behavior, attitudes, and outlook change if the experiences are worked through, something that certainly need not occur.

The two world wars brought with them ruptures of experience and shifts of experience for those involved on a scale that had been unthinkable and unimaginable. There can thus be no doubt that the world wars have imprinted the consciousness of all contemporaries. And if it did not in fact change, then one might readily conclude that prewar consciousness had become false consciousness. At this level of generalization, the proposition that both world wars formed the consciousness of those involved seems uncontroversial. The survivors' memories and stories or the silence or the breaking off of their stories speak an eloquent language.

However, if we ask about social, common, collective consciousness, our answer becomes more difficult. For this presupposes a commonality, a collective mentality that is necessarily based on common experiences, on common preconditions of consciousness. The question then arises: how far does this commonality encompassing all agents and affected extend, and where must we distinguish varying levels of involvement and varying preconditions for the formation of consciousness? Not everyone experienced the same war in the same way. For this reason, we must take several analytical steps in order to determine commonalities and differences. First we must differentiate between the wars themselves and their results. Of course, the two are directly linked in the experience of those involved; in particular, the formation of consciousness arises through both the war and the results of war. Moreover, consciousness in particular is the place where war and the results of war meet up. For this reason we must differentiate analytically between the synchronic factors that have an effect in war itself and the diachronic factors that have been brought forth by the results of war.

I. Synchronous Factors in the Formation of Consciousness

1. The *Wartime Experiences*

a. Meanings, modes of behavior, and attitudes, as well as consciousness affected by and reacting to them, are formed by the direct experiences [*Erfahrungen*] that the events of war call forth—by the experiences [*Erlebnisse*] lived through in each case. All experiences are based in *the events*, in which those affected by or active in the war are involved. They may potentially be as numerous as the people who have endured them.

b. The consciousness-forming content of experience, the so-called experience of war must then be categorized and leads to commonalities that should be organized according to more general typical situations or positions. Similarities and commonalities run through all experiential situations, and they likewise establish common positions of consciousness. Here we must speak of structured events or *event structures* that allow us to infer common formations of consciousness. These include the experiences of trench warfare, bomb warfare, life and death in the camps, work in the war industry, or also the experiences that topple the inventory of emotions, from collective psychosis or mass hysteria all the way to the disruption of personal, intimate life, such that the modes of sexual behavior of civil society are rent asunder, the separation of familial relations, the loss of relatives, the homosexuality encouraged by all-male combat units, the invasion of the respective victors, and everything else that social-anthropological data can reveal. In each case, we are dealing with singular events that, taken together, are similarly structured and point to common formations of consciousness.

2. While the events and experiences depicted thus far achieve their common structures through the war itself, *the consciousness with which the events and experiences are worked through is itself preformed.* There is no consciousness that can be isolated as the consciousness of war. Rather, there are numerous socializing conditions from the prewar time period that have a consciousness-forming effect. Indeed, they operate as something akin to a filter prior to the events and experiences in war itself. These preformations prepare the possibility for which experiences can be made and how; they both condition and limit them. Analytical steps are also necessary here, even if on an empirical level these preformations only ever appear as tightly bundled together and difficult to differentiate.

a. One preformation that is especially difficult to transcend is belonging to a specific *linguistic community.* One's language or dialect sorts the possibilities for experience according to pregivens such as linguistic images, metaphors, topoi, concepts, and textualization, more generally the capacity for articulation and for making statements, which all simultaneously form and limit consciousness. There exist collective linguistic pregivens that experiences of war can alter but not completely disrupt.

b. Another set of preformations that are also closely connected with linguistic traditions are *religious beliefs, world views, self-interpretations, and ideological projections* that have been transmitted and that have the power to set free, inhibit, and sort the data of experience. These pregivens give rise to a common inventory of consciousness that can also transcend linguistic boundaries. Lateral constellations then emerge that can even transcend the wartime boundaries of friend and enemy.

c. Equally formative of consciousness is being part of a *political unit of action*. We should first mention the state, to the extent that it forms the most important political collective agent involved in war. Political organizations also belong to this category, which includes parties, organizations, and churches, for belonging to each of these respective groups calls forth collective opportunities for experience and formations of consciousness. Here we are dealing with organizational, specifically military, administrative, or propagandistic conditions that delimit the space of consciousness and that resist being directly controlled by the individuals affected by them. Similarly to languages or ideologies, political organizations—and especially states—have their own individual traditions that precede consciousness. We also must differentiate between nation-states like France and nations brought together in a single state (such as Russia, Austria-Hungary, or Belgium), something that can be altogether decisive for a particular social position of consciousness [*soziale Bewußtseinslage*].

d. Furthermore, we must differentiate analytically between *generations*. Despite all shared experience, the formative power of experiences of war comes in different doses depending on whether one has them in early youth, as an adolescent, as in adult, or in old age. This alters the mode of reception, and it is especially necessary that we judge the history of the effects of the two wars according to the sedimented layering [*Abschichtungen*] of generational experiences that are politically identical but biologically distinct. The consciousness of the veterans of 1870–71 in World War I differed from that of the volunteers of the youth movement, and the same applies mutatis mutandis to the generational conflicts between World Wars I and II. The elite leaders of the SS largely stemmed from generational cohorts after 1900 who believed that they had missed the Great War and whose breaks in consciousness were brought about by defeat, the civil war after 1918, inflation, the failure of parliamentarian democracy, and world economic crisis. Absolute generational divides exist, depending on whether one actively participated in the war or only passively experienced it. And these generational divides affect consciousness formation in different ways in World Wars I and II respectively.

e. Additionally, we must distinguish between the roles played by *gender and family*. Women would have had to experience the war potentially differently than men. During World War I, the tension between the front and the home was experienced more strongly, formatively, and consciously than in World War II. World War I also affected segments of the population and men and women differently. Only with the blockade and submarine warfare did the war become total. World War II was total in every respect: bombing, terror, genocide, partisan war, this all contributed to the leveling of the dichotomy between front and home as well as between gender roles and intensified the extent to which families were affected by the war. Perhaps the two wars and their aftereffects altered the pregivens of traditional gender roles more than ever before.

f. In order to measure a given social consciousness, we must naturally differentiate according to *criteria of class and social stratum.* Belonging to economically or socially conditioned classes leads, whether covertly or openly, to relatively homogeneous consciousness formations, even if these vary in particular groups according to the factors already mentioned above. To these we must add variants pertaining to social stratification, which give rise supplementarily to consciousness formations. Levels of activity or of compulsion in wartime are highly staggered depending on the social setting, conditioned by the class or social stratum in which the war is experienced. This includes residence in the city or countryside, the position in the process of production, possession of the means of production, and the spectrum of occupations, which is not necessarily identical to social class. Here we are always dealing with the economically and socially created net of conditions of different chances for experience, which in all cases play a role in consciousness formation.

All six of these analytical interventions aim to carve out the consciousness-forming factors that precede particular events and experiences of war and their processing. Put in empirical terms, all of these factors are in effect simultaneously, though with differing weight. But this analytical distinction is necessary in order to investigate the change in consciousness as a result of war events and war experience, for the change in consciousness through the wars is carried out simultaneously on all of these levels with different formative power.

3. It is necessary to differentiate these structures of event and experience and the conditioning structures of social consciousness formations

strictly from the *functions specifically and solely determined by war* that individuals carry out and are obliged to carry out specifically and solely in war. The activities called forth by a war are of a very specific nature and they by no means overlap entirely with the structural preconditions in which any given consciousness is embedded.

Consciousness is formed differently in war depending on whether command structures or strictures of obedience predominate. The mentalities of officers, noncommissioned officers, and soldiers are traditionally distinct, even if, generally speaking, the boundaries between them were stricter during World War I than World War II, which in this regard opened up and forced more porousness between the ranks. We also must distinguish between individuals active in planning committees or in the executive branch of organizations important to the war, individuals who worked in the munitions industry or in other industries important to the war or in food production, people, at any rate, who did not face death at the front. Additionally, we must consider areas of forced activity or enduring, which were much more extensive in World War II, namely, imprisonment or forced labor. We also can include the kinds of functions that were intensified in World War II through the totalization of the war effort, namely, functions of policing and the judiciary and of politically motivated party formations, which became active as instruments of terror and mass murder. In addition, there are also functions purely negative in nature, all the way to the meaninglessness of sacrifice, which could no longer be made for anyone in particular, as in the concentrations camps." On the other hand, certain areas of action greatly expanded and intensified from World War I to World War II, namely, resistance movements in one's own country and partisan activity against the external enemy, which forced the recalibration of all loyalties.

All of these functions specifically determined by war and carried out as such naturally have a retroactive effect back upon the structural pregivens of the entire social system from which they derive. But in both wars, and in each case in distinct and intensifying ways, the social system and thus also consciousness formation were altered through these very functions.

The consciousness-forming effect of the wars can thus be found primarily in the concrete events that affected every person or that these events called forth. The kinds of primary experiences traceable back solely to the war only ever come into being through events and their experiences. Such wartime events had common structures that generated similar, repeated experiences, thus giving rise to commonalities in consciousness.

However, all events could necessarily only become factors of consciousness formation by being perceived in a specific, preformed manner. Wartime experiences could only be made and raised to the level of consciousness because they fitted into a grid of historically pregiven possibilities of experience. As noted above, such structures are formed through language, ideology, political organization, generation, gender and family, class, and social stratum. All of these contributed to the formation of modes of social consciousness.

By the same token, all social pregivens were altered by the events of war. The fundamental question, therefore, is which series of factors is of greater importance: was it primarily the pregiven events of the war and their shared structure that altered consciousness, or the handed-down positions of consciousness listed above that formed the experiences of war in their particularity? Even if we concede that some reciprocity is certainly at play here, it does seem possible to measure the difference between the weight of experiences of war and the weight of social preconditions.

To what extent did language, ideology, political organization, generation, gender and family, or class form the consciousness of war, or to what extent did the events of war and their consciousness forming power themselves alter this series of factors? We might answer this question if our second analytical intervention next measures the power of altering consciousness inherent in all the functions that are only present in and solely called forth by war itself, and that for their part altered social pregivens and at the same time gave rise to the events of war. The wars occasioned a functional transformation in society and as a result necessarily also occasioned changes in consciousness that would never have emerged without the events of war.

2. Diachronic Effects of the Wars on Consciousness

War in the technical sense ends when a ceasefire is implemented. This thereby also alters the status of consciousness of the war. Experience of war becomes memory of war. However, memory of the war is not a stable entity that has a continuous, unchanging effect. Rather, it is subject to the results of the war, which might well reshape, repress, channel in short, alter memory of the war. Many things are forgotten, others remain stubbornly lodged in consciousness, like a thorn. Many things are repressed, others glorified. The war yields results that are filtered by the conscious efforts of memory. If we are then to investigate the effects of wars on collective consciousness, we must distinguish between the effects that came about through the war during the war from those that can be defined as a later effect of the war. On the empirical level, we are dealing once more with a continuous process that our investigation can only divide up analytically into different parts. Isolating those effects of war on consciousness that occurred solely during wartime is an exceptionally difficult methodological problem. How is it even possible to isolate war itself and its immediate effects in the constant flow of consciousness? How is it possible to translate memory effects on consciousness or their repression back into the preceding perception of the war now that it is over? All synchronous factors from the first part of our analysis now reappear in their diachronic effect. Schemata of the translation of experience into language come to the fore and retroactively transform the structure of the space of experience of war. New language contents resulting from the war such as ideologies, stereotypes, or slogans overlay or repress the original experiential content of the war. In addition there are all the experiences that people collected during the war without being able to articulate them in language. These have an effect on the attitudes and modes of behavior without each respective consciousness needing to or necessarily being able to account for it. The factors of the formations of consciousness are thus multilayered; they originate simultaneously in the prewar era, in the past of the war itself, and in the consequences of this war, which continue to have an effect on consciousness. It is therefore difficult for a history of consciousness and a history of mentality precisely to identify the threshold that is crossed once and for all when a ceasefire is implemented.

A decisive difference in the history of consciousness is naturally to be found in the direct conclusion of the war, when the threshold of the ceasefire is crossed: do those affected belong to the victors or the vanquished? Even when the world wars gave rise to numerous common experiences as a unified event, the distinction between victors and vanquished constitutes a hard alternative, which channels *ex post* the effects and work of consciousness in distinct ways. It makes a difference whether one has died for a lost cause or for victory; this also applies to the survivors.

But this hard alternative necessarily gives rise to further differentiations, for not every victory remains a victory, nor every defeat a defeat. Some winners in World War I, such as Italy and Japan, were among the defeated in World War II, and Russia, defeated in World War I, was victorious in World War II as the USSR.

The history of consciousness appears differently again if we consider the course of the war itself. For example, there are wartime losers who emerge victorious at war's end, such as the peoples of the Austro-Hungarian and Russian empires who gained their national independence through World War I and the countries conquered by Germany in World War II where the wartime loss of state sovereignty and the subsequent Allied victory were followed eventually by decisive constitutional transformation. This applies both to France and to the Eastern European states.

And finally one must also include the more or less neutral countries whose political identity was not necessarily interrupted by the wars and remained intact throughout.

It thus is not just victory or defeat but also the kind of victory and the kind of defeat that lead to numerous refractions in the formation of consciousness, such that it becomes difficult to define minimal commonalities of collective spaces of consciousness. Identifying similarities or differences in the social spaces of consciousness must thus be differentiated diachronically by inquiring into continuity and discontinuity. Despite similar and hence comparable kinds of suffering, constraints upon the formation of a common war consciousness among the European nations are placed by sluices of experience that are regulated at different paces and different thrusts of experience. In terms of its historical effects, the transformation of war experience through the direct consequences of the war cannot be overestimated. The influence of the October Revolution [in Russia] created new alternatives throughout all of Europe, to which there were many different reactions. These included civil wars and inflation, which in turn created very different flows of consciousness in different countries and social strata and retroactively stylized the consciousness of the past war in new ways. Even the victors of 1918 sought for a half-decade to improve the outcomes of their peace treaties. Following World War II, the Cold War between the East bloc and the West bloc played an analogous role. Numerous primary experiences of World War II were thus repressed in the different spaces of consciousness or stabilized or transposed into new constellations of meaning that could not be easily reconciled with primary experience.

3. The Political Veneration of the Dead and Its Memorials: Commonalities and Differences after the Two World Wars

Millions of people who were killed in battle, murdered, annihilated, gassed, who went missing, died from hunger or epidemics, millions of dead of every age and sex: this is a finding that in the case of both wars is among the primary experiences of those—now a dwindling number—who survived. This finding applies to different countries in the two wars in different ways. But the veneration of the dead is a common response in the attempt to find meaning, if possible, in mass death.

Every dying person dies alone. But organized mass killing leads to commonalities and to differences in how survivors work through the experience and remember the war, and in what follows I would like to sketch these commonalities and differences.

Suffering can be extended, death can be drawn out, but violent death is itself irredeemable. The inexorability of death in wartime is the central primary experience for all survivors. This is the reason why consciousness faces the question as to the meaning of violent death. To be sure, the political and religious gatekeepers of meaning attempted to formulate answers in both world wars. But we cannot examine the efficacy of the press, propaganda, parties, the pulpit, and the lectern here. The extent to which they met with approbation or dismissal is parsed out in as many ways as the national and social systems of the various countries remain distinct from one another.

We might say in advance that the enthusiasm for war in 1914, which was enormous in part, was not repeated in the same way in any country, including Germany, when war resumed in 1939. To this extent, and despite all nationalisms, we can register a decisive transformation in consciousness. The experience of mass death reaches quite deeply and no specific national responses can overcome it.

In what follows I want to pose the more limited question as to the consciousness-forming function played by the political veneration of the dead in France and Germany, in particular via memorials. I therefore do not claim to make representative statements that apply to all countries.

The compulsion to draw meaning from violent death or attribute meaning to it in advance is as old as humans have been able to kill each other in history. The French Revolution represents the crossing of a threshold in this attribution of meaning. Every death for the cause of the revolutionary fight for freedom should be remembered, individually, on memorials. This was the first time in which the political veneration of the dead transformed the death of the soldier into a national cause, distinct from Christian tradition. The decisive issue here was that those who had fallen did so for the same cause of freedom to which the survivors should dedicate themselves. This represents a new, secular, no longer primarily religious cult (even if some religious forms were appropriated) whose purpose was to fuse the past of dying with the future of the survivors into a unified, overarching amalgam of meaning. The political future replaced the Christian beyond as the site of the dead. This function of war and civil war monuments—up to this point there had only been memorials for victory and for generals or princes—continued up to World War II, and this function is one of the signatures of modernity. This call to remember each fallen individual was first issued by the French revolutionaries, but it was also adopted by the nations that rose up against France and Napoleon. The memory of all individual soldiers brought with it a democratic principle of equality, a principle that became established over the course of the nineteenth century in all European states despite their many different constitutional forms. World War I was the high point of this development. Since World War I, memorials have no longer differentiated among officers, noncommissioned officers, and troops (except for memorials for specific regiments): the equality of death becomes the symbol of the political unit of action.

In the soldier cemeteries of all peoples, guaranteed by peace treaty since 1871, it is common to have graves for everyone whose name can be identified. And the mass graves for those who have fallen anonymously are related back to individuals through inscriptions with their names. And those who can no longer be found due to the technology of mass extermination receive their individual inscriptions in the large memorials for the missing. The number of those remembered in this way often makes up almost or more than half of all the soldiers memorialized, as in the battlefields in Flanders, on the Somme, or Verdun. No name could go missing. The political function of soldier cemeteries and memorials for the missing thus fuse every fallen citizen with the identity of the nation, for which the death of these individuals serves as a pledge. In France, the state oversees the soldier cemeteries, while in Germany a nongovernmental organization came to perform this function after the defeats of the two wars. At the same time we can say that following World War I, both countries cultivated the national and patriotic meaning of the soldier cemeteries in the same way. Of course, this has not prevented families from finding ways to give voice to their own private suffering, beyond the claims of patriotism, at these sites of memorialization.

In France, following World War II, the veneration of the fallen soldier faded in favor of the state-organized memory of the dead of the resistance movement. In Germany, in contrast, the prevalent ideology of the war graves commission was downgraded to a form of humanitarian care, with the widespread admonition: "Never again war!" This had not been a guiding motto in the years between the two world wars.

It was a completely new result of World War II that there were mass graves for those murdered in the concentration camps. Although these are similar in number and were similarly useless in a military sense to the mass death in the attrition warfare of World War I, they are unique in every other way. For we are dealing with the murder, the eradication, the destruction of individuals of both sexes without the murdered having any sacrificial importance attributed to or required of them. These memorial sites (which replace cemeteries) thus lose the function of offering meaning, unless it is survival itself that is thematized.

In the concentration camp memorials (and in municipal memorials for the dead in West Germany after World War II) it becomes especially clear that death is no longer understood as an answer and instead only as a question, death no longer generates meaning, instead it calls out for meaning. This is a sign of a transformation of mentality that can also be witnessed in the history of soldier monuments more limitedly after the two world wars.

Among the monuments specifically for fallen soldiers, the tomb of the unknown soldier under the Arc de Triomphe in Paris naturally stands out. The representative death that stands in for all of the fallen of the nation can be found in almost every European country that participated in the wars, aside from Germany. In Germany, there is no central memorial site for either world war, and this is due to the federal constitution. To this extent, the lack of a national symbol of unity is characteristic of the national consciousness of the Germans and the fact that it has never been fully homogenized.

In both countries there are many types of memorials that lend themselves to comparison and differentiation. These include memorials for regiments, monuments that stand in for the military units of actions that have adopted the service of maintaining tradition. This tradition was undone in Germany after 1945 and has only been tentatively taken back up in the Federal Republic. France faces a similar problem of offering forms of military identification after and despite the lost civil wars / wars of liberation in Vietnam and Algeria.

An additional type of memorial equally common in both countries is the memorialization of specific organizations. Schools, student fraternities, universities (in other words, mainly civic institutions) but also larger units like the postal service, the railways, and gymnastic and singing clubs have all erected their own memorials. Generally speaking we can say that here the state of consciousness of the founders can be directly derived from the social conditions in which they practice the veneration of the dead, as survivors or descendants. While this cult was largely continued after World War I, it more or less died out in the period after World War II. After 1945, these kinds of memorials often seem to be little more than memorials to bygone eras. With the passing of the generations of direct survivors, the veneration of the dead also dies out. These memorials are traces of the past, without any longer pointing toward the future.

There are also many different kinds of soldier memorials on the battlefields in France that don't exist in Germany. In France, upholding tradition is an obligation partly of the state, partly of the military, and also partly of veterans' organizations; Antoine Prost has written a ground-breaking analysis of the history of mentality of the latter.[1]

The most widespread type of soldier memorial is the local municipal memorial. There is hardly a town in Germany or France that did not erect a memorial after World War I of its own accord. If it is possible to register a broadly effectual transformation in consciousness that the wars and the wars alone bring about, then we should be able to do so via these kinds of memorials. The veneration of the dead belongs to the history of the effects of war, the dead themselves belong to the war. At this lowest level of social and political organization, the analysis can come to several empirically grounded conclusions. Prost has done this for France, but several studies of the German context have also been carried out that lend themselves to broader generalizations.

The history of the rise of these municipal memorials in both countries is quite comparable, and in many cases the memorials and practices appear nearly identical. All local towns concluded that they wanted to preserve the memory of the fallen from their midst through a monument. These towns founded committees, and because they often faced financial pressures, they organized subscriptions. It was mostly the middle bourgeoisie who participated in these subscriptions, and mostly with political attitudes that ranged from the center to the right. The state did not intervene in Germany prior to 1933, while in France, the state contributed up to 15 percent of the expenses, depending on what percentage of the town's population the number of the fallen soldiers represented. To this extent, we can see a larger amount of governmental direction and influence in France than Germany.

It stands out in the French case that victory monuments are very much in the minority in the local towns, in contrast to the official politics of the national government. Half to two-thirds of all memorials express a message about civic life, about citizenship, or are mainly focused on mourning. In political terms, the monuments express a range of positions, ranging from conservative Catholics to socialists, who made use of these kinds of memorials to invoke mourning and to take the dead as a pledge for peace, rather than to memorialize the war as a victory. These stand in contrast to a group of patriotic, pathos-infused memorials that are more in the republican tradition. An important but comparatively small group of memorials cultivate explicitly pacifist traditions: these memorials depict widows, orphans, or parents who have lost their children. In France, more so than in Germany, families, women and children as those left behind are demonstratively incorporated into the rite of mourning.

If we compare the French typology with German memorials, we can observe a series of commonalities as well as differences, to the extent that preliminary conclusions are possible.

There are obviously no victory memorials in the German case. At the same time, however, a series of memorials, especially from the bourgeois milieu, seek to offset the loss of World War I. These memorials claim that Germany was (supposedly) undefeated on the battlefield, and they largely come from conservative organizations but can also be found in cities with a conservative majority. Here structures of consciousness that sought to not accept defeat were subliminally stabilized: the possibility of reinstigating the war can certainly be derived from these kinds of monuments, even if this possibility was not made explicit.

In many regards, German and French monuments are similar to the extent that they thematize mourning itself. The allegories are often identical if one disregards the helmets or uniforms. The impossibility of rationalizing death is often compensated for via pathos or sidestepped via aesthetic signals, with the erection of simple stones or steles, stone squares or cubes, whose allegorical meaning is barely accessible today.

Here, though, we can identify a difference in mentality after World War I: while in France, around 30 percent of the memorials contain some reference to fame, honor, and heroes, the German inscriptions memorializing the heroes of the war were more extensive. This too is a sign of overcompensation for defeat, even if the emphasis of these inscriptions would seem to point in a different direction. In Germany, "comrades" and "heroes" were named just as frequently, though not on local municipal monuments. The tendency in Germany is more to identify a male community who together endured World War I on the front. The figural incorporation of family members also occurs in Germany, but apparently less than in France. To this extent, and to the extent that the memorials signal specific meanings, memorializing mourning is directed in different ways. In both countries, mourning is privileged over blunt despair, but in France mourning is directed more toward the victorious peace and in Germany toward the past struggle. However, we shouldn't let these kinds of differences cause us to risk general statements about national mentalities.

An additional criterion of differentiation for the veneration of the dead consists in the involvement or lack thereof of the Church in the cultivation of memory. In France, this was generally regulated through the law of 1905 separating church and state. No Christian symbols were allowed to appear in public squares, and thus not on memorials. If Christian symbols could be used for the veneration of the dead, then only if these memorials were located on church property or at a cemetery. To this extent, the iconography of French monuments reproduce quite precisely the social structures that predominated in the different respective municipalities. This shows especially clearly how the history of consciousness contained in this new veneration of the dead connects up with the social givens already in existence prior to the war. The same applies to the German case, not least because of Germany's regional and federal plurality. In decidedly Catholic towns, the soldier memorials were commonly linked to the Christian veneration of martyrs, as well as to the Church's symbolism of resurrection. In Protestant communities, in contrast, there are many more memorials that do without any Christian references, largely in favor of the Iron Cross, which, to be sure, can certainly be interpreted as Christian.

In sum, we can say that the soldier memorials helped to stabilize the social and political structures that already existed in the towns. Via symbolized memory, mass death was channeled into the dispute between political parties, which also fought each other in the towns. It is rare to find any purely pacifist monuments in Germany because there was no majority of pacifists, while in France there were more, though these too were in the minority.

The National Socialists' seizure of power constituted a caesura. They destroyed all memorials that they found to be too pacifist or defeatist and favored potential victory monuments with heroic pathos. Because the party took over the veneration of the dead, all of the memorials could be repurposed in terms of the new ideology in order to create a military mind-set and stance in the youth coming of age at the time. We are lacking a study of the old frontline fighters' role in this process; their mentality certainly shared much with the French frontline soldiers, even if it was not identical. Here the rising role of the young postwar generations, especially of the Hitler Youth, requires closer study. To point to one parallel in particular: in France, the strongly revanchist memorials to the war of 1870–71 were first put up after 1890 by a private organization called Souvenir-Français. Hitler himself mistrusted the Germans' enthusiasm for war, which he sought to inflame through propaganda. Enthusiasm for Hitler grew less through the commencement of the war and more through the victories of its first half. In general, though, we can say that conservative and nationalistic mentalities preserved the veneration of the dead more in German municipal memorials than in republican France, which was always anxious about its victory.

This then also affected the cultivation of memorials after World War II, where both the paths of the two Germanies and those of France and Germany diverge.

The comparatively few fallen soldiers of the French Army were basically remembered only through supplementary plaques on the municipal memorials. They converged in a space of memory that stressed the continuity of the two wars iconographically. The same also applies to the majority of the soldier memorials in the towns of West Germany, but with one difference: numerous soldier memorials in West Germany—and even more in the later GDR—were removed by the victors or destroyed by left-wing majorities in the towns. If the memorials were minimally altered, it was by excising pathos-laden inscriptions. References to fame and honor were removed, heroes were transformed into victims or the dead. As a minimal consensual basis for a lost consciousness of national identity, Christian symbols began to dominate, without this necessarily indicating any rise in Christianity. In addition, inscriptions in West Germany were expanded to include civilian deaths, later even including deaths in the concentration camps. War and terror came to be memorialized in conjunction, and this brought together different strands of identity whose minimal commonality consists only of a kind of despairing meaninglessness. To this extent, then, the cultivation of memorials (which hardly occurs any more) represents more a loss than a founding of identity. These memorials thus point to a fundamental transformation in consciousness.

The situation was different in France. Here de Gaulle ordered that new memorials could only be erected for the Résistance. The Nazis' regime of terror, not Germany, was defined as the enemy, and under this motto, the new national homogeneity included communists and conservatives alike to the extent that they participated in the resistance movement. The veneration of the deaths was thus placed in the service of the newly founded Fourth Republic, directed through centralized oversight, but also maintained by all French citizens who sought to free themselves from the burden of the former Pétain regime. Municipal memorials thus brought the two world wars together into a continuous space of memory, and the new memorials created a new basis for a future with a new French constitution.

The cultivation of memorials in the GDR is not dissimilar in this regard. Soldier memorials were reserved for the USSR, and these memorials cultivated mourning for its dead and stressed their political function as liberators from fascism. And wherever new memorials were established, they commemorated only the victims of the concentration camps and resistance activities related to the workers' movement. Here too we are dealing with a process of identification directed by the state and the founding of new front lines in the space of memory. Only the dead of the class struggle, civil wars after 1918, and the anti-Nazi resistance are memorialized, as representatives of a particular segment of the political past serving to pledge a socialist future. As a result, the political functionality of the memorials for the dead is much stronger in the GDR than in the Federal Republic. The veneration of the dead in municipal memorials has been more or less forgotten, and this memory is cultivated increasingly in private.

And the attempt to preserve the consciousness of the meaninglessness of wartime death occurs in extra-institutional settings. This is given expression by the common practice of painting over of the soldier memorials with words such as "never again war." Without ritual forms this kind of memory of the millions of dead takes on a new meaning: survival itself becomes the sole challenge. The dead disappear.

14

Beyond the Deadly Line:
The Age of Totality

After the closing of its open Western frontier, the United States entered world politics in 1898. In maritime war against Catholic Spain, it conquered the Philippines in the Pacific and Cuba in the Caribbean, where it created military bases, and in 1901 it began the construction of the Panama Canal. One year later a struggle for world standing arose between Germany and [U.S. President] Theodore Roosevelt, who raised his "big stick" in particular against the German emperor in order to prevent a European intervention in South America, with German gunboats poised to force Venezuela to settle outstanding debts. Invoking the Monroe Doctrine, the United States laid claim to a monopoly over control or intervention. And so it was not just Great Britain but especially the United States that began to perceive the German fleet as a meddling, disruptive factor.

In Africa a crucial confrontation arose at Fashoda [on the White Nile River in southern Sudan] between the British and the French empires, which was resolved through a treaty between the two colonial powers, which in the long term was a precursor to the so-called Entente Cordiale, implicitly directed against the German Empire. This then initially allowed Great Britain free rein to wage one of the most bloody colonial wars ever, the first total war of our century: the Boer War. The British mobilized 450,000 men to subjugate 80,000 Boers, but the bloody victories of the

British forced the Boers into guerrilla warfare. The British responded with scorched earth tactics: around 30,000 farms and the harvests were destroyed, and the civilian population was gathered together in so-called "concentration camps." Around 28,000 white women and children died there, as did around 14,000 of the Boers' black subjects, who were kept in separate camps. This was the first modern war not simply fought for land—at stake were gold and diamond mines—and instead against an entire people. The Boers as a whole were held accountable for the war. To this extent it was an ethnic or national war [*Volkskrieg*], a democratic war that departed from liberal principles of protecting private individuals and their property.

But it did not take long for the British and the Boers to come to an agreement to bear the burden of the white man together against the black, mixed-blood, and Indian majority population. Racist patterns of interpretation emerged, but it took several decades for the banning of extramarital sex between whites and nonwhites (1927) and, finally, of all mixed marriages (1950). In the neighboring German colonial territory, the Germans likewise carried out a war of eradication against the rebellious Hereros (1904), of which about eighty percent—80,0000—died, were killed, or were driven into the desert to die of thirst.

Racist determinations of the enemy also emerged as the Chinese "Righteous and Harmonious Fists," the so-called Boxers, rose up in a bloody rebellion against the expansion of the colonial powers, which led these powers to invade China militarily (1900). With the German emperor calling upon his soldiers to deal with the "yellow peril" in the same way as the Huns—that is, to take no prisoners—defeated China was subjected to debasing moral and financial reparations. In addition, and departing from the typical partitioning according to colonial spheres of influence, the United States called for the famous "open door" in order to open up the Chinese market in its entirety. During these episodes, bloody and ominous signs were entered into a book of history that still has many blank pages and that will continue to be written long into the coming century. The Japanese achieved the first follow-up to the Boxer War in 1904–5 when they defeated a white world power, the Russians. And the "yellow peril"—now Japanese—was once more invoked after the Japanese attack on Pearl Harbor in order to expropriate and intern all Japanese of both sexes in the United States in camps for the duration of the war, including those with U.S. citizenship.

I need not list any more of these dates from the beginning of the twentieth century, dates whose symbolic power reaches far into our own time. It is not that we are necessarily obliged to establish causal chains between events occurring around 1900—the total war of the British, the universal claims of the Americans, the discrimination against all non-whites on the basis of the race, the genocidal campaign of the Germans, the uprising of the Chinese, and the rapid rise of the Japanese—and the time that followed. But these events strikingly illuminate problems for which solutions continue to be sought on all continents to this day. Taken on its own, a date is blind, of no analytical meaning, unless this date is weighed in terms of what happened prior to, after, or at the same time. In contrast, aggregating one hundred years into the concept of a century—something that first became utterable and hence thinkable in German in the seventeenth century—only offers us a formal and questionable arithmetic unit. First invented as a way to collate different masses of material side by side, akin to a handbook, the concept of "century" took on symbolic weight only after contemporaries first started to make use of them. This is how the eighteenth century became that of the Enlightenment, and the following century that of progress. Our current century resists these kinds of simplifications. Is it the century of the failure of Germany and Japan (in the first half) and Russia (in the second)? Or does this make it the century of America? Or is it the century of the catastrophes—and inversely—of technical-industrial expansion? Of mass murder and exile escalated into the millions? Or of the exploration of outer space and of genetic technology? In purely political terms, the concept of the century has already become something malleable and accordion-like: we call the nineteenth century long (1789–1914) and the twentieth century short (1914–89). This suffices to show that the time frame of one hundred years is arbitrary, random, and purely coincidental. Individual dates may well be symbolic, but one hundred years are not, for one can at any rate always go back and recalibrate it from year to year. For this reason we will side with Kant and his call for chronology to follow the lead of history instead of the reverse, history following chronology. Let us then first ask as to the historical factors and constellations that endure longer than our accidental century, that existed prior to it and point beyond it. Viewed from this larger perspective, it becomes clear that many things that seem to stay the same and repeat themselves over and over again have, nonetheless, elicited changes with far-reaching consequences.

We might first mention generative patterns. Population explosions have occurred in places where—and because—things have stayed the same. In sub-Saharan Africa, the population has tripled and at times almost quadrupled in the past forty years. The asymmetry between industrial countries, with relatively stable rates of reproduction, and developing countries—around 80 percent of the world population—is only increasing. The Chinese are seeking in vain to implement their one-child policy so as to postpone crossing the one billion mark. The exponential curve of duplication in ever-shorter time periods—there were one billion people on the earth in 1800, two in 1930, today it is six—may flatten off, whether through family planning or disease or catastrophic starvation. But the dilemma identified by Malthus that the population doubles geometrically while food production doubles at best arithmetically, this dilemma remains a very real danger, even if genetic technologies could supplement the food supply as much as possible. Hobbes's prediction that overpopulation and increasing food scarcity would once more lead to the full manifestation of human nature—being wolves to each other—remains an undeniable threat; it has been apparent throughout our hundred years, and it will determine the future even more than it does today, where we can already see enough of the ubiquitous consequences of the choice between starvation or migration. The proliferation of megacities that cross the ten million mark evokes a call for quality of life precisely because it is disappearing. In the past, shifts in the relation between urban and rural areas have been occasioned but also offset by industrialization (in industrialized nations, the population involved primarily in the agricultural sector has sunk to around 5 percent), but with the rise in recent decades of the information society, this outlet is no longer available. Here too exponential curves are propelled ever upward.

Ever more information can be stored and communicated in ever-shorter intervals. The mechanical origins of computing, think of Leibniz's stepped reckoner, for example, are ancient history. Starting in the middle of our century, ever-smaller and more effective electronic computers have come to transform our lives. Here the curve of acceleration remains entirely open, and every experience of one technology overtaking another prohibits us from imagining any kind of saturation point. But this sort of experience does force us to alter previous modes and inventories of planning for the future. The more data we can store and access, the more we participate in a potential future, which without any experience determines our actions. This applies to the economy, politics, and the military above all. The more pregiven data that can be combined and computed, the larger the compulsion to plan ahead so as to be able to act at all. This transformation overturns the dimensions of the past and future and imbricates them anew, and it is not of one piece with the desire or obsession with future planning that has spread since the early modern period. Indeed, this transformation has even set the constantly repeating preconditions of our social existence into motion. That which withholds itself from direct experience appears as an imaginary reality on the computer screen. The boundary between the factual world of what can be known and the fictive world of what is possible becomes blurry. Behind the screen the two dimensions converge and generate what we are tempted to call an irreal world, but one that is nonetheless quite concrete and real. Once it is grasped by the computer, the imaginable becomes real. The red telephone installed between Washington and Moscow after the Cuban Missile Crisis rests on the table not just symbolically. It represents this structural transformation and is there to help avoid the possible catastrophes that are stored and preprogrammed. By the mid-1970s, nuclear missiles [whose flights were] precalculated and directed by computer had made it possible to obliterate the Soviet Union's entire military and industrial reserves, along with its entire population, in a matter of thirty minutes—with consequences that would have been impossible to control, of course.

The imbrication of the potential for atomic destruction with electronically stored strategic planning data points to preconditions of both, namely, the conditions of scientific research that repeat themselves across all transformation and without which no technical-industrial progress would be possible. For centuries, every hypothesis, every experiment has sought to solve as of yet unsolved problems, and solutions have then generated new problems. However, the generation of new problems does not occur randomly, but instead in linearly irreversible succession (without ruling out researchers returning to previously considered alternatives in new contexts).

At the beginning of our century (though it could have occurred at a different point), quantum physics and the theory of relativity posed new questions with previously unimaginable consequences. And it happened, by the way, at the same time as the development of twelve tone music and abstract art, which both had equally unpredictable consequences in the aesthetic realm. The phenomenon of modernisms seeking to surpass each other seems to indicate a subjectively driven acceleration of artistic movements. That said, the creation of the notion of "postmodernism"—a nonsense word logically speaking—is at best an indication that the speed at which intellectual and aesthetic fashions overtake each other has slowed down. This also applies to sports, whose records are now measurable in thousandths of seconds. This measurement becomes the true increase in achievement, while the speeds or reaches of individual sports run up against their natural upper limits. The sports with an enduring appeal are those that manage to stay surprising across repetition. It is doubtful whether we can expect similar decelerations in the realm of pure research. But a flattening out of exponential curves can be seen in the realm of news reporting and transportation. The nineteenth century brought with it the transition from naturally powered carriages and sailboats to steamboats and trains, which initially overtook these earlier modes slowly and then later supplanted them almost entirely. The concentration and acceleration of transportation, now also via the automobile, have led to a shrinking of space.

But it was only in our hundred years that we could witness a qualitative difference: the third dimension—air—has been conquered by both transportation and communication. Our globe has been transformed into the spaceship that we now experience it to be. It was possible to fly even prior to the French Revolution—thanks to Montgolfier—but Zeppelin was the first to steer his airship with a motor and rudders in 1900. In 1904, the first motorized airplane left the ground, the English Channel was crossed by plane for the first time in 1909, the Atlantic Ocean in 1919, and in 1969 the first humans landed on the moon: all within the span of a single human life. And the exploration of space has moved forward ever since.

These accelerational shifts would hardly have followed so quickly without military competition and without the challenges of the two "hot" wars and the Cold War. But technical progress also generates its own processes of unfolding. Air travel has now replaced sea travel. Crossing the Atlantic is no longer a matter of months, as in the age of the sailboat, weeks as in the age of the steamship, but now only hours. This represents a maximal point, though its efficiency is sometimes impeded by traffic congestion on land and in the air. An analogous end point has also been reached in the accelerational curve of reporting and communication. Already by the nineteenth century, a cable communication network had come to span the globe, but in 1899, the first wireless transmission took place between England and France and two years later the same occurred across the Atlantic. Since then the temporal difference between events and news reporting has shrunk continuously, so as to become identical at a kind of zero point. Earlier, reports and images of events only appeared months, weeks, or days after the events themselves; today they converge ever more.

The assassination of Kennedy occurred at the same time as the famous amateur film about it. This can be extended: in 1960, the socialist party leader was stabbed to death in Tokyo while delivering a speech in front of running television cameras. The political assassination and its transmission to the television public [merge into] one and the same thing. And this would then be repeated in 1963 with Qasim in Iraq, in 1981 with Sadat in Egypt, and in 1989 with the execution of Ceaușescu in Romania. The threshold into the information age has thereby been visibly crossed. Even missiles send the details of their radar-controlled flightpaths back to computer screens all the way up to the moment when they have identified their destination through their own explosion. And wars are now planned and directed in terms of how they will be aesthetically transmitted and received via the screens of the observing citizens. The true misery remains concealed.

Our accelerational curves can be found in numerous additional sectors. But it might suffice to point out that enormous changes came about amid preconditions that have remained identical, and these changes had an effect on all the societies of the globe. Despite exponential curves that flatten out here and there, an absolutely deadly end line is constantly present. The reason is that the capacity for destruction has also increased exponentially. This capacity is both the motor and the flipside of technical-industrial progress: on the one hand, the explosive power of missiles has grown so much that it now even obliterates the corpses. In three days of the war in Flanders, the British discharged ammunition that cost as many pounds sterling as they spent on soldier cemeteries after the war (for 1.2 million fallen). In addition, we have the invention of deadly gas in World War I, which the Germans then used in World War II—over and above their direct acts of murder—to gas five to six million Jews, "gypsies," and Slavic prisoners. Traditional land-based troops and quick tanks remained decisive on the battlefield, but accessing the third dimension above and below the earth's surface became decisive for war. The Germans were defeated in their two attempts at underwater warfare, while the Anglo-Americans won the air war and, with the two atom bombs, could force the Japanese to capitulate more quickly. A potential for destruction was developed that for the first time included the entirety of humanity and all individual humans in what should well be called an apocalyptic threat. We are no longer dealing with the Last Judgment awaited by the believers and repeatedly delayed from prophesy to prophesy; instead, since the end of the war, it has always remained a daily and hourly possibility that the entire human race could be exterminated through atomic radiation. Spoken abstractly, this would represent the self-destruction of humanity. Concretely, though, this would be the decision of a small group of people who could initiate the chain reaction as men of state or terrorists. This state of affairs, which we can certainly call a singular and unique achievement of our scientific-technical-industrial century, then leads into the open field of politics. Following the question guiding our interpretation of technical progress, namely: what is it that changes, even when the preconditions remain the same?—we might conclude that in political history, so much has happened because the preconditions for politics have changed so considerably. However, this only applies very conditionally.

Two major trends of the European nineteenth century have had a lasting effect into our own century and have since encompassed the entire globe, namely, the geopolitically seamless formation of nation-states and the increasing hollowing out of these same nation-states. These occur from above and from within through trans- and international accumulations of political and economic power, as well through movements of both insurgency and partition, which threaten the state monopoly on power from below or the outside. State and sovereignty increasingly diverge and can no longer be reintegrated, as had been the goal of the princely states. Civil wars constantly break out and create ever-new, unsolvable conflicts. The only successful exception to this rule seems to be the European Union, a union of old states. The more recent formation of nation-states has occurred in three pushes and according to identical rules. They always emerge after the collapse of transnational empires. The competing state formations of the Balkan wars occurred at the cost of the Ottoman Empire, and with the collapse of Russia in 1917 and of Austria-Hungary as well as Germany in 1918, a range of nation-states with various lifespans emerged, from Finland and Yugoslavia all the way to the Caucasus.

The second wave followed after the end of World War II. It encompassed the entire Islamic world, from Morocco to the Middle Eastern mandate territories all the way to Indonesia, and it also included the Southeast Asian dominions and partial colonies from India to Vietnam. Afterwards, with the successive end of the European colonial empires, a new world of nation-states emerged. The South African Republic bookended this second wave, emancipating itself twice, once from the Commonwealth, once from the exclusive domination of the whites. The last wave followed with the implosion of the Soviet Union, from which around twenty, mostly Islamic republics emerged between China, Russia, and the Orient. Purely numerically this growing, for now receding high tide of nation-states can be seen in the membership numbers of the League of Nations, which began with twenty-six states and already had sixty members by 1935. The United Nations was founded by fifty signatory nations and now [in 2000] has 188 members. In terms of international law, the globe has been parceled out into nation-states. This process, which can rightly be called secular (in the sense of spanning an entire century), began in each case as a revolutionary, though usually peaceful movement, but ended almost everywhere with a deluge of blood and misery. For the legitimacy of all nation-states depended upon homogeneity. The postulated unity of the people or the nation created resistance of its own kind, whether it was justified through religion, language, economics, history, ethnicity, or however else. These forms of resistance may have originated in the border zones or were called forth from within these young states themselves. A range of different homogenizing measures were carried out in these states, ranging from subjugation, incorporation, or purification to relocation or expulsion all the way to the extermination of minorities that were defined as not belonging. Whether these states were liberal democratic or radical democratic, popular democratic or, as Mussolini defined his fascist state, a *democrazia totalitaria*, the common signature of all was civil war. The political opponent is not recognized as an enemy, and instead is ostracized.

The initial impetus was provided by sorting groups according to ethnic criteria. The victors of 1918 divided the Alsatians into four groups: full, three-quarter, and half French; the rest, defined as imperial German [*reichsdeutsch*], were expelled. It could come to pass that Harry Bresslau, a medieval scholar in Straßburg/Strasbourg, was kicked out over the Rhine bridge in Kehl with two suitcases in his hands, while his son-in-law Albert Schweitzer, after four years of being interned as a German could stay as a full Frenchman with his "half-French" wife. His successor built upon Bresslau's critically prepared source material in developing his own well-known research. This was Marc Bloch, whom the Germans shot in World War II as an officer of the Résistance, and after whom the University of Strasbourg is named. This is one of those histories that appear national only on a superficial level. Above all, though, this story shows that the Germans learned nothing from their defeat in 1918. Just the opposite: in 1939 they once more created a system of four categories, which they applied to conquered Poland to force it to become a homogeneous settlement area through Germanification or expulsion. And they went far beyond this. They began to eradicate the Polish elite, and, even more, all Jews of all ages and both sexes—millions of innocent civilians.

The range extending from expulsion to extermination establishes the moving scale for countless actions of homogenization over the course of nation-state formation. We need only recall the Greek-Turkish population transfer of 1923, which was sanctioned by the victorious powers; the exchange of twelve million expellees between India and Pakistan; the expulsion of over one million Palestinians by the Israelis; the forced resettlement of many millions of blacks in South Africa; the civil war of the peoples of Nigeria, of whom the Ibos above all suffered losses of around one million people; the reciprocal campaigns of eradication carried out by the Hutu and Tutsi in Rwanda and Burundi; the annihilation of the Chinese on Java; the peoples whom Stalin redefined as class enemies and let starve or expel and work to death, not to mention the millions of executed "enemies of the Soviet people." The number of victims of the civil war in Mao's empire is estimated at around sixty million. But enough of these almost randomly selected references.

To be sure, the trail of blood on the path to national unification in each of these countries might well have been self-inflicted. However, it nonetheless brings us back to the international power constellations that have changed fundamentally in our hundred years. All national civil wars are dependent on international politics, in part causally, in part functionally. The Spanish Civil War was just as much a war between fascist states and the Soviet Union, with the liberal-democratic great powers abstaining half-heartedly. The collapse of the pentarchy [i.e., the Vienna system] in World War I was in no way compensated for by the Treaty of Versailles or the League of Nations. Not only the vanquished but also the victors of the war sought to improve the terms of peace, year after year. We might only mention the Polish free corps that entered Upper Silesia in 1921 in order to violently reverse a popular referendum decided in favor of Germany. The promised protection of minorities had no effect. None of the states that emerged from Austria-Hungary were capable of controlling the burdensome legacies of different nationalities in any kind of federal system. Every federation presupposes the equality of unequals, something that requires tolerance and expense. Czechoslovakia and Yugoslavia alike were unable to recognize the equal rights or autonomy of the peoples in these countries. Both states fell apart and failed due to the same problems that the dissolution of the Austro-Hungarian Empire was supposed to have solved. If the shots of Sarajevo were directed solely at an archduke and his wife, the shots of Sarajevo of 1994 were aimed at an entire people, the Muslim Bosnians.

World War II still took place under the sign of forming hegemonial *Großräume*: "Greater Germany [Großdeutschland]" in Europe and "Greater East Asia [Tōyama Mitsuru]" for the Japanese. The reasons for their failure are multifaceted but one suffices. With their racist ideologies, both empires did not simply neglect national realities and potentials, but instead sought to suppress them through unbounded terror, which led them to lose any and all supranational legitimacy. In the postwar situation, what the United Nations seemed to bring to fruition led immediately to the polar tension between the two world powers. Both powers were legitimate heirs to the European Enlightenment, both defended ideologies that applied universally and for that reason excluded the other: the United States as the standard bearer of the liberal-democratic model of statehood, where the separation of powers protects human rights—programmatically postulated by Wilson in 1917; and the Soviet Union as the vanguard of the world revolution, which would realize social justice with the end of all classes—formulated dogmatically by Lenin's Third International in 1919. The result was that the world was tightly divided up into two new regions according to the modern article of faith: *cuius regio, eius oeconomia*. Defining each other ideologically as evil incarnate, the two highly armed military blocs were only capable of avoiding war with one another because the fear of nuclear war forced both parties to adopt a minimum of political rationality.

Still, the East-West conflict impregnated the entire globe: all of the new national formations and many national histories, buffeted by the fall of monarchs, coups d'états, shifts in constitutions, and presidential assassinations, and repeatedly flaring up into genocidal murder, got drawn into the undertow of the two world powers. Countless civil wars, including those that arose genuinely, mutated into proxy wars of the superpowers—from Korea to Vietnam to Palestine, Afghanistan, Algeria, and Cuba, to only name countries in the northern hemisphere. All of the parties involved in civil wars remained dependent upon the help or protection of the world powers if they wanted to complete their national revolutions.

The more nations found themselves caught up in the swirl of this so-called "world civil war," the quicker the front lines shifted, which made it all the easier and more common to change sides. Betrayal offered the chance to stay virtuous. Instead of establishing peace, states themselves became instruments of terror. The polar opposition could be exploited by those who were affected by it, opening up the sluice gates for a range of new alternatives. Neutral movements of the Third World, ethnically or religiously motivated "pan-"movements, above all, transcontinental organizations such as OPEC, held together by economic interests, helped to soften the bipolar opposite. And after China broke off from the Soviet bloc and pursued its own hegemonic politics, a pluralism of new risks emerged. With the implosion of the Soviet empire, this trend was strengthened, because many new political units of action became agents. It then became clear that all nation-states are not only the heirs of the nineteenth century but also remain dependent upon protection and help, whether this protection is mutual, affected by units of action aggregated on a higher level, or by the universally legitimated organizations of the United Nations. Three structural problem areas then emerge, within which and between which future conflicts will break out. One: the global market economy competes universally with the political postulates of social or individual human rights. Two: there is a need for supranational coalitions in regionally defined spaces that will be necessary for survival, in order to protect oneself from and together with others. Three: nation-states will continue to create their own conflicts, which will then influence other problem areas.

15

Forms and Traditions
of Negative Memory

To speak of negative memory is ambiguous, because either the negative in memory implies that the content stored by memory is off-putting, unwelcome, despicable and worthy of scorn, or it means that memory [*das Gedächtnis*] closes itself off to recollection [*Erinnerung*], refuses to become cognizant of the negative: that memory thus represses the negative and thus makes the past responsible for it and relegates it to oblivion. Naturally, these two aspects, both the horrifying content and the refusal to carry over this content from memory to active recollection, are closely connected. The one points to the other and takes us directly to the historical problematic of how crimes are to be remembered at all.

A bloody trail has run through human histories as long as they have existed, and the curse of their actions is transmitted down through the generations, from the Bible and Herodotus up to the present day. The memories [*Erinnerungen*] that accumulate are then repeatedly compensated for: revenge through revenge, through punishments, through acts of atonement. We might recall the marks of shame and the crosses of conciliation that the pope was forced to erect in Rome in the seventeenth century after his Swiss Guard had murdered French subjects; the French king forced the pope to establish a memorial site to recall this murder. Or we might recall the memorial columns that have been erected after the failed uprisings of defeated rebels. This kind of negative memory has always served to hold the curse of evil deeds at bay. In times of civil war, both sides certainly shared in the crimes. For example, in Lyon, after revolutionaries were murdered, so-called counterrevolutionaries were not simply executed, thrown in the water, and drowned, but, in addition, as if by magic, their houses were also torn down. Such action is also evident in the leveling of the city of Warsaw after the uprising of the Poles in 1944, though the Poles who revolted were surprisingly still held as prisoners. The fact that Himmler's Villa in Dahlem was torn down after 1945 because (understandably) no one wanted to live in it is a different story.

But negative memories can also be reinterpreted positively if it seems politically appropriate. The devastating defeat of the British at the Dardanelles in 1915 thus became a national day of celebration in Australia, the country that suffered the largest losses in the battle. Defeat as a national day of celebration, because Australia, a continent that had been looked down upon up to that point, suddenly found itself elevated to a proud and politically conscious society through the act of memorialization. To this day victories and defeats alike are memorialized to an equal degree in Warsaw; all the dead are remembered together as martyrs for their fatherland. [French Prime Minister Georges] Clemenceau's saying of the French defeat at the Brenner Pass in 1870, "Always think about it, never talk about it," similarly reinterprets a negative experience into—in this case patriotic—positive expectation.

What is the point of this kaleidoscopic survey of past histories originally with negative associations, histories that would be easy to add to and create a thick, consistent, and seamless volume of world history? It is characteristic of all of these examples, no matter their scale, that the bloody deeds have been evaluated, in one way or another, in terms of a standard of possible justice, or judged according to a kind of justice that could be demanded or conceived of. No matter whether vendetta was justified through justice—through unwritten law—or whether revenge was additionally legitimized by natural law, through theology, or positivistically, through international or criminal law: justice either seemed to be inherent in the actions themselves or provided a backdrop against which the actions of others could be recognized and defined as crimes.

This standard fails us if we turn today to the crimes from the national socialist period that form our memory. It is not that this or that action was not prosecuted and punished in accordance with the law: we see this in the many trials, begun in Nuremberg and continued in the Eichmann trial and the Auschwitz trial with all of their aftereffects down to the present day. No, it is the magnitude and abysmalness [*Abgründigkeit*]— forgive me the metaphor, which one cannot avoid here—the abysmalness that we continue to confront to this day if we commit ourselves to call to memory and hold in our memories the terror system, the mass murders, and the actions of annihilation of those years.

However, the idea of some kind of supposedly intended justice or of a justice that could be properly enforced in the present day both fall short in the face of the absurdity of what was carried out and what took place. Senselessness [*Sinnlosigkeit*] became an event. There is no attribution of meaning [*Sinnstiftung*] that could retroactively encompass or redeem all the crimes of the National Socialist Germans. This negative finding forms our memory of the events of the first six [Nazi] years, from 1933 to 1939, and especially the events and dates of the second six years, from 1939 to 1945. The all-consuming fear of the prisoners in the camps that had to be swallowed in order to continue to live. The pain with which constantly biting hunger eats away at the body. The shaking of all one's limbs while working, up to the point of total exhaustion. The waiting and yet more waiting, the standing and being forced to stand yet again, standing at attention for hours, for days, for days and nights. The fear of the neighbor that stokes one's own egotism. The slim chances of finding some kind of security or help in the rigorous hierarchy of the camp. Actually helping a fellow man, which was life-endangering and could lead to death. The utter lack of any prospect of finding a way home or out into a freedom that has vanished. Forgetting hopelessness itself in order simply to survive. The contrived categories that only allowed for bonds of solidarity at the expense of others: whether it was the different nations in the camp or the communists or the biblical scholars, the people defined as criminals, and other higher and lower categories, all the way down to the Jews. The constant prospect that one might at any moment be beaten, hanged, or shot.

None of these experiences can be transmitted. They fill the memory of those affected by them, they form their memories, flow into their bodies like a mass of lava, immovable and inscribed. In comparison, all experiences of contemporaries who were not in the camps as well as those who were born later are secondary. And just as the experiences of those who shared in the suffering in the camps were genuine, so too are their memories, they form their memory directly and immediately. It is perhaps possible, though quite difficult, to talk about this, but to deduce from it that there exists some kind of collective memory [*Gedächtnis*] (as one likes to say today) or even a collective recollection [*Erinnerung*] to which one could attest in Germany, this is a false conclusion, however well-intentioned. As a primary experience, the experience of absurd meaninglessness burned into the body cannot be carried over to the memory of others, nor can it be transmitted to the recollection of others who were not affected. Those of us who are contemporaries or were born later must learn to come to terms with this negative message.

But the terroristically enforced senselessness of the camp was far outdone. Up to this point we have only considered the camps within the territory of the old Reich, camps that fed on arbitrary murders and a long-term, ever-increasing routine of killing. Around a half-million people were killed in these old concentration camps. If we turn our gaze to the East, we encounter the camps where, from the very beginning, inmates were being led to complete annihilation with bureaucratically exact planning and direction: Kulmhof (Chelmno), Treblinka, Sobibór, Majdanek, Belzec, Birkenau. These camps were sites of acceleration, technical perfection, and anonymous annihilation; up to this point, in contrast, the massacre was still being done entirely personally in the whole territory behind the Eastern front. These actions of annihilation were carried out primarily and above all on the Jews of all Europe, but also on the gypsies (today redefined as Sinti and Roma and thus removed from the linguistic zone of hate), on numerous members of the peoples then defined as Slavic. The mentally ill (and cases diagnosed as mentally ill without this necessarily making them mentally ill), around 100,000 people, were the first to be gassed in the Reich, before the killing teams and murder wagons began their activity in subjugated Poland. In every case we are dealing with innocent civilians annihilated on the basis of racial-zoological or "national-hygenical" [*volkshygenisch*] criteria. There was rarely even the slightest opening for them to sacrifice themselves for those like them or for others, although [the actions of] rare and laudable exceptions such as Korczak and Kolbe were partially tolerated by the Nazis. With the disposal of their inmates, these camps produced their own finale. Truly an apocalypse without mercy—to put it in Christian terms—but in fact much worse. The death of those destroyed in the camps was denied any reconnection to their life, denied any and all recollection, for their very bodies were dissipated into air and ash. It thus became humanly possible to extinguish the very quality of being human.

We should be all the more grateful to those witnesses who have taken it upon themselves—often in old age—to report about their survival. We should also extend our thanks to those researchers who have made the effort of processing in a secondary manner and transmitting in scholarly fashion what the other contemporaries never experienced. I am thinking here of Poliakov, Hilberg, Saul Friedländer, but also of Broszat and Hillgruber. They have ventured to form hypotheses in order to offer possible rationales for processes that, in general, are held to be incomprehensible. The different experiences [*Fremderfahrungen*] of those who were persecuted, martyred, who disappeared into nothingness, who were annihilated—the innocent of all European nations and social classes, the innocent of all confessions and religions and above all the Jews who were redefined in racial terms all challenge and provoke our memory [*Erinnerung*], the memory of the Germans. These are the preconditions according to which our memory constitutes itself and according to which it must prove itself.

A first conclusion was drawn by our Basic Law in 1949, with its basis for legitimation standing in opposition to the entirety of the National Socialist past. Article 1 reads: "The dignity of man is inviolable. To respect and protect it shall be the duty of all public authority." Article 79 reinforces this, stating that any change to Article 1 is forbidden. This self-obligation of the Germans, issuing from the experience of the National Socialist time, its crimes, and its genocides throughout Europe, this must be remembered in examining the ambivalence and negativity of our memory. There is, as Article 3 reinforces, no ethnic, no racial, no linguistic, no religious, no political, no genetic, and no spatial criterion that can detract from equality before the law. Of course, this is only a normative conclusion that we Germans have subjected ourselves to after 1949. But it is the minimum below which we may not fall. It is the title of legitimacy of our identity in the Federal Republic, which calls us and forces us to treat those who are empirically unequal as equal before the law. And for this reason we recall that the differentiation between unequals, between human and unhuman, between *Übermensch* and subhuman, was the quasi-anthropological premise that served to legitimate murders. So we should accept the fact that our memory is indeed preformed by the negative but remains only secondary and historically transmitted when measured against the genuine experience of the victims. Our experiences are not the same as those of the people whom we killed or who survived. This negative difference remains the leitmotif of our memory.

For this reason we must address the difference between the primary experience of those actually affected and the secondary experience of those living today, which has to be worked through after the fact. This gives rise to certain problems, which I would like to discuss in closing via three questions:

Who should be remembered?

What should be remembered?

How should be remembered?

It is difficult to answer the question as to who. For we in Germany must remember both the perpetrators and the victims, two groups that seem to exclude each other, though not wholly, because this was a shared occurrence called forth by the perpetrators. The Neue Wache ["New Guardhouse"] memorial in Berlin has already misguidedly responded to this question with a pietà that Käthe Kollwitz originally conceived of as a memorial for a volunteer in World War I. In the first place, this has nothing to do with the murders of World War II. Secondly, it is a pietà, which by definition excludes Jews. Thirdly, in depicting a surviving mother mourning her dead son, it excludes the women who were the majority of the civilian victims. In regards to Jews and women, then, the monument perpetuates the separation of peoples and the sexes, and very few can or would want to identify with it.

There were numerous protests by those who felt excluded by the Neue Wache memorial, and I won't report in detail about each one. Numerous organizations objected to this monument, forming a broad front, yet they were unsuccessful. The question then remains: who should be remembered? My thesis is that there is only one possibility for the Germans: the perpetrators and their actions must be incorporated into out memory, rather than solely the victims as such and in isolation. This distinguishes us from other nations, for we are politically responsible, and for that reason we must also remember and memorialize the actions and the perpetrators and not solely the victims. It is difficult to formulate this, and we have missed the chance to do so with the entire debate about the [Berlin] Holocaust Memorial. The curse of the action is thus visible in the negative to this day, to the extent that no solution has been found, no answer as to how the nation of perpetrators is to position itself vis-à-vis its victims.

Earlier this was possible through an act of contrition. This was only conceivable though within the context of religious attitudes and the dispensation of mercy by the Church. This allowed for the negotiation of forgiveness along with contrition. This path is no longer available today, not least because the German state is not a religious institution that could take on the task of creating this kind of meaning.

From the experiential perspective of the nation that provided the perpetrators, we are confronted with one difficult alternative and one alone: either we remember all of the victims individually or all individual victims together. This alternative, which was never correctly debated in the Bundestag, requires that when we single out a victim group—that of the Jews, and understandably so, because they represent the single largest victim group—we as perpetrators are obliged to treat the other groups in the same way, because we killed all the victims in the same manner. I am thinking here of the three and a half million Russian prisoners of war, of whom we let 60 percent starve to death. They have no memorial.

To be sure, the important thing here is not to compare numbers (of the German prisoners, around 40 percent did not return home from the Soviet Union). But numbers are taken here symbolically in order to mark the difference between a memorial for victims—which every group may deserve—and one for perpetrators. A perpetrators' monument [*Tätermal*] should memorialize all the murdered. Homosexuals too were murdered. And almost all gypsies—as they were then called—who could be apprehended were killed. To this day, the promise for a monument for the Sinti and Roma has not been fulfilled.[1] This means, then, that we have bracketed out the memory of the others in favor of the Jewish victims. This is unforgivable from the standpoint of the perpetrators. The standpoint of the victim groups might be different. The possibility naturally exists that memorials be erected for individual victim groups, but then none should be forgotten or excluded. Then we would logically have to erect memorials for all individual victim groups, if not a single one for all of them. And this too has not occurred, although it has been urgently called for.

One difficulty can be found in situations where the victim groups seek to divide themselves up in order to preserve their identity. They thereby unavoidably perpetuate the categories of the SS according to which they were sorted and sent to their deaths. Whether the mourning of the dead necessarily has to make use of these terroristic-bureaucratic characteristics remains an open question here. But as Germans, as the politically responsible nation, we must decide whether we want to remember a single victim group—the Jews—alone: for then we must be consistent in remembering all other victim groups as well. Or we must erect a monument that remembers all victims together. This is a necessary consequence of our responsibility to remember the actions themselves and thereby also the perpetrators. Mourning is not divisible. And we certainly should not be allowed to hide behind victim groups such as the Jews, as if we would get a Holocaust memorial just like other countries in the world. As Germans, we can neither presume nor expect this. We alone are called upon to incorporate perpetration into our reflection.

This much on the question of who should be remembered.

One additional reference is quite useful in view of our own dead. There is a city, in which I happen to live, where an 1870–71 [Franco-Prussian War] victory monument was razed in the 1960s. A small World War I statue of a soldier was decapitated in the 1990s. The World War II registry of births and deaths—belonging to the church—was recently stolen. I can recall no noticeable reaction to any of these actions. It is as though the memory of murdering the Jews obliged us to forget our own dead in the wars of unification and World War I, who had nothing to do with the annihilation of the Jews, as well as those dead who were only partially guilty in World War II. It is as if the millions dead could be counted against each other. The way in which we deal with our own dead, dead who belong to the nation that provided the perpetrators, is so refracted and broken that the escape into an ostensible pacifism that knocks over and destroys so-called military monuments would seem to bring some kind of unburdening. This is a mistake.

We can only remember the victims that we produced murderously and technically when we can attain the self-consciousness that allows us to remember our own dead and thereby also the perpetrators among our own kin, in our own nation. This is part of the difficulty characterizing the negativity of our memory. We must learn to deal with this negativity and not simply postulate positive heroes, such as those of the resistance. It should be clear that those who avoid or despise a monument to the two million [German] soldiers of World War I who were exterminated (and [often] gassed, already at that point) fail to comprehend the dignity that is required of us if we wish to keep the equality of those who have been killed alive in the humanity of our recollection.

What must be remembered? I have spoken about the difficulty of the who, and it became clear that there are no simple solutions. Resolving these paradoxes politically requires much thought and energy.

What, then, is to be remembered? I believe the simplest answer is that we must think the unthinkable, that we learn to speak the unspeakable, and that we attempt to imagine the unimaginable. With these challenges it becomes clear how quickly one runs up against the limits of what is possible. But I might recall the title of the memoirs of Anita Lasker-Wallfisch, published [in German] in 1996–97: *Inherit the Truth*.[2] This title encompasses everything that I intended to say in attempting to guide the unspeakable into language. This is a truth that applies to all of the dead and all of the events we are obliged to remember.

I would like to briefly explore the final question of the How in four points. The first mode of remembering is moral, it is clear and unambiguous. Morally, the judgment of what was carried out in the concentration camps, the mass murders, and the actions of annihilation in the East is clear: this was an injustice and morally uncontroversial. As a result, moral condemnation is necessary, but the insufficiency of moral condemnation is that it can no longer alter the past *ex post*. Moral judgment is necessary, but it does not alter the past. The morality that would have been due earlier was lacking. Even if we recover this morality today through our judgments, we can no longer change what has happened. We find ourselves in an aporetic situation. Moral judgment is necessary, but is not enough to explain or to understand what has happened. To modify Marx: the past cannot be altered, it can only be interpreted anew.

For this reason, the second approach is that of science [*Wissenschaft*]. Science seeks to explain the lack of morality and attempts to analyze the amoral with the methods of sociology, psychology, and other sciences. However, the aporia of scientific explanation is that it too cannot recover what was morally called for. A morally necessary interpretation and a scientific explanation of the same moral deficiency might well supplement each other, but they exclude each other methodologically.

The third possibility is that of religious veneration and memorialization. From the outset this excludes those who belong to a different religion. For this reason, every religious attempt to process the past is equally insufficient and limited in the end. When prayers petition for help, salvation, or mercy and forgiveness in Dachau or Auschwitz, they never reach the majority of the victims, who were not Christians. Religious memory alone is not sufficient, even if it remains necessary for believers. In the active memory of the believer, he or she feels that the moral, scientific, and also religious way of dealing with the past all lead to a dead end. All paths of memorialization remain insufficient, and even if they supplement each other, they can never recover the senselessness of the crime. To this extent the aporia still holds that all knowledge and all belief are not sufficient for adequately remembering the crimes committed.

The fourth possibility of memorialization is the long-standing aesthetic one, and this variety emerged in the debates about memorials mentioned above. This aesthetic variety likewise leads to a dead end. Let me briefly sketch this.

In earlier times, monuments that memorialized those who were violently murdered or killed or who had fallen on the battlefield were always monuments that attributed meaning. Up to World War I, almost all of them communicated a meaning that the death had had for the individuals who had been killed to those who were born later. After World War I, however, countless monuments were erected that simply demanded meaning, because establishing this was something that barely remained possible. The demand for meaning is a first step toward the present-day negative form of memory. A third form of memorialization, which became widespread, though not ubiquitous, after World War II, attempts to show that the question of meaning has itself become meaningless. This means that an aporia, namely the impossibility of generating meaning through memorialization, itself becomes an aesthetic theme.

There have been excellent efforts in this regard. I need only refer to them in theoretical terms. Walls that leave open a slit that allows light to shine through, so that one can see the outside from inside without being able to exit. One sees the light that one cannot reach—this theme characterizes many Holocaust memorials. Another form blocks any escape, even though one can see the saving light. Or hollow forms of people who have disappeared are poured or carved out again and again, the negation of the human being, if you like, as aesthetic form. And finally there are memorials that themselves disappear, like the ones designed by Jochen Gerz in Hamburg-Harburg or in Saarbrücken. Or masses of stones are piled up, blockades that no longer offer protection, as World War I memorials still did. Instead, these stone masses are overwhelming and crushing. That is to say that the central message of these new memorials, which thematize the question of meaning as itself meaningless, lead to statements of negativity, which can then be characterized as successful in aesthetic terms. Crimes are thereby shown only indirectly. The form of an indirect statement certainly belongs to one of the most important messages—I also am thinking here of Art Spiegelman, who wrote and drew "Mauschwitz."[3] His visual histories [*Bildgeschichten*] depict the Jews as mice and the Nazis as cats. Initially, one might view the daringness of this metaphor as unbearable. But whoever picks up these volumes quickly notices that the indirect statement contained within the animal fable can actually have a stronger effect than any form of direct description that exhausts itself in the factual contemplation of misery. We can thus recognize that aesthetic solutions are possible if they thematize unanswerability itself, if they take detours that lead the reader, the viewer, or the reflecting observer into a state that forces him or her to think without knowing how to incorporate everything that has happened into memory. Through this line of thinking I have also indicated some of the difficulties for the future.

It is impossible to plan fifty years ahead. Over the past fifty years, the history of the [Nazi] actions and the perpetrators has already been depicted in many different refractions, in the German public sphere and in scholarship. Retrospectively dealing with the mass murders and the actions of annihilation, above all of the Jews, has always called forth new intellectual approaches without ever having a conclusive answer. We must learn to deal with this challenge; we must learn to communicate it to others, and we must recall it in the debates between all generations in the hope that secondary memory too does not disappear. But I believe that we can be sure that it will not disappear. Yet the question of How must be thought through anew each day.

16

Histories in the Plural and the Theory of History: An Interview with Carsten Dutt

CD: The philosopher and sociologist of religion Jacob Taubes once described you as a "partisan" fighting for histories in the plural against history in the singular.[1] Taubes's characterization refers to a polemical aspect that is indeed prominent in many of your works, starting with *Critique and Crisis*, namely, your critique of the modern philosophy of history. Contrary to its speculative or pseudoscientific claims to comprehensive knowledge of historical procession and contrary to the universal teleologies that the philosophical-historical paradigm has attributed to "history" as a collective singular, you instead remind us of a plurality of histories that tends toward the infinite and of the irreducible heterogeneity and nonconvergence of the actions, events, and states of affairs investigated by historiography—and you do this, by the way, without linking this turn to plural histories to an emphatically narratological or narrativist position that would posit narrative as the only legitimate form of historical representation. My first question then would be: how do you look back upon your critique of the philosophy of history?

RK: Well, the difficulty presented by the philosophy of history lies in the fact that all the idealist systems posited or attempted to prove totalizing accounts of the entirety of history up to its supposed end point. This claim to totality is totalitarian when translated into the political realm and as such it has well-known consequences, in particular with Marxism, which was, after all, a result of these idealist philosophies of history. One can deploy the idea of a plurality of histories theoretically, in opposition to these philosophies, and this is justifiable to my mind, though certainly with an important caveat: that the multiplicity of single histories, which can always be aporetic and rule each other out, which do not permit a common interpretation and instead only breed contradictions, especially contradictions in interpretation—that beginning in the twentieth century, this plurality nonetheless also points to a single common history, but one whose terminology I want to circumvent, for it has been coated over by the philosophy of history. It is impossible to avoid addressing this commonality of the plurality of histories as a modern problem, especially one of the twentieth and twenty-first centuries. That said, it remains an open question to what extent this commonality, which one can at first glance find empirically validated by technology—especially that of communication, news reporting, and transportation—, will, through global interconnectedness, have an effect on the political structure of the plurality of histories, though this is also a problem that neither teleological models of history nor appeals to narrativity can solve.

CD: According to a memorable formulation that you have used on a number of occasions, the central task for the theory of history [*Historik*] after the failure of the philosophy of history consists in elucidating the "conditions of possible histories."[2] If I understand you correctly, despite your use of the language of transcendental philosophy, your approach is pretty straightforwardly object-oriented, more a theory of actual and repetitive patterns of history (and hence less toward a possible historical epistemology, as with Droysen, or a theory of historical representation, as with Ricœur). You are concerned with developing categories that help understand why histories take place in the first place and how they may proceed. You have pursued this theoretical program in various steps, beginning in the 1960s, by developing a spectrum of formal temporal structures that was to encompass the possible forms in which historical occurrences could unfold. Beginning in the 1980s the project then increasingly shifted toward discerning the ways in which histories are anthropologically grounded. Engaging especially with the Heideggerian analysis of *Dasein* but also with the certain theoretical assumptions of your teacher

Hans-Georg Gadamer's philosophical hermeneutics, you have outlined an anthropology of elementary oppositions that lead humans, as potentially conflictual beings, to become enmeshed ever-anew in histories. I would like to ask you to speak once more about this undertaking before we turn to questions of detail that might arise.

RK: Yes, as a framing concept for possible histories the concept of anthropology actually designates the vision for a theoretical program rather than this program's full, empirical realization, for even the formal anthropological categories I have developed are always in need of empirical realization if they are to be translated into a theory of history. But even with this caveat pertaining to the practice of historical research, I would nonetheless say that several formal durable determinations [Dauerbestimmungen] are undoubtedly inherent in human nature, determinations that are then articulated in altogether different ways in actual individual histories. This is the case with Herodotus's histories and all the way up to modern histories of terrorism that can have global effects, as we have seen in recent days.[3] What are these formal categories? Basically, we are dealing with three categories—later I would rediscover these unexpectedly in Goethe, by the way[4]—namely, the oppositions earlier-later, inside-outside, and above-below. These are very formal categories, but ones without which history is unthinkable. And once we take this seriously, we can deduce forms of conflict from these categories—conflicts, because these structural refractions lead quite necessarily to temporal and social determinations of difference. In other words: if I have a theory of conflict that can be potentially applied over and over, then I can take into consideration the spark that ignites possible problems, the seed that creates conflicts. And this seems to me the most important thing, that histories do not thereby end harmoniously, as philosophers of history have time and again alleged, that they do not have diachronic structures of completion, but instead that we can always witness new conflicts breaking out on a different level, whether higher or lower. Along with the aforementioned oppositional pairs, a second anthropological distinction naturally differentiates between language and nonlinguistic history. It is true that this difference can always be called into question by the foundational hermeneutic reflection of Gadamer's philosophy, that it can always be superseded because language conditions everything that the human being thinks and does, but the question is whether this hermeneutic given is sufficient for treating all histories and history in toto as a linguistic occurrence, and I doubt whether this is possible. For this reason, the differentiation between language and history distinguishes all theories of history from hermeneutics of whatever kind.

CD: In *Truth and Method*, Gadamer actually calls history writing "a kind of philology writ large,"[5] which, to my mind, is a rather problematic formulation, because it ignores the fact that the historian's relationship to the textual sources serving as the material for his investigations is completely different from the philologist's to poetry (and equally different from the jurist's to the relevant law or the theologian's to revealed truth). For the historian, the transmitted texts are not the final word. He interrogates these texts for something that lies outside, or, as it were, behind them, something for which they might only give testimony in a distorted manner.

RK: Yes, that is part of the basic phenomenon of all historical studies, the fact that texts are necessary in order to understand it, to retell, repeat or rewrite it. I cannot undertake any kind of history without texts, but the texts are surely not the final word, because no text already reveals what constitutes a history. No source, however one defines it, is sufficient for adequately deriving the history that the source points to. Every history is either more or less than the source can state. This even holds for the event structures of histories, which may well follow quite closely along the lines of the actual events in well-narrated sources, but can never be brought into a one-to-one relationship. And it holds all the more for long-term processes that are not described in any source but whose source material must instead first be constructed, so as to insert long-term operations into a temporal corset that is capable of thematizing the sort of diachronicity that as such is not contained in any source. For this reason, it is always a transcendental undertaking, if you will, that one derives the conditions for possible histories from texts but cannot call any single source "history."

CD: I would like to return to the relationship between the theory of history and anthropology: shouldn't an undertaking that seeks to discern anthropological and hence metahistorical conditions of possible— "humanly possible'"—histories, shouldn't such an undertaking be concerned, not just with the potentials for conflict that are prescribed by the *condition humaine* and are thus structurally unavoidable (e.g., relations between "above" and "below" or "inside" and "outside"), but also with the human ability to resolve conflict, and thus with reason as something that humans have a monopoly on? For, obviously, we are not only capable of killing or defeating each other, we also can agree on things, we can exercise justice, and we can forgive, as Hannah Arendt reminds us so forcefully in her political anthropology.[6] It stands out that these aspects retreat into the background on your account. There is a passage in *Zeitschichten* where you write: "History itself [. . .] is irrational. At most its analysis is rational."[7] Here one might object: isn't this an overly sober reversal of philosophical-historical exuberance and naïveté? Shouldn't it be possible to identify gains in rationality, learning processes in history, shouldn't it be possible to analyze them in their conditions and constitutive features and to thematize them in such a way as to strengthen these processes in a historically reflective manner?

RK: Well, seeking reason in history certainly makes sense as a political postulate or a political program, for it would be absurd to claim that human beings enmeshed in histories and capable of killing each other are a priori irrational. The call to reason certainly belongs to the minimal claim of any sensible politics. The question, though, is whether reason emerges in history when different units of action, each with its own rational projections, yet each not entirely capable of making itself understood, generate new conflicts. One conflict comes to an end only when a new one begins. Conflicts can never be completely resolved, but instead are simply replaced by conflicts with different structures. This is the experience that the entirety of history transmits to us; one can of course interpret this experience in a rational manner, but one cannot derive from it the idea that this series of conflicts brings about a more perfect reason. Undoubtedly, one can hope for it, intend it, work toward it politically, but not with an anthropology of history that posits a process of becoming rational as a foregone conclusion. The danger is that by positing the rationality of history, one is able to evade one's own responsibility. In my doctoral thesis I attempted to show that this was the actual aporia of the Enlightenment.[8]

By the way, something analogous applies to another human monopoly, namely, to morality. It is still my hypothesis that a moral dimension is always present in every field of action: in the religious and theological realms as well as in politics and economics, but that this moral dimension does not serve as the guiding principle or have the final say in how decisions are made. In other words: the greater the lack of morality in political or even military history, for example, or in the history of terror, the stronger the deficient mode of moral implications, but it is possible to draw attention to this deficient mode of moral absence. To this extent, then, the negative judgment of the lack of morality is thus a necessary part of what occurs. For even if one does not assume that history is a form of last judgment that irons out moral mistakes (whether in the beyond or even in history itself), that, in this interpretation of world history, which is in the final analysis terroristic, everything that happens is the carrying out of justice and morality—even if one cannot adopt this position, the negative instantiation of moral mistakes and sources of mistakes remains and one cannot judge any political action without it. I would perhaps say that morality represents the negative monitoring of what actually was the case. But that which was the case is never *eo ipso* moral.

CD: I'd like to turn to the typological and explanatory power of the categories of your *Historik*: it seems clear that as schemata for tensions that generate histories and that can be filled in in a variety of ways, the oppositional pairs of inside and outside, above and below, earlier and later enable comparisons that reveal both commonalities and differences between histories: *semper idem, semper aliter* [always the same, always different]. However, what do these categories contribute to the reconstruction of individual histories and their consequences, to knowledge about their emergence, their unfolding, and their effects? It seems that each case would require additional explanations, ones that were deeper-reaching and often very specific and that could not be derived from the schema of your elementary oppositional pairs.

RK: The concept of reconstruction certainly suggests that one can define histories as those that reveal themselves sufficiently in and through themselves; that what is at stake, in other words, is only a reconstruction, a rendering of what actually was the case, rather than a construction. This is possible in relation to courses of events in which human agents or groups of agents are engaged in empirically understandable actions that can be reconstructed. This is a feature of the histories of diplomacy or political history that contributes to their simplicity; the reconstruction of these histories is possible because the agents and their actions or failures to act can be made visible. In contrast, the actual conflicts extending out across longer spans of time and over many generations of agents cannot be found in any source, as I already mentioned, and for this reason necessitate less a kind of reconstruction and more a projection of a possible history whose plausibility is secured through evidence in the context of the sources by the historian. This is not a process of inventing [*Erfindung*] history, and instead is always only ever one of finding or locating [*Auffinden*] it, but this finding or locating is related to contexts that are in need of preconceptualization. For example, that the historian analyzes generational conflicts across long periods of time, or tracks the means of production and productive forces in the Marxian sense across centuries in order to discern when a qualitative shift in production occurs, through the mechanization of production, for example. There is quite a lot that one can study across longer periods of time that cannot be reduced to individual events, but that nonetheless conditions individual events.

One point is particularly important here, namely, that the concept of duration so frequently taken up in our field, Braudel's longue durée, can lead to a significant misunderstanding, for duration is anything but static. Stasis is everywhere in nature as long as natural, nonhuman pregivens remain constant or change only very slowly, over a million years, as in natural history, or also over tens of thousands of years, as with the Ice Ages. But modes of actions that can be assessed in the short- and mid-term can hardly be defined as long-lasting. Rather, every duration implies repetition, that is, individual events encapsulate innumerable modes of behavior, mentalities, subjectivities, institutional regulations, and so on, which all depend upon being repeated. Repetition is itself also an action and an event; however it is an event that is not legible in terms of its singularity, but instead in terms of what repeats itself in the event and its singularity. It is hard to judge this in percentages, but I would venture that more than 50 percent of all events contain structures of repetition that *in actu* arise again and anew. The concept of duration is thus by all means also a mode of action that is singular in each case, but the summation of singularities contains repetitions that are very difficult to determine on the basis of source material because sources typically refer to singular events. And this calls for a kind of preconceptualization that, as far as I know, no historical writing [*Historie*] has sufficiently considered with regard to the empirical practice of the writing of history—by the way, this also includes me.

In my book on Prussia,[9] I tried to analyze structures of repetition over the course of a century in the legal system in order to uncover what nonetheless changed, namely, the social conditions of the legal system. And it was these conditions that gave rise to conflicts, although the legal system remained the same. Conflicts emerged because of changes in social relations, which themselves were part of the legal system; these conflicts can only be explained through structures of repetition in the legal system, which remained one and the same, but in effect resulted in injustice in the cases that it had to process.

At first glance it would seem that actual history is more rightly characterized by singularity, for individual, day-to-day processes intervene in the daily routine and political decision makers face new alternatives from one day to the next, and one can then derive disagreements and conflicts and their resolutions from these alternatives. But these singularities have an abundance of predispositions to repetition built into them that reach back centuries or half-centuries, chronologically speaking, and that form the conditions of any possible singularity. If everything were singular, one would fall into a black hole. One would not know the direction in which one should act if everything were new. And this gives rise to the question: what is it that actually repeats itself in order to make singularity possible? How many constraints or structures of repetition does one need (do we need) in order to be able to be innovative? This is the central, the theoretically central question that emerges in each and every political context.

Think, for example, of the history of Bismarck's unification of Germany, which has been dealt with extensively from the perspective of the critique of ideology. Structurally, this represents the establishment of a constitution by the princes for the protection of the German people; this was how the constitution was defined at the time, and there are federal pregivens therein that are based on the coalition between princes. This is not identical to the democratic lining that Bismarck introduced through universal franchise, which represents an entirely modern side to his founding of the German Empire. But in regard to the federation of princes, he called upon a model of action that reached back in German history a half-millennium with the experience that this history transmitted again and again, namely, that internal federations both undermine and preserve the empire. The Imperial Chamber Court [*Reichskammergericht*] and the Imperial Court Council [*Reichshofrat*], on the one hand, and continued interventions by neighboring states, on the other, helped to preserve this internal federal structure, which was always endangered. Bismarck made use of a set of instruments that is thus a given in Germany in different ways than it is in other European countries (one might also think of the customs union in the German Confederation). These are structures of repetition that represent the conditions of possible freedoms for action, and Bismarck made use of them in astonishingly pronounced ways. Unification failed in 1848, probably because of an excess of national identification. No one wanted to introduce genuinely federal models under the pressure of the hegemonic positions of Prussia and Austria, and yet nothing would come into being without these two powers. But Bismarck made use of the awareness of this revolution; he implemented the minimal solution, so to speak, of Prussian hegemony at the federal level (which then changed rapidly on a structural level over the course of the Wilhelmine period).

These are ways of accessing history that one must operationalize in order to introduce them into the methodology of historical research, and this is something where we have achieved very little, including myself.

CD: By revealing processes that span multiple generations, structural changes that are long-term and "creeping," so to speak, historical research is able to reveal something that contemporaries themselves do not register, something that cannot be consciously experienced. To this extent there exists a kind of experience of history that is, in a strong sense, dependent upon historical research, that is a result and an achievement of the methodology of the professionalized study of history. You have dealt with the history of historiography in various writings, and what you have found is largely and unambiguously a history of progress, a history, that is, of accumulating various instruments that open up new sources for experience and yield knowledge that can then be stored and enhanced and remains accessible in the memory of institutionalized scholarship. However, you also draw attention to losses, pertaining in particular to the historiographical possibilities for representing what has been understood through research.

RK: Yes, we can naturally find evidence of scientific progress within the framework of rational criteria that apply to the methodological access and interpretation of sources, to the ways sources are created, from archaeology to textual interpretation and the exegesis of contemporary media studies. There are criteria within these framing conditions that enable rational controls and move processes of knowledge irreversibly forward, and this is not affected by the conditions of this process. If we thematize scientific revolutions with Thomas Kuhn,[10] one must conclude that there are insights that nonetheless remain accumulative despite all singularities and generational shifts and paradigm shifts. And it would be terrible if this were not the case, for we would have to admit our complete and utter stupidity. But on the other hand, there are losses that cannot be balanced out or equated with the progress of knowledge. Instead I would say that these represent asymmetrical relations. There are calculations of loss that resist being mastered by rational science, that are in science's blind spot, so to speak, that stand in an oblique relation to science. The classic example of this is Thucydides' invention of speeches in historical writing, which was imitated into the eighteenth century. Even Ranke wove speeches into his narratives, except that he derived them directly from the sources and did not invent any of them, in contrast to Thucydides. But the invented speeches of Thucydides have the great advantage that they say more in a quasi-poetic manner in just a few condensed pages than any kind of speech that was actually delivered at a moment of political struggle would have been capable of. Thucydides is thus able to intervene theoretically in internal and spoken thoughts alike in a way that would otherwise have been impossible. This is an aesthetic achievement that is superior to a reconstructed or source-based speech insofar as it is able to encapsulate the theoretical conditions of possible action better than if these invented speeches were not available. And one can thus say that this is in fact a loss, because the imagination that Thucydides' invented speeches had offered for the theoretical highest forms of historical research came to be limited.

CD: One could perhaps say that in modernity, this deficit is balanced out through a kind of division of labor between the discipline of history, which avoids these and other kinds of strategies of fictional representation, and literary prose, which makes use of them. This might well be seen as a complementary relationship. Many important novels— from Tolstoy's *War and Peace* to Uwe Johnson's *Jahrestage*—should at least partly be valued and appreciated as works of fictionalized historiography, although they are obviously not the kinds of works that are subject to the discursive limitations pertaining to representation that characterize the scientific study of history, which aims to be a "discipline of truth."

RK: Without a doubt, one can certainly call this relationship complementary, but it is also not an equal one; instead this complementarity reveals mutual asymmetries, so to speak. Literary depictions of historical experiences are without a doubt not only more aesthetically exciting than most historical texts, but they also have the considerable advantage that they can symbolically reduce conflict situations down to situations that say more in a few pages than bookshelf-long source editions are capable of saying. In this regard, the narrated history of the novelist is thus much closer to the epic than the critical source edition. Each narrated history leads into a realm that requires the imagination in order to produce a minimum of consistency, a minimum of symbolic expressiveness, a minimum of meaning, something that is impossible without narratives. And there are many good examples of this, such as Kleist's *Betrothal in Santo Domingo*, a love story whose symbolic conflict situations encapsulate the entirety of the French Revolution. The same is true of Melville's story *Billy Budd*: in about a hundred pages, Melville symbolically portrays all of the conflicts of the French Revolution, as well as those between England and France. In fact, there are many poetic achievements that as a historian I value higher in a certain way than a statistically useful source collection, which presupposes an entirely different kind of approach. Condensation is an extremely important part of how humans cope with experience and should not be associated solely with pure fiction. Instead, one must admit that many poets have given expression to historical experiences in entirely plausible and insightful ways. I am thinking here about Faulkner's novels against the backdrop of the American Civil War. One of his greatest themes is the perspectivity of experience, the fact that multiple layers of experience exist that often are mutually exclusive. In other words, Faulkner's novels bring together experiences that are in each case refracted in such a way that one can understand how unsolvable conflicts arise and jam into place.

CD: Recently there have been intense discussions about the literary dimension of historiography, above all in the wake of Hayden White's *Metahistory*;[11] these discussions include the work of professional historians and are not simply limited to the historiography done in literary genres such as the historical "novel." Drawing on Northrop Frye, White developed a poetics of writing history that identifies archetypal forms of the narrative modeling of the world, uncovering romance, comedy, tragedy, and satire in the representations of historical works that are firmly grounded in the critical study of source material. Do you draw on aspects of this work in your own writing? How would you evaluate the discussion about narrativity and poetics that continue to occur in recent theories of historical study?

RK: Well, I edited [the translation of] White myself,[12] so as to make him accessible to a German audience, even though I am critical of aspects of his work, in all friendship to him as an author. He developed a justified approach that thematizes the linguistic status of historical narratives and of writing history in general. To this extent he brings history [*Historie*] into the proximity of genres also discussed in literary studies, literary history, and the history of rhetoric. His expansion of rhetorical categories into generic concepts is a bit clumsy, but this is a problem of secondary importance. The main problem is that the distinguishing feature of historical research is missing in White, namely, the establishment of a regulative, controlling instance in source exegesis; history must always jump over the methodological hurdle of this control in order to present itself as science [*Wissenschaft*]. With White this regulative instance of source exegesis slips through the cracks; his analysis is inspiring and suggestive, but it falls short of circumscribing the difference between writing history and historical research. White's categories cannot achieve this differentiation; this is the main disadvantage. And the contemporary fashion of rediscovering narrativity is, in effect, a reaction against an excessively analytical, sociologizing mode of writing history—this is perhaps also a reaction against sociology in general, though I wouldn't want to gauge this right now. But this does not resolve the problem, for the methodological criteria for writing history embodied in the science of history cannot be overcome by any narrative supplementation, disintegration, or outbidding. We need to preserve the criteria of the science, although this naturally does not entail any kind of prescriptions for how future historians should write. The manner in which the historian writes is, in the end, shaped by his own skill in expressing him or herself, and this certainly points to an affinity with literature. But I would cast doubt upon whether we can conclude from this that narrativity is a basis for identity formation. I believe that the profession of writing history overestimates itself when it presumes to control or produce political identities through its narratives, something that is to a certain extent an idealistic hope of many narrativists.

CD: So you are not an advocate of the thesis that history [*Historie*] has the "function of identity presentation" developed by Hermann Lübbe (who, to be fair, himself noted that this was only a part of history's task)?[13]

RK: This is certainly an overestimation and one that can be traced back to the outsized position attained by history writing in the nineteenth century, which almost outstripped that of the theologians. History's position later declined with the rise of political science, sociology, and so on, above all thereby losing its need for currentness, something that can now be recreated only artificially. This is exactly the point of my critique of the French Annales school, which represents a purely solipsistic history writing of French self-identification. Braudel began by defining the French Revolution as the end point of the longue durée so as to avoid thematizing the complex difficulties that have since intervened in French history. This means that this longue durée is an idealistic postulate in regards to French identity formation. And the same applies to the guardians of identity today. Pierre Nora's sites of memory (*lieux de mémoire*) are specifically only French ones, and, as such, the conflicts with Germany, Great Britain, Italy, or Spain that these sites of memory contain are not considered from the opposing perspectives.[14] But historical research has the duty to represent conflicts in their actual plurality and not to seek out identity. And this is the considerable advantage of historical research and, of course, of history writing, if it articulates scientific insights, namely, that it requires a kind of reading against the grain, that through it one is forced to take into account truths that do not found identity.

CD: So calls for history's "relevance" that arise outside of the field of academic historiography, via politically defined notions of being current or up-to-date, for example, are inherently out of place? Analyses of the present are not "more important" than purely antiquarian research.

RK: Well, I would certainly say analyses of the present may arouse greater curiosity in common readers than topics that seem quite foreign to them, but this is not a claim that applies to the theory of historical science [*Geschichtswissenschaft*] or its institutional politics. You are certainly right; in terms of the theory of knowledge it is a weak argument that proximity to the present day leads to greater currentness or urgency and increased relevance. Instead, relevance and urgency consist in the surveying of conflict zones that transcend individuals and personal associations and that undergo constant regeneration. For this reason, I can learn much more from Thucydides than I can from any randomly selected biography of Helmut Kohl. The foreignness of past histories can be much more important for creating knowledge than instrumentalized attempts to make history be about the present day. Indeed, currently, when religious antagonisms are once more becoming apparent on a global scale, the question is whether it would be better for us to be familiar with histories of Muhammad and read the surahs [of the Quran] than to be aware of the day-to-day unfolding of acts of terrorism. Indeed, here, distance might be more current than proximity. And once one realizes this, it becomes impossible to swallow the facile alternatives of "current" and "purely antiquarian." In fact, in history, everything has to do with everything else, and being able to call forth perspectives in order to increase knowledge or even produce it in the first place is an art that the historian should be in command of.

The advantage of historical science, as Goethe well knew, is that it can draw on a couple thousand years. This allows the study of history to see through the assumption of currentness or urgency as false and in certain circumstances politically dangerous. Orchestrated attempts to make something current tend to become outdated so very quickly. The kinds of identities constantly being created on this basis are short-term and asthmatic. In the same way that the "German *Volk*" constantly invoked in the nineteenth century never existed, there is no such thing as a "European community" that functions today in which to found identity. Of course one can work politically toward such a goal, and one can also draw on historical arguments in doing so, but one cannot access these arguments when one simply functionalizes or instrumentalizes history. History withholds itself from every instrumentalization. It will always take revenge as a force that contains more than what can be corralled by offers of identification.

CD: In an essay of yours which first appeared in a Festschrift for Karl Löwith and has since become famous, you investigate the loss in validity of the *historia magistra vitae* [history is life's teacher] topos, its "dissolution within the horizon of modern, dynamic history."[15] Would you agree with the suggestion that the rehabilitation of this very topos is the point, or at least one of the main points of your "partisan fight" for a theory of history [*Historik*] that elucidates structures of repetition—natural, anthropologically determined and historically contingent structures of repetition—as the conditions of possible histories? If we can identify structures of repetition, then we can likewise develop prognoses, prognoses that perhaps might not allow one to deduce individual events, but that might well allow us to say what can be the case and what probably will be the case.

RK: You are completely right that the evidence for the *historia magistra* topos decreased in the nineteenth century in the wake of the French Revolution, because history in its entirety came to be conceived as unique. This is also the axiom of so-called historicism: each epoch has a direct relationship to God, and is hence always unique. And this uniqueness does not allow me to learn something from a prior case because this case is unique. In reality, though, historicism's theory of uniqueness is a result of an accelerating industrial and revolutionary society that eliminates the old society of orders and introduces the democratic state of equality, as analyzed by de Tocqueville. But the more this uniqueness mounts within the context of modern industrialization, the more it turns out that the conditions that make these singularities possible repeat themselves forcefully. And it is here where the *historia magistra vitae* idea could reassert itself, though on a different theoretical level. We cannot predict specific events; we do not know what President [George W.] Bush will do in the future. But we know the framing conditions, for example, within which the Americans will carry out their fight against terrorism. Indeed, the diagnostic categories employed by the Americans naturally contain elements of repetition of their entire political worldview, which certainly is exemplary with regards to democratic freedoms, but which brings with it significant consequences that have less exemplary effects in other areas of the world.

The characteristic feature of modernity—if we are to sum it up in a single concept—is an acceleration that is not contained by the natural pre-givens of humankind. And this is what fundamentally distinguishes every history since the eighteenth century from all previous histories, because the structural pregivens are themselves changing more quickly than had been previously possible. This process starts with the invention of the steam engine and continues through to the chemical, electronic, and atomic accelerators that have completely altered networks of transportation and communication in such a way that travel around the world in twenty-four hours is no longer just a utopian dream and that events at every location on the globe can be present at the same time in all news media. This means that we can recognize a law, identify a regularity, something, by the way, that Henry Adams had already formulated in 1904 in "A Law of Accelera-tion."[16] This law is based on the fact that technological accelerators have altered the entire structure of society as well as its economic potentialities along with the structure of political decision making. One can no longer wait for decisions to present themselves, but must instead anticipate them in order to still be able to act. One must act more quickly and yet, at the same time, because of possibilities for repetition, one must plan ahead in the long-term so as to be able to act in a manner that is up-to-date. Events and the reports about them increasingly converge. We saw this once more with the terror attack on New York: the event was temporally identical to the images we were viewing. There is no longer any difference between event and political representation and interpretation; instead, these must be theoretically anticipated to be able to influence events. To this extent, then, the acceleration of systems of communication and transportation alter the entire structure of action, and this also applies to the realm of the military. Planning ahead anticipatorily presupposes, nonetheless, that there is a minimum of structures of repetition; otherwise, nothing could be anticipated. This means that, in order to gain any kind of influence over what is happening, what must be anticipated is the anticipation of possible repetitions.

So, *historia magistra vitae*, yes, but not in the sense of the repetition of individual events, but instead in that of a prognostics that surveys the scopes of possibilities of events.

Notes

Introduction

1. "Der Fragebogen," *Forschung und Lehre* 8 (2003): 464.
2. As Koselleck observed in his speech accepting the Sigmund Freud Prize for Academic Prose (Reinhart Koselleck, Vorgriff auf Unvollkommenheit, Dankrede Sigmund-Freud-Preis 1999, Deutsche Akademie für Sprache und Dichtung, www.deutscheakademie.de/de/auszeichnungen/sigmund-freud-preis/reinhart-koselleck/dankrede [accessed 29/11/2017]).
3. Manfred Hettling and Bernd Ulrich, "Formen der Bürgerlichkeit. Ein Gespräch mit Reinhart Koselleck," in *Bürgertum nach 1945* (Hamburg: Hamburger Institut für Sozialforschung, 2005), 40–60, at 55.
4. Christian Geulen, "Plädoyer für eine Geschichte der Grundbegriffe des 20. Jahrhunderts," *Zeithistorische Forschungen / Studies in Contemporary History* 7 (2010).
5. Reinhart Koselleck, "Einleitung," in *Zeitschichten. Studien zur Historik* (Frankfurt am Main: Suhrkamp, 2000), 9.
6. See esp. Helge Jordheim, "Against Periodization. Koselleck's Theory of Multiple Temporalities," *History and Theory* 51 (2012), 151–71; and John Zammito, "Koselleck's Philosophy of Historical Time(s) and the Practice of History," *History and Theory* 43 (2004): 124–35.
7. Koselleck, "Einleitung," in *Zeitschichten*, 9.
8. For a very different, programmatic usage of the metaphor of "sediments" and "desedimentation," see Jacques Derrida, *Edmund Husserl's Origin of Geometry: an Introduction* (Lincoln: University of Nebraska Press, 1989); and id., *Of Grammatology* (Baltimore: Johns Hopkins University Press, 1997), 10.
9. See "'Space of Experience' and 'Horizon of Expectation': Two Historical Categories," in Reinhart Koselleck, *Futures Past: On the Semantics of Historical Time*, trans. Keith Tribe (New York: Columbia University Press, 2004), 255–77, at 260–61.
10. Reinhart Koselleck, "*Historia Magistra Vitae*: The Dissolution of the Topos into the Perspective of a Modernized Historical Process," in id., *Futures Past*. First published as "*Historia Magistra Vitae*. Über die Auflösung des Topos

im Horizont neuzeitlich bewegter Geschichte," in *Natur und Geschichte. Karl Löwith zum 70. Geburtstag,* ed. Hermann Braun and Manfred Riedel (Stuttgart: W. Kohlhammer, 1967), 825–38.

11. Niklas Olsen, *History in the Plural: An Introduction to the Work of Reinhart Koselleck* (New York: Berghahn Books, 2012); Jan Eike Dunkhase, *Absurde Geschichte. Reinhart Kosellecks historischer Existentialismus* (Marbach: Deutsche Schillergesellschaft, 2015). *Begriffene Geschichte. Beiträge zum Werk Reinhart Kosellecks,* ed. Hans Joas and Peter Vogt, (Frankfurt am Main: Suhrkamp, 2011); Carsten Dutt and Reinhard Laube, *Zwischen Sprache und Geschichte* (Göttingen: Wallstein, 2013); Hubert Locher and Adriana Markantonatos, *Reinhart Koselleck und die Politische Ikonologie* (Berlin: Deutscher Kunstverlag, 2013).

12. Paul Ricoeur, *Time and Narrative*. 3 vols. (Chicago: University of Chicago Press, 1984–1988); François Hartog, *Regimes of Historicity: Presentism and Experiences of Time* (New York: Columbia University Press, 2015). See also Alexandre Escudier "Le temps de l'histoire. 'Temporalisation' et modernité politique: penser avec Koselleck," *Annales. Histoire, Sciences sociales* 64 (2009): 1269–1301.

13. Reinhart Koselleck, *Critique and Crisis. Enlightenment and the Pathogenesis of Modern Society* (Oxford: Berg Publishers, 1988).

14. Reviews of Koselleck, *Futures Past*: Hayden White, *American Historical Review* 95 (1987): 1175–76, at 1175; David Carr, *History and Theory* 26 (1987): 197–204.

15. Personal correspondence by Stefan-Ludwig Hoffmann with Michael Geyer, February 28, 2014.

16. Anthony La Vopa, "Conceiving a Public: Ideas and Society in Eighteenth Century Europe," *Journal of Modern History* 64 (1992): 79–116, 81.

17. Reinhart Koselleck, "Dankesrede (2004)," in *Reinhart Koselleck (1923–2006). Reden zum 50. Jahrestag seiner Promotion in Heidelberg* (Heidelberg: Universitätsverlag Winter), 34.

18. See, e.g., *Habermas and The Public Sphere* , ed. Craig Calhoun (Cambridge, MA: MIT Press, 1992; 4th ed., 1996).

19. Review of Koselleck, *Critique and Crisis*: T. C. W. Blanning, *German History* 20 (1989) 265–66.

20. Hans-Ulrich Wehler, "Geschichtswissenschaft heute," In *Stichworte zur »Geistigen Situation der Zeit«,* ed. Jürgen Habermas (Frankfurt am Main: Suhrkamp, 1979), 709–753, at 725, fn. 23.

21. Koselleck, *Critique and Crisis*, 7; trans. modified.

22. Reinhart Koselleck, "Wie neu ist die Neuzeit?" *Dritte Verleihung des Preises des Historischen Kollegs* (Munich: Stiftung Historisches Kolleg, 1991), 37–52, at 38.

23. Jürgen Habermas, "Verrufener Fortschritt—verkanntes Jahrhundert: Zur Kritik an der Geschichtsphilosophie," *Merkur* 14 (1960): 468–477. In a review

of Dirk van Laak's *Gespräche in der Sicherheit des Schweigens. Carl Schmitt in der politischen Geistesgeschichte der frühen Bundesrepublik* (1993), Habermas conceded thirty years later that "some of the most productive and smartest scholars of the postwar years converted to 'Schmittianism' without buying into his political prejudices." Habermas, "Das Bedürfnis nach deutschen Kontinuitäten," *Die Zeit*, December 3, 1993. See also Reinhard Mehring, "Begriffsgeschichte mit Carl Schmitt," in *Begriffene Geschichte*, ed. Joas and Vogt, 138–67.

24. Review of Koselleck, *Critique and Crisis*: Carl J. Friedrich, *American Political Science Review* 54 (1960): 746–48.

25. See Reinhart Koselleck to Carl Schmitt, January 21, 1953, Deutsches Literaturarchiv (DLA) Marbach, A: Koselleck; Olsen, *History in the Plural*, 58–63; id., "Carl Schmitt, Reinhart Koselleck and the Foundations of History and Politics," *History of European Ideas*, 37 (2012): 197–202.

26. Koselleck, "Dankesrede," 55–56.

27. Ivan Nagel, "Der Kritiker der Krise: Über den Historiker Reinhart Koselleck," *Neue Zürcher Zeitung*, January 8–9, 2006; Reinhart Koselleck to Stephen Holmes, May 30, 1989, DLA Marbach, A: Koselleck.

28. Reinhart Koselleck, "Einleitung," in *Taktische Kernwaffen. Die fragmentierte Abschreckung,* ed. Philippe Blanchard, Reinhart Koselleck, and Ludwig Streits (Frankfurt am Main: Suhrkamp, 1987), 13–18.

29. Only two of Koselleck's contributions for the *Geschichtliche Grundbegriffe* are available in English (translated by Manuela Richter): Reinhart Koselleck, "Crisis," *Journal of the History of Ideas* 67 (2006): 357–400; id., "Introduction and Prefaces to the *Geschichtliche Grundbegriffe,*" *Contributions to the History of Concepts* 6 (2011), 1–37.

30. Olsen, *History in the Plural*, 196. Similarly, Helge Jordheim, "Thinking in Convergences—Koselleck on Language, History and Time," *Ideas in History* 3 (2007): 65–90.

31. Edoardo Tortarolo, interview with Reinhart Koselleck, DLA Marbach, A: Koselleck, 17 MS pp., at 12.

32. Melvin Richter to Reinhart Koselleck, November 19, 1987, DLA Marbach, A: Koselleck. See also Melvin Richter, *The History of Social and Political Concepts. A Critical Introduction* (Oxford: Oxford University Press, 1997). Similarly, Kari Palonen, *Die Entzauberung der Begriffe: Das Umschreiben der politischen Begriffe bei Quentin Skinner und Reinhart Koselleck* (Münster: LIT, 2004); Jan-Werner Müller, "On Conceptual History'" in *Rethinking Modern European Intellectual History*, ed. Darrin M. McMahon and Samuel Moyn (Oxford: Oxford University Press, 2014), 74–93.

33. Reinhart Koselleck, "A Response to Comments on the *Geschichtliche Grundbegriffe,*" in *The Meanings of Historical Terms and Concepts*, ed. Hartmut Lehmann and Melvin Richter, Occasional Papers, No. 15 (Washington, DC: German Historical Institute, 1996), 59–70, at 65.

34. Jason Edwards, "The Ideological Interpellation of Individuals as Combatants: An Encounter between Reinhart Koselleck and Michel Foucault," *Journal of Political Ideologies* 12 (2007): 49–66. In fact, Foucault used *Geschichtliche Grundbegriffe* for his lectures on governmentality at the Collège de France in the late 1970s and early 1980s. He first heard about Koselleck in 1977—two years before the publication of the French translation of *Critique and Crisis*—from Walter Seitter at a meeting with Pasquale Pasquino and the Merve Verlag publishers Heidi Paris and Peter Gente in Paris. Tape recordings of the meeting are in the possession of Merve Verlag. We are grateful to Philipp Felsch for making this tape available to us. See also Philipp Felsch, *Der lange Sommer der Theorie. Geschichte einer Revolte, 1960– 1990* (Munich: C. H. Beck, 2015), and Michel Foucault, *The Birth of Biopolitics: Lectures at the Collège de France, 1978–1979*, ed. Michel Senellart (Basingstoke, England: Palgrave Macmillan, 2008), 315, fn. 26, on Manfred Riedel, "Gesellschaft, bürgerliche," in *Geschichtliche Grundbegriffe*, vol. 2, ed. Otto Brunner, Werner Conze, and Reinhart Koselleck (Stuttgart: Klett-Cotta, 1975), 719–800.

34. Jason Edwards, "The Ideological Interpellation of Individuals as Combatants: An Encounter between Reinhart Koselleck and Michel Foucault," *Journal of Political Ideologies* 12 (2007): 49–66. In fact, Foucault used *Geschichtliche Grundbegriffe* for his lectures on governmentality at the Collège de France in the late 1970s and early 1980s. He first heard about Koselleck in 1977—two years before the publication of the French translation of *Critique and Crisis*—from Walter Seitter at a meeting with Pasquale Pasquino and the Merve Verlag publishers Heidi Paris and Peter Gente in Paris. Tape recordings of the meeting are in the possession of Merve Verlag. We are grateful to Philipp Felsch for making this tape available to us. See also Philipp Felsch, *Der lange Sommer der Theorie. Geschichte einer Revolte, 1960– 1990* (Munich: C. H. Beck, 2015), and Michel Foucault, *The Birth of Biopolitics: Lectures at the Collège de France, 1978–1979*, ed. Michel Senellart (Basingstoke, England: Palgrave Macmillan, 2008), 315, fn. 26, on Manfred Riedel, "Gesellschaft, bürgerliche," in *Geschichtliche Grundbegriffe*, vol. 2, ed. Otto Brunner, Werner Conze, and Reinhart Koselleck (Stuttgart: Klett-Cotta, 1975), 719–800.

35. Koselleck, *Zeitschichten*, and—compiled by Koselleck but posthumously published—*Begriffsgeschichten. Studien zur Semantik und zur Pragmatik der politischen und sozialen Sprache* (Frankfurt am Main: Suhrkamp, 2006) and *Vom Sinn und Unsinn der Geschichte: Aufsätze und Vorträge aus vier Jahrzehnten* (Frankfurt am Main: Suhrkamp, 2010). As Koselleck explains in the preface to *Zeitschichten*, the content of these volumes was put together to capture the three main themes of his *Historik*: the theory of historical times, the theory *and* practice of conceptual history, and his historiographical studies in the history of perceptions (*Wahrnehmungen*). For this edition, we included essays from all three volumes; the German footnotes in brackets for essays taken from *Sinn und Unsinn der Geschichte* were supplemented by Carsten Dutt and all other bracketed footnotes are from the editors.

36. See Martin Heidegger, *Der Zeitbegriff in der Geschichtswissenschaft* (1916), 433. See also Heidegger, "Die Trivialisierung der Diltheyschen Fragestellung durch Windelband und Rickert," in *Frühe Schriften, Gesamtausgabe*, vol. 1 (Frankfurt am Main: Klostermann, 1978), and "Prolegomena zur Geschichte des Zeitbegriffs," in *Gesamtausgabe*, vol. 20 (Frankfurt am Main: Klostermann, 1979).

37. Reinhart Koselleck to Carl Schmitt, January 21, 1953, DLA Marbach, A: Koselleck.

38. See also Koselleck, "Transformations of Experience and Methodological Change: A Historical-Anthropological Essay," in id., *The Practice of Conceptual History: Timing History, Spacing Concepts*, trans. Todd Samuel Presner et al. (Stanford: Stanford University Press, 2002), 45–83.

39. Stefan-Ludwig Hoffmann, "Koselleck, Arendt, and the Anthopology of Historical Experiences," *History and Theory* 49 (2010): 212–36; Dunkhase, *Absurde Geschichte*, esp. 48–51.

40. Reinhart Koselleck, "Vielerlei Abschied vom Krieg," In *Vom Vergessen und Gedenken. Erinnerungen und Erwartungen in Europa zum 8. Mai 1945,* eds. Brigitte Sauzay, Heinz Ludwig Arnold and Rudolf von Thadden (Göttingen: Wallstein Verlag, 1995), 19–25; Barbara Stelzl-Marx, "Alltag in Karaganda. Zur Geschichte des Kriegsgefangenen-Lagers 99 Spasozavodsk," *Problemy voennogo plena: istoriia i sovremennost',* vol. 2. (Vologda, 1997), 202–225; Kate Brown, *Dispatches from Dystopia. Histories of Places Not Yet Forgotten* (Chicago: University of Chicago Press, 2015), esp. chap. 6.

41. Eric J. Hobsbawm, *Interesting Times. A Twentieth-Century Life* (London: Allen Lane, 2002), 179.

Chapter 1

Chapter 1, "Sediments of Time," was originally published as "Zeitschichten" in *Zeit und Wahrheit: Europäisches Forum Alpbach 1994,* ed. Heinrich Pfusterschmid-Hardtenstein (Vienna: Ibera, 1995), 95–100. The translation here is from "Zeitschichten" in Koselleck, *Zeitschichten,* 19–26.

1. Arnaldo Momigliano, "Time in Ancient Historiography," *History and Theory* 6 (1966): 1–23. See also Momigliano, *On Pagans, Jews and Christians* (Middletown, CT: Wesleyan University Press, 1987).

2. I learned of Friedrich Cramer's book *Der Zeitbaum. Grundlegung einer allgemeinen Zeittheorie* (Frankfurt am Main: Suhrkamp, 1993) only after first presenting this material. At times his theses overlap with the historical-anthropological lines of thought I have pursued here, though they are grounded more widely and with richer empirical detail, both in terms of natural science and the history of science.

Chapter 2

Chapter 2, "Fiction and Historical Reality," was a talk held at the convention of Germanists (Germanistentag) in Düsseldorf 1976 and originally published as "Fiktion und geschichtliche Wirklichkeit" in the *Zeitschrift für Ideengeschichte* 1, no. 3 (2007): 39–54. The translation here is from "Fiktion und geschichtliche Wirklichkeit" in Koselleck, *Vom Sinn und Unsinn der Geschichte,* 80–95.

1. Charlotte Beradt, *Dreams of the Third Reich* (Chicago: Quadrangle Books, 1968), 21, 135; wording slightly modified.

2. [Aristotle, *Poetics,* trans. Anthony Kenny (Oxford: Oxford University Press, 2013), 1451b.]

3. [Johan Heinrich Alsted, *Scientiarium omnium encyclopaedia,* 4 vols., 3rd ed. (Lyon, 1649), 2: 619, plate.]

4. François Fénelon, *Oeuvres complètes,* vol. 6 (Paris, 1850), 639.

5. Johann Christoph Gottsched, *Versuch einer Critischen Dichtkunst,* reprint of the fourth edition, Leipzig, 1742 (Darmstadt: Wissenschaftliche Buchgesellschaft, 1962), 354.

6. Lucian, "How to Write History," In *Lucian in Eight Volumes,* trans. K. Kilburn, 6 (Cambridge, MA: Harvard University Press, 1959), 65.

7. [Gotthold Ephraim Lessing, "Über den Beweis des Geistes und der Kraft" (1777), in Lessing, *Werke,* ed. Herbert G. Göpfert, vol. 8: *Theologiekritische Schriften III. Philosophische Schriften* (Munich: Hanser, 1979), 9–14, at 12.]

8. Gotthold Ephraim Lessing, *Briefe, die Neueste Literatur betreffend,* letter 63 (October 18, 1759), in id., *Werke,* vol. 5: *Literaturkritik, Poetik und Philologie* (Munich: Hanser, 1973), 207.

9. See Reinhart Koselleck, "Geschichte, Historie," in *Geschichtliche Grundbegriffe,* 2: 693–717.

10. [See George Grosz, *An Autobiography* (Berkeley: University of California Press, 1998), 221–26.]

11. Jean Cayrol, *Lazarus unter uns* (Stuttgart: Schwab, 1959); French orig., *Lazare parmi nous* (Neuchâtel, 1950).

12. [Johann Wolfgang Goethe, "Brief an König Ludwig I. von Bayern," January 12, 1830, in *Goethes Briefe,* vol. 4: *Briefe der Jahre 1821–1832,* ed. Karl Robert Mandelkow (Hamburg: Wegner, 1976), 363.]

13. [See Wolfgang Iser, "The Reality of Fiction: A Functionalist Approach to Literature," *New Literary History* 7, no. 1 (1975): 7–38.]

14. [See note 12 above.]

15. [Alexander Kluge, *The Battle* (New York: McGraw-Hill, 1967).]

16. [Theodor Plievier, *Stalingrad* (New York: Carroll & Graf, 1984).]

17. [Dieter Forte, *Martin Luther & Thomas Münzer. Oder die Einführung der Buchhaltung* (Berlin: Wagenbach, 1971).]

18. Johann Peter Eckermann, *Gespräche mit Goethe in den letzten Jahren seines Lebens,* ed. Christoph Michel (Frankfurt am Main: Deutscher Klassiker, 1999), in Goethe, *Sämtliche Werke. Briefe, Tagebücher und Gespräche,* 39: 616 (conversation of May 6, 1827).

Chapter 3

Chapter 3, "Space and History," was the final keynote lecture delivered in October 1986 at the convention of German historians (*Historikertag*) in Trier. The translation here is from "Raum und Geschichte" in Koselleck, *Zeitschichten,* 78–96.

1. ["O Glück der Mücke, die noch innen hüpft": Rilke, *Dunio Elegies,* no. 8.]

2. Arno Seifert, *Cognitio Historica. Die Geschichte als Namensgeberin der früh-neuzeitlichen Empirie* (Berlin: Duncker & Humblot, 1976).

3. See Wolf Lepenies, "Das Ende der Naturgeschichte und der Beginn der Moderne. Verzeitlichung und Enthistorisierung in der Wissenschafts-geschichte des 18. und 19. Jahrhunderts," in *Studien zum Beginn der modernen Welt*, ed. Reinhart Koselleck (Stuttgart: Klett-Cotta, 1977), 317–51; and Koselleck, "Geschichte, Historie," in *Geschichtliche Grundbegriffe*, 2: 678–82.

4. C. F. v. Weizsäcker, *Die Geschichte der Natur* (Göttingen: Vandenhoeck & Ruprecht, 1948, 1964); Max Jammer, *Concepts of Space: The History of Theories of Space in Physics* (New York: Courier, 1954); Elisabeth Ströker, *Philosophische Untersuchungen zum Raum* (Frankfurt am Main: Klostermann, 1965), with discussion of the anthropological dimension of the concept of space. We also have a brief and clear psychological and political conceptual history of the term *Lebensraum* by A. Lang and J. Debus in *Historisches Wörterbuch der Philosophie* (Basel: Schwabe, 1980), 5: 143–47. The same lexicon also contains a philosophical/natural scientific conceptual history of "space" (8: 67–111); a psychological conceptual history (111–21); and a conceptual history of political space (122–31) by W. Köster.

5. Hermann Overbeck, *Kulturlandschaftsforschung und Landeskunde* (Heidelberg: Heidelberger Geographische Arbeiten, 1965); id., "Die Entwicklung der Anthropogeographie (insbesondere in Deutschland) seit der Jahrhundertwende und ihre Bedeutung für die geschichtliche Landesforschung," in *Blätter für deutsche Landesgeschichte* 91 (1954): 182–244, repr. in: *Probleme und Methoden der Landesgeschichte*, ed. Pankraz Fried (Darmstadt: Wissenschaftliche Buchgesellschaft, 1978), 190–271.

6. Johann Gustav Droysen, *Historik*, ed. Rudolf Hübner (Munich: R. Oldenbourg, 1943), 8–9, and 406–15 on "Natur und Geschichte."

7. See Karl-Georg Faber, "Was ist eine Geschichtslandschaft?" in *Festschrift Ludwig Petry* (Wiesbaden: Steiner, 1968), 1–28; and id., "Geschichtslandschaft—Région historique—Section in History. Ein Beitrag zur vergleichenden Wissenschaftsgeschichte," *Saeculum: Jahrbuch für Universalgeschichte* 30, no. 1 (1979): 4–21.

8. Ernst Bernheim, *Lehrbuch der Historischen Methode und der Geschichtsphilosophie* (1889) (Leipzig: Duncker, 1903), 46.

9. Ludwig Rieß, *Historik. Ein Organon geschichtlichen Denkens und Forschens* (Leipzig: Göschen 1912), 69.

10. Even though it has been newly taken up by Hermann Hambloch, *Der Mensch als Störfaktor im Geosystem* (Opladen: Westdeuscher Verlag, 1986).

11. See note 7.

12. See Peter Schöller, "Wege und Irrwege der Politischen Geographie und Geopolitik," (1957), in *Politische Geographie*, ed. Josef Matznetter (Darmstadt: Wissenschaftliche Buchgesellschaft, 1977), with representative sources and essays on the history of science and its shifting positions.

13. The open, contested, and unresolved question of the location of the eastern borders of the European Union—whether it should skirt Crimea or the southern slope of the Caucasus Mountains—shows how political calculations must take specifically geographical givens into consideration; "geopolitics" thus retains its indisputable importance [1999 addition].

14. Halford J. Mackinder, *Democratic Ideals and Reality* (New York: Holt, 1919).

15. Karl J. Narr, "Vom Wesen des Frühmenschen: Halbtier oder Mensch?" *Saeculum: Jahrbuch für Universalgeschichte* 25, no. 4 (1974): 293–324.

16. Karl J. Narr, ed., *Handbuch der Urgeschichte* (Bern: Francke, 1966), 1: 236.

17. Wolfgang Zorn, "Verdichtung und Beschleunigung des Verkehrs als Beitrag zur Entwicklung der 'modernen Welt'," in *Studien zum Beginn der modernen Welt*, ed. Koselleck, 115–34.

18. A book that remains indispensable is Heinrich von Stephan, *Geschichte der preußischen Post von ihren Ursprüngen bis auf die Gegenwart* (Berlin: Decker, 1859; repr. Glashütten im Taunus: D. Auvermann, 1976). See also Amand von Schweiger-Lerchenfeld, *Das neue Buch von der Weltpost. Geschichte, Organisation, und Technik des Postwesens von den ältesten Zeiten bis auf die Gegenwart* (Leipzig [1901]).

19. Alberto Tenenti, "The Sense of Space and Time in the Venetian World of the Fifteenth and Sixteenth Centuries," in *Renaissance Venice*, ed. J. R. Hale (London: Faber, 1973), 17–46, 29–31.

Chapter 4

Chapter 4, "*Historik* and Hermeneutics," originated as the text of a lecture delivered in honor of Hans-Georg Gadamer at Heidelberg University on February 16, 1985. It was first published as "*Historik* und Hermeneutik" in *Sitzungsberichte der Heidelberger Akademie der Wissenschaften* 1 (1987), 9–28. The translation here is from "*Historik* und Hermeneutik" in Koselleck, *Zeitschichten*, 97–118.

1. Pope Innocent III, *De contemptu mundi* 1.24.

2. Winston S. Churchill, *My Early Life: A Roving Commission* (New York: Scribner, 1930), 191–92.

3. [See in this volume chapter 12, "Concepts of the Enemy."]

4. Hans-Georg Gadamer, "Replik," in *Hermeneutik und Ideologiekritik*, ed. Jürgen Habermas et al. (Frankfurt am Main: Suhrkamp, 1971), 302.

5. Johann Gottlieb Fichte, *The Science of Knowing: J. G. Fichte's 1804 Lectures on the Wissenschaftslehre*, translated with an introduction and notes by Walter E. Wright (Albany: State University of New York Press, 2005), 71.

Chapter 5

Chapter 5, "Goethe's Untimely History," originated as the text of a plenary speech delivered in Weimar at the seventy-third main congress of the Goethe Society in 1993. It was first published as "Goethe's unzeitgemäße Geschichte" in the *Goethe-Jahrbuch* 100 (1993): 27–39. The translation here is from "Goethe's unzeitgemäße Geschichte" in Koselleck, *Vom Sinn und Unsinn der Geschichte*, 286–305.

1. Albert Schweitzer, *Goethe. Gedenkrede gehalten bei der Feier der 100. Wiederkehr seines Todestages in seiner Vaterstadt Frankfurt am Main am 22. März 1932* (Munich: C. H. Beck, 1932), 50.

2. Friedrich Meinecke, *The German Catastrophe: Reflections and Recollections*, trans. Sidney B. Fay (Cambridge, MA: Harvard University Press, 1950), 115. A useful collection of sources is Walter Iwan ed., *Den Manen Goethes. Gedenkreden von 1832 bis 1949* (Weimar: Kiepenhauer, 1957). Useful in understanding the National Socialist appraisal of Goethe is Baldur von Schirach, "Goethe an uns. Eine Rede, gehalten am 14. Juni 1937 zur Eröffnung der Weimar-Festspiele der deutschen Jugend," in *Goethe an uns. Ewige Gedanken des großen Deutschen* (Berlin: Eher, 1942). For a contemporary perspective on the reception history of Goethe, see Karl Robert Mandelkow, "Natur und Geschichte bei Goethe im Spiegel seiner Rezeption im 19. und 20. Jahrhundert," in *Geschichtlichkeit und Aktualität. Festschrift für H.J. Mähl*, ed. K. D. Müller et al. (Tübingen: Niemeyer, 1988), 69–96.

3. Karl Löwith, *My Life in Germany before and after 1933*, trans. Elizabeth King (Urbana: University of Illinois Press, 1994). Löwith's analysis is strikingly lucid in his "Zeit und Geschichte bei Hegel und Goethe," in id., *Von Hegel zu Nietzsche. Sämtliche Schriften* (Stuttgart: Metzler, 1988), 4: 263–95. Ernst Cassirer, *Goethe und die geschichtliche Welt* (Berlin: B. Cassirer, 1932) and Hans Blumenberg also both break important new ground in this regard. Blumenberg shows that neither a philological-critical method nor an account of actual historical events is sufficient on its own for understanding Goethe's relationship to and reflections on history. Blumenberg, *Work on Myth*, tran. Robert M. Wallace (Cambridge, MA: MIT Press, 1985), subtly examines transgressions at the boundaries of history and myth, especially in pt. 4, "Against a God, only a God," 399–560. For a brief, but comprehensive account—and so as to limit further references to secondary literature—see Victor Lange, "Goethes Geschichtsauffassung," *Études germaniques* 38 (1983): 3–16. Horst Günther offers an anthology of primary sources in Goethe, *Historische Schriften. Eine Auswahl in biographischer Folge* (Frankfurt am Main: Insel, 1982).

4. "An Charlotte von Stein, 9/10. Juli 1786," in id., *Gedenkausgabe der Werke, Briefe, Gespräche*, 27 vols., ed. Ernst Beutler (Zurich: Artemis, 1949–), vol. 18: *Briefe der Jahre 1764–1786*, 937. This edition is referred to as AA in subsequent notes.

5. Johann Wolfgang Goethe, "Advice for Young Poets," in Johann Wolfgang von Goethe, *Essays on Art and Literature*, trans. Ellen and Ernest H. von Nardorff (New York: Suhrkamp, 1986), 209.

6. Johann Wolfgang Goethe, *Sämtliche Werke. Briefe, Tagebücher und Gespräche,* (Frankfurt am Main: Deutscher Klassiker Verlag, 1985–2013), vol. 14: *Aus meinem Leben. Dichtung und Wahrheit,* 13. This edition is referred to as SW in subsequent notes.

7. Johann Wolfgang Goethe, *Wilhelm Meister's Journeyman Years, or the Renunciants*, trans. Krishna Winston (New York: Suhrkamp, 1989), 424.

8. See conversation with Eckermann, January 4, 1824, in Goethe, *Conversations with Eckermann, 1823–1832* (San Francisco: North Point Press, 1984), 27–30.

9. Goethe, *Italian Journey,* trans. Robert R Heitner (Princeton, NJ: Princeton University Press, 1994), 346.

10. Goethe, *Wilhelm Meister's Journeyman Years,* 432.

11. *Maximen und Reflexionen,* AA 9: 635.

12. *Wilhelm Meisters Wanderjahre* (Munich: Deutscher Taschenbuch Verlag, 1962), afterword by Wilhelm Flitner, 234.

13. Goethe, *Dichtung und Wahrheit* (Paralipomena, 30), SW 14: 934.

14. Goethe, *Gedichte, 1800–1812*, ed. Karl Eibl (Frankfurt am Main: Deutscher Klassiker Verlag, 1988); SW 2, 5: 765.

15. Goethe, "A Challenge for a Modern Sculptor" (1817), in id., *Essays on Art and Literature,* 93–95 (New York: Suhrkamp, 1986), 95.

16. Goethe, "Zur Farbenlehre," SW 23: 614.

17. Goethe, "Tag- und Jahreshefte als Ergänzung meiner sonstigen Bekenntnisse," AA 2: 623.

18. Ibid., 846.

19. Goethe, "An Zelter, 15. Februar 1830," cited in SW 14: 1035.

20. SW 14: 13.

21. SW 14: 1034.

22. Goethe, "Bildnis jetzt lebender Berliner Gelehrten," AA 14: 228.

23. Goethe, "An Lavater, 28. Oktober 1779," AA 18: 458.

24. Goethe, *Maximen und Reflexionen,* AA 9: 608.

25. Goethe, "Stages of Man's Mind" (1817), in *Essays on Art and Literature,* 203–4. Translation altered.

26. Albrecht Schöne, *Goethes Farbentheologie* (Munich: C. H. Beck, 1987).

27. Goethe, *Tag- und Jahreshefte* (1804), SW 23: 739.

28. Goethe, "Zur Farbenlehre," SW 23: 13.

29. Goethe to Schiller, January 24, 1798, cited in *Correspondence between Goethe and Schiller,* trans. Liselotte Dieckmann (New York: Peter Lang, 1994), 262.

30. SW 23: 613.

31. Goethe, "Notes and Essays for a Better Understanding of the *West-East Divan,*" trans. Martin Bidney and Peter Anton von Arnim, in *West-East Divan: The Poems, with "notes and essays"; Goethe's Intercultural Dialogues,* 173–288 (Albany: State University of New York Press, 2010), 244.

32. SW 23: 634. To be sure, Goethe placed superstition—here used as a concept in opposition to unbelief—much higher than unbelief, which he called a sign of faintness of heart. Superstition is an unavoidable anthropological pregiven, similar to Gadamer's "prejudice." See also AA 9: 515 and 563.

33. SW 23: 613.

34. Goethe, *Wilhelm Meister's Journeyman Years,* 435.

35. Vincenz von Lerin, "Commonitorium primum," in *Patrologia Latina,* ed. Jacques-Paul Migne, 50 (1865): 666: "Si prophana est novitas, sacrata est vestustas [. . .] ut cum dicas nove, non dicas nova."

36. Goethe, *Tag- und Jahreshefte* (1793), AA 11: 631.

37. Goethe, "Ilmenau," SW 1: 266, SW 2: 337.

38. Goethe, *Campaign in France, 1792,* trans. Thomas P. Saine (New York: Suhrkamp, 1987), 745.

39. Goethe to Schiller, March 9, 1802, AA 20: 885.

40. Goethe, conversation with Eckermann, January 10, 1825, in *Conversations with Eckermann*, 64.

41. Goethe, "Benvenuto Cellini, Anhang X," AA 15: 883.

42. See Roger Dufraisse, "Goethe und Valmy, zwischen Legende und Wirklichkeit," in *Goethe in Trier und Luxemburg. 200 Jahre Campagne in Frankreich: Katalog der Ausstellung der Stadtbibliothek Luxemburg und der Stiftung Weimar Klassik,* 197–206 (Trier: Stadtbibliothek Trier, 1992).

43. Goethe, *Campaign in France, 1792,* trans. Thomas P. Saine (New York: Suhrkamp, 1987), 640.

44. Ibid., 773.

45. "Heine to Varnhagen, February 28, 1830," cited in Blumenberg, *Work on Myth,* 667.

46. Bettine von Arnim, *Goethes Briefwechsel mit einem Kinde,* ed. Walter Schmitz and Sybille von Steinsdorff (Frankfurt am Main: Suhrkamp, 1992), 251.

47. Goethe to Karl von Reinhard, November 14, 1812, in *Goethe und Reinhard. Briefwechsel in den Jahren 1807–1832,* ed. Otto Heuschele (Wiesbaden: Insel, 1957).

48. From a passage that was later cut from a draft of the letter to Reinhard, ibid., 477.

49. Ibid., 191.

50. Pierre-Victurnien Vergniaud, "Les Ides de Mars, seance du 13 Mars 1793," in *Les grands orateurs républicains,* ed. Michel Lheritier (Monaco: Hemera, 1949–50), 187.

51. Goethe, *Gedichte, 1800–1812,* ed. Eibl; SW 2: 746; see also the commentary by Eibl, 1247.

Chapter 6

Chapter 6, "Does History Accelerate?" originated as a lecture at the Rhenish-Westphalian Academy of Science in 1976. It was first published in part as "Fortschritt und Beschleunigung: Zur Utopie der Aufklärung" in *Der Traum der Vernunft: Vom Elend der Aufklärung,* ed. Berliner Akademie der Künste (Darmstadt: Luchterhand, 1985), 75–103. The translation here is from "Gibt es eine Beschleunigung der Geschichte?" in Koselleck, *Zeitschichten,* 150–76, and draws on the English translation by James Ingram, "Is There an Acceleration of History?" in *High-Speed Society: Social Acceleration, Power and Modernity,* ed. Hartmut Rosa and William E. Scheuerman (University Park: Pennsylvania State University Press, 2008), 113–34.

1. Schnell! Schnell, mein Schmied! Mit des Rosses Beschlag! / Dieweil Du zauderst, verstreicht der Tag.—/ "Wie dampfet Dein ungeheures Pferd! / Wo eilst Du so hin, mein Ritter wert?"

2. Adelbert von Chamisso, *Chamissos Werke,* ed. Max Sydow, 5 vols., 1: 1: *Gedichte* (Berlin: Bong, 1907), 66.

3. "Mein Dampfroß, Muster der Schnelligkeit, / läßt hinter sich die laufende Zeit / Und nimmt's zur Stunde nach Westen den Lauf, / Kommt's gestern von Osten schon wieder herauf." Ibid.

4. "Ich habe der Zeit ihr Geheimnis geraubt, / Von gestern zu gestern *zurück* sie geschraubt." Ibid.

5. From "Lieder eines deutschen Mädchens," cited in Manfred Riedel, "Vom Biedermeier zum Maschinenzeitalter," *Archiv für Kulturgeschichte* 43:1 (1961): 100–123, at 109. Riedel gathers numerous examples from a variety of literary genres of the rapid shift in experience through the steamship and railroad.

6. Heinrich Heine, *Lutetia,* LVII, May 5, 1843, in *Sämtliche Schriften,* ed. Klaus Briegleb, (Munich: Hanser, 1976), 9: 448–49.

7. Beurmann cited in Riedel, "Vom Biedermeier zum Maschinenzeitalter," 102.

8. "Die Dampfwagen," in *Gedichte des Königs Ludwig von Bayern* (Munich, 1847), pt. 4, 275; with thanks to Erich Maschke for the reference. For an analysis of the context and meaning, see Wolfgang Frühwald, "Der König als Dichter, Zu Absicht und Wirkung der Gedichte Ludwigs des Ersten, Königs von Bayern,"

Deutsche Vierteljahresschrift für Literaturwissenschaft und Geistesgeschichte 50 (1976): 146.

9. See Jacques Le Goff, "Merchant's Time and Church's Time in the Middle Ages" (1960), in Le Goff, *Time, Work and Culture in the Middle Ages*, trans. Arthur Goldhammer (Chicago: University of Chicago Press, 1980), 29–42, and Gerhard Dohrn-van Rossum, *Die Geschichte der Stunde. Uhren und moderne Zeitordnungen* (Munich: Hanser, 1992), which downplays the opposition between Church and merchant time, because the mechanical clocks were used above all by the nobility in tandem with the Church, even if over time they were introduced to the benefit of merchants. See also Arno Borst, *Computus. Zeit und Zahl in der Geschichte Europas* (Berlin: Wagenbach, 1990), which brings together his extensive research on this topic.

10. On this and for the following dates and thoughts, see E. P. Thompson, "Time, Work-discipline and Industrial Capitalism," *Past and Present* 38 (1967): 56–97.

11. Klaus Maurice, *Die Französische Pendule des 18. Jahrhunderts. Ein Beitrag zu ihrer Ikonologie* (Berlin: De Gruyter, 1967), 102.

12. See Johann Amos Comenius (1592–1671), *De rerum humanarum emendatione consultatio catholica* , 2 vols. (Prague: Academia Scientiarum Bohemoslovaca, 1966), 2: 511: "In omni Republica sit una suprema potestas, cui caeterae subordinentur: in uno judicio unus judex, quem admodum in una civitate unum commune Horologium esse expedit, ad quod omnia publica negotia disponantur."

13. "Le monde est une horloge, qui était une fois montée continue aussi longtems [*sic*] que Dieu s'est proposé de la laisser aller." J. H. S. Formey, "Conservation," in *Encyclopédie ou dictionnaire raisonné des sciences, des arts et des métiers*, 4 vols. (Paris: Briasson, 1754), 4: 38.

14. Karl Marx, *Die Klassenkämpfe in Frankreich, 1848–1850* (1850) (Berlin: Vorwärts, 1895), 90, cited in Karl Griewank, *Der neuzeitliche Revolutionsbegriff* (Weimar, 1955; 2nd ed., Frankfurt am Main: Europäische Verlagsanstalt, 1969), 218.

15. B. G. Niebuhr, *Geschichte des Zeitalters der Revolution* (1829), 2 vols. (Hamburg: Agentur des Rauhen Hauses, 1845), 1: 55.

16. See Wolfgang Zorn, "Verdichtung und Beschleunigung des Verkehrs als Beitrag zur Entwicklung der 'modernen Welt,'" in *Studien zum Beginn der modernen Welt*, ed. Koselleck, 115–34. See also Philip S. Bagwell, *The Transport Revolution* (London: Routledge, 1988), and Brian Austin, *British Mail Coach-Service, 1784–1850* (New York: Garland, 1986).

17. Illustrative and with extensive supporting material: Hermann Kellenbenz and Hans Pieper, *Die Telegraphenstation Köln-Flittard, Geschichte der Nachrichtentechnik* (Cologne: Rheinisch-Westfälisches Wirtschaftsarchiv, 1973).

18. Johann Georg Büsch, *Abhandlung von dem Geldumlauf in anhaltender Rücksicht auf die Staatswirtschaft und Handlung*, pt. 2 (Hamburg: C. E. Bohn, 1800), 43.

19. Karl August Espe, *Conversations-Lexikon der Gegenwart*, 4 vols. (Leipzig: F. A. Brockhaus, 1838), 1–2: 1115–36, §41; by the same author, see "Die Eisenbahnen, eine europäische Notwendigkeit," in *Scherz und Ernst* (Leipzig, 1836). The overcoming of spatial separations through convergence in time is treated ironically by Heine (*Lutetia* VII, 449): "Even the basic concepts of space and time have become unstable. Space is killed through the railroad, and all we have left is time. If only we had enough money to also properly kill the latter!"

20. In 1848, an article entitled "Dampfüberschuss und Zeitüberschuss," *Der bayerische Gewerbefreund* 13 (1848): 55, asked what was to be done with the millions of hours freed up by the use of the railroad and the steamship. The author feared that "this enormous existing capital of time made free" would not be used for moral improvement by the growing proletariat. Cited in *Aufbruch ins Industriezeitalter,* vol. 3: *Quellen zur Wirtschafts-und Sozialgeschichte Bayerns*, ed. Konrad von Zwehl (Munich: Oldenbourg, 1985), 140. The challenge of time that is not economically usable is a direct consequence of increased and thus accelerated production.

21. Büsch, *Abhandlung von dem Geldumlauf,* 2: 17.

22. See Rolf Peter Sieferle, *Bevölkerungswachstum und Naturhaushalt: Studien zur Naturtheorie der klassischen Ökonomie* (Frankfurt am Main: Suhrkamp, 1990).

23. Henry Adams, *The Education of Henry Adams: An Autobiography* (Boston: Houghton Mifflin, 1918), chap. 34: "The Law of Acceleration" (1904). Until a new equilibrium is attained, the law of acceleration rules: "A dynamic theory would begin by assuming that all history, terrestrial or cosmic, mechanical or intellectual, would be reducible to this formula if we knew the facts" (489). Adams musters examples from all realms of life to support his claim that all the spirit can do now is simply react, and that it has learned to do this; in the future, however, it will have to learn to jump in order to adapt.

24. Johann Wolfgang von Goethe, *Elective Affinities*, trans. R. J. Hollingdale (London: Penguin Books, 1971), 88.

25. F. C. Perthes, undated letter (ca. 1815), in *Friedrich Perthes' Leben nach dessen schriftlichen und mündlichen Mittheilungen aufgezeichnet von Clemens Theodor Perthes* (1848), 3 vols. (Gotha: F. A. Perthes, 1872), 2: 146. See also the analogous and exaggeratedly dualistic polemic from the "Council of Five Hundred" in Félix Bonnaire, Corps législatif, Conseil des Cinq-Cents: Rapport fait par Bonnaire sur le calendrier républicain, séance du 4 thermidor an VI ([July 22,]1798), Bibl. Nat. Le 43: "Dèhors la France présenta le spectacle de deux nations ennemis"; their two moralities, languages, and opinions stand

in strict opposition. The one nation follows the reign of philosophy ("règne de la Philosophie"), the other its prejudices, the one freedom, the other servitude; the republic stands in opposition to monarchy: "en un mot, l'intervalle de deux siècles entre les habitants de la même patrie." Thanks to Michael Meinzer for this reference.

26. Georg Friedrich Rebmann, *Der revolutionäre Kalender* (n.d.), reprinted in the *Insel-Almanach auf das Jahr 1966* (Frankfurt am Main: Insel, 1966), 80–85.

27. Joseph Görres, *Teutschland und die Revolution* (1819), in *Gesammelte Schriften*, ed. Wilhelm Schellberg, vol. 13, ed. Günther Wohlers (Cologne: Gilde, 1929), 81. See also Reinhart Koselleck, "Geschichte, Historie," in *Geschichtliche Grundbegriffe*, 2: 677.

28. See Reinhart Koselleck, "Krise," in *Geschichtliche Grundbegriffe*, 3: 639–40.

29. G. W. F. Hegel, *Die Vernunft in der Geschichte*, ed. J. Hoffmeister (Hamburg: F. Meiner, 1955), 9.

30. G. W. F. Hegel, *Einleitung in die Geschichte der Philosophie*, ed. J. Hoffmeister (Hamburg: F. Meiner, 1959), 62, 64.

31. See also Reinhart Koselleck, "Zeitverkürzung und Beschleunigung: Eine Studie zur Säkularisation," in id., *Zeitschichten*, 177–202.

32. Jean-Antoine-Nicolas de Caritat, marquis de Condorcet, *Esquisse d'un tableau historique des progrès de l'esprit humain* (1793), trans. Wilhelm Alff as *Entwurf einer historischen Darstellung der Fortschritte des menschlichen Geistes* (Frankfurt am Main: Europäische Verlagsanstalt, 1963), 27, 43, 371, 385; see also Koselleck, *Futures Past,* 52.

33. See note 26 of Koselleck, "Zeitverkürzung und Beschleunigung." On the different scales of pronouncements of acceleration, see *Die Französische Revolution. Berichte und Deutungen deutscher Schriftsteller und Historiker,* ed. Horst Günther (Frankfurt am Main: Deutscher Klassiker Verlag, 1985), 552, 831, 837 (Wieland), 652 (Forster), 1054, 1070 (Wilhelm Schulz).

34. Joseph Görres, *Europa und die Revolution* (1819), in id., *Gesammelte Schriften*, 13: 188–89.

35. Claude-Henri de Saint-Simon, "Esquisse d'une nouvelle encyclopédie," in *Œuvres de Saint-Simon et d'Enfantin,* 47 vols. (Paris: E. Dentu, 1865–78), 15: 89, cited in Rolf Peter Fehlbaum, *Saint-Simon und die Saint-Simonisten: Vom Laissez-Fair zur Wirtschaftsplanung* (Basel: Kyklos, 1970), 12.

36. Auguste Comte, *Cours de philosophie positive*, ed. Charles Le Verrier, 2 vols. (Paris: Garnier, 1949), 2:114, 157–58.

37. See note 19.

38. Chamisso, *Chamissos Werke*, 1: 1, 136.

Chapter 7

Chapter 7, "Constancy and Change of All Contemporary Histories: Conceptual-Historical Notes," was originally published as "Begriffsgeschichtliche Anmerkungen zur 'Zeitgeschichte'" in *Die Zeit nach 1945 als Thema kirchlicher Zeitgeschichte*, ed. Victor Conzemius, Martin Greschat, and Hermann Kocher (Göttingen: Vandenhoeck & Ruprecht, 1988), 17–31. The translation here is from "Stetigkeit und Wandel aller Zeitgeschichte. Begriffsgeschichtliche Anmerkungen" in Koselleck, *Zeitschichten*, 246–64.

1. Hellmuth Auerbach, "Die Gründung des Instituts für Zeitgeschichte," *Vierteljahrshefte für Zeitgeschichte* 18, no. 4 (1970): 529–54.

2. Johann Heinrich Alsted, *Scientiarum omnium Encyclopaedia*, vol. 4 of 4 (Lyon: Huguetan & Ravaud, 1649), 37, 65.

3. Eberhard Jäckel, "Begriff und Funktion der Zeitgeschichte," in *Die Funktion der Geschichte in unserer Zeit*, ed. Eberhard Jäckel and Ernst Weymar (Stuttgart: Klett, 1975), 162–76.

4. Fritz Ernst, "Zeitgeschehen und Geschichtsschreibung: Eine Skizze," in id., *Gesammelte Schriften*, ed. Gunther G. Wolf (Heidelberg: Hermes, 1985), 289–341.

5. Byron, *Manfred*, monologue cited by Franz Freiherr von Lipperheide, *Spruchwörterbuch*, 8th unabridged ed. (Berlin: Haude & Spenersche Verlagsbuchhandlung, 1907), 264 Goethe, *Gedichte,1800–1832*, ed. Eibl, 2: 554.

6. Goethe, "Lebensregel," in *Gedichte, 1800–1832*, ed. Eibl, 2: 422.

7. *The Confessions of Saint Augustine* 11.28, trans. Edward B. Pusey (New York: Modern Library, 1949), 277.

8. Raymond Aron, *Introduction to the Philosophy of History: An Essay on the Limits of Historical Objectivity* (Boston: Beacon Press, 1961), 179; Reinhard Wittram, *Zukunft in der Geschichte: Zu Grenzfragen der Geschichtswissenschaft und Theologie* (Göttingen: Vandenhoeck & Ruprecht, 1966), 5; Niklas Luhmann, "Weltzeit und Systemgeschichte," in *Soziologie und Sozialgeschichte: Aspekte und Probleme*, ed. Peter Christian Ludz, *Kölner Zeitschrift für Soziologie und Sozialgeschichte* (Opladen: Westdeutscher Verlag, 1972), 81–115.

9. Sigmund von Birken, *Ostländischer Lorbeerhain. Ein Ehrengedicht von dem Höchstlöblichen Erzhaus Österreich* (Nuremberg: Endtern, 1657), 233; Wilhelm Vosskamp, *Zeit- und Geschichtsauffassung bei Gryphius und Lohenstein* (Bonn: Bouvier, 1987).

10. Kaspar von Stieler, *Der teutschen Sprache Stammbaum und Fortwachs oder Teutscher Sprachschatz* (Nuremberg: Hofmanns, 1691), cited by Jäckel, "Begriff und Funktion der Zeitgeschichte," 165.

11. Christian Friedrich Schwan, *Nouvelle Dictionnaire de la langue allemande et françoise*, vol. 2 of 2 (Mannheim: Schwan & Fontaine, 1783), 676.

12. Gottlieb Jakob Planck, *Geschichte des Pabstthums in den abendländischen Kirchen von dem Anfang des vierzehnten Jahrhunderts bis zu der*

Reformation, vol. 1 of 5, Preface (Hannover: Hahn, 1805), cited by Peter Meinhold, *Geschichte der kirchlichen Historiographie* (Freiburg: Karl Albert, 1967), 2: 106.

13. Cited in Jäckel, "Begriff und Funktion der Zeitgeschichte," 165.

14. Joachim Heinrich Campe, *Wörterbuch der deutschen Sprache*, vol. 5 of 5 (Braunschweig: Schulbuchhandlung, 1811), 833; here cited in Jäckel, ibid., who interprets the first definition from our contemporary viewpoint as a "misunderstanding."

15. Jacob and Wilhelm Grimm, *Deutsches Wörterbuch*, vol. 15 of 16 (Leipzig: S. Hirzel, 1956), rev. Moriz Heyne, Henry Seedorf, and Hermann Teuchert (repr., Munich: Deutscher Taschenbuch, 1984), 31: 550–83.

16. Reinhart Koselleck, "Neuzeit: Remarks on the Semantics of Modern Concepts of Movement," in id., *Futures Past*, 222–54.

17. Also see Reinhart Koselleck, "Archivalien—Quellen—Geschichten," in Koselleck, *Vom Sinn und Unsinn der Geschichte* , 68–79.

18. Wilhelm von Humboldt, *Das achtzehnte Jahrhundert*, in *Werke*, vol. 1 of 5, ed. Andreas Flitner and Klaus Giel, 376–505 (Darmstadt: Wissenschaftliche Buchgesellschaft, 1960), 398.

19. An analogous threshold was also crossed at earlier points, e.g., from Herodotus to Thucydides; see Reinhart Koselleck, "Transformations of Experience and Methodological Change: A Historical-Anthropological Essay," in id., *Practice of Conceptual History*, 65–70.

20. John Keegan, *The Face of Battle: A Study of Agincourt, Waterloo and the Somme* (London: Jonathan Cape, 1976), 24, 221, 311 and elsewhere.

Chapter 8

Chapter 8, "History, Law, and Justice," is the text of a lecture at the twenty-sixth convention of German legal historians in September 1986. It was first published in *Akten des 26. Deutschen Rechtshistorikertages 1986*, ed. Dieter Simon (Frankfurt am Main: Klosterman, 1987), 129–49. The translation here is from "Geschichte, Recht und Gerechtigkeit" in Koselleck, *Zeitschichten*, 336–58.

1. See Fritz Loos and Hans-Ludwig Schreiber, "Recht, Gerechtigkeit," in *Geschichtliche Grundbegriffe*, 5: 231–311.

2. See, for the critical sociohistorical discussion of this methodological debate in the faculty of law, Marcel Senn, *Rechtshistorisches Selbstverständnis im Wandel. Ein Beitrag zur Wissenschaftstheorie und Wissenschaftsgeschichte der Rechtsgeschichte* (Zurich: Schulthess, 1982), and Diethelm Klippel, *Juristische Zeitgeschichte. Die Bedeutung der Rechtsgeschichte für die Zivilrechtswissenschaft*. Gießener Rechtswissenschaftliche Abhandlungen, vol. 4 (Gießen: Brühl, 1985); in what follows, I

attempt to give a more differentiated account of Klippel's premises dealing with temporality. Both works include good overviews of the literature on the topic.

3. Cicero, *De oratore* 2.15.64.

4. On this topic, see Hayden White, *Tropics of Discourse: Essays in Cultural Criticism* (Baltimore: Johns Hopkins University Press, 1978).

5. For a more differentiated account of this, see Hermann Strasburger, *Herodot als Geschichtsforscher* (Zurich: Artemis, 1980), 54.

6. Carolus Linnaeus, *Nemesis Divina*, ed. Michael John Petry (Dordrecht: Kluwer Academic, 2001). Also Julian H. Franklin, *Jean Bodin and the 16th Century Revolution in the Methodology of Law and History* (New York: Columbia University Press, 1963).

7. Thucydides, *The War of the Peloponnesians and the Athenians*, ed. Jeremy Mynott (Cambridge: Cambridge University Press, 2013), 3.45.189–90.

8. See Wolfgang Schadewaldt, *Die Anfänge der griechischen Geschichtsschreibung* (Frankfurt am Main: Suhrkamp, 1982), and Christian Meier, *Die Entstehung des Politischen bei den Griechen* (Frankfurt am Main: Suhrkamp, 1980).

9. Agrippa d'Aubigné, "La confession du Sieur de Sancy," in id., *Œuvres complètes*, vol. 2 of 6 (Paris: 1877), 369ff. See also Koselleck, *Critique and Crisis*, 19.

10. See Alexander Cartellieri, *Weltgeschichte als Machtgeschichte* (Munich: Aalen, 1927).

11. See the satirical war memorial by Edward Kienholz in the Museum Ludwig, Cologne.

12. Jörg Fisch, *Die europäische Expansion und das Völkerrecht: Die Auseinandersetzungen um den Status der überseeischen Gebiete vom 15. Jahrhundert bis zur Gegenwart* (Stuttgart: Steiner, 1984).

13. See the legal conceptual history by Hans Hattenhauer, "Pax et Justitia," *Berichte aus den Sitzungen der Joachim Jungius-Gesellschaft der Wissenschaften*, vol. 1, no. 3 (Hamburg, 1983).

14. See St. Augustine, *De civitate Dei contra paganos* 20.19 [English trans., *The City of God against the Pagans*, ed. R. W. Dyson (Cambridge: Cambridge University Press, 1998), 1007–10]: the condemned are seduced, the seduced are condemned, and, moreover, the condemned are seduced according to judgments that are just by virtue of being secret and justifiably secret—"judiciis Dei occulte justis, juste occultis"—judgments that God has ceaselessly inflicted on rational creatures ever since the Fall. On Dante's necessary conclusion that punishments carried out on earth continue to be imposed in the beyond, in an unrelenting and eternal manner, and that this is proof of divine mercy, which thereby becomes the most radical, quasi-unmerciful executor of justice, see Hugo Friedrich, *Die Rechtsmetaphysik der Göttlichen Komödie; Francesca da Rimini* (Frankfurt am Main: Klostermann, 1942).

15. G. W. F. Hegel, *Die Vernunft in der Geschichte: Einleitung in die Philosophie der Weltgeschichte*, ed. Johannes Hoffmeister (Hamburg: Felix Meiner, 1955), 147–48. Translated by Robert S. Hartman as *Reason in History: A General Introduction to the Philosophy of History* (New York: Macmillan, 1987).

16. Franz Wieacker, "Pandektenwissenschaft und Industrielle Revolution," *Juristen-Jahrbuch* 9 (1968–69): 1–28; Stephan Buchholz, *Abstraktionsprinzip und Immobiliarrecht: zur Geschichte der Auflassung und der Schuld* (Frankfurt am Main: Klostermann, 1978); Heinz Wagner, *Die Politische Pandektistik* (Berlin: Arno Spitz, 1985).

17. [A case in the 1770s that led later to the independence of the judiciary and the codification of the Prussian Civil Code.]

Chapter 9

Chapter 9, "Linguistic Change and the History of Events," originated as the seventh George Lurcy Lecture, "Language and History," delivered at the University of Chicago on November 15, 1988. It was first published as "Sprachwandel und Ereignisgeschichte" in *Merkur* 486 (August 1989): 657–73. The translation here is from "Sprachwandel und Ereignisgeschichte" in *Begriffsgeschichten: Studien zur Semantik und Pragmatik der politischen und sozialen Sprache* (Frankfurt am Main: Suhrkamp, 2006), 32–55, and draws on the English translation by Stephen Duffy, "Linguistic Change and the History of Events," *Journal of Modern History* 61 (December 1989): 649–66.

1. See John E. Toews, "Intellectual History after the Linguistic Turn: The Autonomy of Meaning and the Irreducibility of Experience," *American Historical Review* 92:4 (1987): 879–907.

2. See further Koselleck's "*Historik* and Hermeneutics" (chapter 4 in this volume) and two of his essays in *The Practice of Conceptual History*: "Social History and Conceptual History" (20–37) and "Transformations of Experience and Methodological Change: A Historical-Anthropological Essay" (45–83).

3. See Hans-Friedrich Bornitz, *Herodot-Studien: Beiträge zum Verständnis der Einheit des Geschichtswerks* (Berlin: De Gruyter, 1968).

4. See *Neuer Teutscher Merkur*, March 1798. See also Koselleck, "The Unknown Future and the Art of Prognosis," in id., *Practice of Conceptual History*, 131–47.

5. See John H. Finley, *Thucydides* (Cambridge, MA: Harvard University Press, 1942).

6. See Heinrich Ryffel, *Metabolē politeiōn. Der Wandel der Staatsverfassungen* (PhD diss., Bern, 1949; New York: Arno Press, 1973).

7. Here I draw on a research program carried out at Bielefeld that has compared the forms of address, the lexicography related to the *Bürgertum*, and the arguments for emancipation in Germany, England, and France. See Reinhart Koselleck et al., "Three *bürgerliche* Worlds? Preliminary Theoretical-Historical Remarks on the Comparative Semantics of Civil Society in Germany, England, and France," in Koselleck, *Practice of Conceptual History*, 208–17.

8. See the article "Revolution, Rebellion, Aufruhr, Bürgerkrieg" in *Geschichtliche Grundbegriffe*, 5: 653–788.

9. See chapter 8, "History, Law, and Justice," in this volume.

Chapter 10

Chapter 10, "Structures of Repetition in Language and History," was originally published as "Wiederholungsstrukturen in Sprache und Geschichte" in *Saeculum: Jahrbuch für Universalgeschichte* 57, no. 1 (2006): 1–15. The translation here is from "Wiederholungsstrukturen in Sprache und Geschichte" in Koselleck, *Vom Sinn und Unsinn der Geschichte*, 96–116.

1. Johann Nestroy, *Lektüre für Minuten. Gedanken aus Büchern,* ed. Egon Friedell (Frankfurt am Main: Insel 2001), 42.

2. See Manfred Fuhrmann, "Persona, ein römischer Rollenbegriff," in *Identität,* ed. Odo Marquard and Karlheinz Stierle (Munich: Fink, 1979), 83–106.

3. Johann Gottfried Herder, "Eine Metakritik zur Kritik der reinen Vernunft," in: Herder, *Werke in zehn Bänden,* vol. 8, ed. Hans Dietrich Irmscher (Frankfurt am Main: Deutscher Klassiker, 1998), 360.

4. Friedrich Cramer, *Der Zeitbaum. Grundlegung einer allgemeinen Zeittheorie* (Frankfurt am Main: Insel, 1993).

5. Rahel Varnhagen, diary entry July 15, 1821, cited in *Die Weisheit des Judentums,* ed. Walter Homolka and Annette Böckler (Gütersloh: Gütersloher Verlagshaus, 1999).

6. [See Crane Brinton, *The Anatomy of Revolution* (New York: Norton, 1938).]

7. See Ferdinand de Saussure, *Linguistik und Semiologie. Notizen aus dem Nachlaß. Texte, Briefe und Dokumente,* trans. and ed. Johannes Fehr (Frankfurt am Main: Suhrkamp, 1997); and Eugenio Coseriu, *Synchronie, Diachronie und Geschichte. Das Problem des Sprachwandels,* trans. Helga Sohre (Munich: Fink, 1974). Coseriu brings together Saussure's ostensible oppositions between speech and language, diachrony and synchrony, languages and language, and movement and system in order to describe every linguistic system as a system in becoming or a "structural history."

8. Heinrich Lausberg, *Elemente der literarischen Rhetorik* (Munich: Hueber, 1963), 39.

Chapter 11

Chapter 11, "On the Meaning and Absurdity of History," was originally published as "Vom Sinn und Unsinn der Geschichte" in *Merkur* 51 (April 1997):
319–34. The translation here is from "Vom Sinn und Unsinn der Geschichte" in
Koselleck, *Vom Sinn und Unsinn der Geschichte*, 9–31.

    1. [*Letzte Briefe aus Stalingrad* (Frankfurt am Main: Quadriga, 1950). English
trans. *Last Letters from Stalingrad* (London: Methuen, 1956).]

    2. [See Ernst Topitsch, *Stalins Krieg. Moskaus Griff nach der Weltherrschaft*
(Herford: Busse Seewald, 1985).]

    3. [King Friedrich II of Prussia, *Réflexions sur les talents militaires et sur le car-
actère de Charles XII, roi de Suède: de main de maître* (1786), cited in *Aufklärung
und Kriegserfahrung. Klassische Zeitzeugen zum Siebenjährigen Krieg*, ed. Johannes
Kunisch (Frankfurt am Main: Deutscher Klassiker, 1996), 547–87.]

    4. [See Thomas Mann, "Deutsche Hörer! Fünfundfünfzig Radiosendun-
gen nach Deutschland," broadcast on September 27, 1942, in Thomas Mann,
Gesammelte Werke, vol. 2, *Reden und Aufsätze 3* (Frankfurt am Main: Fischer,
1960), 1053: "There exists an exact and authentic report about the killing of no
fewer than 11,000 Polish Jews with poison gas. They were brought to a special
field of execution near Konin in the Warsaw district, put into airtight trucks, and
within fifteen minutes they were transformed to corpses. We have the detailed
description of the entire process, of the screams and prayers of the victims and
the good-natured laughter of the SS-Hottentots who organized the fun and
games." There is no mention of the expression "SS-kaffirs" [*Kaffern*] in this context. Mann did speak of "bloody kaffirs" a week later, though, in relation to
Baldur von Schirach and his speech at the Nazi "European Youth-Congress" in
Vienna (ibid., 1057).]

    5. Sabine R. Arnold, *Stalingrad im sowjetischen Gedächtnis: Kriegserinnerung
und Geschichtsbild im totalitären Staat* (Bochum: Projekt, 1997).

    6. [See Theodor Lessing, "Über logificatio post festum," in *Geschichte als
Sinngebung des Sinnlosen* (1919) (Munich: Matthes & Seitz 1983), 56–63.]

    7. [Friedrich Schiller, "Resignation" (1786), in Schiller, *Werke* (Nationalaus-
gabe), vol. 1: *Gedichte, 1776–1790* (Weimar, 1943), 168. For an interpretation of this
verse and its reception history, see chapter 8, "History, Law, and Justice," in this
volume.]

    8. [See Wilhelm von Humboldt, "Über die Aufgabe des Geschichtsschreibers"
(1821), in Humboldt, *Werke in fünf Bänden*, ed. Andreas Flitner and Klaus Giel,
vol. 1: *Schriften zur Anthropologie und Geschichte*, (Darmstadt: Wissenschaftliche
Buchgesellschaft, 1960), 585–606.]

    9. [Bernard de Fontenelle, "A Digression on the Ancients and the Moderns"
(1688), trans. Donald Schier, in *The Continental Model: Selected French Critical*

Essays of the Seventeenth Century, in English Translation, ed. Scott Elledge and Donald Schier (Ithaca, NY: Cornell University Press, 1970), 358–70.]

10. [See Karl Löwith, *Meaning in History: The Theological Implications of the Philosophy of History* (Chicago: University of Chicago Press, 1949).]

11. [See Paul Ricœur, *Memory, History, Forgetting,* trans. Kathleen Blamey and David Pellauer (Chicago: University of Chicago Press, 2004).]

12. [See Immanuel Kant, "Idea for a Universal History with a Cosmopolitan Purpose" (1784), in Kant, *Political Writings,* trans. H. B. Nisbet (Cambridge: Cambridge University Press, 1970), 41–53.]

13. [See G. W. F. Hegel, *The Philosophy of History,* trans. J. Sibree (Kitchener, Ont.: Batoche, 2001), 47.]

14. [See *6,000,000 Accusers: Israel's Case against Eichmann. The Opening Speech and Legal Argument of Mr. Gideon Hausner, Attorney-General,* ed. Shabtai Rosenne (Jerusalem: Jerusalem Post, 1961), 27–175.]

Chapter 12

Chapter 12, "Concepts of the Enemy," was originally published as "Feindbegriffe" in the Deutsche Akademie für Sprache und Dichtung's *Jahrbuch, 1993* (Göttingen: Wallstein, 1993), 83–90. The translation here is from "Feindbegriffe" in Koselleck, *Begriffsgeschichten,* 274–86.

1. See Koselleck, "The Historical-Political Semantics of Asymmetric Counterconcepts," in id., *Futures Past,* 155–91.

2. Cited in Hans Wagener, *René Schickele, Europäer in neun Monaten* (Gerlingen: Bleicher, 2000), 277 [emphasis in original]. As Schickele recognized early on, like every civil war, worldwide civil war eats away at the power and clarity of linguistic concepts. Concepts congeal into ideological stereotypes, behind which horror collects itself and hides.

Chapter 13

Chapter 13, "Sluices of Memory and Sediments of Experiences: The Influence of the Two World Wars on Social Consciousness," is based on a talk at a conference on the comparison of the two worlds wars hosted by the Polish Academy of Science in 1984. It was originally published as "Der Einfluß der beiden Weltkriege auf das soziale Bewußtsein" in *Der Krieg des kleinen Mannes: Eine Militärgeschichte von unten,* ed Wolfram Wette (Munich: Piper, 1992), 324–43. The translation here is from "Erinnerungsschleusen und Erfahrungsschichten. Der Einfluß der beiden Weltkriege auf das soziale Bewußtsein" in Koselleck, *Zeitschichten,* 265–86.

1. [Antoine Prost, *In the Wake of War:* Les anciens combattants *and French Society* (Providence, RI: Berg 1992).]

Chapter 14

Chapter 14, "Beyond the Deadly Line: The Age of Totality," was originally published as "Hinter der tödlichen Linie. Das Zeitalter des Totalen" in the *Frankfurter Allgemeine Zeitung*, November 27, 1999. The translation here is from "Hinter der tödlichen Linie. Das Zeitalter des Totalen" in Koselleck, *Vom Sinn und Unsinn der Geschichte*, 228–40.

Chapter 15

Chapter 15, "Forms and Traditions of Negative Memory," was originally published as "Formen und Traditionen des negativen Gedächtnisses" in *Verbrechen erinnern. Die Auseinandersetzung mit dem Holocaust und Völkermord*, ed. Volkhard Knigge and Norbert Frei (Munich: C. H. Beck, 2002), 21–32. The translation here is from "Formen und Traditionen des negativen Gedächtnisses," in Koselleck, *Vom Sinn und Unsinn der Geschichte*, 241–53.

    1. [The Berlin memorial to the Sinti and Roma victims of National Socialism opened in 2012.]

    2. [Anita Lasker-Wallfisch*, Ihr sollt die Wahrheit erben. Breslau-Auschwitz-Bergen-Belsen*, with a foreword by Klaus Harpprecht (Bonn: Weidle, 1997). Translated as *Inherit the Truth, 1939–1945: The Documented Experiences of a Survivor of Auschwitz and Belsen* (London: Giles de la Mare, 2012).]

    3. [See Art Spiegelman, *Maus: A Survivor's Tale* (New York: Pantheon Books, 1992).]

Chapter 16

Chapter 16, "Histories in the Plural and the Theory of History: An Interview with Carsten Dutt," was originally published as "Geschichte(n) und *Historik*: Reinhart Koselleck im Gespräch mit Carsten Dutt" in the *Internationale Zeitschrift für Philosophie* 2 (2001): 257–71. The translation here is from "Geschichte(n) und *Historik*" in Reinhart Koselleck and Carsten Dutt, *Erfahrene Geschichte. Zwei Gespräche* (Heidelberg: Winter, 2013), 45–67.

    1. Jacob Taubes, "Geschichtsphilosophie und *Historik*. Bemerkungen zu Kosellecks Programm einer neuen *Historik*," in *Geschichte—Ereignis und Erzählung*, ed. Reinhart Koselleck and Wolf-Dieter Stempel (Munich: Fink, 1973), 490–499, at 493.

    2. See chapter 4, "*Historik* and Hermeneutics," in this volume.

3. [The interview took place only a few days after the terrorist attacks of September 11, 2001.]

4. See chapter 5, "Goethe's Untimely History," in this volume.

5. Hans-Georg Gadamer, *Truth and Method*, 2nd rev. ed. (New York: Continuum, 1996), 339. Translation modified.

6. See Hannah Arendt, "Irreversibility and the Power to Forgive," in id., *The Human Condition* (Chicago: University of Chicago Press, 1998), 236–42.

7. Chapter 4, *"Historik* and Hermeneutics," in this volume.

8. See Koselleck, *Critique and Crisis.*

9. Reinhart Koselleck, *Preußen zwischen Reform und Revolution. Allgemeines Landrecht, Verwaltung und soziale Bewegung zwischen 1791 und 1848* (Stuttgart: Klett, 1967).

10. Thomas S. Kuhn, *The Structures of Scientific Revolution* (Chicago: University of Chicago Press, 1962).

11. Hayden White, *Metahistory: The Historical Imagination in Nineteenth Century Europe* (Baltimore: Johns Hopkins University Press, 1973).

12. Hayden White, *Auch Klio dichtet, oder, Die Fiktion des Faktischen* (Stuttgart: Klett-Cotta, 1986), translation of *Tropics of Discourse: Essays in Cultural Criticism* (Baltimore: Johns Hopkins University Press, 1978).

13. See Hermann Lübbe, "Zur Identitätspräsentationsfunktion der Historie," in *Identität,* ed. Odo Marquard and Karlheinz Stierle (Munich: Fink, 1979), 277–92.

14. See *Les lieux de mémoire*, ed. Pierre Nora, 7 vols. (Paris: Gallimard, 1984–92).

15. Koselleck, "Historia Magistra Vitae: The Dissolution of the Topos into the Perspective of a Modernized Historical Process," in id., *Futures Past,* 26–42.

16. Henry Adams, *The Education of Henry Adams: An Autobiography* (Boston: Houghton Mifflin, 1918), chap. 34: "The Law of Acceleration" (1904).

Index

Ability to kill (*Totschlagenkönnen*), xii, 45–46

Above and below, as conditions of history, xxv, 51–52, 139, 164, 252, 255

Absurdity: of concentration camp experience, 240–41; existential, 127–28; of history, xxvii, 72–73, 123–24, 177–79, 181, 185–86, 190–96; of mass death, xix, xxvii

Acceleration, of experience in time, 34, 36–38, 79–99, 229–32; apocalypse and progress as categories for understanding, 93–98; as historiographical concern, 110–13, 160; modernity and, 149, 230, 265; technology and denaturalization of time experience, 81–93

Adages. *See* Maxims

Adams, Henry, 90, 265, 280*n*23

Aging: experience of time as affected by, 41; metaphors of, in conceptions of history, 192–93

Air travel, 230–31

Alsted, Johann Heinrich, 101

Amphiktyonic leagues, 129

Annales school, 262

Anthropogeography, 25, 28

Anthropology, 34, 44–45, 50, 67, 68, 127, 138–39, 151, 159–61, 163, 165, 173, 186, 198, 243, 251–54

Apel, Karl-Otto, 56

Apocalyptic tradition, 93–98

Archives, 111

Arendt, Hannah, xxii, xxvii, 50, 114, 124, 254; *Origins of Totalitarianism*, xxi

Aristotle, 11, 13, 68, 129, 161

Arndt, Ernst Moritz, 203

Arnold, Sabine, 182

Aron, Raymond, 102, 114

Athens and Athenians, 52, 121–22, 144, 155

Aubigné, Agrippa d,' 121

Augustine, Saint, 95, 102, 122–27, 151, 156; model of justice, 123

Auschwitz. *See* Holocaust

Baader, Franz von, 149

Barbarians, 199–200

Basic Law (Germany), 242

Bauer, Bruno, 111

Beethoven, Ludwig van, 89

Being toward death (*Sein zum Tode*), xii

Below. *See* Above and below

Bengel, Johann Albrecht, 168

Beradt, Charlotte, 11, 15

Berlichingen, Götz von, 108

Bernheim, Ernst, 26, 35

Berr, Henry, 30

Betti, Emilio, 129

Beurmann, Eduard, 81

Bible, x, xxix, 57, 94, 238

Binary categories. *See* oppositional concepts

Birken, Sigmund von, 104

Bismarck, Otto von, 145, 257–58

Blanning, T. C. W., xix

Bloch, Marc, 234

Blumenberg, Hans, x. 285*n*3

Boer War, 225–26

Bonaparte, Napoleon, 62–63, 80, 86, 115, 120, 121, 143, 169, 180, 188, 203

Bonhoeffer, Dietrich, 114

Boxer War, 226

Braudel, Fernand, xiii–xiv, 160, 256, 262

Brecht, Bertolt, 73

Bresslau, Harry, 234

Brezezinski, Zbigniew, xx

Brezhnev, Leonid, 115

Brinton, Crane, 168

Brockhaus (publisher), 89

Brockhaus der Gegenwart (Brockhaus Dictionary of the Present), 87, 89

Brockhaus encyclopedia, 81, 98

Broszat, Martin, 242

Büchner, Georg, 41

Buffon, Georges-Louis Leclerc, 163

Bund (union), 149–50, 173–74

Burckhardt, Jacob, x, 92, 112

Bürger (bourgeoisie), 146–48

Büsch, Johann Georg, 86, 88

Busch, Wilhelm, xv–xvi, 7, 184

Bush, George W., 264

Byron, George Gordon, Lord, 101

Caesar, Julius, 62, 121

Cambridge School of Intellectual History, xxiii–xxiv

Campe, Joachim Heinrich, 108, 114

Carr, David, xvii

Carriages, 85

Cartellieri, Alexander, 122

Cayrol, Jean, 17

Ceauşescu, Nicolae and Elena, 231

Century, concept of, 227

Chamisso, Adelbert von, 99; "Das Dampfroß" (The Steam Steed), 79–81

Change, 103, 108, 113

Charles XII of Sweden, 120, 169, 180

China, 226

Christianity: conception of time in, 109; concept of the enemy formulated by, 200–201; and justice, 123. *See also* Judeo-Christian tradition, time in; Last Judgment

Church Fathers, 95

Churchill, Winston, 45–46, 104, 121, 151

Cicero, 36, 83, 119

Civil wars, 204, 235

Class, as influence on experience of war, 211

Clemenceau, Georges, 239

Clocks, 82–85

Cold War, xx–xxii, 236

Collective consciousness. *See* Social consciousness, influence of war on

Columbia University, xviii

Communication, 231

Commynes, Philippe de, 104, 151

Computers, 228–29

Comte, Auguste, 97–99

Concentration camps, xiv, xxviii, 17, 218, 226, 240–42. *See also* Holocaust

conceptual history (*Begriffsgeschichte*), xix, xxiii–xxv

Condorcet, Marquis de, 97, 99

Copying (*Abschreiben*), xxvi, 153

Coseriu, Eugenio, 286*n*7

Cramer, Friedrich: *Der Zeitbaum*, 271*n*2

Cromwell, Oliver, 142

Cyclical model of time, 161

Darius, 137, 141–42

Dasein (existence), 44–47

Death: meaning of genocidal, 240–42; meaning of war-related, 216–18, 247–48. *See also* war memorials

De Gaulle, Charles, 31, 223

Diderot, Denis, 143, 146, 149

Dilthey, Wilhelm, 53

Dreams, 11–12, 14–17

Droysen, Johann Gustav, 26, 112, 251; *Historik*, xxv

Dualism. *See* oppositional concepts

Dubček, Alexander, 52, 114, 122, 144

Duration: legal history and, 130–36; measures of, 82–83; repetition as

characteristic of, 160; representation
of, xiv, 103, 109–11, 256
Dutt, Carsten, xvi, 250–65

Earlier and later, as conditions of
history, xxv, 138–39, 165, 252, 255
Eichmann, Adolf, 195, 240
Einstein, Albert, 27, 164
Endurance (*Leiden, Erleiden*), xxxi
Enemies: concepts of, 198–206; friends
in oppositional pairing with, 46–
47; prelinguistic conditions for
conceiving of, 198–99, 203–5
Engels, Friedrich, 149, 150, 168, 174
Enlightenment, xxii, xxvii, 10, 12, 14,
63, 71, 108, 236, 254
Epictetus, 157
Ernst, Fritz, 101
Europe, 24, 27, 37, 204, 232, 263–64
European Economic Community, 33,
130
Eusebius, 156
Events: defined, ix; disruptions of time
manifest in, xiii; language in relation
to, xxvi, 137–57; legal history and,
130–32; meaning of, 178, 182–84;
narration of, xxvii, 13, 18–21, 73–75,
94, 188–91, 231, 265; singular nature
of, ix, 4–7, 26, 264; structure of, ix,
xi, xiv, xvi, 12, 94, 157–74, 186–87,
208–11, 253, 256, 264
Expectation: apocalyptic, 93–97, 109,
168; as structure of history, xiv–xv,
7, 14, 19, 34, 82; as structure of time,
102; utopian, xv, 98
Experience: of concentration camp
inmates, 240–41; concept of,
187; history as science of, xxvi, 4;
history in relation to, 187; language
in relation to, xxvi; primary vs.
secondary, xxvi; as structure of
history, xiv–xv, 7, 14; of war, 208–
9

Faber, Karl-Georg, 30

Family, as influence on experience of
war, 211
Faulkner, William, xxvii, 184, 260
Federal Republic of Germany, 6
Fehr, Hans, 133
Fénelon, François de, 12
Fichte, Johann Gottlieb, 59, 64, 203
Fiction: historical reality in relation to,
10–23; historiography in relation to,
259–60
Finitude, 49–50
Fisch, Jörg, 122
Fontenelle, Bernard de, 193
Ford, Henry, 84
Forster, Georg, 128
Forte, Dieter, *Die Einführung der
Buchhaltung* (The Introduction of
Accounting), 21–23
Foucault, Michel, xii, xxiv, 270*n*34
France, war memorials in, 217–24
Frankfurt School, xii
Franz Ferdinand, archduke of Austria,
235
Frederick (Friedrich) the Great, 62, 104,
113, 121, 143, 151, 169, 180
Freedom, 72–73, 191
French Revolution, 63, 72–73, 76, 86,
87, 91–92, 96–98, 108, 110, 128, 146–
48, 203, 217
Friedländer, Saul, 242
Friedrich, Carl J., xx
Friend and enemy, as basic oppositional
pair, 46–47
Frye, Northrup, 261
Fugger, Jacob, 22–23
Furet, François, xviii, xxiv
Future: acceleration and, 87, 91, 96;
apocalypse as orientation toward,
93–98; concept of, 100–103;
considerations for action in, 81,
143, 168–70, 229; historiographical
interpretations based on, 63–
64; memorialization of the dead
conceived in light of, 217, 219, 224;
modernity and, 79–81; progress

oriented toward, 93–98, 109–10. *See also* Expectation

Gadamer, Hans-Georg, xi, xvii, xxv, 41–43, 53–54, 56–57, 59, 171, 252; *Wahrheit und Methode* (Truth and Method), 43, 54, 253
Garve, Christian, 88
Die Gegenwart (journal), 89
Gehlen, Arnold, 34
Gender, as influence on experience of war, 210–11
Generations and generational boundaries: as precondition for thought and action, 8, 50, 68–70, 138–39; preconditions of experience surpassing, 8–9, 165, 258; technological transformation of experience available to, 81, 90–91; temporal transformations in, 81, 90–92; transitions involving, 50–51; war experiences inflected by, 210
Generativity, 50–51, 138–39, 228
Genghis Khan, 36
Geographical pregivens, 28–37
Geography, 25–27. *See also* Historical geography
Geopolitics, 30–33
German Customs Union, 130
German Democratic Republic (GDR), 6, 223–24
Germany, war memorials in, xxix–xxx, 217–24, 243–48. *See also* Nazi Germany
Gerz, Jochen, 248
Geschichte (history). *See under* History
Goblet, Yves-Marie, 30
Goebbels, Joseph, 177–78, 204
Goethe, Johann Wolfgang von, xv–xvi, 18, 20, 23, 60–76, 90, 101, 108, 113, 252, 263
Gondi, Jean François Paul de, Cardinal de Retz, 104
Görres, Joseph, 91, 97
Gottsched, Johann Christoph, 12

Grimm, Jacob, 109
Grimm, Wilhelm, 109
Grosser, Alfred, 105
Grosz, George, 16
Grünewald, Matthias, 11
Guicciardini, Francesco, 151
"Gypsies" (Sinti and Roma), xxx, 170, 232, 241, 244

Habermas, Jürgen, x, xviii–xxi, 56, 269*n*23; *Structural Transformation of the Public Sphere*, xviii
Hácha, Emil, 114, 122, 144
Hanseatic League, 129
Hardenberg, Karl August von, 134
Hartog, François, xvii
Heathens, 201–2
Hecataeus, 106
Hegel, Georg Wilhelm Friedrich, 60, 66, 67, 93, 108, 124–26, 128, 168, 193, 195; *Grundlinien der Philosophie des Rechts* (Elements of the Philosophy of Right), xiii
Heidegger, Martin, xi–xii, xx, xxv, 34, 41, 251; *Being and Time*, 43–54, 102
Heine, Heinrich, 75, 81, 111
Helmholt, Hans Ferdinand, 26
Herder, Johann Gottfried, 4, 25, 26, 63, 163–64, 203
Hereros, 226
Heretics, 201–2
Hermeneutics, 41–43, 53–59, 253
Herodotus, 12, 32, 104, 105, 107, 118, 123–26, 137, 141–43, 145, 155, 187, 238, 252; model of justice, 120–21
Hilberg, Raul, 242
Hillgruber, Andreas, 242
Himmler, Heinrich, 239
Historia magistra vitae (history is life's teacher), 264–65
Historical geography, 28, 30
Historical reality: dreams in relation to, 11–12, 15–16; fiction in relation to, 10–23
Historicism, 80, 113, 189, 264

Historie (history writing), xxv; concept of, 4; Gadamer's hermeneutics and, 42–43; modern historiography vs., 188–89; Nietzschean critique of, 190–93; the novel in relation to, 14

Historik (theory of history): categories underpinning, 45–52; defined, 42; hermeneutics and, 42, 53–59; historiographer's role and perspective in, xxvi; interview concerning, 250–65; language's role in, xxv–xxvi; linguistic innovations in, x, xii; maxims related to, xv–xvi; overview of, ix–x, 43–53; and plurality of histories, 250–51; pregivens (*Vorgaben*) as central to, xi; reception of, xvii–xxv; time in, xii–xvi, xxiii, 3–9. *See also* Historiography

Historiography: fiction in relation to, 259–60; Goethe and, 67–68; intentions of, beyond factuality, 19; and language, 151–57; literary history and, 23; misconceptions of, 3–4, 22–23; the novel in relation to, 14; outline of history of, 187–88; paradoxes of, 183–89; prelinguistic conditions of, xxvi, 151–52; progress and loss in, 258–59; rational constraints on, 20, 23, 58; role of texts and sources in, 58–59; and space, 25–27; and time, 25–27. *See also Historik*

History: absurdity/meaningless of, xxvii, 123–25, 127–28, 177–79, 181, 185–86, 190–96; actual, 12, 185–86, 188; concept of, 187–90; *Geschichte* (history), xxv, 14; Goethe and, 60–76; Heideggerian philosophy and, 43–53; hermeneutics and, 42–43, 253; and "histories in the plural," 14, 16, 43, 183–87, 250; and identity formation, 262; ideological use of, xxvii; justice in relation to, 118–28, 191–92; language in relation

to, xxv–xxvi, 17–21, 137–57, 184, 252–53; law in relation to, 128–36; literary analysis of, 261; meanings of, xxvii, xxxi, 23, 42, 177–96; natural pregivens of, 28–29, 31–33; nature in relation to, 24–25; perspectival nature of, 183–85; philosophy of, 188, 250–51; poetry and fiction in relation to, 11–14, 20, 68; prelinguistic conditions of, xxv–xxvi, 17, 19–21, 43–54, 138–41, 163–65, 251–52; relevance of, 262–63; role of texts and sources in, 253; as science of experience, xxvi, 4; space and, 24–40. *See also Historik*; Historiography; Possible histories; Structures of history

Hitler, Adolf, 31, 33, 114, 115, 120, 122, 169–70, 180–81, 205, 223; *Mein Kampf,* 58–59, 179

Hitler Youth, 223

Hobbes, Thomas, 228

Hobsbawm, Eric J., xxviii

Hochhuth, Rolf, 115

Hofer, Andreas, 86

Holocaust, xxvii–xxx, 58–59, 115, 124, 128, 180–81, 195, 240, 248. *See also* Concentration camps

Holocaust Memorial, Berlin, xxix, xxx, 244

Huber, Ernst Rudolf, 133

Human/suprahuman (*Übermensch*)/ unhuman (*Unmensch*)/subhuman (*Untermensch*), 192, 201–2, 243

Humboldt, Alexander von, 26

Humboldt, Wilhelm von, 26, 113, 189

Identity formation, 262

Idioms. *See* Maxims

Industrial Revolution, 81–82, 87, 148

Innocent III, Pope, 44

Inside and outside, as conditions of history, xxv, 47–49, 139, 164, 197–98, 252, 255

Inventory (*Haushalt*): concept of, xv;

of experience, 7–8, 154, 156, 185;
    linguistic, 145–46, 148, 154, 171, 181
Iser, Wolfgang, 19
Islam, 233
Israel, 195

Jacobi, F. H., 90
Jahn, Friedrich Ludwig, 203
Japan, 226
Jaspers, Karl, xi
Jews. *See* Concentration camps;
    Holocaust
Johnson, Uwe, 260
Judeo-Christian tradition, time in, 93–
    96. *See also* Christianity
Jünger, Ernst, 115
Justice: history in relation to, 118–28,
    191–92; negative memories and, 239
Justinian, 38

Kafka, Franz, 11
Kant, Immanuel, xviii, 4, 25, 26, 41,
    49, 63, 96–97, 108, 125, 163, 185, 187,
    194–95, 227
Kapp, Christian, 26
Kennedy, John F., 231
Keynes, John Maynard, 114
Khrushchev, Nikita, 99
Kleist, Heinrich von, 11, 41; *Verlobung
    in St. Domingo* (Betrothal in Santo
    Domingo), 23, 260
Kluge, Alexander, *Schlachtbeschreibung*
    (Battle Description; *The Battle* [of
    Stalingrad]), 20–21
Kohl, Helmut, xxix–xxx, 194, 263
Kolbe, Maximilian, 114, 242
Kollwitz, Käthe, xxx, 243
Korczak, Janusz, 242
Kuhn, Thomas, 259

Lamprecht, Karl, 26
Language: and concepts of the enemy,
    198–99, 203–5; experience in
    relation to, xxvi; hermeneutics
    and, 53–59; historical events and,

141–50; historiography and, 151–
    57; history in relation to, xxv–xxvi,
    17–21, 137–57, 184, 252–53; and
    social consciousness, 209; speech
    in relation to, 5; systemic character
    of, 286*n*7. *See also* Prelinguistic
    conditions
Lasker-Wallfisch, Anita, 246
Last Judgment: in apocalyptic tradition,
    95, 109; human enactment of, 201;
    world history as, xiii, 67, 97–98,
    123–25, 189, 255
Later. *See* Earlier and later
Lausberg, Heinrich, 172–73
La Vopa, Anthony, xviii
Law: hermeneutics and, 56–57; history
    in relation to, 128–36; power in
    relation to, 121; repeated applicability
    as essential to, 130–32, 166
Lea, Homer, 30
League of Nations, 233
Legal history, 117–18, 129–36
Le Goff, Jacques, 82
Leibniz, Gottfried Wilhelm, 27, 161,
    164, 228
Lenin, Vladimir, 236
Lessing, Gotthold Ephraim, 13, 20, 96
Lessing, Theodor, 186
Life, Nietzschean concept of, 192–93
Linnaeus, Carolus, 120
List, Friedrich, 99
Literary history, 23
Livy, 113
Louis XIV of France, 84
Love, 158–59
Löwith, Karl, xi, xv, 44, 61, 194, 264;
    Meaning in History, xxi
Lübbe, Hermann, 262
Lucian, 12–13, 152
Ludwig I of Bavaria, 81
Luhmann, Niklas, x, 102
Luther, Martin, 21–23, 95, 149, 150, 173

Machiavelli, Niccolò, 74, 122, 151, 156
Mackinder, Halford, 30, 32

Mahan, Alfred Thayer, 30
Mährlen, Johannes, 110
Malthus, Thomas Robert, 228
Mann, Thomas, 181, 205
Mao Zedong, 99, 235
Marx, Karl, 85, 105, 111, 149, 150, 151,
    156, 165, 168, 174, 191, 247
Marxism, 251
Master and slave, as conditions of
    history, 51–52, 139. *See also* Above
    and below, as conditions of
    history
Matthias, Holy Roman Emperor, 104
Maxims, xv–xvi
McCarthy, Thomas, xvii
Meinecke, Friedrich, 60
Melian Dialogue, 52, 114, 121–22, 144
Melville, Herman: *Benito Cereno*, 23;
    Billy Budd, 260
Memoirs, 121
Memorials. *See* War memorials
Memory, xiv; negative, 238–49; of war
    experience, 214; and war memorials,
    xxix–xxx, 217–24, 243–48
Metahistorical conditions. *See*
    Prelinguistic conditions
Metaphors, x, xii–xv, 3, 12–13, 170–71
Metaphysical truths, 8–9
Michelet, Jules, 111
Mill, John Stuart, 145
Mitterand, François, 194
Modernism, 230
Modernity (*Neuzeit*), 90, 109–10, 190,
    192, 201, 204, 265
Momigliano, Arnaldo, 3
Monroe Doctrine, 225
Montaigne, Michel de, x
Montgolfier brothers, 230
Morality, 246–47, 254–55
Mozart, Wolfgang Amadeus, 89
Muhammad (prophet), 263
Münzer, Thomas, 21–22
Mussolini, Benito, 234

Nagel, Ivan, xxii

Nation-states, and world politics, 232–
    37
Nature: Goethe's conception of, 72–73;
    history in relation to, 24–25; time in
    relation to, 82–93
Nazi Germany, xi, xix–xx, xxii, xxvii,
    xxix, 11, 15, 50, 172, 181, 222–23, 240.
    See also Hitler, Adolf
Necessity, of history, 191
Negative memory, 238–49
Nestroy, Johann Nepomuk, ix, 158–59
Neue Wache Memorial, xxix, 243
New School for Social Research, xviii
Newton, Isaac, 27
Niebuhr, Barhold Georg, 85, 112
Nietzsche, Friedrich, 57, 190–94
Nora, Pierre, 262
Novels, 14
Nuremberg trials, 240

Oetinger, Friedrich Christoph, 168
Olsen, Niklas, xvii
Oppositional concepts, 45–55, 67–72,
    75, 139–40, 164–65, 197–202, 205–6,
    252, 255
Oroites, 137
Orosius, 156
Otto-Peters, Louise, 80
Outside. *See* Inside and outside

Past, concept of, 101–3
Perceptions, xxvii, 26, 178, 183–87, 190
Perthes, F. C., 90, 111
Pétain, Philippe, 224
Peter the Great, 120, 169
Phidias, 13
Philology, 57–58
Philosophy of history, 188, 250–51
Pianos, 88–89
Pius XII, Pope, 115
Planck, Gottlieb Jakob, 107
Planning, 169–70, 229, 265
Plato, 51–52, 161
Plessner, Helmut, 34
Plievier, Theodor, 20–21

Plutarch, 113
Pocock, John, xxiii–xxiv
Poetik und Hermeneutik group, xxiii
Poetry: history in relation to, 11–14, 20,
    68, 259–60; truth in relation to, 68
Poliakov, Léon, 242
Polybius, 92, 104, 142, 151, 156, 161
Popper, Karl, 180
Possible histories, x–xii, xiv, xvii, xxiii,
    xxv–xxvi, 8, 19, 27, 29, 42–58, 70,
    91, 92, 119, 138–39, 142, 160, 251–53,
    256, 264
Postmodernism, 230
Poststructuralism, xvii
Power, 121–22, 125
Pragmatics, of language, 172–73
Pregivens (*Vorgaben*): geographical,
    28–37; of historical experience, xi,
    22, 45–52, 152, 213, 265; linguistic,
    19–20, 23, 53, 148, 154, 203, 209;
    of meaning, 56, 189–90, 192–
    93; temporal, 34–39, 49, 95, 167;
    zoological, 50–51, 139, 164. *See also*
    Prelinguistic conditions
Prelinguistic conditions: of dreams,
    16–17; of enmity, 198–99, 203–
    5; for experiences of war, 209–11;
    of historiography, xxvi, 151–52; of
    history, xxv–xxvi, 17, 19–21, 43, 138–
    41, 163–65, 251–52. *See also* Pregivens
Prescient past (*vorausgewußte
    Vergangenheit*), x
Present: concept of, 83, 101–3; future in
    relation to, 102–3; history of, 103–16,
    262–63; past in relation to, 102–3;
    transitional character of, 64
Prognoses, 168–69, 264
Progress, 69–70, 80
Prophesies, 168
Prost, Antoine, 220
Public and secrecy, as conditions of
    history, 48–49

Qasim, Abd al-Karim, 231
Quran, 263

Racism, 181, 226, 235
Radbruch, Gustav, 133
Railroads, 79–81, 84, 85, 87
Ranke, Leopold von, 12, 22, 32, 68, 112,
    119, 125, 127, 156, 185, 259
Rationality, 254
Ratzel, Friedrich, 26, 28, 30, 32, 33
Reality. *See* Historical reality
Rebmann, Georg Friedrich, 91
Reception history, 42
Recht (law, legal system, right, justice),
    xiii. *See also* Justice; Law
Reconciliation, 194–95
Reformation, 109
Reinhard, Duke Carl Friedrich von, 75
Religion: and *Bund* concept, 149–
    50, 173–74; memorialization and
    veneration in context of, 244, 247;
    structures of repeatability in, 8–9,
    166. *See also* Christianity; Judeo-
    Christian tradition, time in;
    Theology
Renaissance, 109
Repetition, as structure of history,
    x, xiii–xvi, 5–9, 114–16, 158–
    74, 256–58, 264–65; biological
    structures, 164–65; extrahuman
    structures, 163–64; institutional
    structures, 165–67; linguistic
    structures, 170–74; in singular
    events, 167–70
Res factae, xxv, 10, 12–16
Res fictae, xxv, 10, 12, 14–16
Res gestae (occurrences), xxv, 151, 187
Retz, Cardinal. *See* Gondi, Jean
    François Paul de
Revolution, xxiii, 22–23, 51, 52, 73,
    91. 142–43, 168. *See also* French
    Revolution
Rewriting (*Umschreiben*), xxvi, 65, 113,
    154–55
Rhetoric, 172–73
Richter, Melvin, xxiii–xxiv
Ricœur, Paul, xvii, xxv, 194, 251
Rieß, Ludwig, 26–27

Rilke, Rainer Maria, 24
Ritter, Moritz, 26
Robespierre, Maximilien, 97
Roma, xxx, 241, 244. *See also* Gypsies
Roosevelt, Theodore, 225
Rousseau, Jean-Jacques, 62–63
Ruge, Arnold, 149

Sadat, Anwar, 231
Saint-Just, Louis-Antoine de, 203
Saint-Simon, Henri de, 97
Sallust, 142, 151
Sattelzeit (mid-eighteenth to -nineteenth centuries), x–xi
Saussure, Ferdinand de, 286*n*7
Schelling, Friedrich Wilhelm Joseph, 108
Schickele, René, 205
Schiller, Friedrich, xiii, 41, 67, 71, 73, 97, 124, 189
Schmitt, Carl, xviii, xx–xxi, 269*n*23
Schöller, Peter, 30
Schopenhauer, Arthur, 185
Schumpeter, Joseph, 114
Schwan, Christian Friedrich, 107
Schweitzer, Albert, 60, 234
Secrecy. *See* Public and secrecy
Secularization, 96, 103, 201, 217, 233
Sediments: concept of, xiii–xiv; of experience, xiv, xxix, 15, 17, 69, 207–24; as metaphor, xiii, 3; operationalization and value of concept of, 6, 9; of time and history, 3–9, 74, 92, 160–61, 189
Semantics, 172
Ships, 86
Simmel, Georg, 34
Simultaneity of the nonsimultaneous (*die Gleichzeitigkeit des Ungleichzeitigen*), xiii, 45
Singularity: historical role of, 4–5, 158–74, 257; historicism and, 113; repetition in relation to, 158–74; surprise as element of, 7–8; *Zeitgeschichte* and, 113–14

Sinti, xxx, 241, 244. *See also* Gypsies
Skinner, Quentin, xxiii–xxiv
Slave. *See* Master and slave
Smith, Adam, 87–88
Social consciousness: factors in preformation of, 209–11; influence of war on, 207–24
Sohm, Rudolph, 133
Sömmering, Thomas, 86
South Africa, 225–26, 233
Souvenir-Français, 223
Soviet Union, 181–82, 233, 236
Space: acceleration and the disappearance of, 87; historiography and, 25–27; history and, 24–40; human-created, 29–30; as metaphorical basis of conceiving of time, xii–xv; pregivens of, 28–29, 31–33; time in relation to, 34–39
Spengler, Oswald, 161
Spiegelman, Art, 248
Stalin, Joseph, xxi, 169–70, 179, 182, 205, 235
Stalingrad, battle of, 20–21, 177–82
Stein, Karl Freiherr vom, 134
Stein, Lorenz von, 111, 128, 135
Stereotypes, 205, 206
Stieler, Kaspar von, 106
Stoicism, 199, 201
Strahlheim, Karl, 110
Stuart, Charles Edward, Prince of England (Bonnie Prince Charlie), 85
Superstition, 71, 277*n*32
Surprise, 7
Sybel, Heinrich von, 111, 112
Syntax, 172

Tacitus, 104, 105, 106, 115, 142, 151, 156
Talmon, Jacob, *Origins of Totalitarian Democracy*, xxi–xxii
Taubes, Jacob, 250
Telegraph, 86
Teleology, 190–91, 194–95
Theodicy, 179
Theology, and hermeneutics, 57

Theory of history. See *Historik*

Thiers, Adolphe, 111

Third Reich. *See* Nazi Germany

Thrownness, 49

Thucydides, 31–32, 52, 92, 104, 105, 107, 114, 121–25, 133, 142–45, 151, 155, 259, 263; model of justice, 122–23

Time: acceleration and, 79–99; *Dasein* and, 44; denaturalization of, 81–93; hermeneutics and, 42; historiography and, 25–27; in Koselleck's theory of history, xii–xvi, 3–9; linear conceptions of, xiii, 3–5, 42, 71–72, 161–62, 193; measurement of, 82–84; space in relation to, 34–39; spatial metaphors used for, xii–xv; traditional conceptions of, 3–4. *See also* Sediments of time (*Zeitschichten*)

Tōyama Mitsuru, 235

Tocqueville, Alexis de, 264

Tolstoy, Leo, xxvii, 260

Topitsch, Ernst, 179

Tortarolo, Edoardo, xxiii

Toynbee, Arnold, 161

Transcendence, 8–9

Truth: actual history as, 12, 185–86, 188; after the fact, 186; historiographical method and, 119; poetry in relation to, 68

Turner, Frederick Jackson, 30

Übermensch. See Human/suprahuman/ unhuman/subhuman

United Nations, 233, 236, 237

United States, 225, 236

University of Bielefeld, xviii, xix

University of Chicago, xviii

Unmensch/Untermensch. See Human/ suprahuman/unhuman/subhuman

Vanquished. *See* Victors and vanquished

Varnhagen, Rahel, 165

Veneration of the dead. *See* War memorials

Vergniaud, Pierre-Victurnien, 76

Vico, Giambattista, 106

Victors and vanquished, as conditions of history, 105, 151–52, 214–16, 235

Vidal de la Blache, Paul, 30

Vincent of Lérins, 72

Volk (Nation), 62, 263

Voltaire, 123

War: diachronic effects on social consciousness, 213–16; meaning of, 179–80; memorials of, xxix–xxx, 195, 217–24; social consciousness formed by, 207–24; sociocultural factors in, xxix; synchronous factors in formation of consciousness, 208–13; technology of, 232

War memorials, xxix–xxx, 195, 217–24, 238, 243–48

Weber, Alfred, xx

Weber, Max, 127, 133

Wehler, Hans-Ulrich, *The German Empire*, xix

Weizsäcker, Viktor von, xi, 34

Wellington, Arthur Wellesley, duke of, 87

White, Hayden, xvii–xviii, xxiv, xxv, 184, 261

Wieacker, Franz, 129

Wieland, Christoph Martin, 63, 143

Wilhelm II, 22, 111

William of Orange, 31

Wilson, Woodrow, 236

Wittram, Richard, 102

Work, as repeatable structure, 165–66

World War I, 115, 180, 195, 204; experiences of, 207–16; war memorials for, 217–21

World War II, xi, xix, xxvi–xxx, 169–70, 177–82; experiences of, 207–16; and national unification, 235–36; war memorials for, 218–24

Writing down (*Aufschreiben*), xxvi, 152–53, 155

Yellow peril, 226

Zeitgeschichte (contemporary history), 100–116; common features of, 105; and concepts of past, present, and future, 101–3; diachronicity and synchronicity connoted by, 106–8; history and meaning of the term, 104–7; narrowing of concept of, 110; professional historians and, 111–12; singularity of, 113–14; structures of repetition in, 114–16

Zeppelin, Ferdinand von, 230

Cultural Memory | *in the Present*

Devin Singh, *Divine Currency: The Theological Power of Money in the West*

Stefanos Geroulanos, *Transparency in Postwar France: A Critical History of the Present*

Sari Nusseibeh, *The Story of Reason in Islam*

Olivia C. Harrison, *Transcolonial Maghreb: Imagining Palestine in the Era of Decolonialization*

Barbara Vinken, *Flaubert Postsecular: Modernity Crossed Out*

Aishwary Kumar, *Radical Equality: Ambedkar, Gandhi, and the Problem of Democracy*

Simona Forti, *New Demons: Rethinking Power and Evil Today*

Joseph Vogl, *The Specter of Capital*

Hans Joas, *Faith as an Option*

Michael Gubser, *The Far Reaches: Ethics, Phenomenology, and the Call for Social Renewal in Twentieth-Century Central Europe*

Françoise Davoine, *Mother Folly: A Tale*

Knox Peden, *Spinoza Contra Phenomenology: French Rationalism from Cavaillès to Deleuze*

Elizabeth A. Pritchard, *Locke's Political Theology: Public Religion and Sacred Rights*

Ankhi Mukherjee, *What Is a Classic? Postcolonial Rewriting and Invention of the Canon*

Jean-Pierre Dupuy, *The Mark of the Sacred*

Henri Atlan, *Fraud: The World of Ona'ah*

Niklas Luhmann, *Theory of Society, Volume 2*

Ilit Ferber, *Philosophy and Melancholy: Benjamin's Early Reflections on Theater and Language*

Alexandre Lefebvre, *Human Rights as a Way of Life: On Bergson's Political Philosophy*

Theodore W. Jennings, Jr., *Outlaw Justice: The Messianic Politics of Paul*

Alexander Etkind, *Warped Mourning: Stories of the Undead in the Land of the Unburied*

Denis Guénoun, *About Europe: Philosophical Hypotheses*

Maria Boletsi, *Barbarism and Its Discontents*

Sigrid Weigel, *Walter Benjamin: Images, the Creaturely, and the Holy*

Roberto Esposito, *Living Thought: The Origins and Actuality of Italian Philosophy*

Henri Atlan, *The Sparks of Randomness, Volume 2: The Atheism of Scripture*

Rüdiger Campe, *The Game of Probability: Literature and Calculation from Pascal to Kleist*

Niklas Luhmann, *A Systems Theory of Religion*

Jean-Luc Marion, *In the Self's Place: The Approach of Saint Augustine*

Rodolphe Gasché, *Georges Bataille: Phenomenology and Phantasmatology*

Niklas Luhmann, *Theory of Society, Volume 1*

Alessia Ricciardi, *After La Dolce Vita: A Cultural Prehistory of Berlusconi's Italy*

Daniel Innerarity, *The Future and Its Enemies: In Defense of Political Hope*

Patricia Pisters, *The Neuro-Image: A Deleuzian Film-Philosophy of Digital Screen Culture*

François-David Sebbah, *Testing the Limit: Derrida, Henry, Levinas, and the Phenomenological Tradition*

Erik Peterson, *Theological Tractates*, edited by Michael J. Hollerich

Feisal G. Mohamed, *Milton and the Post-Secular Present: Ethics, Politics, Terrorism*

Pierre Hadot, *The Present Alone Is Our Happiness, Second Edition: Conversations with Jeannie Carlier and Arnold I. Davidson*

Yasco Horsman, *Theaters of Justice: Judging, Staging, and Working Through in Arendt, Brecht, and Delbo*

Jacques Derrida, *Parages*, edited by John P. Leavey

Henri Atlan, *The Sparks of Randomness, Volume 1: Spermatic Knowledge*

Rebecca Comay, *Mourning Sickness: Hegel and the French Revolution*

Djelal Kadir, *Memos from the Besieged City: Lifelines for Cultural Sustainability*

Stanley Cavell, *Little Did I Know: Excerpts from Memory*

Jeffrey Mehlman, *Adventures in the French Trade: Fragments Toward a Life*

Jacob Rogozinski, *The Ego and the Flesh: An Introduction to Egoanalysis*

Marcel Hénaff, *The Price of Truth: Gift, Money, and Philosophy*

Paul Patton, *Deleuzian Concepts: Philosophy, Colonialization, Politics*

Michael Fagenblat, *A Covenant of Creatures: Levinas's Philosophy of Judaism*

Stefanos Geroulanos, *An Atheism That Is Not Humanist Emerges in French Thought*

Andrew Herscher, *Violence Taking Place: The Architecture of the Kosovo Conflict*

Hans-Jörg Rheinberger, *On Historicizing Epistemology: An Essay*

Jacob Taubes, *From Cult to Culture*, edited by Charlotte Fonrobert and Amir Engel

Peter Hitchcock, *The Long Space: Transnationalism and Postcolonial Form*

Lambert Wiesing, *Artificial Presence: Philosophical Studies in Image Theory*

Jacob Taubes, *Occidental Eschatology*

Freddie Rokem, *Philosophers and Thespians: Thinking Performance*

Roberto Esposito, *Communitas: The Origin and Destiny of Community*

Vilashini Cooppan, *Worlds Within: National Narratives and Global Connections in Postcolonial Writing*

Josef Früchtl, *The Impertinent Self: A Heroic History of Modernity*

Frank Ankersmit, Ewa Domanska, and Hans Kellner, eds., *Re-Figuring Hayden White*

Michael Rothberg, *Multidirectional Memory: Remembering the Holocaust in the Age of Decolonization*

Jean-François Lyotard, *Enthusiasm: The Kantian Critique of History*

Ernst van Alphen, Mieke Bal, and Carel Smith, eds., *The Rhetoric of Sincerity*

Stéphane Mosès, *The Angel of History: Rosenzweig, Benjamin, Scholem*

Pierre Hadot, *The Present Alone Is Our Happiness: Conversations with Jeannie Carlier and Arnold I. Davidson*

Alexandre Lefebvre, *The Image of the Law: Deleuze, Bergson, Spinoza*

Samira Haj, *Reconfiguring Islamic Tradition: Reform, Rationality, and Modernity*

Diane Perpich, *The Ethics of Emmanuel Levinas*

Marcel Detienne, *Comparing the Incomparable*

François Delaporte, *Anatomy of the Passions*

René Girard, *Mimesis and Theory: Essays on Literature and Criticism, 1959–2005*

Richard Baxstrom, *Houses in Motion: The Experience of Place and the Problem of Belief in Urban Malaysia*

Jennifer L. Culbert, *Dead Certainty: The Death Penalty and the Problem of Judgment*

Samantha Frost, *Lessons from a Materialist Thinker: Hobbesian Reflections on Ethics and Politics*

Regina Mara Schwartz, *Sacramental Poetics at the Dawn of Secularism: When God Left the World*

Gil Anidjar, *Semites: Race, Religion, Literature*

Ranjana Khanna, *Algeria Cuts: Women and Representation, 1830 to the Present*

Esther Peeren, *Intersubjectivities and Popular Culture: Bakhtin and Beyond*

Eyal Peretz, *Becoming Visionary: Brian De Palma's Cinematic Education of the Senses*

Diana Sorensen, *A Turbulent Decade Remembered: Scenes from the Latin American Sixties*

Hubert Damisch, *A Childhood Memory by Piero della Francesca*

José van Dijck, *Mediated Memories in the Digital Age*

Dana Hollander, *Exemplarity and Chosenness: Rosenzweig and Derrida on the Nation of Philosophy*

Asja Szafraniec, *Beckett, Derrida, and the Event of Literature*

Sara Guyer, *Romanticism After Auschwitz*

Alison Ross, *The Aesthetic Paths of Philosophy: Presentation in Kant, Heidegger, Lacoue-Labarthe, and Nancy*

Gerhard Richter, *Thought-Images: Frankfurt School Writers' Reflections from Damaged Life*

Bella Brodzki, *Can These Bones Live? Translation, Survival, and Cultural Memory*

Rodolphe Gasché, *The Honor of Thinking: Critique, Theory, Philosophy*

Brigitte Peucker, *The Material Image: Art and the Real in Film*

Natalie Melas, *All the Difference in the World: Postcoloniality and the Ends of Comparison*

Jonathan Culler, *The Literary in Theory*

Michael G. Levine, *The Belated Witness: Literature, Testimony, and the Question of Holocaust Survival*

Jennifer A. Jordan, *Structures of Memory: Understanding German Change in Berlin and Beyond*

Christoph Menke, *Reflections of Equality*

Marlène Zarader, *The Unthought Debt: Heidegger and the Hebraic Heritage*

Jan Assmann, *Religion and Cultural Memory: Ten Studies*

David Scott and Charles Hirschkind, *Powers of the Secular Modern: Talal Asad and His Interlocutors*

Gyanendra Pandey, *Routine Violence: Nations, Fragments, Histories*

James Siegel, *Naming the Witch*

J. M. Bernstein, *Against Voluptuous Bodies: Late Modernism and the Meaning of Painting*

Theodore W. Jennings Jr., *Reading Derrida / Thinking Paul: On Justice*

Richard Rorty and Eduardo Mendieta, *Take Care of Freedom and Truth Will Take Care of Itself: Interviews with Richard Rorty*

Jacques Derrida, *Paper Machine*

Renaud Barbaras, *Desire and Distance: Introduction to a Phenomenology of Perception*

Jill Bennett, *Empathic Vision: Affect, Trauma, and Contemporary Art*

Ban Wang, *Illuminations from the Past: Trauma, Memory, and History in Modern China*

James Phillips, *Heidegger's* Volk: *Between National Socialism and Poetry*

Frank Ankersmit, *Sublime Historical Experience*

István Rév, *Retroactive Justice: Prehistory of Post-Communism*

Paola Marrati, *Genesis and Trace: Derrida Reading Husserl and Heidegger*

Krzysztof Ziarek, *The Force of Art*

Marie-José Mondzain, *Image, Icon, Economy: The Byzantine Origins of the Contemporary Imaginary*

Cecilia Sjöholm, *The Antigone Complex: Ethics and the Invention of Feminine Desire*

Jacques Derrida and Elisabeth Roudinesco, *For What Tomorrow . . . : A Dialogue*

Elisabeth Weber, *Questioning Judaism: Interviews by Elisabeth Weber*

Jacques Derrida and Catherine Malabou, *Counterpath: Traveling with Jacques Derrida*

Martin Seel, *Aesthetics of Appearing*

Nanette Salomon, *Shifting Priorities: Gender and Genre in Seventeenth-Century Dutch Painting*

Jacob Taubes, *The Political Theology of Paul*

Jean-Luc Marion, *The Crossing of the Visible*

Eric Michaud, *The Cult of Art in Nazi Germany*

Anne Freadman, *The Machinery of Talk: Charles Peirce and the Sign Hypothesis*

Stanley Cavell, *Emerson's Transcendental Etudes*

Stuart McLean, *The Event and Its Terrors: Ireland, Famine, Modernity*

Beate Rössler, ed., *Privacies: Philosophical Evaluations*

Bernard Faure, *Double Exposure: Cutting Across Buddhist and Western Discourses*

Alessia Ricciardi, *The Ends of Mourning: Psychoanalysis, Literature, Film*

Alain Badiou, *Saint Paul: The Foundation of Universalism*

Gil Anidjar, *The Jew, the Arab: A History of the Enemy*

Jonathan Culler and Kevin Lamb, eds., *Just Being Difficult? Academic Writing in the Public Arena*

Jean-Luc Nancy, *A Finite Thinking*, edited by Simon Sparks

Theodor W. Adorno, *Can One Live after Auschwitz? A Philosophical Reader*, edited by Rolf Tiedemann

Patricia Pisters, *The Matrix of Visual Culture: Working with Deleuze in Film Theory*

Andreas Huyssen, *Present Pasts: Urban Palimpsests and the Politics of Memory*

Talal Asad, *Formations of the Secular: Christianity, Islam, Modernity*

Dorothea von Mücke, *The Rise of the Fantastic Tale*

Marc Redfield, *The Politics of Aesthetics: Nationalism, Gender, Romanticism*

Emmanuel Levinas, *On Escape*

Dan Zahavi, *Husserl's Phenomenology*

Rodolphe Gasché, *The Idea of Form: Rethinking Kant's Aesthetics*

Michael Naas, *Taking on the Tradition: Jacques Derrida and the Legacies of Deconstruction*

Herlinde Pauer-Studer, ed., *Constructions of Practical Reason: Interviews on Moral and Political Philosophy*

Jean-Luc Marion, *Being Given That: Toward a Phenomenology of Givenness*

Theodor W. Adorno and Max Horkheimer, *Dialectic of Enlightenment*

Ian Balfour, *The Rhetoric of Romantic Prophecy*

Martin Stokhof, *World and Life as One: Ethics and Ontology in Wittgenstein's Early Thought*

Gianni Vattimo, *Nietzsche: An Introduction*

Jacques Derrida, *Negotiations: Interventions and Interviews, 1971–1998*, edited by Elizabeth Rottenberg

Brett Levinson, *The Ends of Literature: The Latin American "Boom" in the Neoliberal Marketplace*

Timothy J. Reiss, *Against Autonomy: Cultural Instruments, Mutualities, and the Fictive Imagination*

Hent de Vries and Samuel Weber, eds., *Religion and Media*

Niklas Luhmann, *Theories of Distinction: Re-Describing the Descriptions of Modernity*, edited and introduced by William Rasch

Johannes Fabian, *Anthropology with an Attitude: Critical Essays*

Michel Henry, *I Am the Truth: Toward a Philosophy of Christianity*

Gil Anidjar, *"Our Place in Al-Andalus": Kabbalah, Philosophy, Literature in Arab-Jewish Letters*

Hélène Cixous and Jacques Derrida, *Veils*

F. R. Ankersmit, *Historical Representation*

F. R. Ankersmit, *Political Representation*

Elissa Marder, *Dead Time: Temporal Disorders in the Wake of Modernity (Baudelaire and Flaubert)*

Reinhart Koselleck, *The Practice of Conceptual History: Timing History, Spacing Concepts*

Niklas Luhmann, *The Reality of the Mass Media*

Hubert Damisch, *A Theory of /Cloud/: Toward a History of Painting*

Jean-Luc Nancy, *The Speculative Remark: (One of Hegel's bon mots)*

Jean-François Lyotard, *Soundproof Room: Malraux's Anti-Aesthetics*

Jan Patočka, *Plato and Europe*

Hubert Damisch, *Skyline: The Narcissistic City*

Isabel Hoving, *In Praise of New Travelers: Reading Caribbean Migrant Women Writers*

Richard Rand, ed., *Futures: Of Jacques Derrida*

William Rasch, *Niklas Luhmann's Modernity: The Paradoxes of Differentiation*

Jacques Derrida and Anne Dufourmantelle, *Of Hospitality*

Jean-François Lyotard, *The Confession of Augustine*

Kaja Silverman, *World Spectators*

Samuel Weber, *Institution and Interpretation: Expanded Edition*

Jeffrey S. Librett, *The Rhetoric of Cultural Dialogue: Jews and Germans in the Epoch of Emancipation*

Ulrich Baer, *Remnants of Song: Trauma and the Experience of Modernity in Charles Baudelaire and Paul Celan*

Samuel C. Wheeler III, *Deconstruction as Analytic Philosophy*

David S. Ferris, *Silent Urns: Romanticism, Hellenism, Modernity*

Rodolphe Gasché, *Of Minimal Things: Studies on the Notion of Relation*

Sarah Winter, *Freud and the Institution of Psychoanalytic Knowledge*

Samuel Weber, *The Legend of Freud: Expanded Edition*

Aris Fioretos, ed., *The Solid Letter: Readings of Friedrich Hölderlin*

J. Hillis Miller / Manuel Asensi, *Black Holes / J. Hillis Miller; or, Boustrophedonic Reading*

Miryam Sas, *Fault Lines: Cultural Memory and Japanese Surrealism*

Peter Schwenger, *Fantasm and Fiction: On Textual Envisioning*

Didier Maleuvre, *Museum Memories: History, Technology, Art*

Jacques Derrida, *Monolingualism of the Other; or, The Prosthesis of Origin*

Andrew Baruch Wachtel, *Making a Nation, Breaking a Nation: Literature and Cultural Politics in Yugoslavia*

Niklas Luhmann, *Love as Passion: The Codification of Intimacy*

Mieke Bal, ed., *The Practice of Cultural Analysis: Exposing Interdisciplinary Interpretation*

Jacques Derrida and Gianni Vattimo, eds., *Religion*